D0215208

The Ethnomusicologists'
Cookbook

The Ethnomusicologists' Cookbook

Complete Meals from Around the World

Sean Williams

Routledge
Taylor & Francis Group
New York   London

Routledge is an imprint of the
Taylor & Francis Group, an informa business

JACKSON COUNTY LIBRARY SERVICES
MEDFORD OREGON 97501

Routledge
Taylor & Francis Group
270 Madison Avenue
New York, NY 10016

Routledge
Taylor & Francis Group
2 Park Square
Milton Park, Abingdon
Oxon OX14 4RN

© 2006 by Taylor and Francis Group, LLC
Routledge is an imprint of Taylor & Francis Group, an Informa business

Printed in the United States of America on acid-free paper
10 9 8 7 6 5 4 3 2 1

International Standard Book Number-10: 0-415-97819-X (Softcover) 0-415-97818-1 (Hardcover)
International Standard Book Number-13: 978-0-415-97819-4 (Softcover) 978-0-415-97818-7 (Hardcover)
Library of Congress Card Number 2006004799

No part of this book may be reprinted, reproduced, transmitted, or utilized in any form by any electronic, mechanical, or other means, now known or hereafter invented, including photocopying, microfilming, and recording, or in any information storage or retrieval system, without written permission from the publishers.

Trademark Notice: Product or corporate names may be trademarks or registered trademarks, and are used only for identification and explanation without intent to infringe.

Library of Congress Cataloging-in-Publication Data

The ethnomusicologists' cookbook / edited by Sean Williams.
    p. cm.
    Includes bibliographical references and index.
  ISBN 0-415-97818-1 (hb) -- ISBN 0-415-97819-X (pb)
  1. Cookery, International. 2. Ethnomusicology. I. Williams, Sean.

TX725.A1E86 2006
641.59--dc22   2006004799

Visit the Taylor & Francis Web site at
http://www.taylorandfrancis.com

and the Routledge Web site at
http://www.routledge-ny.com

Contents

1
Prelude

WORLD MUSIC, WORLD FOOD

Sean Williams

> If music be the food of love, play on.
>
> Shakespeare, *Twelfth Night*

This cookbook comes to you from over forty contributors from around the world, almost all of whom are academics in music (ethnomusicologists in particular) or attached in one way or another to music and musicians. We have created this book as a way of celebrating the delicious and enduring connection between music and food.

I had been living in West Java, Indonesia, for about two months when Gugum Gumbira, the patriarch of my host family, paused between bites of fried rice one morning. "Soni!" he burst out. "You can already eat rice!" I tried to keep the shadow of a frown from my forehead, having heard this expression so many times and always with a tone of utter amazement. I had learned to use chopsticks at about the same time I learned to use a knife and fork as a toddler, so rice had always been an important part of my West Coast American upbringing. But Mr. Gumbira wasn't finished. "If you keep eating this rice," he said, "you'll become completely Sundanese. It doesn't matter how long you spend studying our music. You could be here for a lifetime if you want, and become the finest *kacapi* player in the country. You could be fluent in speaking Sundanese. You could dance *jaipongan* like a deer. But if you can't eat the food we eat—and love every bite of it—you will never understand what it means to be Sundanese." At the time I was still learning to tolerate the brilliant red spicy *sambal* sauce on my fried rice every morning, and to simply scoop out the dead ants that had discovered the sweetened condensed milk and coffee grounds in the bottom of my cup only to meet their doom in the form of boiling water. When he made that statement, I confess to having had a momentary longing for cornflakes, strawberries, and fresh milk in the bright sunshine (emotional and physical) of my parents' kitchen. But he had a point.

In Indonesia (and in some other parts of the world), rice *is* food. Rice is what ascribes humanity to its consumers: when you eat rice, you become human. In other areas of the world, it might be kasha, or quinoa, or oats, or corn that makes you belong, locally. I recall my Sundanese friends being astonished to learn that Americans do not have a particular staple defining who we are, and that we do not expect foreigners to "learn" to eat what we eat in order to absorb American-ness. Yet people everywhere (including in North America) seem proud and delighted when an outsider grasps what it means to thoroughly enjoy local food. The need of a group of people to "claim" music ("This is what tells us—and you—who we are") is at least as strong as their need to "claim" food-ways ("This is what tells us—and you —who we are").

Ethnomusicologists (those of us who study music in cultural context) will tell you that we enjoy listening to music, playing music, thinking about music, and talking about music. Our connection to food, however, might be less obvious. On no fewer than five separate occasions in the past ten years, I have overheard ethnomusicologists jokingly say that they selected a particular area of the world to do research based on the compatibility and overall deliciousness of the local food. Many models of fieldwork hold sway in ethnomusicology, from our roots among the people running colonial empires to more contemporary efforts involving the Internet and electronic media. For years, however, ethnomusicologists have attempted to get close to music and the musicians who play it by living *in situ*, working frequently with one or several individuals or groups, learning the language(s) of the area, and practicing the classic fieldwork methodology of participant observation. While conducting fieldwork, some of us can easily purchase food imported (expensively) from our home nations, but many of us choose not to; local food is often all that is available, and local food is often absolutely delicious. Many of us, therefore, spend at least part of our lives in the role of musician-researcher-student of cooking.

The links between music and food are quite strong in many areas of the world; for some people, both are a vaguely threatening or sinful form of "entertainment." For others, food and music must be "consumed" together for fulfillment. The parallels between learning to cook and learning music are often startlingly obvious: one person might be told to "watch what I do [on this instrument/with this whisk] and then try this on your own," while a researcher in another part of the world might be told "put your hands right here [on this instrument/on this whisk] and I'll help you make them do the right things." Similarly, in one place it is appropriate to have absolute silence and solemnity during a meal and during a concert. In another place, uproarious laughter and ribald jokes are essentially healthy for both eating and listening. It is the rare ethnography that explores foodways in addition to music; this volume, therefore, represents a small step in the direction of what might be called *gastromusicology.*

The search for authenticity—in the field of ethnomusicology and in related fields of folklore and anthropology—has led directly to contested territory. Who gets to proclaim one musical style or language or political system or foodway as any more authentic than any other? Many ethnomusicologists (including several of this volume's contributors) were born and raised in the "host country" from which these recipes originate. Others were not (myself included). For those born and raised in the country from which the recipes originate, these recipes might well represent some kind of national dish or must-have meal, or be a reflection of the creativity of members of that individual's family. They might also represent a new creation as a result of being part of an immigrant or diasporic community. But we all have important ideas in common: a deep respect for the musicians with whom we work, a recognition that food and music are often conjoined in live context, and an understanding that we have much to learn from understanding food as a signifier of identity. As is the case with music, one could go blithely through this cookbook sampling bits of this and that cuisine, never extending below the surface. But I and the other contributors invite you to explore much more deeply: make a whole meal with all its constituent parts, listen to several CDs, ponder the included proverb, read the essay, talk to each other, and dig further for more information.

Perhaps the question should be whether we are all culinary and musical tourists in disguise, using food and music to explore, satisfy our curiosity, and redefine ourselves in our observations of the culinary and musical ways of others. I refer readers interested in this subject to Lucy Long's excellent edited volume, *Culinary Tourism* (2004), which covers wide ranging issues in the arenas of tourism, foodways, and authenticity. In cautioning us against automatically championing the notion of authenticity, Arjun Appadurai claims that authenticity "measures the degree to which something is more or less what it *ought* to be" (Appadurai 1986, 25). He also points out that authenticity depends to a great degree on who is making the claim. It would be easy for any of the contributors to claim authenticity for themselves or their recipes, but you can rest assured that for every recipe or decision made about the contents of this book, a hundred others would rise to dispute it with great passion, all in the name of authenticity.

It might be useful to remember that you can't have an "authentic" experience without a hefty dose of reality, often in the form of some negative experience involving, for example, extremely loud motorcycles, exhaust fumes from buses and trucks, startlingly large flying cockroaches, or hordes of ants. Sometimes "authenticity" includes food poisoning, more chili peppers than you might think humans could possibly eat, or items that the people of one's home country do not necessarily think of as consumable. Americans rarely think twice about drinking water "purified" by chlorine, a known carcinogen, but some visitors to America are surprised and nauseated by its smell and taste, and can instantly detect its effect on the flavor of coffee and tea. Conversely, some

Americans are somewhat challenged by the idea of eating entrails and profoundly challenged by the idea of eating bugs. I shouldn't have to point out the physical similarities between the large exoskeletal creatures that Americans treat as delicacies (lobster, crab) and small, equally edible, ones (spider, locust).

I used to fret at my students' fond attachment to Irish-American hit songs like "When Irish Eyes Are Smiling," until I realized that it gave them firm emotional ground on which to stand, as Irish-Americans, while they began to explore the much more difficult musical territory of Irish-language *sean-nós* (old-style) songs. At the time I was dismissive of the entire Irish-American repertoire, failing to recognize its uniquely liminal authenticity for my students and its exploration of Irish-American experiences. For my students and for many Irish-Americans, that whole body of songs references for them an experience they need and understand; one that feels "just about right." Of course you are, to some extent, attempting to stage an authentic event when you cook a meal and play CDs for your guests. Just be mindful that any attempt at authenticity is (and possibly should be, in this context) idealized.

Even as melodies or timbres of sound can take you back to your childhood, it is another sense—smell—that can have an even deeper effect. Knowing the impact of sounds and scents (and, by extension, tastes) on our deepest feelings can help us to recognize our vulnerabilities in determining what foods and sounds to trust. The sense of trust, of "just about right," is part of what allows us to be adventurous. So although you won't be instantly transported to Thailand, Tonga, or Tokyo by these meals and essays and CDs, they can at least start you on a fascinating and enjoyable path toward further exploration.

> A good recipe is closer to a musical notation than to a blueprint. As a musician, I learned that the notes on the page represent what the composer intended but cannot possibly convey all of the nuances. Ultimately, the performer should decide just how loud *ff* is, just how short a staccato sequence should sound, or just how bouncy those triplets should be. One can recognize every performance as Mendelssohn's Violin Concerto, but each will reveal a different interpretation. In the same way, ten cooks can make a classic Burgundian *Coq au Vin* from the same recipe. Each recipe will taste like *Coq au Vin*, but likely no two will taste the same.
>
> Harvey Steinman, quoted in *The Recipe Writer's Handbook*, 1997, 179

The intent of this volume is to offer sets of recipes from specific areas of the world. Each set of recipes makes enough food to feed six people, sometimes more. The recipes for these meals are intended to help you to create an entire meal, whatever the local definition of that meal is. In some areas of the world, one makes the main meal at noon and the family simply enjoys leftovers all the rest of the day and evening. For others, the food must be eaten at night. Sometimes men and women eat separately, or the children are fed elsewhere. Some people eat first while others wait their turns. Some people use only their right hand for eating, while others use chopsticks, a fork, a folded piece of bread, or an elaborate set of rules governing which fork or spoon serves a particular purpose. Each detail reveals much about the people in a community, just as the details of musical concepts/behaviors/sounds illuminate values, histories, and relationships.

Not one of the recipes in this book is exotic; each one is local, familiar, and just right to somebody. Exoticism is a matter of what we ourselves bring to the table or to the musical experience. After all, you (I'm talking to *you*: the one holding this book) are impossibly exotic to someone. Your manner of dress, idiomatic speech, choice of snack food, bathing habits, and tunes that you hum in the shower are funny, strange, frightening, and possibly even dangerous. The recipes for this book are different, in some cases, from what you might see in a standard cookbook from your region of the world, but they're also just about irresistible. The contributors deliberately wanted to strike a balance between what is interesting and fun to try on the one hand, and too difficult to find or simply too far outside the "gotta try this" sensibility for large portions of the world. So we left out the grubs, dogs and horses, whole roasted kangaroos, fish head soup, and water buffalo lung chips that are nonetheless prized delicacies in parts of the world. Remember what I said about "exotic" foods; these, too, are just right.

Representation of world cultures is not uniform in this book. Instead, contributions have been welcomed from everywhere. For each set of recipes you will see a basic estimate of the amount of time it would take to complete the preparation of an entire meal. You will also find a translation of a pithy food-related proverb for each area represented, suggested recordings to listen to during the meal, and a list of resources for further exploration.[1] In addition, each contributor offers an essay discussing food and music locally, with the individual emphasis that each area required. In requesting these essays, I deliberately asked the contributors to use their normal "voices" in a reflection of the ways in which we actually speak to each other and to other musicians. Many ethnomusicologists enjoy hanging out with musicians, spending late nights hearing "just one more song" or enjoying yet another encore. We rarely try to impress musicians with the brilliance of our postmodern academic discourse (although it can happen). Instead, we listen and talk naturally about food and politics and spirituality and sex and history…and music. We often eat while we talk, and many of us eat while we listen to music. Some people eat while they *play* music. It is the inherently interdisciplinary nature of ethnomusicologists and what we do that enables us to get excited about the many cultural products that extend beyond music.

The cover photograph of this book combines the rich flavors and textures of essential foods from around the world: rice, corn, quinoa, kasha, and lentils, together with a variety of essential musical instruments from every continent. Like the grains, some of the instruments are specific to one region, while others (like the fiddle) have found a home nearly everywhere.

My thanks go to Martin Kane of the Evergreen State College for his outstanding artistry in arranging and capturing my rough idea with his camera. Piper Heisig gave me the unforgettable tagline for the back cover of this book, and our mutual friend Joe Vinikow offered other options from the world of Indian food: "My Pappadum Told Me," "Oh, You Beautiful Dal," and "Paperback Raita." I would like to express my gratitude to Margaret Sarkissian for (literally) dreaming up the idea for this volume, to the Board of Directors of the Society for Ethnomusicology for agreeing to the project, and to the many contributors from around the world. Rebecca Ungpiyakul was my office assistant, and deserves my gratitude for keeping track of the many different contributions and permissions forms through the development of a handy spreadsheet. My husband Cary Black and daughter Morgan gamely sat through multiple meals—both successes and failures—as I tested them out. In addition, Richard Carlin, former music acquisitions editor of Routledge, was instrumental, so to speak, in supporting this book's development. I would also like to thank Khrysti Nazzaro for deftly shepherding the project through to completion. The many ethnomusicologists (and their families and friends) who volunteered to test out these recipes had much to do with the overall ease of use and readability of the recipes. All these people—contributors, testers, editors, and people who like to eat—know that in many parts of the world, food and music are closely entwined. It is one of our many joys as working ethnomusicologists to bring the richness of our fieldwork experiences—including the wonderful food we eat—to our current lives and to the lives of others. Thank you for giving us the opportunity to bring some of that richness to you.

HOW TO USE THIS BOOK

All these meals are designed to serve six people. While it would be delightful to always have six people at the table, few of us regularly invite five of our closest friends over for a meal. According to my tests, however, every one of these meals works extremely well as leftovers the next day. I have created a website [http://academic.evergreen.edu/w/williams/cookbook.htm] for more information about the meals, including photographs of many dishes, and a printable shopping list for each meal, which should enable you to avoid trekking back and forth through a store or from bakery to butchery and back by listing the ingredients in logical groupings (meat, dairy, produce, grains, miscellaneous). No one should have to be thinking, "What? I have to go back to produce for *another* onion?" Should you choose not to cook the entire meal, a quick scan of any individual recipe will tell you precisely which ingredients you need and in what quantities and what order.

Because this book is being published in the United States, all measurements conform to American standards. We understand that most of the world uses the metric system, and we hope that our metrically inclined readers will take advantage of the many excellent conversion and substitution tools that exist online. Recipes here are presented using the standard North American cookbook shorthand of c. (cup), t. (teaspoon), lb. (pound), and T (tablespoon). Inches are represented with double prime marks, as in 2" fresh ginger root. Temperatures are in Fahrenheit.

If you are a vegetarian, several meals are entirely vegetarian and many others can be easily modified. If you are a vegan, you will find that many of the vegetarian recipes are, in fact, vegan as well. If you keep kosher, we have indicated that as well as vegan and vegetarian recipes in the section titled I Can't Eat That! Dietary Modifications (p. 282).

Some standard kitchen equipment will help you to be successful with these recipes. A rice cooker is a necessity for many cooks; perhaps a third of the recipes in this book call for rice. No longer the expensive commodity they once were, rice cookers are widely available in either simple versions or loaded with bells and whistles. Many recipes call for a large cooking pot with a tight-fitting lid; my tests have shown that a 6-quart pot is large enough for most meals. Recipes that call for multiple cloves of garlic (and many recipes do) would benefit from the use of a simple rubber tube called a garlic roller: place the cloves inside, roll a couple of times, and the garlic comes out peeled cleanly. It would also be helpful to invest in a large roasting pan suitable for a whole chicken or two pounds of beef/pork/lamb. However, you can buy an inexpensive (one-time) foil version at a grocery store. Some recipes require an unusual item for cooking, such as a cotton pudding bag (Newfoundland) or a springform pan (Norway). Both are available from any kitchen store or even a supermarket.

Finally, though, it is not so much the physical equipment in your kitchen as the adventurous spirit of your friends and family members that counts, and their willingness to try something new. These recipes are much more fun to prepare when a couple of people are working simultaneously; however, the projected cooking times are for the person laboring away solo in the kitchen. Remember that each time you make a recipe or a meal, you get better and more efficient at it and start making modifications to suit your tastes and cooking style. Cooking times are always approximate and vary wildly according to each cook's experience, easy access to ingredients, willingness to invite guests into the kitchen to help, and excellent sense of humor!

Read through each recipe carefully before you begin. Some recipes require you to do some preparatory work the night before, such as soaking dry beans or herring or cooking and cooling a particular type of meat. You may also have to locate unusual ingredients. North American sources for hard-to-find ingredients include www.hashems.com (Middle Eastern spices), www.exoticmeats.com (e.g., snake and venison), www.thespicehouse.com (South Asian spices), www.worldspice.com (any kind of spices), and www.uwajimaya.com (East and Southeast Asian foods and spices).

You should also consider establishing a friendly relationship with your local Mexican, Indian, Vietnamese, and others, shops and restaurants, because some ingredients (such as curry leaf or salam leaf or particular kinds of chilis) are difficult to acquire without an inside source (restaurant owners can be your allies). And don't let anything stop you! Good luck and happy cooking!

Quick Conversions (Approximate)

1 teaspoon = 5 milliliters
1 tablespoon = 15 milliliters
1 cup = 236 milliliters
1 quart = 946 milliliters
1 pound = 454 grams
1 inch = 2.5 centimeters
300°F = 149°C
350°F = 177°C
400°F = 204°C

NOTES

1. As one of the co-editors—with Terry Miller—of volume 4 (Southeast Asia) of *The Garland Encyclopedia of World Music* (New York; London: Routledge), I would like to recommend this entire series to anyone interested in more information about any of the areas covered by these recipes. And in the interest of full disclosure, Taylor & Francis is the parent company of Routledge, publisher of both the Garland Encyclopedias and this volume.

REFERENCES

Appadurai, Arjun. 1986. On culinary authenticity. *Anthropology Today* 2.
Long, Lucy. 2004. *Culinary Tourism*. Lexington, KY: The University Press of Kentucky.
Ostmann, Barbara Gibbs, and Janet L. Baker. 1997. *The Recipe Writer's Handbook*. New York: John Wiley & Sons.

2
Africa

KENYA

Jesse Samba Wheeler

S/he refused ugali = "S/he died."

Menu: *Mchuzi Wa Ng'ombe Na Tamarindi* (Beef Stew with Tamarind), *Maharagwe Ya Nasi* (Kidney Beans in Coconut), *Sukumawiki* (Greens), *Ugali* (White Corn Meal, optional), *Chapati* (Flat Bread, optional), *Wali Wa Nasi* (Coconut Rice, optional), *Chai Maziwa* (Milky Tea), and *Kahawa Ya Tangawizi* (Ginger Coffee). A mango, bananas, pineapple—these alone or with vanilla ice cream can be eaten for dessert. Serve with White Cap, Tusker or Pilsner lagers, Coca-Cola, or Fanta.

Preparation Time: 3 hours (or more, depending on your use of fresh or canned coconut milk and dried or canned beans).

Cooking Process: Decide whether you plan to make your own coconut milk or buy canned coconut milk; it will take extra time to make the milk and you should allow for that. Similarly, decide on which grain you plan to have—white corn meal or coconut rice or *chapati*—so that you do not buy the ingredients for all of them. Make the stew first, start the beans, then the grain/starch (whichever you choose), then the greens. Serves six people.

The Recipes

MCHUZI WA NG'OMBE NA TAMARINDI (BEEF STEW WITH TAMARIND)

10 tamarind pods (*ukwaju*) or ½ c. tamarind paste (to taste)
2 T brown sugar
½ t. pepper
1" length of ginger, minced
1 t. cardamom
1 t. cumin
1 t. cinnamon
½ t. allspice
2 lb. tender cut of beef
½ c. flour
2 large yellow onions, chopped
1 T vegetable oil
1 T butter
2 large carrots
2 slightly underripe plantains

The easiest option is to buy prepared tamarind paste. If this is unavailable, you can make your own in the following way: Boil tamarind flesh from 10 pods with 2 c. water and 2 T brown sugar until flesh begins to fall from seeds. Separate pulp from seeds (discarding seeds), return to sauce pan and add ½ t. pepper, 1" length of minced ginger, 1 t. cardamom, 1 t. cumin, 1 t. cinnamon, and ½ t. allspice. Reduce, adding more water, a little sugar to taste, and more of the spices until you have a sauce that tastes good. Cut 2 lb. beef into cubes. Put into plastic bag, toss in ½ c. flour, covering each piece as much as possible. In a large pot, sauté the onions in 1 T vegetable oil and 1 T butter. Add meat and brown. Add enough water to completely cover the meat

10

and chopped onions. Cut 2 large carrots and 2 plantains into chunks, then add to the meat and onions with the tamarind sauce. Cook covered on medium heat for 30 minutes. Lower the heat and cook for another half hour, or until beef and plantains are cooked thoroughly. Add more water and spices (cardamom, cumin, and cinnamon) during cooking if desired. Keep covered.

MAHARAGWE YA NASI (KIDNEY BEANS IN COCONUT)

4 c. fresh or canned coconut milk (see recipe below)
4 c. cooked kidney beans
1 t. salt
½ t. allspice

If you wish to make your own coconut milk, you will need to do the following: scrape the flesh from 2 coconuts and place it in several layers of cheesecloth (traditionally a long cone of woven reed or straw). Then run boiling water through the cloth, catching the liquid in a pan. Squeeze the cloth to extract the milk. Do this three times, keeping the milk from each run separate. For this recipe you will need 4 c. coconut milk. As you boil the beans, add first the weakest milk (the top of the can will also have the weakest milk). As it soaks into the beans, add the second run's milk. When almost finished, add the strongest milk. (This is the same method used when making coconut rice). Or you can buy 4 c. canned coconut milk, in which case it can be all added at once. Soak 1⅓ lb. kidney beans for 24 hours or use 4 c. canned beans. Boil with water, 1 t. salt and ½ t. allspice until soft. When nearing desired softness, add 4 c. coconut milk (or the milk you make from fresh coconut). Stir in and simmer until a thick cream forms around the beans.

Maharagwe ya nasi (Kidney beans in coconut, Kenya). Photo by Sean Williams.

SUKUMAWIKI (GREENS)

3 large bunches of spinach (or kale or collards)
1 large yellow onion
1–2 cloves garlic
1 t. salt
½ t. pepper
½ c. chopped golden raisins
2 T butter or vegetable oil
3 roma tomatoes, chopped
1 c. vegetable stock

Shred 3 large bunches of spinach or 1½ bunches of kale or collards. Sauté 1 large yellow onion, 1–2 cloves of garlic, 1 t. salt, ½ t. pepper, and ½ c. chopped golden raisins in 2 T butter or vegetable oil. Add roma tomatoes and sauté until thick. Mix in greens well. Add 1 c. vegetable stock. Cover and simmer until greens are tender, but still a dark green color.

UGALI (WHITE CORN MEAL) [FIRST OF THREE OPTIONS]

1 t. salt
2 c. corn meal

In a large, heavy pot, bring 4 c. water and 1 t. salt to a boil. Over a high flame, sprinkle 2 c. corn meal into the water, stirring as you go. As the mix gets thicker you will have to really stir, with force. When all the meal has been added, turn the flame to medium-low, and cook for 10 minutes or so, stirring constantly, and mashing any lumps against the side of the pot. Do not let it stick. It will get thick and smooth, and begin to pull away from the sides of the pot. Turn off the flame, cover and allow to cool a bit. Upcountry it is then turned out on to a central plate and scored with a knife tip like a chessboard to make breaking off pieces easier. On the coast it is sometimes taken out of the pot, formed into large balls, and placed on each person's plate. As I spent a fair amount of time on a *dhow*, we ate it directly from the pot. While it's steaming hot (scalding), break off a piece with your right hand, form a scoop, pick up stew, greens, or beans with it, and push it out of the hand and into the mouth with the thumb. It's efficient and graceful when done correctly.

Sukumawiki—sautéed greens (Kenya). Photo by Jesse Samba Wheeler.

CHAPATI (FLAT BREAD) [SECOND OF THREE OPTIONS]

3 c. flour
salt
2 T vegetable oil or butter

Mix 3 c. flour with 1¼ c. water and a pinch of salt; knead, and if you have time, set aside for a few hours. Then divide into 12 balls, making 2 *chapati* per person. Roll a ball out flat, then form a long, thin worm. Coil the worm up into what resembles a cinnamon bun. Drizzle butter/oil in the seams, then roll out flat. Repeat this process at least 4 times per ball. This creates layers in the *chapati*, so that it is flaky when cooked. Do this with each ball. Place a dry frying pan over a medium flame, and place a *chapati* face down on it (it curls up when you roll it out—this is face up) long enough to dry. Flip it over to dry the other side. Now brush with butter/oil and place face down. Bubbles should slowly appear. If not, press around the edges—this sometimes causes trapped air to form bubbles. When golden brown with dark spots, turn over. It should be served hot and soft.

WALI WA NASI (COCONUT RICE) [THIRD OF THREE OPTIONS]

2 c. white rice
2 c. coconut milk

Wash 2 c. rice 3 times. You will need about 5 c. liquid for the rice to absorb. If you made your own coconut milk, bring the weakest coconut milk, 2 c. water, and a little salt nearly to a boil in a heavy saucepan. Over medium heat, stir in the rice. Add the second run of milk. Keep stirring. As this is absorbed, add in the thickest of the milk. Cover tightly and let simmer for 20 minutes or so, adding a little more water if necessary. An alternative is to wash 2 c. rice and add it to a rice cooker with 2 c. coconut milk and 3 c. water, then start the rice cooker.

CHAI MAZIWA (MILKY TEA)

3 c. milk
2 T black tea
4 T sugar

In a saucepan place 3 c. water, 3 c. milk, 2 T black tea, and 4 T sugar. Boil. If you add a little cardomom, cinnamon, clove, and black pepper (all crushed), it becomes the delicious *chai special*. For those who don't like milk, make *Chai Kavu* (Dry Tea), boiling ginger, sugar, and tea in 1 cup of water per person. For those who prefer herbal teas, I used to drink in Mombasa a sweet hibiscus tea in small glass cups, especially in the mornings.

Kahawa Ya Tangawizi (Ginger Coffee)

Kenyans on the island of Lamu make a delicious coffee by boiling grounds with plenty of ginger. It makes a strong, hot, spicy cup. Sugar may be added to each cup. It is served in small glass cups.

Pushing the Week in Kenya

Stews are popular throughout Kenya, made with beef, goat, lamb, chicken, guinea fowl, and fish. Some are as basic as a broth with salt, pepper, and meat. Others add fruit, vegetables, and a variety of spices. Coastal and island cuisine make use of more spices, a result of centuries of trade with Arab and Indian lands. The culinary influence of these cultures is contained in the word *tamarindi*, which joins the Arabic word for "date," *tamr*, to *hindi*, as in "of India."

Another legacy of contact with Indian cuisine is the *chapati*. Kenyan *chapati* are more like Indian *naan* than *chapati*, tending to be thicker and oilier than their Indian namesakes. Beside *chapati*, I have included two other grain options. *Ugali*, made from white corn, is the national mainstay. Upcountry it tends to be stiffer, while on Lamu it was almost always smoother. This is a result of the flour-to-water ratio. Cooking it is a workout! The other option is coconut rice, the least likely to be served with beef stew, but delicious nonetheless. In this case you may want to omit the coconut milk from the *maharagwe ya nasi*, and cook the beans alone (this is actually a more common way of eating them, especially upcountry). Whichever your choice, it should be remembered that these are alternatives; they are not served together.

Sukumawiki, whose name literally means "push the week," is served throughout Kenya. The name derives from the practice of using this dish to feed the household when money for meat has run out, usually at the end of the week. As such, most anything can be added to the base of greens, onions, and tomatoes. The raisins are good if you use kale, which can be quite bitter.

Welcome your guests with a sincere "*Karibuni!*" (Welcome!) Serve the meal communally, in the middle of the table or on a cloth on the floor with pillows for sitting. Give each person a plate to keep individual portions, pieces of food, etc. Before the meal, walk from person to person with a pitcher of water and a basin and pour water over the guests' hands. This is repeated after the meal. The guests should eat *with their right hands only*, though the left hand may be used *as long as it doesn't come into contact with food that may be eaten by another.*

I lived in Kenya in 1990 and 1991, both upcountry in Machakos in Akamba territory (Ukambani), and on the island of Lamu. I returned to both for a brief stay in 1993. At the time of my first stay, the most popular musical styles upcountry were *benga*, a Western Kenyan guitar-based music, and what was called "Lingala music," the guitar-based music from then-Zaïre, often generically referred to as *soukous*. *Benga* was, in general terms, a mixture of certain Kenyan "dry" guitar styles (which at times resemble *palm-wine*) and "Lingala music," brought to Kenya beginning in the 1960s on records, over radio waves, and by musicians, some on tour, others coming to stay. Popular artists included Pepe Kalle of Zaïre, Simba Wanyika of Tanzania (and the Kenyan off-shoots Les Wanyika and Wanyika Super Les Les), Zaïri transplant Samba Mapangala and Orchestra Virunga, and the Kenyans Maroon Commandos, Kakai Kilonzo, and H.O. Kabaselleh. Aziz Abdi's "Sina kazi" ("I am unemployed") and Sam Muthee's "Dereva, chunga maisha" ("Driver, protect life!") were smash hits.

On the island of Lamu, I heard three kinds of music blaring from people's houses and storefronts, carried by the sea breeze over roofs and into the narrow streets thronged with handcarts, scampering sheep and idle donkeys, children skittering barefoot to and from *madrasa*, and adults ambling to the square, the mosque, or their homes. One was *tarabu*, which in the Lamu archipelago is more likely to feature the harmonium than a string section, as in the Zanzibari and Mombasa versions. The biggest singer at the time, even more popular than Zein, was Lamu-born Malika, and the song of hers on everyone's lips was "Wape, wape," whose refrain went

> Wape, wape, vidonge vyao.
> Wakimeza, wakitema,
> Ni shauri yao.

> (Give them, give them, their pills.
> If they swallow them or if they spit them out
> Is their business.)

Though not specified, because of then-president Daniel Arap Moi's position on reproductive rights, the pills mentioned were universally understood to refer to contraceptives.

The other two types of music heard were roots reggae and Tracy Chapman. Tracy represented a type as well as an example, because her music was unique in that context—no other U.S. or European artist was heard, except in isolated cases where a tourist had left behind a tape (one such instance was David Byrne/Brian Eno's *My Life in the Bush of Ghosts*). Tracy's look, voice, and singing style appealed to reggae fans, I think. My friend Dickson Kombi Yeri, who played her music daily, refused to believe that she was a woman, as her voice (and the ambiguous image on her debut album's cover) did not jive with his gendered imaginings.

When I returned in 1993, *tarabu* had declined in popularity, while dancehall reggae and a smattering of U.S. music had gained ground on Lamu. Upcountry one heard less "Lingala music" and almost no *benga*, whereas Camerounian *makossa*, dancehall, and U.S. hip-hop were playing in the discos.

RECOMMENDED LISTENING

Chapman, Tracy. *Tracy Chapman*. Elektra, 1988.
Malika. *Tarabu*. Shanachie, 1997. (Or try to find her numbered albums, especially #8, which contains the mentioned song.)
Mapangala, Samba. *Virunga Volcano*. Earthworks, 1998.
Various. *Before Benga, Vol. 1: Kenya Dry*. Original Music, 1988.
Various. *Kenya Dance Mania: East Africa's Finest Rumbas & Other Styles*. Earthworks, 1995.

FOR FURTHER INFORMATION

Barz, Gregory F. 2001. Meaning of "Benga" music in Western Kenya. *British Journal of Ethnomusicology* 10/1.
Mboya, Tom. 1970. *Challenge of Nationhood*. Portsmouth, NH: Heinemann.
Mwangi, Meja. 1976. *Going Down River Road*. Portsmouth, NH: Heinemann.
Ngugi wa Thiong'o. 1986. *Decolonising the Mind: The Politics of Language in African Literature*. Portsmouth, NH: Heinemann.
———. 1969. *Weep Not, Child*. New York: MacMillan.
Ntarangwi, Mwenda. 2001. *Gender, Performance & Identity: Understanding Swahili Cultural Identy Through Songs*. Trenton, NJ: Africa World Press.

NORTHERN GHANA (DAGOMBA ETHNICITY)

David Locke (learned from Alhaji Dolsi-naa Abubakari Lunna)

Eat the same food every day so you know what killed you.

Menu: *Sima Zeri* (Groundnut Soup) and *Sakoro* (aka *Fufu*, Boiled and Pounded Cassava, Yams, and Plantain).
Preparation Time: 1 hour.
Cooking Process: This extremely basic, very simple version of a classic West African meal is for a bachelor or family man away from home. First find a "tropical market" that caters to migrants from Africa and its diaspora to buy the powdered *fufu* and shrimp flavorings. With the ingredients on hand, cook the soup and keep warm; at mealtime prepare the *sakoro* and eat immediately. Rice or thick mashed potatoes can be substituted for the *sakoro*. Serve the soup in one large bowl; form the *sakoro* into fist-size balls and serve on a separate platter. Eat by hand in a communal manner. Serves six people.

The Recipes

SIMA ZERI (GROUNDNUT SOUP)

6–10 pieces of chicken (legs, thighs with bones)
1 medium-sized onion
2 cloves garlic
9 oz. peanut butter
3 oz. tomato paste
1 shrimp bouillon cube
1 T shrimp flakes or powder
⅛ t. red pepper to taste
salt to taste

In a large saucepan start 4 c. water to boil. Skin the chicken pieces; trim away fat. Put chicken into boiling water. Finely chop 1 medium-sized onion and 2 cloves of garlic; add to pan. Add 9 oz. peanut butter, 3 oz. tomato paste, 1 shrimp bouillon cube, 1 T shrimp flakes, and pinch of red pepper. Boil gently for 15–20 minutes, stirring occasionally, until the oil separates from the peanut butter and rises to the surface. Skim off the oil and discard it. Remove the soup from the heat and let stand for 10 minutes.

Sima zeri (Groundnut soup, Northern Ghana). Photo by Sean Williams.

SAKORO (FUFU, BOILED AND POUNDED CASSAVA, YAMS, OR PLANTAINS)

1 box of powdered plantain *fufu*

"Instant" *fufu* in a box is readily available at tropical food markets; follow the directions on the package. Have a sturdy wooden spoon on hand for stirring, which requires considerable physical strength. If you are unable to find *fufu*, you can make either mashed potatoes or rice. (I am not fond of *sakoro* and prefer Japanese rice made in a rice cooker.)

Bachelor Living in Northern Ghana

Groundnut soup with *fufu* is a hallmark of West African cuisine. My teacher of Dagomba music, Dolsi-naa Abubakari Lunna, improvised this "bachelor" version for his daily meal while living with my family in the United States. When our children were young we called it "Skippy Soup." After Dolsi-naa Abubakari Lunna had a stroke, we developed this low salt, low fat recipe. Watching me trim off the skin and fat, Alhaji would ruefully muse, "That is the sweetest part!", but the improvements in his blood pressure more than made up for the diminished flavor. At home in Ghana, Alhaji's wives would never allow him to cook, not only because he would be useless in the kitchen but because household chores are divided by gender. For years I resisted learning how to make it because I knew it would become my obligation; now I can whip up a pot of peanut butter stew in half an hour. I offer this "man, a can, and a plan" recipe for this project with a large measure of ironic humor. The idea that a Dagomba man is the source of this recipe is pretty strange: may African women forgive us!

Fufu, boiled root crops and/or plantain pounded to a paste, is a staple in the forested regions of West Africa. In Africa the preparation of *sakoro*, the word for *fufu* in *Dagbani*, the mother tongue of the *Dagomba* people, is a graceful, musical ritual. Standing on opposite sides of a large wooden mortar, several women beat the hot boiled starch with large wooden pestles. Deftly following their rhythmic beating, a third woman turns *fufu* until it has become a gleaming glutinous mass. The intricately coordinated, rhythmicized group effort of food preparation perfectly mirrors the exciting multipart, call-and-response style of African music for the dance.

Eating by hand from communal bowls also is an aesthetically stylized occasion. After "cutting" off a bite-sized portion of the *sakoro*, one dips the dollop into the sauce, and taking care not to allow the sauce to touch the lips, swallows it without chewing. Bites of meat are eaten separately from the starch. A bowl of soapy water and a hand towel is made available after eating.

In Dagomba culture, many of life's activities are segregated along lines of family heritage, sex, and age. Preparing and eating food is no exception. People eat together in groups according to age and sex: children of both sexes eat together, male and female adolescents eat separately, as do adults. Meals usually are eaten privately, quickly, and quietly. Typically, there is only one course. The idea is to feel full, well fed, and ready for whatever challenges life may bring. Once the stomach is satisfied, socializing happily follows.

Regarding the proverb: Violent jealousy is a problem in West African societies, making poisoning a constant anxiety. Disease from microorganisms and unhygienic food preparation is another concern. For these reasons, many people prefer to eat homecooking, prepared by a trusted family member.

RECOMMENDED LISTENING

Drum Damba, Featuring Abubakari Lunna, A Master Drummer of Dagbon. White Cliffs Media Company, 1996. WCM 9508.
Exponent of Bamaya: Traditional Music from Northern Ghana. Zadonu Records, 2001. ZR 3263. Zadonu Records, P.O. Box 950667, Mission Hills, CA 91345.

FOR FURTHER INFORMATION

http://www.ghana.co.uk/history/
http://www.allghanadata.com/culture/index.asp

CAPE VERDE ISLANDS, ATLANTIC WEST AFRICA

Susan Hurley-Glowa

> *A beautiful party has to have music, dance, and food!*
>
> Norberto Tavares

Menu: *Catchupa* (Hominy with Lima Beans and Meat), *Salada de Alface* (Green Salad with Vinaigrette), and *Fruta Fresca* (Fresh Mango, Papaya, and Banana). Serve with Portuguese *viño verde* wine or cold beer.

Preparation Time: 3 hours (not counting the time to soak the hominy and beans overnight).

Cooking Process: The night before you make this meal, soak the hominy and beans separately. When you are ready to cook make the *catchupa* first, then the green salad. Just before the *catchupa* is ready, peel and cut up the fresh fruit. To prevent the banana from turning dark, sprinkle a little lime juice over the cut pieces. Serves six people.

The Recipes

CATCHUPA (HOMINY WITH LIMA BEANS AND MEAT)

2–3 c. dried white hominy corn (available in the Spanish/Mexican section of the grocery store)
½ lb. dried lima beans
3–4 chicken or beef bouillon cubes
1 bay leaf
2 T olive oil (Portuguese Azeite, if possible)
2 large onions
6 cloves garlic
2 lb. beef (or other meat) for stewing, cut into bite-sized cubes
1 small cabbage, sliced fine (to make 2 cups), or kale
1 yucca or manioc root (8" long, 2"–3" in diameter), cut into pieces (to make 2 cups)
1–2 c. hard winter squash (optional)
salt
pepper

Soak the corn and beans overnight, separately. Wash and strain the corn and beans. Boil the corn in a large, heavy kettle for about 10 minutes, discarding the froth that collects on the top. Add the beans, bouillon cubes, 1 bay leaf, 2 T of olive oil, and enough water to cover the corn and beans, and bring to a boil. Partially cover the top and simmer at a low boil for 1 hour. Stir and add water periodically so that the beans and corn are always covered. In a large skillet, sauté the onions and garlic in the olive oil until soft. Add the pieces of beef and brown. When the corn and beans have begun to soften after about an hour of cooking, add the browned meat, onions, and garlic. Add additional water, if necessary. Cook partially covered at a gentle boil over low heat for an additional 90 minutes. Add the cabbage and yucca pieces (and optional squash) about half an hour before serving, adding more water as it evaporates. Add salt and pepper to taste. The stew can be served with varying degrees of liquid remaining—it always a rather thick soup, and it is okay if virtually all the water is absorbed when it is reheated and served for breakfast as leftovers.

SALADA DE ALFACE (GREEN SALAD)

Wash and shred enough salad greens to feed six people. Prepare a vinaigrette by combining olive oil and red wine vinegar with fresh or dried herbs to taste.

FRUTA FRESCA (FRESH FRUIT)

Peel and cut up a variety of fresh fruit (mango, papaya, banana) and arrange in a bowl or plate. To keep the fruit fresh-looking, squeeze the juice of 1 lime over the cut pieces. Serve after dinner.

Sharing Catchupa in Cape Verde

Catchupa is a favorite dish from the Cape Verdean islands, and there are as many variations of this recipe as there are cooks making it. It is a stew based on dried corn, beans, onions, and garlic that are boiled together for many hours. Other added ingredients depend very much on what is available at the right price on any given day. *Catchupa rica* (rich *catchupa*) has meat (beef, pork, bacon, goat, chicken, or fish) and an abundance of vegetables, while a more basic version is called *Catchupa povera*. The recipe can be easily adapted for vegetarians by omitting the meat. It is often made with tuna or other firm fish in Cape Verde with excellent results. This dish is a hearty meal in itself and needs only a green salad with a vinaigrette dressing as accompaniment. It goes well with a cold beer or a well-chilled Portuguese *viño verde* wine. It is sometimes served with *piri-piri*, a local homemade hot sauce made from tiny hot peppers marinated in whiskey, vinegar, olive oil, and a little salt. Leftover *catchupa* tastes wonderful warmed up for breakfast, served on a bed of browned onions with a fried egg on top (*Catchupa ku ova strelado*) and a spicy fried *linguiça* sausage on the side.

I had heard about *catchupa* long before I visited the islands, as it is a comfort food and symbol of home for Cape Verdean immigrants I met in southern New England. Food takes on a special significance in Cape Verde because the islands have had such a tragic history of drought and famine over the past 500 years; sharing food together is always a time to be thankful and joyful. Making *catchupa* is quite labor intensive in its original village context. After the corn is harvested and dried, the hulls are removed from the tough corn kernels by pounding them with long wooden pestles in heavy, drum-shaped vessels made from tree trunks, similar to those found in mainland Africa for pounding grain. Women often do the *pilão*, or pounding of the corn in tandem, standing across from each other and alternating strokes. The action forms a polyrhythm pattern that is the basis for many Cape Verdean folk songs, and women often sing as they beat the corn. The corn and beans are generally soaked for a day or so to soften them, reducing the overall boiling time.

I first saw *catchupa* cooking in 1991 when I visited the home of the *funana* accordion player Kodé di Dona, in the dusty little village of São Francisco located along the eastern coast of the island of São Tiago (also called Santiago). Kodé's young daughters were in charge of the *catchupa*, a typical chore for adolescent females. The *catchupa* simmered in a large, cast iron footed pot that sat directly over the wood and charcoal fire in a small, stone cooking-shack, located behind the main house. This thatched hut provided shelter from the endless wind that blows in from the sea across the stony, barren Cape Verdean hills. Firewood, charcoal, and fresh water are precious commodities in the bone-dry countryside, and the young girls had the formidable responsibility to keep the fire burning and making sure that the stew did not dry out and burn during its many hours in the pot.

Because *catchupa* takes a long time to cook, it is often saved for special gatherings of family and friends called *catchupada* (other staple dishes based on rice are more economical for daily consumption). *Catchupa* is generally not an expensive dish to eat in a local restaurant, although the tourist hotels on the island of Sal have begun to charge outrageous prices to foreigners who want to sample the native cuisine. When a big pot of *catchupa* is prepared in a typical village family context, the meal often develops into an impromptu *festa*, as Cape Verdeans like more than anything else in the world to hear their music, dance, tell stories, and socialize with other *Krioulos*, especially when their stomachs are full! Cape Verdean party food is not served with a high degree of ceremony; everyone simply fills a plate, grabs a fork, and looks out for a wooden stool for a seat. Shots of *groggo* (local rum) may well be distributed until the bottle runs dry. At Cape Verdean gatherings throughout the diaspora, someone always has a guitar, a *cavaquinho*, or an accordion handy to share a *morna* or *coladeira,* and folks don't wait to be asked to dance. Once a *festa* gets started, a good one may well continue until the sun begins to rise. This gusto for living, always fused with a large dose of *saudade* or bittersweet nostalgia, is something that remains a central part of the Cape Verdean character, following its people from the remote Atlantic islands located west of the coast of Senegal to new communities spread across the four corners of the globe.

RECOMMENDED LISTENING

Cape Verde. Putumayo World Music, 1999. PUTU 156-2.
Cesaria Evora. *Miss Perfumada.* Lusafrica, 1992. 79540-2.
de Barros, Maria. *Nha Mundo Music of Cabo Verde.* Narada Productions, 2003.
L'âme du Cap Vert. Lusafrica, 1996. COL 486631-2.
Lura. *Di Korpu ku Alma.* Lusafrica, 2005. 462362.

FOR FURTHER INFORMATION

http://www.umassd.edu/specialprograms/caboverde/
http://capeverde-islands.com/
http://www.caboverde.com/evora/evora.htm

NAMIBIA

Minette Mans (with thanks to my mother Minn Stewart, Eli Hausiku, and Kyllikki Nampala)

If you want to eat, you must work.

Menu: *Braaied* (Grilled Goat or Lamb Chops), *Mahangu* (Sorghum or Maize Meal Porridge with a Spicy Tomato Sauce), *Ekaka* (Spinach), and *Oshikuki* (Doughnuts or Pumpkin Fritters). Serve with copious amounts of *Tafel Lager, oshikundu* or careful sips of *omagongo* liquor.

Preparation Time: Approximately 3 hours.

Cooking Process: You will need a supply of good quality wood (ideally camelthorn or mangetti) to make a fire, and a metal grill on which to grill the meat. Accompanying dishes should be prepared before cooking the meat, which is quick (about 10–15 minutes). The outdoor fire should be made well ahead of time, so that flames have died down and the grid can be placed over a bed of red-hot coals. The best temperature for the meat is when you can hold your hand for just over 10 seconds above the grid. Serves six people.

The Recipes

BRAAIED (GRILLED GOAT OR LAMB CHOPS)

6 lamb or goat chops
salt
pepper

The 6 chops should be removed from wrapping, patted dry, and placed in a container until ready to grill. Meat is placed on the grill without spices, because at this stage spices would tend to draw out the juices. Do not turn the meat until one side has sealed and is browned. Then turn and season the brown side with salt and pepper to taste. Repeat when other side is done. Remove and eat as soon as possible.

Mahangu (Sorghum or Maize Meal Porridge with a Spicy Tomato Sauce)

5 c. sorghum meal

2 medium yellow onions

1 T vegetable oil

1 clove garlic

4 tomatoes

salt

pepper

½ t. coriander

½ red chili pepper (optional), seeded and chopped

Bring 1 quart of water to a boil in a heavy, deep saucepan. Mix 1 c. *mahangu* (sorghum) meal in 2 c. water in a separate bowl. Pour *mahangu* mixture into saucepan and stir. Reduce heat and cover pot to simmer for 5–10 minutes. Then add 4 c. *mahangu* to the mixture and stir well for about 5 minutes until the mixture has thickened nicely. Reduce heat, cover, and simmer for another 10 minutes. In the meantime, make the tomato sauce by finely slicing 2 onions and sauté in a little oil until transparent. Crush 1 garlic clove and roughly chop 4 tomatoes, and add to the onions. Simmer for about 10 minutes, stirring occasionally. Stir the *mahangu* again for about 3 minutes with a large wooden spoon. Cover once more and simmer for 15 minutes. Now go back to the tomato sauce: add salt and pepper to taste, and ½ t. coriander. You may wish to add half a chopped, seeded chili (optional). Simmer for another few minutes until the tomato sauce is soft but still visibly chunky. Check the *mahangu*; the consistency should be firm, so that portions can be eaten by hand and dipped into sauces. Usually the porridge should pull away from the side of the saucepan. Serve together with the tomato sauce for dipping.

Ekaka (Fresh Spinach) or Evanda (Dried Spinach)

1 large bunch spinach

1 medium yellow onion

1 medium tomato

1 T vegetable oil

1 T flour

1 T butter

Chop or tear a large bunch of washed spinach into pieces and add to 1 c. cold salted water. Bring to a boil. In a separate saucepan, gently sauté 1 finely chopped onion and 1 chopped to-mato in 1 T of cooking oil until translucent. Add to spinach. Simmer gently until the spinach has wilted and cook until tender (about 30 minutes). Moisten 1 T flour in a little cold water and add with 1 T butter to mixture. Stir until sauce has thickened.

OSHIKUKI (DOUGHNUTS OR PUMPKIN FRITTERS FROM MY 88-YEAR-OLD MOTHER)

1 medium butternut or pumpkin squash
2 T flour or maize flour
½ c. cold milk
1 egg
salt
2 t. cinnamon
1 c. sugar
1 c. vegetable oil for frying

Slice 1 medium butternut squash or pumpkin in half; place face down on a lightly greased cookie sheet and bake at 350°F until soft; about 1 hour. Blend 2 T flour or maize flour with ½ c. cold milk, and add 1 egg and a pinch of salt. Mix well. Soften cooked squash with a fork, and slowly blend in the egg and milk mixture, until it develops a soft, smooth consistency (like soft ice cream); set aside. Mix 2 t. cinnamon and ½ c. sugar and set aside. Heat 1 c. oil in a deep frying pan until the oil begins to shimmer (not so hot that it smokes). Add one spoon of squash mix at a time to the pan, taking care to keep the blobs apart as they will spread a bit. Fry a few minutes on each side until golden brown (remember to turn carefully so as not to break them). Sprinkle some of the sugar in the bottom of a serving dish. Add a layer of fritters and sprinkle some sugar over. As they are done, add further layers, with a layer of sugar on each. Serve hot and still crispy.

Slowing Down in Namibia

The dishes offered here are more or less representative of the broad Namibian population. However, diverse cultures mean diverse menus, and Namibian cultures include German and Afrikaner as well as Owambo, Damara, Nama, Herero, and other groups. But meat and porridge prevail across the country. Meat is usually eaten by hand, not using a knife and fork. Go ahead—tear the meat off with your teeth—it tastes great! Often in Namibia, the meat is cooked in a black iron pot over the fire, but as this tends to collect sauces, the meat is more likely to toughen. While chops have been recommended, almost any portion of an animal might be cooked this way (ribs, shoulder, neck, and unrecognizable chunks). Toughness is often not considered a problem, as the process of tearing meat with your teeth slows the eating, and allows for companionable chatter.

Most of the recipes above are typical of the central and eastern north, as well as the central region. In general, singing and dancing take place on specific occasions such as weddings and funerals, and while both food and music are important components of most important events, music is not a part of daily mealtimes. *Omahangu* is the major food resource in the north, but several other wild fruits, nuts, groundnuts, and wild vegetables are used creatively. *Mahangu oshifima* is a pap or firm porridge (maize meal is smoother and cooks more quickly, but *mahangu* is a sorghum grain, more coarse and more tasty). The preparation of the *mahangu* meal in a more old-fashioned home means that the grain needs to be stamped in a wooden mortar with large wooden pestles. This task, performed by women and girls, requires strength and commitment, and is eased by singing to coordinate the stamping actions—two or three pestles to a mortar. These songs, responsorial in form, are called *oshiimbo shokakukula* in the Oshikwanyama language, and the variations in stamping rhythms provide an interesting, ever-changing counterpoint to the quiet singing. To eat the *mahangu*, break off a small portion of the porridge by hand, and gently form into a ball with your fingers (one hand) and then dip this into the tomato sauce or the *ekaka* (or both). It is also delicious when served with *ekaka* (spinach), *omatalanga* (tripe), or *okapenda* (sardines). The fritters are also eaten by hand. Namibians are likely to have beer as a beverage, because we brew very good beer! *Tafel Lager* is the beer of choice. The daily local drink is *oshikundu*, which consists of a small amount (about a cup) of *mahangu* meal (dry) mixed with a little over a quart of water and a little sugar. As it starts to ferment in the course of the day it becomes more potent toward evening. It is made fresh every day.

In a typical Owambo household, the children are responsible for household chores and cooking the food, especially the *mahangu*. In the meantime, adults gather in the *oshoto*, an outdoor eating and gathering place with a fire in the center. They might enjoy a sweet drink (usually the tinned variety) or beer. The latter is generally bottled, but many people prefer the homemade variety, *omalovu*, prepared from millet, sugar, and water and left to ferment for a few days in a calabash container. Before eating, a bowl of water, soap, and a cloth is passed around for everybody to wash their hands. Adults eat first and enjoy a leisurely conversation, while dipping firm, handheld balls of the *mahangu* porridge into a sauce or eating it plain. The firm porridge is usually served on a large communal platter accompanied by a smaller bowl of the sauce (chicken, sardine, or vegetable). If the occasion is somewhat more special, such as entertaining special visitors, a goat might be slaughtered and the fresh meat grilled on the grid on the fire.

When the adults have finished, the children enter the *oshoto* area and enjoy their meal. The children might afterward play outside the homestead—play meaning singing and dancing *uudhano*, for example. Adults might take up hymn books and sing for an hour or more. Alternatively, older men might gather for drinking of *marula* liquor, *omagongo* (pronounced aw-mah-horn-gaw), a startlingly potent distillation of this indigenous fruit. There is also a milder beer brewed from the same fruit. These drinking songs, *oshiimbo shomagongo*, are sung in praise of the liquor, but as the effect takes hold the songs tend to sound more and more mournful.

Probably the most important music and food event in Owambo tradition is the wedding (*ohango*). Even Christian weddings are huge, and often last for several days with vast numbers of friends, relatives, and others. People gather and usually need to be accommodated and fed somehow. On attending such a wedding of a close friend, my son and I shared a three-room house with 23 others, and we were the few honored ones who slept inside! The bride accommodated about 120 guests and probably the groom did as well. She slaughtered three heifers, five goats, and untold numbers of chickens, and guests brought along some as well. *Mahangu* was constantly simmering, and doughnuts frying. At mealtimes there was carrot salad and potato salad to accompany grilled meat. Singing began early in the evenings and continued throughout the night. Interestingly, it is the norm for men to sing hymns all night, while the women sing traditional weddings songs, blow whistles, and dance throughout the extended homestead. Whenever people were hungry, they headed for the huge pot of *mahangu* simmering on the coals, or found pieces of meat to grill. The singing didn't stop until after sunrise. Following the church service, the singing of hymns by men and wedding songs by women once again accompanied the two-hour procession back to the bride's home. Here the two families approached one another ritually with loud competitive singing, dancing, and ululating. Once they had ritually met and embraced and given gifts, the real feasting began. Praise singers addressed their songs to the bridal couple, followed by eating—more meat, fruit, rice, vegetables, but no *mahangu*. After the meal, the music system, speakers, and disc jockey made an appearance and the dancing to *soukous*, *kwaito*, and hip-hop began.

The Namibian hunger for meat is considered so basic that it has been effectively used as an argument to defend cattle poaching! Cattle, therefore, not surprisingly feature as a core part of much Namibian music and dance. There are songs specifically for cattle praise, the dance movements echo cattle movements and arm attitudes symbolize cattle, strength, and ownership (wealth). The importance of meat is not only real to people of African descent, but also to those of European descent. Hence meat on an open fire, sizzling on the coals, is an image and an aroma found across the country on any weekend.

RECOMMENDED LISTENING

Namibia. Ju/'hoansi Bushmen Instrumental Music. Ocora-Radio France, France.
Namibia. Songs of the Ju/'hoansi Bushmen. Ocora-Radio France, France.

(These two rare albums give a wonderful overview of the most important Ju/'hoan songs and instrumental music, including games, hunting, and trance songs. Recorded by ethnomusicologist Emmanuelle Olivier in the Nyae Nyae area during her doctoral field research.)

Set-son & the Mighty Dreads. *Kula Umone.* (Self-produced cool *shambo* music—an Owambo contemporary music, blending traditional and reggae sounds.)
Various. *A Handful of Namibians & Papa Wemba.* Hothouse Productions, 2003. FNCC.

FOR FURTHER INFORMATION

http://www.grnnet.gov.na/ (general information, official take).
http://ijea.asu.edu/v1n3 (Mans, Minette. 2000. Using Namibian music/dance traditions as a basis for reforming arts education. *International Journal of Education and the Arts* 1.)

3
East Asia

CHAOZHOU, CHINA

Mercedes DuJunco

Better to be deprived of food for three days than tea for one.

Menu: *Jia Cai Bao* (Mustard Greens and Pork Stew), *Luo Bo Gan Chao Dan* (Daikon Radish Cake Omelet), *Ku Gua Tang* (Bitter Melon, Short Ribs, and Pickled Vegetable Soup), *Zheng Hai Yu* (Steamed Fish with Ginger and Soy Sauce), *Zhou* (Congee/Rice Porridge), Fresh Sliced Fruit in Season, and Gongfu Tea.

Preparation Time: 2 hours to soak the beans, then another 2 hours to cook the meal.

Cooking Process: If possible, purchase a live fish and do the gutting and scaling yourself at home. Start cooking the pork stew first, then start on the soup. Make the steamed fish, then the daikon radish cake omelet while the fish is steaming. After dinner, slice up some fresh fruit and serve with tea. Serves six people.

The Recipes

JIA CAI BAO (MUSTARD GREENS AND PORK STEW)

5 dried *shiitake* mushrooms
5 T vegetable oil
1½ lb. pork meat
2 bunches mustard greens
2 t. salt
3–5 thin slices fresh ginger
dash of fish sauce

Place 5 dried *shiitake* mushrooms in warm water to soak. Heat 5 T oil in a medium-sized clay stew pot or Dutch oven for about 1 minute and add 1½ lb. pork meat, chopped into bite-sized pieces. After the pieces of meat have been browned a bit, add 2 bunches of washed and chopped mustard leaves. Sauté until the leaves turn a bright green, then sprinkle in 2 t. salt, all the while turning the leaves over and around the vessel. Now add 1 c. water, the chopped mushrooms, and 3–5 slices of fresh ginger cut into matchstick pieces. Bring the liquid to a boil, then lower the heat. Simmer for 15–20 minutes or until the meat is completely tender. Stir a bit, then turn off the heat. Add a dash of fish sauce to taste and serve.

Luo Bo Gao Chao Dan (Daikon Radish Cake Omelet)

1 8-oz. package of daikon radish cake
3 T vegetable oil
6 eggs, beaten
salt
pepper

Thaw, rinse, and cut daikon radish cake into lengthwise pieces. Heat 3 T vegetable oil in a medium-sized, flat-bottomed, nonstick frying pan. Add the pieces of daikon radish cake and sauté until light brown. Then pour in the eggs. Tilt the pan in all directions so that the liquid spreads to most of the surface of the pan, forming a circle. Sprinkle a pinch of salt and pepper. Keep the fire in medium heat until the egg liquid bubbles and fully coagulates, then lower the heat. Using a turner, flip the omelet in order to also cook the other side. Then fold it into a roll. Turn off the heat. Cut folded or rolled omelet crosswise into many pieces and serve.

Ku Gua Tang (Bitter Melon, Short Ribs, and Pickled Vegetable Soup)

1 c. yellow soybeans
2 bitter melons
1 lb. pickled leafy vegetables
3–5 lb. beef short ribs
3 T fish sauce
salt

Soak 1 c. yellow soybeans for 2 hours before cooking to soften and remove the husks. Pour 6 c. water into a large stockpot. Drain the soybeans and discard the husks that have come off after soaking. Put in 2 bitter melons (halved, seeded, and chopped), 1 c. yellow soybeans, 1 lb. pickled leafy vegetables, and 3–5 lb. short ribs. Bring to a boil, then lower heat and simmer until meat is tender. Lastly, add 3 T fish sauce and salt to taste.

Zheng Hai Yu (Steamed Fish with Ginger and Soy Sauce)

1 large flounder, monkfish, or other freshwater fish (about 3 lb.)
3 T salt
6 slices fresh ginger
1 T vegetable oil
2 c. soy sauce

First bring 2–3 c. water to a boil in a large covered vessel, then reduce to moderate heat. Rub the inside of 1 large freshwater fish fillet with 3 T salt, then place in a steam basket. Arrange 6 slices of fresh ginger on top of the fish. Lower the basket into the vessel with the water. Make sure the steam basket is not submerged in the water. Cover the vessel and steam to cook the fish until tender. Uncover the pot and douse the fish with 1 T vegetable oil; simmer for 1 more minute, then turn off the heat. Serve with dipping soy sauce on the side.

ZHOU (CONGEE/RICE PORRIDGE)

½ c. Jasmine rice, uncooked, washed

2 T cooking oil

Put rice and 6 c. water into a saucepan and pour in the oil. Bring quickly to a boil, then lower the heat and stir. Cover with the saucepan lid slightly ajar and allow to simmer for 30–40 minutes after which the congee should be ready.

Tea and Sympathy

Chinese people's high regard for tea is legendary, as affirmed by the opening proverb of this article. Chinese lore tells of tea connoisseurs parting with small fortunes in exchange for a few grams of premium, high-grade tea. This should not elicit too much wonder; after all, tea had originated in China and, having made the first brew, the Chinese went on to perfect the preparation of tea and elevate it into an art form well ahead of the Japanese with their tea ceremony. Much of the esoteric knowledge and culture surrounding tea, however, have fallen by the wayside in mainland China in the face of modernity and the social and political upheavals of the twentieth century. In many parts of the country today, people drink tea as they do water and brew tea as Westerners normally brew coffee—with a minimum of fuss.

One place where the preparation and drinking of tea in everyday life retains some of the serious character and attention to detail described in *Chajing* ("Book of Tea"), the classical treatise on

Gongfu Tea (Chaozhou, China). Photo by Mercedes DuJunco.

tea written by Lu Yu in 780 C.E., is the region of Chaozhou in eastern Guangdong Province in south China. One of the things that Chaozhou is well known for is *gongfucha* (*gongfu* means "laborious time" and *cha* means "tea")—a name alluding to the time-consuming practice needed to master the knowledge and etiquette of preparing strong, black Wulong tea in tiny cups using an elaborate tea set with its host of implements. However, Chinese from this area, who refer to themselves as Teochiu in their native dialect, appreciate good food as well as a strong brew of *gongfucha* and often consume them in tandem with each other. In Chaozhou culture, feasting and drinking *gongfucha* form a whole complex of normative, ritualistic social behavior together with the performance of Chaozhou traditional string ensemble music and the singing of Chaozhou opera excerpts. Many Teochiu (mostly men) indulge in them within the privacy of their homes or within the confines of numerous music clubs and native place associations found throughout the region and within many Teochiu diasporic communities abroad. Together, banquets, rounds of *gongfucha*, and hours of smoke-filled music sessions help facilitate the forging and renewal of bonds of trust, friendship, and ethnic affinity, without which Teochiu businessman would find it nearly impossible to even gain a foothold in the competitive world of rice trading, the export of Chinese medicines, remittance banking, and other businesses.

I used the word "banquets" above because Chaozhou meals, even the simplest ones cooked and eaten at home, normally consist of several dishes. They are clearly not meant to be eaten alone. There are usually two kinds of soup, two to three main dishes, steamed rice or, more commonly, plain congee, a warm or cool dessert of either beans cooked in syrup or fruits in season—all topped with *gongfucha* to help digest everything. In the meals I have eaten with my Teochiu friends, it was common practice to eat the dishes unaccompanied by rice or congee and to save these for last. When I asked the reason for this, I was told that eating rice or congee at the outset of a meal would make me full right away and leave no room for the main dishes. The nutritional wisdom of this practice was really brought home to me when I found myself actually weighing five pounds less (!) at the end of a 2-week visit to Chaozhou, despite the fact that I had eaten these huge meals throughout my stay. Teochiu had obviously discovered the secret of maintaining one's ideal weight through a healthy, low-carb, fish protein-rich diet, coupled with the regular consumption of *gongfucha*, long before the invention of the Atkins and the South Beach diets or the recent Western discovery of the wonders of tea.

Chaozhou cuisine is one of the "three main flavors" of Guangdong, the other two being the Cantonese and Hakka cuisines. It derived a lot of elements from southern Fujian (Minnan) cooking, but has also absorbed influences from the cuisines of Guangzhou (Canton), east-central China, and Southeast Asia. It is known for its seafood, sweet dishes, and the numerous condiments that go with the cooking that give the food their distinctive tastes. The cooking style reflects a reliance on the sea for food and efforts by cooks to remove the fishy smell from the food. Consequently, there are quite a lot of processed fish products such as dried fish, fish balls, fish dumplings, etc., and many different locally manufactured condiments for dipping, which unfortunately are not easily available elsewhere outside the region.

Many Chaozhou restaurants specialize in fresh seafood and often feature rows of see-through glass tanks containing varieties of live marine animals, both freshwater and seawater, which could rival the marine exhibits in many U.S. city aquariums. There are typically no written menus in these restaurants. Instead, one just points to the fish, prawn, crab, lobster, oysters, clams, mollusks, abalone, or sea slugs of choice and discuss the price with the server and how you want it cooked: boiled, steamed, grilled, or fried. It is then fished out of the tank, gutted, cleaned, and custom cooked for you in a matter of minutes.

There is less emphasis on meat such as beef and pork in this regional cuisine. These are frequently cooked in a dish or a soup in combination with other ingredients, such as mushrooms, bamboo shoots, leafy vegetables, carrots, and other root crops. For poultry, duck and goose are preferred over chicken. These are either braised or roasted. However, chicken must be used on certain occasions according to local custom. For example, on the occasion of young males reaching the age of 15 years, a whole chicken is served and the boy must eat the head of the cooked bird.

Rice and wheat are the two staple foods. But due to the high population density of the Chaozhou region (it is one of the densest area in Guangdong) and limited cultivable land, there has constantly been a shortage of rice and a need for it to be imported from Southeast Asia, mostly from Thailand. In former times, economic conditions were reportedly so bad that there were often threats and actual periods of famine. The need to make do and adapt to conditions of near-starvation resulted in the substitution of rice with root crops such as boiled sweet potatoes or cooking watery rice which we now know as congee. Teochiu have gotten so used to eating congee even in times of plenty that they seldom eat steamed rice. In fact, I have yet to see a Teochiu person refuse a bowl of congee when they are offered it toward the end of a meal. They tend to eat it plain, as though it is a dish by itself. The gusto and relish with which Teochiu eat congee reveals it to be a comfort food.

The limited amount of cultivable land in Chaozhou also meant that the little that is there is devoted to the planting of rice and wheat, leaving hardly anywhere to grow vegetables. Consequently, these have to be imported from other regions and, barring that, Teochiu had to resort to pickling whatever vegetables they could get their hands on, along with root crops (carrots, beets, turnips, etc.), and even tofu. These pickled foods are often eaten together with congee in the mornings for breakfast, which tends to be light. Since I am not particularly fond of pickles and congee, I often skip breakfast or eat steamed buns made of wheat together with soymilk bought from a street vendor.

My favorite meal of the day is late at night before going to bed. Many Teochiu often eat a midnight snack (*yexiao*) and, for this, it is common to go out on the streets to patronize one of the countless food stalls offering all kinds of *xiaochi* (literally, "little meals" or snacks). These may include fried dumplings, glutinous rice cakes, fried radish cakes, spring rolls, fried noodles, noodle soup, and savory congee (cooked with chicken broth). My Teochiu friends were often concerned about me going to bed hungry, so every night they would take me out for a midnight snack and a few rounds of *gongfucha* before we all turned in. For those who have a problem sleeping after drinking caffeinated beverages a few hours before bedtime, I recommend that you skip the *gongfucha* and refrain from drinking it after 3 pm. since it is quite strong. Otherwise, drink away, for there is nothing better to wash down and neutralize those rich, delicious Chaozhou snacks.

RECOMMENDED LISTENING

Chaozhou Folk Music Troupe of Shantou and the Linhai String and Wind Ensemble. *Chaozhou String Music.* Hugo Production. HRP 7227-2. http://www.hugomedia.com/regional/HRP7227-2.htm
Lin Maogen. *Jackdaws Gambol Water—Chaozhou Zheng Music.* Hugo Production. HRP 735-2.

FOR FURTHER INFORMATION

DuJunco, Mercedes. 2001. Melodic variation, regional identity, and meaning in the *xianshi* string ensemble music of Chaozhou, South China. *Tongyang Umak* [Journal of the Asian Music Research Institute, Seoul National University] 23:17–54.
———. 2003. The birth of a new mode? Modal entities in the Chaozhou *xianshi* string ensemble music tradition of Guangdong, South China. *Ethnomusicology Online* 8. http://research.umbc.edu/eol/8/dujunco/index.html

SICHUAN, CHINA
Su Zheng

Even a clever woman can't cook a meal without the rice.

Menu: Zheng Family Dishes with Sichuan Flavor, *Bangbang Ji* (Bangbang Chicken) with optional chicken soup, *Yuxiang Qiezi* (Fish-Flavored Eggplant), *Mapo Doufu* (Mapo Tofu with Basil), *Su Chao Mogu Qingcai* (Stir-Fry Shanghai Cabbage with Mushrooms), *Qing Chao Xiyang Qin* (Stir-Fry Watercress), *Cong Bao Daxia* (Stir-Fry Crown Shrimps with Scallions), and *Bai Mi Fan* (Cooked White Rice). Serve with fruit juice, tea, water, or Wu Liang Ye, China's top liquor, produced in Sichuan.
Preparation Time: 2–2½ hours.
Cooking Process: Boil the chicken first (it takes about 1½ hours). During this time, cut and chop ingredients, cook the rice, fry the eggplants, then make the tofu, Shanghai cabbage, watercress, and shrimps, in the given order. Cooking times for the greens can be varied according to your taste (slightly crunchy or soft and well cooked). Note that my preferred ingredients are Chu yong Shaoxing jia fan jiu (Shaoxing Cooking Wine), Zhujiangqiao pai sheng chou wang (Pearl River Bridge Superior Light Soy Sauce), Zhenjiang xiang cu (Chinkiang Vinegar), and Li jin ji xiongmao pai xianwei haoyou (Lee Kum Kee Panda Brand Oyster Flavored Sauce). Serves six people.

The Recipes

BANGBANG JI (BANGBANG CHICKEN) WITH OPTIONAL CHICKEN SOUP

1½ lb. chicken breast meat
½–1 t. cooking wine
salt
4 scallion stalks
6 thin slices ginger
½ lb. carrots, shredded
6 T soy sauce
4 T vinegar
2 T sesame oil
2 t. sugar
2 T Szechuan Salad Sauce or Dan Dan Noodle Sauce
8 mushrooms, sliced
1 c. bean sprouts

Boil 1½ lb. chicken breast meat in a cooking pot with water covering the meat. Add ½ to 1 t. cooking wine, salt to taste, 2 stalks of scallions sliced into 1½" long pieces and 6 thin slices of ginger when the water boils. Reduce heat to just keeping the water boiling. Cook for about 1½–2 hours (add water to keep the meat covered in the water) until the meat pieces are tender yet still holding their texture. Remove the chicken meat and tear into thin shredded pieces, each about 1½" long (like small sticks, hence the name *bangbang*). Add ½ lb. carrots (shredded) and 2 more stalks of thinly sliced scallions (slice them on a long angle at 1" intervals), placed around, under, and top. Make the sauce by mixing 6 T soy sauce, 4 T vinegar, 2 T sesame oil, 2 t. sugar, and 2 T Szechuan Salad Sauce or Dan Dan Noodle Sauce (both by Spicy King, called Chuan Bawang in Chinese. If this is not available, substitute with any other Sichuanese spicy

33

Bangbang ji (Bangbang chicken, Sichuan, China). Photo by Su Zheng.

sauce). Serve with the sauce separated or pour the sauce onto the chicken before serving. Add the sliced mushrooms and a handful of bean sprouts to the broth and boil for 5 minutes; serve it as a chicken soup.

YUXIANG QIEZI (FISH-FLAVORED EGGPLANT)

6 Chinese eggplants (about 7" long, slender)
¾ qt. corn oil
2 scallion stalks
2 thin slices ginger
2 cloves garlic
2 T soy sauce
2 T Spicy Eggplant Sauce
1 t. sugar
1 t. vinegar

Cut 6 Chinese eggplants at an angle, 1 to 1½" long. Heat ¾ quart of corn oil for deep fry in a wok, then put part of the eggplant chunks into the oil. Do not put too many at one time; they should be covered by the oil. Fry till the eggplants get tender (do not over-fry, as the original purple color of the eggplants' skin should be kept as much as possible). Use a strainer to take them out and leave them in a drainer. Repeat the same steps for the rest of the eggplants. When finished frying, pour out the remaining oil from the wok (you can use the oil to cook the other dishes). Also drain out the excess oil from the eggplants. Finely chop 1 scallion stalk, dice 2 thin slices of ginger, and thinly slice 2 cloves of garlic. Heat the wok with 2 T oil, lightly sauté

Chinese eggplant (Sichuan, China). Photo by Su Zheng.

the tiny scallion pieces, garlic and ginger, add the eggplant pieces, 2 T soy sauce, 2 T Spicy Eggplant Sauce (by Spicy King, called Chuan Bawang in Chinese. If this is not available, substitute
with any other Sichuanese spicy sauce), 1 t. sugar, 1 t. vinegar, and a scallion sliced into thin 1"
pieces. Stir for 2 minutes and serve hot. Note that the "fish flavor" comes from the ginger, scallion, and garlic, because these are the ingredients Sichuanese use for cooking fish.

Mapo Doufu (Mapo Tofu with Basil)

2 scallion stalks
2 lb. fresh firm or soft bean curd (tofu)
4 T corn oil
2 T soy sauce
½ t. five spices powder
1 t. sugar
2 T Bean Curd Sauce
A few fresh basil leaves

Chop 1 stalk of scallion into tiny pieces. Cube 2 lb. fresh bean curd (½" cubes). Heat 4 T corn
oil for stir-fry in a wok, lightly fry the tiny scallion pieces, add the tofu, stir for 3 minutes, add
2 T soy sauce, ½ t. five spices powder, 1 t. sugar, and 2 T bean curd sauce (by Spicy King, called
Chuan Bawang in Chinese. If this is not available, substitute with any other Sichuanese bean
curd sauce). Stir for 2 minutes, then add a few fresh chopped basil leaves and another scallion
cut into small pieces, stir for 1 more minute and serve hot. Note that the standard recipe for
this dish would include ground pork and no use of basil; however, this is a family recipe that
stands on its own with basil added and without the pork.

Su Chao Mogu Qingcai (Stir-Fry Shanghai Cabbage with Mushrooms)

1 lb. Shanghai cabbage
10 mushrooms
4 T corn oil
1½ T oyster sauce
salt

Cut up 1 lb. Shanghai cabbage into 2" x 1" pieces. Slice 10 mushrooms. Heat 4 T corn oil for stir-fry in a wok, add the cabbage and stir for 5–8 minutes. Add the mushrooms, 1½ T oyster sauce and salt to taste. Stir for 5 more minutes and serve hot.

Qing Chao Xiyang Qin (Stir-Fry Watercress)

1–1½ lb. watercress
2–3 T corn oil
1 clove garlic
1½ T oyster sauce
salt

Cut 1 to 1½ lb. watercress into 1½" lengths. Heat 4 T corn oil for stir-fry in a wok, lightly fry a few slices of garlic, add the watercress, stir for 5 minutes, add 1½ T oyster sauce and salt to taste. Stir for 3 more minutes and serve hot. The watercress shrinks dramatically, but it should be served in combination with the other dishes.

Cong Bao Daxia (Stir-Fry Crown Shrimps with Scallions)

4 scallion stalks
2 thin slices ginger
2 cloves garlic
6 T corn oil
1½ lb. jumbo shrimp
2 T cooking wine
4 T soy sauce
½ t. five spices powder
1 t. sugar
1 t. vinegar

Cut 3 stalks of scallions in 1" pieces at an angle; set aside. Cut 1 stalk of scallion into tiny pieces, cut 2 thin slices of ginger into narrow sticks, and thinly slice 2 cloves of garlic. Heat 6 T corn oil in a wok for stir-fry, then lightly sauté the tiny scallion pieces, garlic, and ginger until you smell the flavors (they get blackened easily; do not overcook them). Add 1½ lb. jumbo shrimp; let one side turn red and then turn them over. When both sides are red (do not overcook, otherwise the shrimps lose their tenderness), add 2 T cooking wine, 4 T soy sauce, ½ t. five spices powder, and 1 t. sugar. Stir for about 2 more minutes, add the angled scallion pieces and 1 t. vinegar, stir for 1 more minute and serve hot.

Bai Mi Fan (Cooked White Rice)

3 c. white rice

Bring 6 c. water to a boil. Rinse and add 3 c. white rice; cover and simmer until rice is tender, about 20 minutes. Fluff gently with a fork and allow to rest, covered, for 10 more minutes.

Out of Sichuan, China—A Family Tradition

For thousands of years, food has been a central focus of Chinese culture. Countless archaeological objects, novels, poems, and paintings have depicted or described raw or cooked food as major themes. In China, food and music have been closely related to each other for their similar communal functionality and immediate sensuous pleasure. Important historical events occurred at banquets where music, dance, and food complemented each other. Until today, a meal with abundant dishes is a must for religious ceremonies, which often include music; while traditional opera is often performed at village or state rituals and festivals where food is often served. Banquets are organized for business deals, family gatherings, reunions, and musicians' free-spirited celebrations after their performances. Following a lecture or performance by visiting musicians and scholars, a luxurious banquet is always offered by the host, accentuated by locally produced liquor. Friendship is not established until people have eaten meals together. In restaurants, most often one person hosts the rest of the group. Splitting the meal cost is culturally unacceptable and considered a loss of face for everyone.

Food is so central in Chinese everyday life that until about twenty years ago, the standard greeting phrase among the mainland Chinese was not "How are you?" but "Have you eaten?" Since the 1980s when China entered its economic reform era, restaurants, either run by family or private entrepreneurs, have mushroomed throughout China. Increasingly people have chosen to entertain their friends or to celebrate traditional festivals (such as the Chinese New Year) with their families in restaurants rather than at home, often accompanied by karaoke entertainment.

Amazingly, in the engulfing wave of modernization since the late nineteenth century, while most age-old Chinese customs and cultural forms, including music, have been greatly transformed and altered in association with Western ideas, even the most radical revolutionaries have surrendered to their Chinese stomachs when it has come to food. Having survived the wars, revolutions, and ideological battles, Chinese food has kept its authentic traditionality and micro-regional flavors. In addition, it is fascinating to note that in a country that has been promoting nationalism for over a century, under which circumstances many national styles or forms were invented (e.g., national music, national opera, national painting school, national language, etc.) for the need of a new national identity, there has never been a national food in China; instead, many regional, city, or family styles continue to exist.

With the wide dispersal of Chinese immigrants in the world, Chinese restaurants have become an essential means for the survival of generations of immigrants in their new homelands. Early Chinese migration was dominated by the Cantonese, thus Cantonese cuisine was the most common style of food found in traditional Chinatowns. Since the 1970s, however, new waves of emigrants from Hong Kong and Taiwan, many of whom were dislocated from various parts of mainland China due to the civil war, brought Shanghai, Hunan, and Sichuan styles to the West, and these styles have ventured beyond the Chinatowns. Beginning from the late 1980s, Chinese takeout food has proliferated in the United States by new emigrants from mainland China. A recent survey indicated that the number of Chinese restaurants in America surpassed any of the mainstream big-name food franchises. People in the world have come to know "Chinese food" mostly through these overseas Chinese restaurants. Yet, unless one spends an extensive amount of time in China, it is impossible to gain a proper sense of the extraordinarily rich and nuanced taste of various Chinese cooking styles.

Sichuan cuisine is one of the Eight Great Traditions of Chinese cooking. Beloved by people in and outside Sichuan, Sichuan restaurants can be found throughout China. The most distinctive feature of Sichuan cuisine is its complex spicy taste. Typical Sichuan dishes are covered with a thick layer of red (hot chili pepper) oil, and the typical scene of eating Sichuan dishes is sweating from head to toe due to its extreme spiciness. Sichuan, the most populous and one of the largest Chinese provinces, is situated in southwest inland China. It was the center of the independent Shu Kingdom in the third century C.E., and has kept many distinct local traditions due to limited road access to the province from outside world until the mid-twentieth century.

Sichuan has a long history of both folk and classical music. *Chuan ju* (Sichuan opera), famous for its high-pitched vocal style, lead and chorus singing form, and unique face-changing technique, is the most well-known Sichuan music/drama genre. In the late 1990s, in the spirit of "dialoguing with the Empire," *Chuan ju* artists appropriated the story of Puccini's opera Turandot and infused it with "Chinese perspective" by creating a new *Chuan ju* Du Landuo (Turandot), which caused a sensation and heated debate in Beijing. Sichuan is one of the most important centers for Daoism, with numerous Daoist temples. Music is frequently played by Daoist priests at various religious ceremonies both in and outside of temples. A well-known Sichuan folk song genre is "Chuan jiang haozi" (work songs sung by boat trackers on the Yangtze River). A number of contemporary compositions have drawn their musical materials from this dying-out folk genre. The most successful contemporary composer from Sichuan is Guo Wenjing, who has been frequently invited to appear at various international music festivals in the past two decades. Guo uses folk songs and *Chuan ju* creatively and imaginatively in his otherwise avant-garde music. His most recent chamber opera, *Ye Yan* (*The Night Banquet*, 2001), toured in Europe, the U.S., and China, and is inspired by an ancient Chinese painting which depicts a private banquet and music enjoyment scene as part of an intricate power struggle imparted from the imperial court.

The recipes offered above are a hybrid of my family tradition and my own personal creation, rooted in the Sichuan cuisine style. My grandmother spent most of her youth in her birth city— Chongqin, a major city in Sichuan Province until 1996 when it became an autonomous municipality directly under China's central government. Searching for personal fulfillment and a new life, my grandmother left her family secretly in her early 20s to take a week-long boat journey to Shanghai to study music and physical education in a school sponsored by the YWCA. Upon graduation, she became one of the first female teachers in her hometown to teach female students music and European folk dances in public school in the early twentieth century. Although she never went back to Sichuan in the last 30 years of her life, she had Sichuanese dishes at home every day. Growing up with her in Shanghai, I inherited her Sichuanese taste for strong flavor (salty and very spicy). When I returned to live with my mother in Beijing in my teens, I began to learn from my mother how to cook those family dishes. But cooking has always been a creative process for me, involving personal choices, improvisation, and some magic inspiration—quite similar to making music, one might say. Therefore in my kitchen, for example, basil, a non-Chinese vegetable, has been added to Mapo Tofu for its complementary intricate taste, while pork has been eliminated. Similarly, shredded carrots have been added to Bangbang Chicken for its contrasting texture and enriching color. Readers trying out my recipes are encouraged to adjust ingredients according to their own tastes.

RECOMMENDED LISTENING

It is very hard to find Sichuan music from outside China. People could try the following:

Zhang Jian Ping and Chen Xue. *Jin Zi, Sichuan Style Opera*. 2004 (China Version), DVD. Bao dao yinxiang chuban she, PAL format. YesAsia 1003319119. Available at http://us.yesasia.com
Guo Wenjing, Nieuw Ensemble. *She Huo*. Zebra 001.

FOR FURTHER INFORMATION

Dunlop, Fuchsia. 2003. *Land of Plenty: A Treasury of Authentic Sichuan Cooking*. New York: Norton.
Lee, Elsa. 1997. An introduction to the gushi drummer of the Chuanju Percussion Ensemble. *Asian Music* 28/2:1–26.
Provine, Robert, Tokumaru, Yosihiko, and Witzleben, Lawrence, eds. 2002. *The Garland Encyclopedia of World Music, Vol. 7: East Asia: China, Japan, and Korea*. New York: Routledge.

TOKYO, JAPAN
Marié Abe

Eat food that is grown within 3 miles from where you are, then you'll stay healthy and live long.

Menu: *Chawan Mushi* (Savory Steamed Egg Custard with Shrimp and Vegetables), *Goma Dofu* (Sesame Tofu), *Gomoku Mame* (Soybeans with Vegetables), *Tofu to Kinoko no Takikomi Gohan* (Rice Cooked with Tofu and Mushrooms), *Sakana no Foiru Yaki* (Fish Steamed in Foil with Miso and Vegetables), and *Kiwi Kanten* (Kiwi Jelly).
Preparation Time: 2 hours the night before, 2 hours on the day of the meal.
Cooking Process: It is relatively easy to order any hard-to-find Japanese ingredients from Uwa-jimaya, a supermaket in Seattle with a thriving online business (www.uwajimaya.com). For the *chawan mushi* you will need 6 teacup-sized ceramic cups. The night before, make the *dashi* (broth) for several of the dishes, soak the soybeans for the *gomoku mame*, and make the *goma dofu* and *kiwi kanten* to chill overnight. Serves six people.

The Recipes

DASHI (BROTH FOR SEVERAL DISHES)

3 thick seaweed pieces (*kombu*), 4" each
3 T shaved bonito flakes (*katsuo bushi*)

Prepare the *dashi* broth first. In a pot, soak 3 *kombu* pieces (4" each) in 5 c. water for 20 min-utes. Then place over medium heat. Just before boiling, once you start to see small bubbles around the *kombu*, take the *kombu* pieces out. Bring the water to boil and add 3 T *katsuo bushi* (shaved bonito). Bring down the heat, and cook for 2–3 minutes. Turn off the heat and leave un-till shaved bonito sinks to the bottom of the pot. Using a fine strainer or paper towel, strain the shaved bonito out of the broth (do not squeeze the shaved bonito). Set the *dashi* broth aside.

CHAWAN MUSHI (SAVORY STEAMED EGG CUSTARD WITH SHRIMP AND VEGETABLES)

12 small shrimp, deveined
4 T sake
salt
6 ginkgo nuts
2 carrots
3 *shiitake* mushrooms
1 chicken breast
6 eggs
4½ c. *dashi* broth (see recipe, above)
3 t. soy sauce

1½ t. *mirin* (rice vinegar)
6 slices fish cake (*kamaboko*)
Japanese parsley (*mitsuba*) for garnish

Prepare the topping: Cook 12 small deveined shrimp in a small pot with 3 T sake, a pinch of salt, and 6 T water. Once cooked, take off the shell. Peel 6 ginkgo nuts, and cook in a small pot with a little water and salt. Peel and thinly slice 2 carrots into 12 slices. Use cookie molds (for example, a waffle cut) for aesthetics. Briefly blanch in salted boiling water. Cut off and discard the stems of 3 *shiitake* mushrooms, and slice the remaining mushrooms thinly. Cut 3 pieces of white-meat chicken into bite size pieces, and sprinkle with a little sake and salt. Now make the eggs: in a large bowl, mix 6 eggs well (without making bubbles—keep the fork or chopsticks touching the bottom of the bowl while stirring.) Add 4½ c. *dashi* broth, 1½ t. salt, 3 t. soy sauce, 1½ t. *mirin* (rice vinegar), and 1½ t. sake to the eggs, mix well, and filter the mixture using cheese cloth or fine strainer. Prepare to use a steamer; get the water boiling. In a small teacup-size ceramic cup, place 2–3 small pieces of chicken. Pour the egg mixture carefully to ³/₅ of the height of the cup. Place the cup into a steamer. Place a thin cloth between the steamer and a lid (placed slightly off the pot to let the steam out), and cook for 1 minute over high heat. Then turn down the heat to low, and steam for 6–7 more minutes. Once the surface is a little bit firm, place shiitake mushrooms, a *kamaboko* (fish cake) slice, 2 shrimp, 2 ginkgo nuts, and 2 carrot slices in each cup. Add more egg mixture to ²/₅ of the height of the cup, and steam for 1 minute over high heat. Bring down the heat to low and steam for 6–7 more minutes. Check by sticking a bamboo skewer inside; if a clear *dashi* broth comes out from the hole, the dish is ready. To serve, top it off with *mitsuba* (Japanese parsley) pieces. Do not discard the rest of the *dashi*, as you will need it several more times (see below).

GOMA DOFU (SESAME TOFU)

1 T powdered gelatin
½ bag powdered agar-agar (*kanten*) (a jelly-like substance from seaweed)
1 c. soymilk
salt
2½ T sesame paste
1 T soy sauce
2 T *dashi* (see recipe, above)
1 t. rice vinegar (*mirin*)

Sprinkle 1 T powdered gelatin into 3 T water in a small bowl, let it sit. In a large pot, dissolve ½ bag powdered *kanten* in 1 c. water over low heat. Stir constantly. Once *kanten* is completely dissolved, add 1 c. soymilk and a pinch of salt and keep heating while stirring. Just before boiling, add moistened gelatin and take the pot off the stove. Put 2½ T sesame paste in a separate small bowl. Add the liquid little by little to the sesame paste, and mix well until it is thinned to water-like consistency. Pour everything back into the large pot and mix well. Pour it into a square container, and let it cool. Meanwhile, make the sauce by mixing together 1 T soy sauce, 2 T *dashi*, and 1 t. *mirin* (rice vinegar). *Kanten* will solidify at room temperature. You can put it in the fridge also. Cut into cubes, take out of the container and serve with the sauce.

Japanese tofu (Japan). Photo by Sean Williams.

GOMOKU MAME (SOYBEANS WITH VEGETABLES)

1 c. soybeans
¼ c. diced (¼") lotus root
¼ c. diced (¼") carrot
¼ c. diced (¼") *konyaku* (a gelatinous starchy vegetable available at Asian markets)
2 T soy sauce
1–2 t. sugar

In a large pot, soak 1 c. soybeans in 2 c. water for 10 hours. Cook gently over medium heat with a lid (slightly off, to let steam out) for about an hour until the beans are soft. Be careful not to let it boil over. Reduce heat and add ¼ c. diced lotus root and/or *gobo* root. At this point water should be reduced to half as much as the soybeans. If not, adjust with additional water. Add ¼ c. each ¼" diced carrot and *konyaku* and cook over low heat for 30 more minutes. Add 2 T soy sauce, and cook for 10 more minutes. Lastly, add 2 t. sugar, cook for 5 more minutes, and turn off heat. This can be served hot, or at room temperature.

Tofu to Kinoko no Takikomi Gohan (Rice Cooked with Tofu and Mushrooms)

4 c. rice
1 package firm tofu
1 4" x 5" piece of fried tofu (*abura age*)
1 branch *shimeji* mushrooms
6 *shiitake* mushrooms
2 branches *enoki* mushrooms
2 T vegetable oil
4 T sake
2 t. sugar
2 T rice vinegar (*mirin*)
4 T soy sauce
½ t. salt

30 minutes before cooking rice, rinse the rice in a bowl, changing the water 3 times. Drain and set aside in a strainer. Wrap 1 package of firm tofu in a paper towel, and put a weight on top to drain water for awhile (alternatively, wrap in paper towel and heat in a microwave for 2 minutes). Then break it into medium size pieces with hands. Place 1 piece of *abura age* (fried tofu) on a strainer, and pour boiling water over it to get rid of its oiliness. Then cut into ½" long thin pieces. Cut the root of 1 branch of *shimeji* mushrooms and break it into small bits. Remove and discard the stems of 6 *shiitake* mushrooms and slice the rest of the *shiitakes* thinly. Cut off the root of 2 branches of *enoki* mushrooms, and cut in half. In a pot, heat 2 T vegetable oil, and add the mushrooms and cook. Add tofu and stir-fry some more, until they're lightly cooked through. Then add 4 T sake, 2 t. sugar, 2 T *mirin*, 4 T soy sauce, and ½ t. salt. In a rice cooker, put the rinsed rice, 2½ c. *dashi* (see *dashi* recipe on p. 40) and mushrooms and mix, then cook rice. Once rice is cooked, let it sit for 10 minutes. Serve with green beans that are blanched in salted water and sliced thinly sprinkled on top.

Sakana no Foiru Yaki (Fish Steamed in Foil with Miso and Vegetables)

6 large pieces of fish (such as mackerel, cod fish, salmon; use fairly thin fillets/medallions)
2 scallion stalks
3 *shiitake* mushrooms
1 bunch spinach leaves, blanched and cut into 1½" pieces
⅔ c. miso paste
4 T sugar
⅓ c. *sake*
2 T rice vinegar (*mirin*)
1 T grated fresh ginger (optional)

Cut a large piece of aluminum foil. Butter the inside surface slightly. Wash and pat dry 6 pieces of fish; place one piece of fish in the center of the foil, arrange some scallions, chopped pieces of 3 *shiitake* mushrooms and small pieces of spinach on top and around the fish. Create the *miso* sauce by mixing ⅔ c. *miso* paste, 4 T sugar, ⅓ c. *sake*, and 2 T *mirin* (rice vinegar). Pour the *miso* sauce on top. Depending on the fish, you could add some grated ginger as well. Envelope all this loosely with the remaining part of the foil, making sure to leave some room over the fish. Seal the package by folding tightly the edges and the top, so as not to let the fish juice, steam, or *miso* sauce escape. Repeat five times with the other pieces of fish. Cook the packages in a heated oven at 360°–400°F for 10–15 minutes, depending on the size and thickness of the fish.

Kiwi Kanten (Kiwi Jelly)

6 kiwis
¼ c. sugar
2 t. powdered agar-agar (*kanten*)
1½ T lemon juice

Peel and puree, or cut into small pieces, 5 kiwis. Peel the remaining kiwi, cut into half lengthwise, and slice thinly for decoration; set aside. In a deep pan, boil 2 c. water, ¼ c. sugar, and 1 bag of powdered *kanten* (2 t.) together while constantly stirring (important!). Once boiling and *kanten* is dissolved, remove from heat and set aside to cool to room temperature. Before it starts to congeal, add pureed kiwi and 1½ T lemon juice to the *kanten*. Pour into a square container, place decorative kiwi slices on the surface (*kanten* liquid might be starting to get a little bit firm at this point, which makes it easy for the decorative kiwi slices to float on top), and cool in fridge. To serve, take it out of the mold and cut into desired pieces.

The Search for Perfection

As the popular film *Tampopo* or the famous TV show *Iron Chef* might suggest, the near-obsessive dedication to perfecting certain kinds of food, or searching out the ultimate serving of a certain dish, often drives the social lives of my friends, family, and many of our fellow Tokyo residents (myself included, of course). There are countless "gourmet" food shows and cooking shows on TV; Japanese TV viewers' curiosity about high-quality and unique cuisines from various parts of Japan and the world is boundless. In Tokyo, food is serious business—figuratively and literally.

As a native of Tokyo, with a mother who is a nutritionist and chef, I have learned quite a bit about contemporary Japanese culinary styles, which are quite different from what one might consider "traditional" Japanese food. I find that "Japanese cuisine" outside of Japan is often synonymous with sushi, but in fact, sushi does not necessarily resemble stereotypical home dishes—dishes that have what we call *ofukuro no aji*, or "a mother's taste." My family meals, like many others' in Japan, take broad inspiration from diverse cuisines—Indian, Chinese, Korean, French, Italian, American, etc.—and my mother creatively incorporates them into her own style. The resulting dishes often feature subtler flavoring, addition of more or less "Japanese" ingredients, etc. Thus, if you do happen to find yourself at an everyday family dinner table, it's more likely that you'll be served "Japanized" versions of curry, hamburger, croquette, omelette, or spaghetti than sushi and sake.

The meal introduced here does not include the most typical "traditional" Japanese dishes you would find at the Japanese restaurants outside of Japan. Instead, I chose these dishes as representative of a homecooked meal that my mother would serve the family on a somewhat special occasion. In a way, this meal is an "authentically hybrid," typical, contemporary homestyle Tokyo meal: *Chawanmushi*, now considered a classic Japanese side dish, has Chinese influence; *sakana no foiru yaki* is my mother's creation, inspired by the French parchment cooking method; and *kiwi kanten* and *goma dofu* are products of similarly creative approaches. Reviewing the dishes I chose, though, I see that they do incorporate characteristics that are often considered typical for Japanese cooking.

First, a typical Japanese meal consists of rice as the main item, with soybeans, vegetables, seaweeds, and fish as accompaniments; all of these components appear in this meal. Second, the menu employs commonly used, low fat Japanese cooking methods: boiling for *gomokumame*, grilling for *sakana no foiru yaki*, and steaming for *chawan mushi*. Third, because Japanese cooking is sensitive to the four seasons, the dishes above can (and should!) be modified to use of the freshest seasonal ingredients. For example, you can always use whatever the fresh-caught fish of the day is to make *sakana no foiru yaki*, or add other seasonal vegetables to the fish in the foil packet. Additionally, I would suggest experimenting with other seasonal fruit for the dessert dish (my summertime favorite is white peaches).

Finally, for many, the decoration and presentation of a dish are considered as essential as the flavor of the dishes. In this menu, you can show off your personal visual aesthetics through the arrangement of the ingredients for *chawanmushi* and *kiwi kanten*. A sense of color is quite important—my mother would always emphasize how each meal must have at least five colors, not only for aesthetics but also for nutritional reasons. Even better is when you can cover five colors in one dish—*gomokumame* is a fine example. *Gomoku* means "five items," and is often used to describe dishes that have an assortment of ingredients cooked together. It naturally adds colors to the dishes and invites appetite.

Some might notice that the most common, popular Japanese dish is missing from this meal: *omisoshiru* (miso soup). This is because *chawanmushi* is considered to serve the same role as miso soup: *osuimono* (soup dish). For those who are curious, *misoshiru* can be made by adding one sour plum-sized dollop of *miso* paste per person to one cup of *dashi* (you need to dissolve the miso paste into a small amount of *dashi* first). You can then add tofu cubes, *wakame* seaweed, finely sliced *daikon* radish, and/or *shiitake* mushrooms.

Based on my experiences, social gatherings in Tokyo almost always involve food, even if you go out "just for drinks." More often than not these gatherings take place outside one's house, typically in restaurants, pubs, and other public spaces. Thus, house dinners or potlucks are rarer, more formal events than I've found them to be in the United States. As for music to go with cooking or eating, these days in Tokyo the most common background music to a meal is a TV, radio, or whatever CD happens to be in the stereo, chattering voices, noises from the streets, or all of the above. Here, I've provided a few recommended recently released albums (a bit on the "experimental" side) that for me would make wonderful music to cook by.

RECOMMENDED LISTENING

CICALA MVTA. *Ghost Circus.* Little More Records, 2004. TLCA1011.
OOIOO. *kila kila kila.* Thrill Jockey, 2004. THR 117 CD.
Ruins. *Vrresto.* Magaibutsu, 2005. MGC-14.
Satoko Fujii Orchestra Nagoya Version. *Nogoyanian.* Bakamo Records, 2005. BKM-001.

FOR FURTHER INFORMATION

http://metropolis.japantoday.com/default.asp
http://www.japaneselifestyle.com.au/culture/culture.html
Wade, Bonnie. 2004. *Music in Japan: Experiencing Music, Expressing Culture* (Global Music Series). New York: Oxford University Press.

OKINAWA, JAPAN
Marié Abe

Food is life's medicine.

Menu: *Gôya Champurû* (Stir-Fry with Bitter Gourd), *Mâminâ Usachi* (Bean Sprouts and Tofu with Sesame Dressing), *Rafutê* (Cooked Pork), *Nâberâ Mbushi* (Sponge Gourd with Miso), *Irichi Châhan* (Fried Rice with *Kombu* Seaweed), and *Sâtâ Andagî* (Doughnut Balls). Serve with water or green tea.
Preparation Time: 2½ hours.
Cooking Process: Prepare the pork first, then the sponge gourd, the stir-fry with bitter gourd, and fried rice. Make the bean sprouts with tofu shortly before you plan to eat. Prepare the doughnut balls after dinner so they are still warm. Serves six people.

The Recipes

GÔYA CHAMPURÛ (STIR-FRY WITH BITTER GOURD)

2 packages firm tofu
2 medium *gôya* (bitter gourd)
¼ lb. pork
2 T lard or vegetable oil
salt
¼ c. sliced onion (optional)
1 egg, beaten
¼ c. soy sauce

Wrap 2 packages of firm tofu in a paper towel. Put a weight on top for a while to drain the water. Alternatively, you can wrap the tofu in a paper towel, and heat for 2 minutes in a microwave. Cut *gôya* (gourd) in half lengthwise. Scoop the seed and spongy part out with a spoon, wash, and slice thinly. Chop ¼ lb. pork (or spam) into bite-size pieces. Tear the tofu into large pieces with hands and fry in 2 T lard or vegetable oil in a heated wok. Add a little salt. When browned on both sizes, take them out of the pan and set aside. In the same frying pan or wok, add the rest of lard oil. Cook *gôya* with salt, and add the pork (and ¼ c. sliced onion, if you are using it). Put the browned tofu back into the pan and mix together with *gôya* and pork. Pour 1 beaten egg evenly into the pan and cook quickly. Add soy sauce around the pan, mix together.

MÂMINÂ USACHI (BEAN SPROUTS AND TOFU WITH SESAME DRESSING)

½ lb. bean sprouts
1 T rice vinegar (*mirin*)
1 cucumber
1 piece of fried tofu (*abura age*)
5 T white sesame seeds, gently roasted in a pan to get the aroma
3 T sugar
1 t. salt

46

2 t. soy sauce
6 T rice vinegar (*mirin*)

Blanch ½ lb. bean sprouts quickly in salted boiling water. While hot, sprinkle 1 T rice vinegar. Let it cool, and drain water. Sprinkle salt generously on 1 peeled cucumber, and roll it strongly against a cutting board. Wash with water, and cut into 1½" slices. Pour boiling water on fried tofu on a strainer. Cut into 1½" thin pieces. Grind the roasted white sesame seeds with a mortar and pestle. Add 3 T sugar, 1 t. salt, 2 t. soy sauce, and 6 T rice vinegar in that order and keep mixing. Add bean sprouts, cucumber, and fried tofu into the sesame mixture and mix well.

RAFUTÊ (COOKED PORK)

½ lb. tender cut of pork
3 c. Okinawan spirits (*awamori*; substitute with shôchû or sake)
½ c. sugar
½ c. soy sauce
⅔ c. shaved bonito flakes (*katsuo bushi*)

Boil ½ lb. pork (whole) in plenty of water, on high heat. Once boiling, turn down the heat to continue boiling just barely, while keeping scooping out the floating foam-like impurities coming from the pork for 40–50 minutes, until pork is soft (a wooden skewer goes right through the meat). Take out the pork and let it cool, then cut it into 2" cubes. Keep the broth. In a deep pot, place the pork cubes, add 3 c. *awamori*, ½ c. sugar, and ¼ c. soy sauce. Bring to a boil, then turn down the heat to low. Do *otoshi-buta* ("dropping lid": use a lid smaller than the pot, so that the lid sits directly onto what is cooking in the pot) and cook for 1 hour. Add the remaining ¼ c. soy sauce and ⅔ c. shaved bonito flakes, and cook for 30 more minutes. Set aside 2 cups of the broth for the fried rice, below.

NÂBERÂ MBUSHI (SPONGE GOURD WITH MISO)

1 small sponge gourd (*hechima*)
¼ lb. pork
1 T potato starch (*katakuriko*)
1 package firm tofu
vegetable oil for frying
4 T miso paste
1 t. chicken stock powder or bouillon
3 T Okinawan spirits (*awamori*)
2 T sugar

With a spoon or knife, scrape off the surface skin of 1 small *hechima* (sponge gourd). Slice into ½" pieces. Prepare ¼ lb. pork in the same manner as the process of the *rafutê* recipe, up until the step where you boil and cool the meat (above). Cut into bite-sized pieces, and mix with 1 T *katakuriko* powder (potato starch). Wrap 1 package firm tofu in a paper towel. Put a weight on top for at least 2 hours to get the water out. Once drained well, cut into bite-sized pieces. Fry the *hechima* and pork in lard or oil in a heated frying pan. Add 1 T water used for boiling pork, 4 T *miso*, 1 t. chicken stock powder or bouillon, 3 T *awamori* and 2 T sugar. Bring to boil, and add tofu pieces. Cook until *hechima* is soft and the sauce is reduced to gain a little bit of viscosity.

Irichi Châhan (Fried Rice with Kombu Seaweed)

3 c. white rice
2½ T oil or lard
6 *shiitake* mushrooms, sliced
⅓ c. fresh seaweed (*kombu*)
2 c. pork broth from *rafutê*, above
1½ T sake
2½ T sugar
1½ T rice vinegar (*mirin*)
5 T soy sauce
3–4 T vegetable oil

Cook the white rice: bring 6 c. water to a boil, rinse, and add 3 c. white rice. Cover with a tight-fitting lid and simmer until tender, about 20 minutes. Set aside and let the rice rest for 10 extra minutes. In a heated pot, put in 2½ T lard/oil and the sliced *shiitake* mushrooms and cook for a brief while. Add ⅓ c. fresh *kombu* (seaweed), and add 2 c. of the pork broth from the *rafute*, 1½ T *sake*, 2½ T sugar, 1½ T rice vinegar (*mirin*), and 4 T soy sauce. Once boiling, reduce heat and continue cooking until the broth is almost gone. Drain and set aside. In a wok, heat up 3–4 T vegetable oil. Stir in 6 c. cooked rice and fry for briefly until the rice does not stick in lumps. Add the mushroom mixture to the rice, and mix thoroughly and cook. Once cooked through, add 1½ t. soy sauce for aroma and mix.

Sâtâ Andagî (Doughnut Balls)

⅓ c. flour
⅓ t. baking powder
salt
1 t. crushed almonds
2 eggs
¼ c. brown sugar
1 c. vegetable oil for frying

Mix and shift together flour and baking powder. Add and mix in a pinch of salt and 1 t. crushed almonds. Beat 2 eggs and ¼ c. brown sugar together, then add to flour mixture and mix well. Heat enough oil for deep frying to 320°F. Roll the dough into ½" balls, and fry. Once the balls start to color, heat up the oil and fry until the balls are nicely browned.

Uchinâ Food

Japan's southernmost prefecture Okinawa, which consists of a few dozen islands called the Ryukyu Islands, is known to have the longest average life expectancy in the world. The secret for long life is often attributed to Okinawa's unique cuisine, and there has been a recent surge of studies and media coverage about the relationship between longevity and Okinawan food. As the proverb *shoku wa nuchigusui* (food is life's medicine) implies, food is considered as important to one's health as medicine, and the local cuisine is known for its well-balanced, nutritious content, and medicinal effects. Regardless of any relationship between longevity and diet, Okinawa's distinct produce and cooking style offer more than just culinary inspiration.

Okinawa's tropical climate provides unique vegetables, fruit, and seafood that are not easily accessible elsewhere, such as *umibudou, shima rakkyo, sîkwâsâ*, etc. Here, I tried to choose some dishes that might be do-able outside Okinawa, but you might need to trek a little to find some of the key ingredients (I'm sure you'll find that the effort is worth it after tasting these dishes, however). Once you gather the ingredients, Okinawan cooking is generally quite simple. It usually entails mixing and stir-frying the ingredients without much labor or multi-step preparations.

The simplicity of Okinawan cooking shouldn't be celebrated innocently, however. The particularity of the preparation and use of certain ingredients must be understood in the context of the contested histories of Okinawa. Some of the key historical markers include Okinawa's past as an independent kingdom called Ryukyu, the dual subjugation to China and Japan, annexation by Japan, a series of famines, the horrific battle fought during WWII on the island, and the subsequent 30-year long U.S. military occupation. In conversations with my friends in Okinawa, I have heard numerous times how the innovative uses of simple ingredients were borne out of necessary wartime thrift; this is also a common explanation for the modest, economical nature of many common homestyle dishes. Pork, which became part of Okinawan cooking 400 years earlier than in Japan, is also often cited as an example of a thrifty attitude toward food. As the Okinawan saying goes, "every part of a pig is used but the squeal," from the meat down to the legs, ears, blood, intestines, and tail.

The word *champurû* as it appears in one of the dishes above, *gôya champurû*, offers great insight into the relationship between Okinawa's food and its distinct histories and geography. *Champurû* literally means "mixing" or "mish-mosh" in the local dialect, and often describes dishes that have numerous ingredients stir-fried together. This "mish-moshing" is found not just in a single dish, but also in the overall style of Okinawan cooking, which is informed by various places. It's often claimed that Okinawan food bears the stamp of Chinese cuisine—an observation easily explained by the fact that before being annexed by Japan, the Ryukyu kingdom maintained extensive ties with China and other Southeast Asian areas as well as Japan. Ryukyu court cuisine, just like its architecture, therefore incorporates explicitly Chinese elements.

Additionally, very distinct influences on Okinawan food were brought by the longstanding presence of the U.S. Army on the island. Canned food provided by the U.S. military during the occupation, most notably SPAM, made its way into homestyle dishes such as *onipô* and *pôku tamago*. Another instance of Okinawan food serving as a lens through which to understand Okinawa's translocal historical connections is a dish called *taco rice*. I was struck by *taco rice* on my first visit to Okinawa—it has everything you'll get in a Mexican taco, but with tortillas replaced by white rice. This dish was allegedly invented in the 1960s to serve American soldiers, although some other accounts attribute this unique fusion of Okinawan and Central American cuisine to the diasporic connections established through the Okinawan history of immigration to the Pacific Islands and Central/South America.

While *champurû* signifies dishes that have ingredients "mixed up" together, it is also used to describe the processes of "mixing" in other aspects of life, such as architectural styles, people, languages, and musical sounds. While great traditional Okinawan singers and *sanshin* (a snakeskin lute instrument) players abound, actively performing for locals and tourists at *minyô sakaba* (folk song pubs), there has been a surge in the "mixing" of sounds and styles in Okinawan popular music. For example, the rock band Murasaki started performing in the U.S. military base town Koza in the 1970s, and is known to be the innovator of the "Okinawan rock" sound. Around the same time, the Jackson Five–like family band Finger Five also adopted and incorporated classic Motown sounds to perform for U.S. servicemen, and became extremely popular throughout Japan. The Latin/rock band Diamantes is another interesting case; it was formed by a third-generation Okinawan from Peru. Today, popular music from Okinawa frequently appears in Japan's pop music chart, drawing from punk rock, soul, hip-hop, as well as Okinawan "traditional" sounds, while musicians from other parts of Japan have also drawn on "Okinawan" sounds. Like its food, Okinawa's music can be seen as a confluence of Okinawa's interconnections—both real and imagined—with the peoples, histories, places, and forces that are beyond Okinawa's geographical boundaries.

RECOMMENDED LISTENING

Daiku Tetsuhiro. *Houraikou, exo-Pai Patirohma*. Off Note Records, 2003. On-43.
Daiku Tetsuhiro and Daiku Naeko. *Yui—Yaima No Kajigu*. Off Note Records, 1996. ON -12.
Diamantes. *Okinawa Latina*. Universal, 1993. PHCL-5006.
Finger Five. *Golden Best Finger 5*. Universal International, 2003. UICZ-6036.
Murasaki. *First*. Tokuma Japan, originally released in 1976. TKCA-70485.
Seijin Noborikawa and China Sadao. *Seijin Noborikawa and Sadao China*. Respect Records, 2004. RES-7.

FOR FURTHER INFORMATION

http://www.okinawa.com
http://www.pref.okinawa.jp/english/
http://www.japan-guide.com/list/e1247.html

KOREA
Okon Hwang

A drunken man tells the truth.

Menu: *Galbi-jjim* (Braised Beef Short Ribs), *Bap* (Steamed Rice), *Gamja Jorim* (Soy Sauce Potato), *Sigeumchi Muchim* (Seasoned Spinach), and *Beoseot Bokkeum* (Mushroom Sauté). Serve with *kimchi* (from a Korean or Asian grocery store) and Korean *Cheongju* or *Munbaeju*. For dessert, serve *Yaksik* (Sweet Glutinous Rice) or fresh peeled fruit.
Preparation Time: 3 hours, not including the braised beef short ribs being started in advance.
Cooking Process: Start the braised beef short ribs the day before. Also, soak the glutinous rice for the *yaksik* the night before. The side dishes are all served at room temperature, so they can be made several hours before eating, while the short ribs are finishing the cooking process. Serves six people.

The Recipes

GALBI-JJIM (BRAISED BEEF SHORT RIBS)

8 beef short ribs (about 5 lb.)
1 pear
⅓ c. scallions
4 T minced garlic
⅔ c. soy sauce
6 T sugar
4 T rice wine
4 T sesame oil
black pepper
24 chestnuts, peeled

This is a good winter dish. If your refrigerator space is tight, you may leave the pot in the garage or other cool place overnight before skimming off the fat. You may also like to serve this dish with mashed potato or mashed sweet potato, which is not Korean at all in its presentation, but creates a very good combination. One day before serving, immerse the beef short ribs in cold water for about an hour to remove the blood. Rinse and dry the ribs. In a large cooking pot about 11" diameter, bring 10 c. water to boil. Place the ribs in the water in one layer and return water to a boil. Reduce heat to medium high and boil for 30 minutes. Turn the ribs every 10 minutes to ensure even cooking. Meanwhile create the seasoning by mixing 1 peeled and finely chopped pear, ⅓ c. finely chopped scallions (white and green parts), 4 T minced garlic, ⅔ c. soy sauce, 6 T sugar, 4 T rice wine, 4 T sesame oil, and a dash of black pepper. Move the ribs to another container, but reserve the broth.

Once the ribs have cooled down, slash the meat part of the ribs so that the seasoning can penetrate; mix the seasoning with the ribs in the container and cover, then refrigerate overnight. Allow the reserved broth to cool; refrigerate it overnight. Rotate several times so that the ribs are marinated evenly. On the day of serving, skim the hardened fat from the broth. Place the ribs and marinate in the broth so that the ribs are just immersed; bring to a boil over high heat. Reduce the heat to medium and simmer, uncovered, until half the broth has evaporated. Rotate the ribs a couple of times to ensure even cooking. Add 24 chestnuts to the ribs and continue to simmer, rotating the ribs several more times. Simmer it down until about 2 cups of the broth remains; this may take several hours. Place the ribs on a warm plate and cover with foil to keep warm. Pour the broth into a fat separator to skim off the fat, then pour the rest of the broth over the ribs and serve immediately.

BAP (STEAMED RICE)

Version 1:

2 c. short-grain white rice

Place 2 c. of short-grain white rice (brands such as Han Kuk Mi, Kyong Gi Rice, Sam Su Gab San, Wang Hanmi Rice, Wang Hangawee Rice, Kagayaki, Kokuho Rose, or Nishiki) and 2 c. of water in a rice cooker and push start; do not open the lid while the rice is cooking. After about 20 minutes the rice will be done; wait another 10 minutes before opening the lid. Thoroughly fluff the rice with a serving spoon and serve warm.

Version 2:

1½ c. short-grain brown rice (use same rice brands as above)
2 c. dark kidney beans

Place 1½ c. short-grain brown rice in a rice cooker. Open a can of dark kidney beans; drain, reserving the liquid. Add the beans to the rice cooker and mix with the rice. Add enough water to the reserved bean liquid to make 3 cups. Add it to the rice cooker, close the lid and push start. Do not open the lid. After about an hour the timer will go off, but let it sit for another 15 minutes or so without opening the lid. Thoroughly fluff the rice with a serving spoon and serve warm.

GAMJA JORIM (SOY SAUCE POTATO)

3 c. peeled and cubed Yukon gold potatoes (about 1 lb.)
½ c. soy sauce
3 T sugar
3 T sake
1 T sesame oil
2 cloves garlic
½" slice fresh ginger root
black pepper

Place the following ingredients in a shallow pan to accommodate potato cubes in a single layer, and bring to a boil: 3 c. cubed (about 1" square) Yukon gold potato, ½ c. soy sauce, 3 T sugar,

1½ c. water, 3 T sake, 1 T sesame oil, 2 cloves garlic, roughly chopped, ½" slice of fresh chopped ginger root, and a dash of ground black pepper. Reduce heat to medium and cook at a gentle boil until the potato is soft. Serve at room temperature.

SIGEUMCHI MUCHIM (SEASONED SPINACH)

1 large bunch fresh spinach
2 scallion stalks
3 cloves garlic
2 T soy sauce
2 T sesame oil
black pepper
salt

Rinse the spinach under cold running water. Bring a large pot of water to a boil, then dunk the spinach in and quickly remove it (if necessary, do it in two or three batches). Squeeze all the water out of the spinach and set aside. Mix 2 finely chopped scallions with 3 minced garlic cloves, 2 T soy sauce, 2 T sesame oil, and a dash each of ground black pepper and salt. Mix with the spinach and serve at room temperature.

BEOSEOT BOKKEUM (MUSHROOM SAUTÉ)

1 lb. fresh oyster or *shiitake* mushroom, cleaned, trimmed, and sliced
4 T olive or corn oil
salt
black pepper
1 t. minced garlic

Place the cleaned, trimmed, and sliced mushrooms in a large, deep skillet or wok. Add 4 T olive or corn oil and a dash each of salt and pepper. Mix well with the mushroom slices. Place the skillet over high heat and cook, stirring occasionally, until tender (about 10 minutes). Reduce heat to low; add 1 t. minced garlic and stir, cooking for about 2 more minutes. Turn off the heat and let the mushrooms sit for about an hour; serve at room temperature.

YAKSIK (SWEET GLUTINOUS RICE)

4 c. glutinous rice (*chapssal*)
6 T sesame oil
1 c. brown sugar
2 T soy sauce
2 t. cinnamon
30 peeled chestnuts
30 dried jujube dates, washed and pitted
4 T pine nuts
4 T raisins

Soak 4 c. glutinous rice overnight. Pour 6 T sesame oil into a pressure cooker and swirl it to coat its inside. Add 1 c. brown sugar with 2 T soy sauce and melt them. Drain the water from the rice and pour the rice into the pressure cooker. Add the rest of the ingredients and mix them well, include 2 c. water. Seal the pressure cooker with its lid and bring pressure to the first red ring (I use the Kuhn Rikon Duromatic 5 Liter Pressure Cooker for this recipe) over high heat. Adjust the heat to stabilize the pressure at first red ring. Cook for 10 minutes. Turn the heat off and let the pressure release naturally (about 13 minutes). Open the lid and mix the contents. Serve at room temperature.

Holiday Food in South Korea

As I was growing up in Seoul, one of my most vivid memories comes from the smell of the food my mother prepared for Korea's many holidays. Festival foods are typically linked with holidays based on the lunar calendar. For example, *Daeboreum* (the fifteenth day of the first month of the lunar calendar) is the first full moon of the year. Koreans say that this moon is the biggest full moon, compared the brightest full moon of *Chuseok* in the fall. The main focus of this holiday is to prevent a disaster and ward off evil spirits. On the morning of this holiday, an elderly person of the family would pour cold wine in shot glasses for younger ones. This practice, known as *guibalgi sul* (literally translated as "wine that sharpens your ear") is said to enhance your listening ability for any good news for the rest of the year. Since eating nuts on this day is said to scare bad spirits away, strengthen one's dental health, and prevent skin rash, a bowlful of various types of nuts in their shells are set out as a special snack. Nine different types of reconstituted dried vegetables from the last year's harvest are also an important part of this holiday's practice. In addition, two different types of rice dishes are prominently featured: *ogokbap* (five grain rice) is made with five different types of grains (rice, two different types of millet, adzuki bean, and black bean) and *yaksik* is made with sticky rice seasoned with sugar, soy sauce, cinnamon, sesame oil, chestnuts, pine nuts, and dates. Koreans usually share these special rice dishes with neighbors to promote good will. Some even believe that one must have nine small meals throughout the day to ensure extra good luck and may organize a special song and dance parade called *"Jisinbalgi"* as a form of exorcism.

Samwol samjinnal (the third day of the third month of the lunar calendar) is believed to be the day of the reappearance of swallows, signaling the return of spring. To celebrate this day and to hasten the spring, people serve rice cakes decorated with azalea flowers and young boys make flutes with branches of newly sapped willow trees. *Dano* (the fifth day of the fifth month of the lunar calendar) is believed to be the beginning of summer and the day with the most vital power in a year. People usually serve a rice cake mixed with a mountain vegetable as a symbol for worshiping the sun god. Many festivals take place on this day throughout the country, and a western seashore city called Gangneung is particularly famous for its *Dano* festival, featuring traditional song and dance performances. *Chilseok* (the seventh day of the seventh month of the lunar calendar) is the day when two lovers in a Korean mythical story can finally be reunited for just one day after waiting for a whole year. The story is described in a folk song called "Chilseokyo" sung during this day. Because of the lovers' tears of joy from the reunification and sadness from the imminent farewell, this day tends to be cloudy or rainy. Along with a fruit punch and a rice cake topped with adzuki beans, various types of food made from flour are served throughout this day. *Dongji*, or Winter Solstice, is the day Koreans eat a bowl of thick porridge made of red adzuki beans dotted with sweet rice cake balls. Some Koreans also place a bowl of this porridge in various parts of their houses because they believe that the red color of the beans drives away evil spirits.

Chuseok (the fifteenth day of the eighth month of the lunar calendar) celebrates the brightest full moon of the year. Known in English as the Harvest Moon Festival, this is the Korean equivalent of Thanksgiving Day in the United States. According to many Koreans this is the biggest holiday of the year. Most people travel back to their hometowns to spend this holiday with their family members and pay respect to their ancestors. Since this holiday marks the end of the grueling agricultural endeavor, people celebrate it by various types of traditional holiday games and cooking rice from the new crop to rejoice the harvest. In addition, girls and women form a circle to sing and dance *"Kang kang suwollae"* under the moonlit night. By far, the most prominent food associated with this holiday is *songpyeon*, a crescent moon-shaped rice cake filled with sweet and savory fillings. It is a favorite snack for children and adults alike. Some *songpyeons* are steamed in a basket lined with pine needles to give additional aroma. When I had my first *Chuseok* in the United States while attending graduate school, my fellow Korean students and I decided to make this rice cake infused with the pine needle aroma to celebrate this important Korean holiday. We scavenged pine needles from our college campus to steam the rice cake, only to find out that the pine needles used in Korea come from a very different species of a pine tree. Although our rice cakes did not come close to what we ate in our homeland, we nevertheless consumed all of them because we were all very homesick.

Although many Koreans consider *Chuseok* to be the biggest holiday, others believe *Seolnal* (the first day of the first month of the lunar calendar) to be the most auspicious and important holiday of the year. Since it is imperative to greet the New Year with a clean slate, Korean families tidy up not only their houses inside and out but also cleanse their bodies. Therefore, the day before *Seolnal* used to be the busiest day of the year for the public bath facilities around the country. Even to this day when almost everybody has access to private bathrooms in their own houses, these public bath facilities still conduct a brisk business on the day before *Seolnal* because people want to take extra care in cleansing themselves.

On the morning of *Seolnal*, most Korean families perform a Confucian ritual to honor their ancestors. Afterward, the young children perform a ceremonial bow to each of the elder living family members, wishing them health and happiness for the New Year. In return, the elder family members give the children a small amount of money ("bow-money") in white envelopes. Then everybody gathers together to eat a bowl of rice cake soup. In Korea, there are two different methods to count one's age. One method is based on one's true age based on the exact birth date. This method is used to determine important matters in one's life, such as a child's readiness for school or the interpretation of one's *saju* (astrological chart) that would determine who would be a suitable spouse or the auspicious date for marriage. The other method is based on turning of the calendar year on New Year's Day. This other method is more commonly used in everyday life, and therefore *Seolnal* is everybody's birthday. Eating a bowl of rice cake soup on the New Year's Day symbolizes growing a year older, and little children, who are impatient to grow up but not yet mature enough to understand the symbolism, attempt to eat several bowls of rice soup in hopes of growing up faster.

In my family, *Seolnal* was the biggest holiday of the year. My brothers and I all anxiously waited a whole year for this holiday. We could not wait to get older. We also liked to wear special Korean costumes to celebrate the day. We particularly liked to receive the "bow-money" from our elders. But to me, the most special aspect of this holiday was the food. My mother used to spend several days prior to this holiday to prepare the feast that would last for three days. Some meals were for our immediate family members and visiting relatives and neighbors. But the third day of the New Year tended to be the biggest feast day in my house because that was the day the crowd of my father's coworkers descended on us. The party, although usually starting out with genteel conversation, soon inevitably turned to a lively affair with everybody clapping and taking a turn in singing their best repertoire, usually from Korean popular songs. For this annual event, my mother, with the help of her maids, worked very hard to prepare various dishes in advance. Along with the obligatory rice cake soup and other holiday menus items that would include *chapchae* (noodles with vegetable and meet), *bulgogi* (barbeque beef), *bindaetteok* (mung bean pancake), *mandu* (dumpling), various types of *jeon* (pan-fried dishes), *haepari naengchae* (jellyfish salad), *sikhye* (sweet rice punch), and *sujeongwa* (persimmon and cinnamon punch), my mother always served her signature dish called *galbijjim* (braised beef short ribs) for this occasion, which I have included here as my interpretation of her recipe. Even to this day in this faraway land, its aroma immediately sends me back to my childhood days filled with images of my parents' happy faces in the midst of boisterous singing parties on New Year's Day.

RECOMMENDED LISTENING

If you have a Korean grocery store near you, it may carry CDs of Korean popular music and some traditional music.

Korean Traditional Music Ensemble: Traditional Music from Korea [LIVE]. Arc Music, 2000. 1561.
Traditional Korean Music. Buda Musique, 2004.

I would also highly recommend a viewing of a Korean film called *Chunhyang* (DVD, 2001), now available through Amazon.com. Yesasia.com is another good source of Korean CDs and DVDs. When you purchase DVDs, however, make sure to check its "region encoding" to be compatible with your DVD players.

FOR FURTHER INFORMATION

Chung, Soon Yung. 2001. *Korean Home Cooking* (Essential Asian Kitchen Series). North Clarendon, VT: Tuttle Publishing.
Hidden Korea. 2001. PBS Home Video. ASIN: B00005A464.
http://www.asiafood.org/koreafood.cfm
http://english.tour2korea.com
Korean Overseas Culture and Information Service. 1999. *Hello From Korea.*
Lee, Cecilia Hae-Jin. 2005. *Eating Korean: From Barbecue to Kimchi, Recipes from My Home.* Hoboken, NJ: John Wiley & Sons.

MONGOLIA
Peter K. Marsh

Listen to your elders and never turn down prepared food.

Menu: *Buuz* (Meat Dumplings), *Baitsaany Salad* (Cabbage Salad), and *Süütei Tsai* (Salted Tea).
Preparation Time: About 1½ hours.
Cooking Process: Make the dough mixture first; while various dumplings are steaming, make the cabbage salad. Serves six people.

The Recipes

BUUZ ["BOZE"] (MONGOLIAN DUMPLINGS)

2½–3 c. all-purpose flour
1½ lb. mutton or beef (the more fat, the juicier the dumplings!)
3–4 cloves garlic
2–3 scallions
2 T vegetable oil
2 t. coriander
½ t. black ground pepper to taste
2 t. salt

First prepare the dough mixture. Put about 2½–3 c. flour into a large mixing bowl. Slowly mix in 1½ c. water to make dough that is not too dry or too moist. Knead the dough on a floured board for a few minutes. Cover it with the bowl and let sit (or "rest" as the Mongolians say) for about 15 minutes. In the meantime, finely cut 1½ lb. mutton or beef and place it in a bowl, and mix in 3–4 cloves of finely chopped garlic and 2–3 finely chopped scallions. (Vegetarians often replace the meat with mashed potatoes and thinly sliced cabbage.) Add additional spices to taste (herders sometimes use about 2 t. coriander and ½ t. pepper), along with 2 t. salt. Finally, mix in about ½ c. water "to give the meat its juices." After the dough has rested, knead it again for 2–3 minutes and then slice it into long strips about 1" wide. Roll each strip on a floured board to make long dough "snakes," which you then cut into small pieces, about 1" x 1". Squish each piece flat in the palms of your hands to make what look like small round cookies. Lightly coat these pieces with flour in the bowl and then flatten each with a rolling pin into a thin round piece of dough.

Now you are ready to fill them. Holding the dough piece in the palm of one hand, scoop a heaping teaspoon of the meat mixture into the middle of the dough piece. With the thumb of one hand and the fingers of the other, fold the dough up and over the meat, pinching the edges together to create the dumpling shape. Mongolians make their *buuz* in different shapes, but the round *yurt*-shaped dumplings are the most common. There are usually small holes at the top of each dumpling where the edges of the dough come together and the steam will escape out. Dip the bottom of each *buuz* in vegetable oil to keep it from sticking to the base of the steamer pan and then place each onto a steamer pan, making sure that they not touch each other. Steam the dumplings in a boiling steamer for 20 minutes. Before taking the dumplings out of the steamer, it is important to waft air over them with the steamer lid for 30 seconds or so, so as to keep the flour from becoming doughy. Pile the *buuz* onto a serving plate and take immediately to the table to serve with cabbage salad and milk tea. Mongolians usually eat *buuz* with their fingers, biting into each and then sucking out the hot juices before consuming the rest of the dumpling. They also love to eat *buuz* dipped in soy sauce, ketchup, and even hot chili sauce.

Baitsaany Salad (Cabbage Salad)

1 head of cabbage
2–3 medium-sized carrots
½ c. vegetable oil
½ t. sugar
½ t. salt
1 T white vinegar to taste

Chop the cabbage and carrots into very thin strips, mix together and place in a bowl. Add the vegetable oil and stir; add the sugar and salt and stir; and then add the white vinegar. If the vinegar is very strong, you only need 1 t. of it, otherwise add a bit more. Cover and place the salad in the refrigerator for 10–20 minutes. Be sure to taste the salad; the cabbage and carrots should become soft after adding the vinegar. Serve chilled.

Süütei Tsai (Salted Tea)

black tea (most varieties; loose or in bags)
⅔ c. milk
½ t. salt

Combine 1 qt. water and tea mixture, and bring to boil. Add ⅔ c. milk (the more fatty the milk, the better!) and ½ t. salt and boil another 5–10 minutes. The salt should be just enough to taste, but not enough to make the tea taste outright salty.

Mongolian Buuz

Mongolia has been increasingly working its way into the popular consciousness of North Americans and Europeans for much of the past 15 years, roughly corresponding to the period of the nation's emergence from under nearly seven decades of Soviet political, economic, and cultural dominance. In recent years, well-publicized exhibits of nomadic art and imperial treasures have wowed audiences across the United States; a documentary film about a "weeping camel" was nominated for an Oscar; a book highlighting the role of Genghis Khan (known to Mongolians as Chinggis Khaan) and the Mongol Empire in the making of the modern world has been a national bestseller; and hordes of young Mongolian musicians have swept through concert halls on both continents, amazing audiences with their famous *khöömii* ("throat singing") and *morin khuur* ("horse-head fiddle") virtuosity.

By contrast, Mongolia's cuisine remains little known outside of the country's national boundaries. This is in part because the Mongolians have never packaged and marketed their food culture to others as have, say, their southern neighbors, the Chinese and Taiwanese. Mongolian cuisine centers on the products produced from the animals they have traditionally herded—sheep, goats, cows or yaks, camels, and horses. Of these, the meat from sheep (principally mutton) and cows form the basis of the diet, which is mostly consumed during the winter and spring months when few other food sources are available. Milk, on the other hand, is drawn from all of these animals throughout the year, that of the mare being the most preferred. The summer and fall are the seasons when the "white foods," those made from milk, are the most abundant. When they can, the Mongols also supplement their diet with what they can hunt, gather, and grow (and sometimes fish) in their surrounding environment.

By the nineteenth century, the growth of trade with Russia and China began to allow regular access to such basic foodstuffs as tea, wheat flour, rice, and salt, among others, greatly expanding their diet. Throughout the twentieth century, Russian cooking had a profound influence on Mongolian cuisine. Post 1990, Korean and Chinese foods have added new dimensions to the Mongolians' eating habits, as has the growth in fast food restaurants (all domestic—there are no McDonald's yet in Mongolia!) and supermarkets in the nation's urban centers. Despite these influences, however, Mongolian cooking remains distinctly conservative.

The Mongols in the countryside cook their foods, even today, in metal, dung-fired stoves in their round traditional house-tents called *gers* (*yurt*, in Turkish). The Mongol women of the household usually cook all the meals over this one stove, passing out dishes as they are finished. The family sits on the floor around the fire, men on one side of the *ger* and women on the other, eating their meals out of bowls with their fingers, chopsticks, or silverware.

Mongolian *buuz* appears to be part of a wide dissemination of steamed dumplings throughout the region. Each of their neighbors has some form of dumpling in their national cuisine, but the linguistic links with China seem the most strong. The name *buuz* (pronounced "boze") comes from the Chinese word for steamed dumpling, *baozi*.

But the Mongols celebrate *buuz* as one of their own. It is consumed in enormous quantities throughout the country, throughout the year, but most famously during the *Tsagaan sar* festivities that mark the beginning of the Lunar New Year (which is calculated somewhat differently than the Chinese Lunar New Year). During this three-day holiday, usually falling in February, when Mongolia remains locked in its frigid winter, the Mongols dress up in their traditional *deel* robes to visit and host the visits of their close relatives and friends. These visits can last up to several hours, depending on how close you are to the host, and will feature endless plates stacked high with hot, steaming *buuz*, jugs of milk-tea, bowls with all sorts of salads and fried breads, and of course vodka (the Mongols make traditional forms of "brandy" by distilling milk). Families typically prepare hundreds of *buuz* in the weeks leading up to the holiday, setting them outside their doors and windows to freeze. Young Mongolian men often compete with each other during their visits to see who can consume the most *buuz* in a sitting—a competition of machismo often accompanied by a great deal of vodka, and one that foreign visitors will in all likelihood lose!

RECOMMENDED LISTENING

The Art of Morin Khuur. World Music Library 65. King Records, 1991. KICC 5165.
Melodies of the Steppes: White Moon. Tsagaan Sar: Traditional and Popular Music from Mongolia. Pan Records, 1992. PAN 2010.
Mongolia: Traditional Music. Auvidis, 1991. D8207.
Mongolian Epic Song: Zhangar. World Music Library 36. King Records, 1991. KICC 5136.
Vocal and Instrumental Music of Mongolia. Topic, 1994. TSCD909.

FOR FURTHER INFORMATION

Marsh, Peter K. 2006. *The Horse-head Fiddle and the Cosmopolitan Reimagination of Tradition in Mongolia*. Current Research in Ethnomusicology. New York: Routledge.

Pegg, Carol. 2001. *Mongolian Music, Dance, and Oral Narrative: Performing Diverse Identities*. Seattle; London: University of Washington Press.

4
South Asia

NEPAL

Anna Marie Stirr

As much as I eat of the food you cook, I keep on wanting more;
As much as I hear of the songs you sing, I keep on wanting more.

Menu: *Bhaat* (Cooked Rice), *Palungo ra Kagatiko Dal* (Spinach-Lemon Lentils), *Rajma ra Tofu* (Kidney Beans and Tofu), *Saag* (Cooked Greens), *Kukhurako Maasuko Jhol* (Chicken Curry), *Aluko Achaar* (Spiced Potato Salad), *Golbedhako Achaar* (Tomato Chutney), and *Dahi ra Phalphul* (Yogurt and Fruit Dessert). Serve with water, beer, or other alcohol.
Preparation Time: 2 to 3 hours.
Cooking Process: The yogurt and fruit dessert can be assembled the day before and refrigerated, adding oranges when ready to serve. If using dried kidney beans, begin soaking the night before. On the day of the meal, first prepare vegetables and set aside until needed. To save time, commercially packaged ginger and garlic paste can be used. It is available at Indian grocery stores and can sometimes be found at other supermarkets. Boil potatoes for potato salad, and begin cooking *dal*. While the *dal* is cooking, sauté tofu and set aside. Make the *rajma ra tofu* up until the step before tofu is added; while it is cooking, sauté the remaining *dal* ingredients. Finish *dal* and set aside; same for *rajma ra tofu*. These recipes taste better if they sit for a little while before being served, and can be kept in a warm oven. Make the potato salad and set aside at room temperature. Put the rice on to cook, and prepare the chicken curry. While these are cooking, prepare greens (*saag*). Finally, at the last minute, prepare tomato chutney, which should taste as fresh as possible. Note: everything is vegan except the chicken and the yogurt dessert; omitting the chicken still leaves you with a bountiful feast, and the yogurt dessert can be made with cultured soy (but I would suggest using vanilla yogurt instead of plain). Nepalis also make and use soy milk. Serves six people.

The Recipes

BHAAT (COOKED RICE)

3 c. white or brown basmati rice

Bring 6 c. water to a boil; rinse and add 3 c. white or brown basmati rice. Reduce heat and simmer, covered, until the rice is done (about 45 minutes). It will expand quite a bit. Rice should be cooked so the grains are separate, not sticky or gooey. Or, if you have a way of cooking rice that works well for you, use that method instead of this one.

PALUNGO RA KAGATIKO DAL (SPINACH-LEMON LENTILS)

1 c. red lentils (*massoor da*l)
½ t. turmeric
½ t. salt
1 T vegetable oil
2 bay leaves
½ t. cumin
1 T ginger paste

62

1 T garlic paste
3 whole cloves
1 stick cinnamon
1 small onion, chopped
1 c. chopped fresh spinach
2 tomatoes, chopped
1 lemon, juiced
¼ c. fresh cilantro

Wash and drain 1 c. *massoor dal* (red lentils). Add ½ t. turmeric and ½ t. salt and cook in 5 c. water until lentils fall apart. Heat 1 T vegetable oil and fry 2 bay leaves until dark; add remaining spices (½ t. cumin, 1 T ginger paste, 1 T garlic paste, 3 whole cloves, 1 stick cinnamon) and onion and fry until translucent. Add 1 c. chopped fresh spinach and cover until it is soft. Add spinach mixture to cooked *dal* and boil for 1 minute. Add the chopped tomatoes, the juice of 1 lemon, ¼ c. fresh cilantro, and serve.

Rajma ra Tofu (Kidney Beans and Tofu)

1 12-oz. can kidney beans or 1 c. dried
1 package firm tofu
4 T vegetable oil
1 t. fenugreek seeds
2 bay leaves
1 medium yellow onion, chopped
salt
¼ t. turmeric
1 T ginger paste
1 T garlic paste
½ t. cumin
½ t. coriander
¼ t. chili powder
½ c. chopped tomatoes
⅛ t. cinnamon

Soak 1 c. kidney beans overnight, or open a can. Press some of the water out of 1 package of tofu with paper towels, and cut tofu into small cubes. Heat 2 T oil in pan and lightly fry tofu until golden brown. Remove from heat and set aside. Heat 2 T oil in pressure cooker (note: you don't need a pressure cooker if you use canned beans) and brown 1 t. fenugreek seeds. Then add 2 bay leaves and let them darken. Add 1 medium onion and fry until light brown. Add the beans, 1 t. salt and ¼ t. turmeric, and stir to mix. Add 1 T ginger paste, 1 T garlic paste, ½ t. cumin, ½ t. ground coriander, ¼ t. chili powder, stir to mix and fry for a minute. Add ½ c. chopped tomatoes and fry a few more minutes. Add 1½ c. water. Boil for 5 minutes or so, adding more water if necessary to maintain a gravy-like consistency. Close the pressure cooker (or just cover the pan if you used canned beans) and cook 20 minutes. Let sit 5 minutes, uncovered, then add the fried tofu and boil for a minute or two. Remove from heat, add ⅛ t. cinnamon, and serve hot. Note: Though tofu is not a "traditional" Nepali food, it is available in Kathmandu markets and has become a favorite of vegetarian families. More traditionally, this dish would be made with sundried vegetable balls called *maseura*.

SAAG (COOKED GREENS)

1 large bunch of spinach, watercress, or mustard greens
2 T mustard oil
1 dried whole red chili
½ T lovage seed
¼ t. turmeric
salt
¼ lemon, juiced

Wash and coarsely chop greens (spinach and watercress, or mustard greens). Heat 2 T mustard oil and fry 1 dried whole red chili, ½ T lovage seed, and ¼ t. turmeric until it browns (a few seconds). Add greens and stir; then add ¼ t. salt; cover and cook until wilted, stirring several times. If greens begin to stick to pan, add a small amount of water. Juice of ¼ lemon can also be added.

KUKHURAKO MAASUKO JHOL (CHICKEN CURRY)

3 T mustard or vegetable oil
2 bay leaves
1 medium yellow onion, thinly sliced
½ t. fenugreek seeds
½ t. turmeric
salt
½ t. cumin
½ t. coriander
¼ t. red chili powder
1 T crushed ginger
1 T crushed garlic
3 skinless, boneless chicken breasts
2 c. chicken stock
1 medium tomato, quartered
¼ c. chopped cilantro

Heat 3 T mustard or vegetable oil and add 2 bay leaves and onion; fry until onions are golden brown. Add all spices (scant ½ t. fenugreek seeds, ½ t. turmeric, ½ t. salt, ½ t. cumin, ½ t. coriander, ¼ t. powdered red chili pepper) with 1 T crushed ginger (or paste) and 1 T crushed garlic (or paste), and mix well. Add 3 skinless, boneless chicken breasts (cut into small pieces) and mix to coat with spice mixture. Stir-fry until chicken is slightly cooked (doesn't have to be cooked all the way through); about 5 minutes. Add 2 c. chicken stock or water, plus the quartered tomato, and boil until chicken is cooked through. The broth will not cook down into gravy; it remains thin. Add cilantro for garnish and serve.

Aluko Achaar (Spiced Potato Salad)

10–12 new red potatoes
1 small onion or shallot, chopped
½ c. ground roasted sesame seeds
salt to taste
1 T mango powder (or juice of 2 lemons)
1 t. red chili powder
2 T vegetable oil
½ t. fenugreek seeds
½ t. turmeric
¼ c. cilantro

Peel 10–12 new red potatoes and cut them into ½"–1" chunks, then boil until tender (about 10 minutes). Mix the potatoes with the onion or shallot, ½ c. ground roasted sesame seeds and ½ t. salt. In another small bowl, mix 1 T mango powder or the juice of 2 lemons and 1 t. powdered red chili powder with a tablespoon or two of water. (If you are using lemon juice, just add lemon juice to the chili powder). Mix with your fingers until no lumps remain, then mix with the potatoes. This ensures that the spices are evenly distributed. Heat 2 T vegetable oil in a pan and add a scant ½ t. fenugreek seeds; fry until they blacken (blackening is what makes them edible). At the last second, add ½ t. turmeric to the oil and fry; you can do this after turning off the heat. Pour the oil mixture into the potatoes and mix. Mix in ¼ c. cilantro, then let cool, and serve.

Golbedhako Achaar (Tomato Chutney)

3 medium tomatoes
3 green chili peppers (serrano or jalapeño)
½ c. cilantro
4 cloves garlic
¼ t. turmeric
¼ lemon, juiced
salt

Cut 3 medium tomatoes in half and place cut-side down on a broiler pan. Roast the tomatoes for a few minutes under the broiler and peel off their skins. Alternately, if you don't have a broiler, place the tomatoes directly on the flame of a gas stove until they blacken and the peel is easily removed. If desired, you can also roast the chilies; it's not necessary to peel them though. Put peeled tomatoes and all other ingredients (3 green chilies, ½ c. cilantro, 4 cloves garlic, ¼ t. turmeric, the juice of ¼ lemon, and ¼ t. salt) in a blender and blend into a smooth sauce. Add salt to taste.

DAHI RA PHALPHUL (YOGURT AND FRUIT DESSERT)

3 c. plain yogurt
1 T sugar
¼ t. cinnamon
¼ t. cardamom
1 apple
1 Asian pear
1 orange

Mix 3 c. plain yogurt in a bowl with 1 T sugar, ¼ t. cinnamon, and ¼ t. cardamom. Peel and chop 1 apple and 1 Asian pear into ½" pieces; add to yogurt and set aside. Just before serving, peel an orange, divide into sections, and cut each section into ½" pieces (if it's a small orange, you can leave the sections whole). Spoon yogurt and fruit mixture into small bowls and top with orange pieces. Note: if you add the orange earlier, it will make the mixture taste bitter.

Pounding wheat (Nepal). Photo by Terry E. Miller.

Music and Food in Nepal

"Batti gayo!" ("Electricity out!") The all-too-familiar cry echoes through our neighborhood in Bhaktapur, a city about 15 miles from Kathmandu, and subject to the electrical load-sharing difficulties that plague the Kathmandu Valley. The only light in my kitchen is the flame from the gas stove, and the world around us is suddenly dominated by sound.

Ssssssssssss! The whistle of pressure cookers fills the air. My visiting neigbor Elija jokes that "this must be the sound of Nepal." Through the window across the street, Puja's flickering stove illuminates her face as she cuts potatoes into a simmering pot while humming the high melody of a Hindi film song. Our pressure cooker sputters and bubbles, getting ready for the full-blown whistle that will announce to us that our rice is ready.

In a small room downstairs, a flute-and-drum ensemble is preparing for the festival of the Newar New Year, *Bisket Jatra*, when they will march from our neighborhood to join groups from all over the city at the festival square, for days of music making and nights of feasting as part of a 10-day celebration. Looking forward to the festival, the men today sip cups of *raksi* alcohol and teach their songs to new group members. The melody of the song *Basanta* (Spring) floats up to the kitchen accompanied by the beat of drums and crash of cymbals.

The teenager next door, his prized amp temporarily deprived of its functionality, sits on his roof terrace and picks out a barely audible, arrhythmic version of "Take Five" on his electric guitar. Motorcycles whoosh around the blind corner, their growling engines and squealing tires sending Puja's sons running screaming into the safety of their doorway. "Dinner's ready! Come eat," we hear her call.

We improvise—"Take Five" takes on a new rhythm, and Elija concocts a delicious *achaar* out of my remaining tomato, garlic, chili, and cilantro, rhythmically pounding them together with mortar and pestle. When the electricity returns, we hear it before we see it: Is that Nepal Television's jingle coming from across the way? A flick of the lightswitch illuminates our dinner: a combination of *dal, bhat,* and *tarkari* (lentils, rice, and vegetables) with a spicy *achaar*.

The connection between music and food in Nepal is perhaps most evident at festivals such as Bhaktapur's Bisket Jatra, varying widely among the country's diverse regions. Learning festival music in Newar communities involves worshiping Nasadyah, the god of music, a process that includes regular offerings of fruit, incense, rice, and flowers and at the culmination of the learning process, a sacrificial chicken or goat which then becomes the basis for a feast to celebrate the newly initiated musicians' accomplishments. Different festivals have their associated songs and foods; at Tihar in late October, boys and girls go from house to house singing songs known as *Bhailo* and *Deusi*, collecting money and perhaps enjoying one of Tihar's special delicacies: rice flour doughnuts called *sel roti*. More frequent rituals also combine music and food. In the village of Pharping, south of Kathmandu, the shrine of Dakshinkali attracts pious Hindus on the days of the week dedicated to the goddess Kali. Down in a small gorge at the confluence of two rivers, a PA system blasts religious *bhajans* at full volume while Kali receives sacrifices of goats, chickens, or from vegetarians, pumpkins and coconuts. Meat and vegetables alike are returned, now blessed as *prasad*, to be consumed in meals full of religious merit. Up on the hills above the gorge, Buddhist monks and nuns in several monasteries perform rituals for the animals whose lives have been taken for Kali. The clanging of cymbals and the low tones of chanting echo down to the bus park, where the weekly influx of Hindu devotees is confronted with the sonic manifestations of conflicting theologies, in the few quiet moments between the revving of engines and the blaring of musical bus horns.

Beyond the festival and ritual setting, music is rarely absent from daily life. Television channels are dedicated to Nepali, Hindi, and English music videos and *dohori* contests where men and women face off in improvising suggestive lyrics; radio stations provide a steady diet of Nepali and Hindi pop, hip-hop, Anglo-American pop and classic rock, Nepali national folk, and classical raga music. Everyday activities of cooking, eating, working, and shopping take place accompanied by a wide variety of melodies and beats. A gathering of a few friends turns into a party with a plateful of meat or vegetable dumplings called *momos*, or perhaps dried soybeans fried with garlic and dried meat, perhaps some alcohol, and of course, songs. Few are shy to sing, and a favorite party game—now turned into a game show on Nepal Television—is *antakshari*, a competition where teams alternate in singing songs that begin with the ending syllable of the opposing team's last song. In the Kathmandu Valley and in the New York diaspora, those who play *bansuri* flute, guitar, or the *madal* drum will rarely go to a party without their instruments, knowing that they will be expected to contribute to the music making without which the party would be incomplete.

The recipes here are my own, based on meals prepared together in Kathmandu, Bhaktapur, Wisconsin, and New York kitchens, often to the accompaniment of friends and family members' music practice, Radio Nepal, favorite Nepali bands' recordings, or most often, our own renditions of popular songs while chopping vegetables or blending an *achaar* with the mortar and pestle. I am indebted to the Malakar, Mali, Vaidya, and Thapa families, for the informal culinary education that they've given me over the years, and to the University of Wisconsin Year in Nepal's culinary tutor, Neesha Shrestha, whom I have never met but whose recipe for *rajma ra tofu* came my way through circuitous routes and is included here with minor modifications. Though I've learned to cook mosty in Newar households, these recipes are not particularly Newari. The combination of *dal, bhat, tarkari*, and *achaar* is standard for most of Nepal's Tarai and mid-hills regions, with different grains and vegetables as staples higher in the hills and Himalayan regions. Thus a full meal should contain all four components, adding more types of *tarkari* and meat for special occasions. An everyday dinner might contain only the *dal*, rice, greens, and tomato *achaar*; for more of a feast, add the other *tarkari*, the potato *achaar*, the chicken, and the yogurt dessert. Put on one of the recommended recordings, or listen for the whistle of your pressure cooker if you use one, and savor the sounds of Nepal.

RECOMMENDED LISTENING

Find contemporary Nepali music of many styles online at http://www.gorkhali.com/playmusic.cgi/
Available in streaming Real Audio format, with large folk and pop selections and even some videos. As most recordings of Nepali artists are difficult to find outside of Nepal, the Internet is probably your best bet. To begin with, try Jhalakman Gandharva (folk); Dr. Pilots or 1974 AD (pop); and Arun Thapa (Modern Song).

Nepathya. *Bhedako Oon Jasto (Like Sheep's Wool)*. 2003. (Rock and pop adaptations of folk tunes learned on bandleader Amrit Gurung's trips around Nepal, plus originals. English liner notes). Recording, accompanying documentary film, and more information available at http://www.bhedakoooonjasto.com
Wegner, Gert-Matthias. *Master Drummers from Nepal: Traditional drumming from Bhaktapur*. Available, along with others, at http://www.ecohimal.org/english/shop_e.htm

FOR FURTHER INFORMATION

Greene, Paul. 2005. Mixed messages: Unsettled cosmopolitanisms in Nepali pop. In *Wired for Sound*. Edited by Paul Greene and Thomas Porcello. Middletown, CT: Wesleyan University Press.
Liechty, Mark. 2005. "Carnal Economies: The Commodification of Food and Sex in Kathmandu. *Cultural Anthropology* 20(1): 1–38.
Widdess, Richard. 2003. Time, space and music in the Kathmandu Valley. *International Institute for Asian Studies Newsletter* 32. Available at http://www.iias.nl/iiasn/32/RR_time_space_and_music.pdf

NORTH INDIA
Amelia Maciszewski

The more food there is, the more songs there will be.

Menu: *Toor Dal* (Yellow Lentils), *Tamatar Chutney* (Tomato Chutney), *Dahi Murgh Masala* (Chicken Curry with Yogurt Marinade), *Aloo Patta Gobi* (Cabbage-Potato Curry), *Raita* (Yogurt Salad), *Chawal* (Steamed Rice), and *Chapati* (Flat Bread). For dessert, serve *Kheer* (Coconut Raisin Pistachio Dessert). Serve with water and/or cocktails.
Preparation Time: 3–4 hours.
Cooking Process: Soak the lentils for the *dal* first, make the *chapati*, then prepare the chicken curry. Make and chill the *raita*, then make the chutney and the cabbage-potato curry. Make and chill the *kheer*. Start the rice about 40 minutes before you plan to eat. North Indians often keep a stash of various sweets that they pass out to those who have room in their stomachs after dinner and want to sweeten their palates. Serves six people.

The Recipes

TOOR DAL (YELLOW LENTILS)

1 c. yellow lentils
1 t. turmeric
salt
¾ t. ground cumin
¾ t. ground coriander
pinch of cayenne powder
3 tomatillos
2–3 chili peppers
pinch of asafetida
1–2 T vegetable oil
3 garlic cloves
1 t. *panch phoron* (mix of cumin, onion, fennel, white mustard, and fenugreek seeds)

Soak 1 c. yellow lentils in approximately 3 c. water for 45 minutes to 1 hour, then rinse once or twice. Bring to a boil on high heat and then reduce to slightly more than a simmer, adding 1 t. each of turmeric and salt. Add ¾ t. each of ground cumin and coriander, a pinch of cayenne powder, 3 chopped tomatillos, and 2–3 finely chopped chili peppers after about 15 minutes. Continue the high-paced simmer for about another 15 minutes, finally adding a large pinch of *hing* (asafetida). In a skillet, heat 1–2 T cooking oil and add 3 thinly sliced garlic cloves and 1 t. *panch phoron* (a mixture of cumin, onion, fennel, white mustard, and fenugreek seeds) and brown. Just as the seeds begin popping and the garlic becomes brown, pour one or two serving spoons of the *dal* into the skillet and watch it sizzle! Then pour the mixture back into the saucepan, mixing it together with the rest of the *dal*. Garnish with a handful of fresh chopped coriander leaves.

Tamatar Chutney (Tomato Chutney)

2 medium yellow onions
5–6 cloves garlic
2–3 serrano chili peppers
2 T vegetable oil
1 t. cumin seeds
1 t. onion seeds
2–3 bay leaves
pinch of salt
pinch of sugar
pinch of *garam masala*
1 t. turmeric
6 large ripe tomatoes

Chop 2 yellow onions, 5–6 cloves of garlic, and 2–3 serrano chili peppers finely. Pour enough oil into a pan to cover the bottom and heat at a high temperature. Add 1 t. cumin seeds, 1 t. *kalonji* (onion) seeds, and 2–3 bay leaves to the hot oil. Stir in the onions, garlic, and peppers and brown everything together. Lower the flame slightly and mix in a pinch each of salt, sugar, and *garam masala*, and 1 t. turmeric. Add 6 large, very ripe tomatoes, finely chopped, and mix everything together evenly; cover the pan. Cook on low heat, stirring occasionally, until the mixture becomes a thick sauce. Add a little water only if necessary.

Dahi Murgh Masala (Chicken Curry with Yogurt Marinade)

1½ lb. chicken meat
2 T turmeric
salt
pepper
2 c. yogurt
3 large yellow onions, chopped
3 heads garlic
3" fresh ginger root
3 t. ground cumin
3 t. ground coriander
1 T paprika
1 T cayenne
½ c. vegetable oil
5–6 large pods of cardamom
2–3 cinnamon sticks
1 t. whole cloves
4–5 medium bay leaves
1 t. cumin seeds
2–3 dried chili peppers
1 bunch fresh cilantro

Wash 1½ lb. chicken meat in cold running water until all traces of blood are removed. Drain. Coat meat generously with 1 T turmeric powder, a pinch each of salt and pepper, using your hands to massage it in (doing it with a spoon doesn't work as well). Add 2 c. yogurt, mixing it in the same way. Cover and set aside to marinate for 1–2 hours. In a blender, combine onions, 3 heads of garlic, several inches of chopped fresh ginger root, 1 T turmeric, 3 t. ground cumin, 3 t. ground coriander, 1 T paprika, 1 T cayenne, and a bit more salt if desired. In a heavy-bottomed pot, heat approximately ½ cup of oil. When the oil is very hot but not smoking, add 5–6 large pods of cardamom, 2–3 cinnamon sticks, 1 t. whole cloves, 4–5 medium bay leaves, 1 t. cumin seeds, and several dried chili peppers; brown slightly, adding carefully the fresh spices from the blender (the mixture will probably splatter). Reduce the heat to medium, stir, and cover. Brown for approximately 10 minutes, opening the cover occasionally to stir. Add the marinated chicken, stir to coat everything evenly, reduce the heat to medium low, and cover. Cook until the meat cuts easily and is whitish inside. If necessary, lower the heat even further; you should not have to add water. Garnish with fresh chopped cilantro if desired.

ALOO PATTA GOBI (CABBAGE-POTATO CURRY)

1 head green cabbage
1 medium potato
1 small tomato
3 large cloves of garlic
1 T fresh ginger root
1 t. mustard seeds
1 t. cumin seeds
2 T vegetable oil
2–3 serrano or Thai chili peppers
salt
1 T turmeric
1 t. ground cumin
1 t. ground coriander
½ t. *garam masala*
½ t. paprika
dash of cayenne
½ c. green peas
pinch of asafetida
pinch of sugar

Slice 1 head of green cabbage into thin slivers, then cut them in half. Chop 1 medium peeled potato into 1" cubes, brown in oil in a separate pan, and set aside. Chop 1 small tomato somewhat finely and set aside. Grind 3 large cloves of garlic and 1 T fresh ginger root in a mortar and pestle or chop finely. Fry 1 t. each mustard and cumin seeds in hot oil until they begin to pop, then add the ginger, garlic, and 2–3 serrano or Thai chili peppers to brown. Fold in the tomato, mixing in ½ t. salt, 1 T turmeric powder, 1 t. ground cumin, and 1 t. ground coriander and cook for about 3 minutes on slightly lower heat. Then add the cabbage, potato, ½ t. *garam masala*, ½ t. paprika, and a dash of cayenne. Cook together for another few minutes, stirring occasionally. Add ½ c. green peas and a large pinch of *hing* (asafetida) powder; stir, cover, and cook another 10 minutes or so on low heat. Add water only if you have to; if so, add very little. Add a pinch of sugar just before turning off the flame. (This dish should have a slight bit of gravy but should not be watery.)

Raita (Yogurt Salad)

2 c. plain yogurt
1 medium cucumber
salt
pepper
1½ t. coriander seeds
1½ t. cumin seeds
¾ t. cayenne powder
dash of paprika
½ lime, juiced

In a medium-sized bowl mix 2 c. plain yogurt until creamy. Peel and grate 1 medium cucumber and mix it in with the yogurt, adding salt and pepper to taste. In a skillet, brown 1½ t. each of coriander and cumin seeds, then add to the yogurt. Roast ¾ t. cayenne powder and a dash of paprika very quickly, adding to the yogurt mixture. Stir everything together, adding the juice of ½ lime. Serve slightly chilled.

Chawal (Steamed Rice)

3 c. white rice

Bring 6 c. water to a boil; rinse and add 3 c. rice. Reduce heat to a simmer, cover, and let it cook undisturbed until done (about 20 minutes). Let the rice sit for another 10 minutes.

Chapati (Flat Bread)

2 c. flour
pinch of salt
1 t. vegetable oil

Mix 1 part water with 2 parts flour, a pinch of salt, and a few drops of oil; let it sit for about half an hour, covered. Use your hands to make a round, very flat piece of bread, fold it up, then roll it out again so that it is even thinner. Place in a dry frying pan until it's slightly brown on each side. It should puff up as you're browning it.

Kheer (Coconut Raisin Pistachio Dessert—also known as Sewian)

5 T ghee

½ lb. vermicelli, broken into 1" pieces

5–6 whole cloves, roughly crushed

2–3 large cinnamon sticks

2 T ground unsweetened coconut

1½ c. hot milk

¾ c. turbinado sugar

2 t. raisins

2 t. chopped pistachio nuts

pinch of saffron

½ t. whole cardamom (shelled but not ground)

Heat 5 T *ghee* in a heavy bottomed pan. Add ½ lb. vermicelli, 5–6 whole cloves, 2–3 large cinnamon sticks, and 2 T ground unsweetened coconut and brown lightly. Add 1½ c. hot milk and ¾ c. sugar. Cover and simmer, stirring frequently. Add 2 t. raisins, 2 t. chopped pistachio nuts, a pinch of saffron, and ½ t. cardamom when thickened. Continue to simmer until the mixture becomes nearly dry. Serve chilled. Can be garnished with fresh mint leaves. This may be followed by the final palate freshener and digestive, *pan,* a wad of betel nuts, lime paste, and digestive seeds such as fennel (and, in some cases, either gooey sweet condiments or a pinch of tobacco), wrapped neatly in a delicate, easily chewable green leaf. Or a plate may be passed around containing *sawf,* a mixture of fennel, anise, and other digestive seeds with tiny slivers of betel mixed in.

Khao aor Gao: Eat and Sing

In Sanskrit-derived languages, the word *rasa* refers both to juice or sap and to the experience of aesthetic delight, particularly that felt when witnessing the performing arts. Similarly, words such as the Bengali *aamej* and the Urdu *zaiqa,* both of which mean "taste or relish," are used to refer to both food and music. This clearly suggests that the delight that comes from the sensation of taste is similar to that experienced when hearing pleasing music. Music making and the preparation and sharing of food are integral parts of a wide spectrum of social/cultural events and festivals. These include communal worship, both Hindu and Sufi Muslim, where *bhajan*-s or *kirtan*-s and *qaw-wali*-s, respectively, are sung; planting and harvest festivals, where regional songs and dances are performed; and the elite *mehfil,* or salon concert, in which a lavish meal follows the performance.

Although individual variations abound, both cooking and music making are taught orally. Teaching methods can range from the teacher demonstrating, followed by the student imitating (and then practicing on her/his own); to an apprentice's observation of the chef's or maestro's performance, to teaching through talk and stories. Musicians and serious music lovers like to get their children started learning well before the age of 10, often around 6. Girls in traditional families often begin helping out in the kitchen around age 8 or 9, although they usually don't cook themselves until at least adolescence. Boys usually don't learn to cook until circumstances such as living away from home for college require that they do. A disciple of a music guru who is serious about cooking, however, is most likely to help in the kitchen and observe how various dishes are prepared, so that at a certain point she or he has their cooking debut, not unlike the performance debut.

Decorum while eating varies almost as much as that during different types of performances. At a wedding, for example, it is all right for family members (particularly men) to tell raucous jokes while eating—which they actually do well after the guests, many of whom make polite, quiet conversation while eating, have been served. Similarly, people are often not particularly attentive to music at a wedding. Musicians tend to carry on lively conversation while eating together at any occasion, often trying to outwit each other. Topics of conversation vary from music to food to gossip to politics.

North Indians traditionally eat with their right hand, either tearing pieces of their *chapati* to gather together the other food, or using their fingers to mix the rice together with other things on the plate into sort of a ball that they will then pop into their mouth. Traditionally an area on the floor was prepared for people to sit by laying a straw or fabric floor covering. The food was then served, often by women and children, on brass or steel *thali*, large round tray-like plates holding the various courses in small bowls called *katori*. People would then sit cross-legged on the floor to have their meal. This custom continues in villages, but in cities more people are using dining tables.

Similar to this, audience members at a house concert would generally sit on the floor to listen to the performers. Even if there is furniture in the room, it is usually considered rude for audience members to sit somewhere where they are higher than the performers, who always sit on the floor (often without a dais). In concert halls people sit in chairs, and the musicians are on stage. However, because the musicians and dancers always remain barefoot during their performance, the area where the musicians sit (or dancers dance) is meant to be shoe-free. Therefore, it is preferable for the musicians to have a dais to sit on where they can avoid any shoes. Although audience members are expected to listen respectfully during a performance, an artist feels inspired if listeners make noises of approval, such as "Vah! Vah! (Bravo!)" or "Kya bat! (Way to go!)" The former exclamation of approval may also be used to compliment a fine dish.

In a traditional home, women tend to remain busier than men with food preparation and serving the guests, while men take care of entertaining the guests with conversation and, in some cases, liquor and *pan*. Guests are often served before the hosts, regardless of gender or age. There is generally little separation of men and women listening to music in a public place, although at a house concert the women may be busy in the kitchen, as indicated above. In the case of many folk musics, women's genres and music-making contexts are separate from men's. Women in North India have a rich tradition of wedding songs (including songs to console the bride who is kin and leaving her natal home, songs to welcome the bride from outside, songs to both welcome and tease the groom, songs of abuse to the new in-laws, etc.), songs to welcome the newborn child, various seasonal songs, etc. These can be performed at all-female gatherings, although it is not uncommon for the women to sing these collectively at mixed-gender community gatherings. Men also sing certain genres as an activity of male solidarity. During such events, children tend to move about seamlessly and relatively quietly. Foreigners may be present; the amount of special attention paid them has decreased in the last two decades, as they have become more commonplace, similar to the proverb "the household chicken has become like the everyday *dal*."

Hereditary, professional Hindustani musicians, historically itinerant artists who spent long periods away from home, moving from one place of patronage to another, considered cooking an important survival skill. Part of a male musician's complex relationship with his patron was the appropriateness of his demanding fine ingredients with which to prepare his dishes. The lore about Hindustani musicians includes not only nearly superhuman dedication to practice under adverse conditions but also a remarkable ability to consume enormous amounts of lavishly prepared food, particularly meat curries, *biryani* (layers of spiced meat and rice cooked together), and breads such as *nan* and *paratha* dripping with *ghee*. The ability to prepare delicious dishes is considered an important part of a hereditary Hindustani musician's aesthetic sensibility, another medium in which to create. Although the women of these communities rarely performed publicly, they were expected to be highly skillful cooks and knowledgeable listeners. For a hereditary professional women performer, or *tawaif,* hosting a lavish meal (either prepared or directed by her) in her salon after a performance was considered an elegant finishing touch to an inspiring evening. On the darker side, a *tawaif* might be poisoned by her rival, who could put a substance in her food or beverage that would harm her voice. For this reason, when two such woman meet to share food or tea, the guest would wait for the host to begin.

My engagement with the world of Indian cuisine has been much like that with Hindustani music: I have learned by doing and making mistakes over and over again until I have been able to create something pleasing. This entails understanding how to use a basic "vocabulary" of ingredients, mastering the preparation of several basic dishes, and finally beginning to improvise on those dishes to create novel versions. Just as one has to listen extensively to good Hindustani music to begin to conceptualize how it should sound in order to sing or play well, one has to be aware of the taste of good food in order to cook it. The recipes below reflect my composite realization of, and improvisation on, the teachings of several distinguished musicians, including my gurus Ustad Aashish Khan and Dr. Girija Devi. Although they are mainly North Indian, there remains an influence of Bengali sensibility in these recipes, as that is my first Indian language, culinary and otherwise.

RECOMMENDED LISTENING

Akhtar, Begum. *The Golden Collection.* The Gramophone Co. of India, 1997. CDNF 13109394.

Devi, Girija, and Gurtu, Shobha. *Jugal Bandis,* Vols. 1 and 2. The Gramophone Co. of India, 1997. CDNF 150191, 150192.

Khan, Aashish, Khan, Sultan, and Hussein, Zakir. *Jugalbandhi: Sarod & Sarangi Duet.* Chandra Dhara, 1997. SNCD 70197.

Khusrau, Amir. *The Best of Amir Khusrau,* Vols. 1 & 2. Living Media India, 1992. CD-B 0385A/B.

Parveen, Abida. *The Golden Collection.* The Gramophone Co. of India, 1998. SS 1188.

FOR FURTHER INFORMATION

http://www.indianfoodsco.com
http://www.khanakhazana.com/recipes/

KERALA, SOUTH INDIA
Zoe Sherinian

It is not the food that brings the relationship, but the relationship that blesses the food.

Menu: *Beef Ollathiyathu* (Fried Beef), *Kuthari Matta* (Red Rice), *Vendakka Ollathiyathu* (Fried Okra), *Moru Kachiyathu* (Cooked Yogurt), and *Payasam* (Rice Pudding). Serve with water, beer, or chai.
Preparation Time: 3 hours.
Cooking Process: Start the rice pudding first, then the beef, the rice, the yogurt, and the okra. When serving, put rice on the plate and pour the yogurt sauce on top with the beef and okra on the side. Mix yogurt, beef and rice together with each bite. Serves six people.

The Recipes

BEEF OLLATHIYATHU (FRIED BEEF)

2 lb. beef
1 t. cumin
2½ t. cayenne (or to taste)
2½ t. coriander
2 t. black pepper
3 t. white vinegar
8 whole cloves
1" cinnamon stick
4–5 cloves garlic, finely chopped
2 T ginger root, finely chopped
1 large yellow onion
2 T coconut oil
10 or more curry leaves (best found at an Indian grocer)
½ c. dried coconut flakes
salt

Cube 2 lb. beef and place in medium-sized bowl. Combine 1 t. cumin, 2½ t. cayenne (or to taste), 2½ t. coriander, and 2 t. black pepper in a small cup and mix with 3 t. white vinegar to create a paste. Crush 8 cloves and 1" cinnamon stick in a mortar and pestle until they turn into small pieces (not powder). Add these and spice paste to beef along with garlic and ginger. Mix well (with hands is best). You can let this sit for 30 minutes, or overnight in the refrigerator if you want a deep flavor; or, if in a hurry, cook the meat right away. Fry 1 large thinly sliced onion until nicely browned in a large frying pan in 1–2 T of coconut oil (run the bottle of oil under hot water to liquefy it). When the onions are almost brown add 10 or more curry leaves (best found through an Indian grocer) and continue frying another minute or two. Remove onion mixture to a small bowl. In this same pan fry ½ c. dried coconut flakes until toasted brown but not scorched. Add coconut to beef and then cook or let it sit longer. In either a large cast-iron frying pan or Indian-style cooker place beef mixture, about 1 t. salt and 1½ c. water not quite covering the beef. Boil at high temperature. Then cover and turn down to low and cook until beef is tender and water begins to cook down, about 30 minutes. If you have too much water you may have to take the lid off for the last 5 minutes, turn the heat up to medium and let the water cook down. Continue to let the water cook down until it becomes like a thick gravy and begins sticking to the bottom of the pan. At this point begin stirring and turning the meat. Turn the heat up to medium high. When it really begins to fry, add the onion and curry leaf mixture. Fry for another 10–15 minutes depending on how crispy you want your beef. Serve in a bowl. You may want to prepare more if you have "Indian-style" eaters who like opportunities for seconds and thirds. You may also crave this in the middle of the night or for breakfast.

KUTHARI MATTA (KERALA RED RICE)

2 c. Kerala red rice

This rice is a whole grain rice with a red streak in it. Bring 4 c. water to a boil. Rinse and add 2 c. rice, then cover, reduce heat and allow to cook for approximately 45 minutes. When cooked it is larger then most grains Americans are used to.

VENDAKKA OLLATHIYATHU (FRIED OKRA)

2 T vegetable oil
1 t. black mustard seeds
2 dried red chili peppers
10 curry leaves
1 medium yellow onion, chopped
1 small green chili
1 lb. okra
½ t. cumin
⅛ t. coriander
salt

In a frying pan or wok heat 2 T vegetable oil until hot but not smoking. Add 1 t. black mustard seeds, 2 dried red chili peppers, and 10 curry leaves. Cover until the seeds are not popping out of the pan, then uncover and add 1 onion and 1 small sliced green chili. Fry until the onions are just turning brown. Add 1 lb. okra and fry for a few minutes. Add ½ t. cumin and ⅛ t. coriander. Continue stirring at medium to high heat until the okra is a little brown and crispy, at least 10 minutes. Add 1 t. salt.

Moru Kachiyathu (Cooked Yogurt)

1 qt. plain yogurt
salt
1 T vegetable oil
1 t. mustard seeds
½ medium yellow onion, finely chopped
2 whole dried red chili peppers
1 T minced garlic
1 T minced fresh ginger root
10 curry leaves
¼ t. fenugreek
¼ t. cumin
¼4 t. turmeric

Put 1 qt. of plain yogurt in a bowl along with ¼ c. water and 1 t. salt. Whisk until smooth and creamy with a wire whisk. Let sit. In a medium pot, heat 1 T vegetable oil until it is hot, not smoking. Add a few mustard seeds. If they begin to bubble it is hot enough. Add rest of the mustard seeds (1 t.) and cover with a lid until they pop for 15 seconds. Do not let them burn. Add onion, 2 whole dried red chili peppers split in half, 1 T minced garlic, 1 T minced ginger, and 10 curry leaves. Turn down heat to medium and cook, stirring, until onions are just getting a little brown. Remove from heat and add ¼ t. fenugreek, ¼ t. cumin, and ¼ t. turmeric powders. Mix well. Slowly add the yogurt mixture to this pot, whisking to prevent curdling. Then stir constantly with a small wooden spoon at low heat until you can see steam coming from the spoon. Never boil. Remove from heat and serve, adding more salt if necessary.

Payasam (Rice Pudding)

3 T unsalted cashews
3 T raisins
1 T *ghee*
1 qt. milk
4 T basmati rice
⅓ c. sugar
½ t. cardamom

Fry 3 T unsalted cashews (broken into pieces) and 3 T raisins in 1 T *ghee* until just golden brown. Boil 1 qt. milk and 4 T uncooked rice in a heavy saucepan over low heat. Stir every few minutes for about 20 minutes until rice is soft. Add ⅓ c. sugar, ½ t. cardamom, and the nuts and raisins. Continue simmering over low heat, stirring periodically, until thickened and reduced to about half the volume, at least 90 minutes. Serve with chai or Indian coffee (a thick decoction with chicory and mostly made of milk).

Beef, Folk Music, and Social Justice in South India

The idea that Indians are primarily vegetarians is a great fallacy that accompanies the hegemony of classical music and dance as *the* representative of Indian culture in the West. The majority of Indians eat some sort of meat or fish and many Brahmins from Bengal eat every kind of meat except beef. Homologously, the majority of Indians patronize or participate in folk music or Bollywood film music, not Indian classical music. At least 16% of the population of India are placed in the category of "Scheduled Caste." These people, who primarily live in villages and work as agricultural day laborers, construction workers, or toilet cleaners were formerly called untouchables, *harajins*, and other pejorative terms. Since the Dalit liberation movement of the 1940s led by Dr. Babasahed Ambedkar (a great critic of Gandhi), and the civil rights movement in India since the 1970s, many Scheduled Caste people today refer to themselves by the self-chosen political term "Dalit" (oppressed) and proudly declare their affinity for and habit of eating beef. Dalits have eaten beef for a very long time. Some believe that they were vegetarians until the Aryans invaded and forced them to eat the dead carnage of cattle, reaffirming their polluted status in the caste system. Others say that Brahmins ate meat when they were nomadic people before settling in the area now known as India.

Today many people in India eat fish, chicken, and lamb (or mutton-goat *briyani*), but refuse to eat beef. Last I heard (before the 2004 elections) one could not buy beef anywhere in New Delhi. Perhaps the decline of the Hindu Nationalist BJP has relaxed this prohibition. Beef is available, however, in most southern cities; especially in Kerala, where most of the Christian population (20%) (and a few of their close Hindu friends that visit frequently) freely indulge in this delicacy. Middle class Dalit activists—with whom I worked in rural areas of Tamil Nadu in summer 2002—proudly proclaimed their beef-eating status, threatening to shake their fist and yell profanities at anyone who negatively judged them for doing so. This was my first step toward Dalit beef-eating conversion. Upon returning from this research trip and spending a lot of time with friends from Kerala, I began making fried beef and moru curry. Then I discovered I could buy Kerala red rice (*kuthari matta*—a whole grain rice). I had been introduced to it many years earlier while visiting Kerala, and thoroughly enjoyed it for its nutty flavor and large grain.

The heart of this meal is fried beef, moru curry, and rice. You can add whatever green vegetable to it that you prefer (beans with coconut, okra, spinach, or even broccoli). Any sort of rice will also do. Furthermore, any Indian dessert will work, while *payasam* is a light sweet finish to the spicy core of the meal. You might just need to make enough extra beef to satisfy your craving the next morning for breakfast and on and on. ...

Moru kachiyathu or moru curry as it is commonly known is a unique dish in India. It is eaten throughout the south, but in Kerala it is ubiquitous as part of a Tali-style meal (blue plate special) in any common restaurant or roadside eating hut. In Tamil Nadu they refer to it as buttermilk and often eat it (or drink it) as a watered-down yogurt (with rice and mango pickle) poured on rice as a refreshing finish for the end of a large midday meal. In this case it does not have the garnishing of fried onions, curry leaves, garlic, etc., or the light yellow color from turmeric that is included in the Kerala moru curry recipe. This is a Kerala specialty. I have also heard of people adding coconut to this recipe, but coconut is added to everything in Kerala. The word "curry" in this case refers to a thick sauce. It generally means some sort of meat cooked in a sauce that includes a mixture of spices. This is usually not the mix of spices that you find in "curry powder" (a British invention) that you can buy (for way too much money compared to the cost of spices in any Indian grocery) in your local grocery. Each cook has her/his own particular mixture of spices (*masala*) for every type of meat or vegetable dish.

The most important cultural aspect of this meal is to cook and serve it for your close friends and family or for those whom you wish to treat with this sort of love. If you have a desire to welcome your guests in a special way you can say the following: "Uṇavu koṇḍu Oṟavu ille. Oṟavu koṇḍu uṇavu āsīrvadām. Amen." ("It is not the food that brings the relationship, but the relationship that blesses the food.") This Tamil Dalit "grace" is in the linguistic form and rhyme schema of a *parimoṟi* or old saying. Old women in Tamil villages commonly walk around saying one *paṟamoṟi* after another instead of normal conversation. The Rev. Jacquolin Jothi of the Protestant Church of South India created this grace when she was in seminary and studying with the Reverend Theophilus Appavoo; he encouraged his students to use folk music and other folk media to create and transmit liberation theology. Have fun with your friends and don't hesitate to satisfy your craving for more curry and beef at breakfast the next morning!

RECOMMENDED LISTENING

You might try to find some Indian folk music to listen to—not always easy—or you might watch a Bollywood film afterwards (which you can rent from the Indian grocery store where you buy the curry leaves). Most films available in DVD format even include English subtitles, including the songs!

FOR FURTHER INFORMATION

Ambedkar, Bhimrao Ramji. 2002. *The Essential Writings of B.R. Ambedkar.* New York: Oxford University Press.
Arnold, Alison, ed. *The Garland Encyclopedia of World Music*, Vol. 5 (South Asia: The Indian Subcontinent). 2000. New York: Garland Publishing.
Holmstrom, Lakshmi, trans. 2000. *Bama, Karuukku.* Chennai: MacMillian India Limited.
http://www.beatofindia.com
http://www.dalitchristians.com
Webster, John C. B. 1992. *A History of the Dalit Christians in India.* San Francisco: Mellen Research University Press.
Zelliot, Eleanor. 1996. *From Untouchable to Dalit: Essays on the Ambedkar Movement.* New Delhi: Manohar.

5
Southeast Asia

LUZON, PHILIPPINES

Mercedes DuJunco

If it's work, do it fast. If it's food, eat it little by little.

Menu: *Ukoy* (Shrimp Fritters), *Lumpia* (Fresh Spring Roll), *Adobo* (Stewed Chicken and Pork), and *Ginataang Halo-Halo* (Sweet Rice Balls in Coconut Milk).
Preparation Time: About 3 hours.
Cooking Process: Prepare the mixtures for the *ukoy* and *lumpia* first, then make them while the *adobo* is cooking. Before you eat, place the rice balls in the oven. Serves six people.

The Recipes

UKOY (SHRIMP FRITTERS)

½ lb. small shrimp
1 c. flour
1 c. cornstarch
1½ t. baking powder
1½ t. salt
½ t. black pepper
1 T annatto seeds
1 egg, beaten
2 T vegetable oil for frying
2 c. bean sprouts
1 c. chopped scallions
1 package firm tofu, drained
1 c. white vinegar
1 t. crushed garlic
salt
pepper

Crush the heads of ½ lb. small shrimp and place in 1½ c. water; allow to soak. Drain and reserve the liquid. In a bowl, sift 1 c. flour, 1 c. cornstarch, 1½ t. baking powder, 1½ t. salt, and ½ t. black pepper together. Add the annatto seed water (¼ c. water in which 1 T annatto seeds have been soaked), 1½ c. shrimp juice (water in which crushed shrimp heads have been soaked), and 1 beaten egg; mix well. Heat enough cooking oil in a large pan for frying. Place a small handful of bean sprouts on a saucer. Pile some of the chopped scallions, some cubes of bean curd, and some shrimp on it. Measure ⅓ c. of the batter and pour on the saucer. Gingerly place the batter with the shrimp mixture into the frying pan with the heated oil. Fry until crisp. Remove and drain on paper towels. Repeat until all the batter and the shrimp mixture are used up and there are several fried rounds. Serve with a dipping sauce of vinegar seasoned with crushed garlic, salt, and pepper according to taste.

LUMPIA (FRESH SPRING ROLL)

2 T vegetable oil
1 T minced garlic
½ lb. ground pork
3 T soy sauce
½ c. sugar
1 cake firm tofu
1 c. grated carrots
1 c. chopped green beans
1 c. chopped cabbage
1 c. trimmed bean sprouts
salt
1 c. chicken broth
1 T cornstarch
2 cloves garlic
1 package *lumpia* wrappers
1 head of lettuce
1 c. crushed roasted peanuts

Preparing the filling: Heat 2 T cooking oil in a wok or a large frying pan and sauté 1 T minced garlic and ½ lb. ground pork. Season with 2 T soy sauce and 1 t. sugar. Add 1 cake of firm tofu and 1 c. each of grated carrots, chopped green beans, chopped cabbage, and trimmed bean sprouts. Mix well until well cooked. Season with salt according to taste.

Preparing the sauce: Mix ¼ c. sugar, 1½ t. soy sauce, ½ t. salt, and 1 c. chicken broth. Bring to a boil and then thicken with 1 T cornstarch dissolved in ¼ c. water. Add 2 cloves minced garlic.

Preparing the lumpia (available at Asian food stores): Place a leaf of lettuce on a *lumpia* wrapper. Spoon in some of the vegetable mixture, a teaspoon of the sauce, and some chopped peanuts. Fold in such a way so that one end is open. Add more sauce and peanuts according to taste.

ADOBO (STEWED CHICKEN AND PORK)

½ lb. chicken
½ lb. pork
⅓ c. white vinegar
3 T minced garlic
1 bay leaf
3 T soy sauce
½ T peppercorns
2 T vegetable oil

In a large Dutch oven, mix ½ lb. each pieces of chicken and pork together with ⅓ c. white vinegar, 1 T minced garlic, 1 bay leaf, 3 T soy sauce, and ½ T peppercorns. Cover until the mixture comes to a boil, and then uncover and simmer for 10 minutes. Add some water after liquid appears to have dried up. Cover again and cook until meat is tender. In a wok or a large frying pan, heat 2 T cooking oil and sauté the remaining 2 T of minced garlic until light brown. Add the stewed chicken and pork pieces. Sauté until brown before adding the liquid they were stewed in. Simmer for another 15 minutes before serving.

Adobo (Filipino stewed meat). Photo by Sean Williams.

GINATAANG HALO-HALO (SWEET RICE BALLS IN COCONUT MILK)

1 c. rice flour
4 c. coconut milk
1 c. chopped yam
1 c. chopped sweet potato
1 c. chopped purple sweet potato
4 plantain bananas, chopped
½ c. chopped jackfruit
1 c. sugar
vanilla extract

Set aside ¼ c. of the rice flour for thickening. Mix the rest of the rice flour with some water and make into dough. Roll pieces of the dough with palms into small balls. Pour 4 c. coconut milk into a casserole dish. After bringing this to a boil, add 1 c. each of yam, sweet potato, and purple sweet potato, and simmer. When these have become soft, add 4 chopped plantain bananas and ½ c. chopped jackfruit together with the balls of rice dough. Add 1 c. sugar according to taste. If desired, flavor with a few drops of vanilla extract. Thicken with ¼ c. of the rice flour mixed in with some of the coconut milk and brought to a boil. Serve medium hot.

Talk Doesn't Cook Rice

Whenever I am asked what is Filipino food, I find myself hard-pressed to give a simple answer, just as I find it difficult to come up with a nice and pat description of what is the music of the Philippines. One reason is that in a country with more than 7,000 islands and inhabited by 120 different ethnic groups, regional diversity is the norm. To point to one dish or even a group of dishes from only the Tagalog region of Luzon as being representative of Filipino cuisine would therefore be a gross simplification of the wide-ranging palette of flavors and cooking styles found across the whole country. Another reason is that dishes from a variety of cultures—Spanish, Chinese, American, and Southeast Asian—have made their way onto the Filipino table (albeit mostly those of the Christianized lowlanders), in the same way that Spanish and American music and their derivative styles have filled the Philippine airwaves, their names often giving away their origins. This is especially true with the Spanish-, Chinese-, and American-derived dishes. But despite their foreign-sounding names, they have become indigenized, adapted to Philippine regional and local tastes and conditions.

For example, Filipino *adobo*, which stews chicken, pork, seafood, or even vegetables such as okra in vinegar, garlic, and peppercorns tastes unlike any *adobo* made in the Spanish or Mexican style. The use of white vinegar, whose astringent sourness is tempered by soy sauce and spices such as bay leaf and peppercorns, remains a distinct feature and can be traced back to the days before refrigeration when pickling and brining were the only ways to preserve foods that are easily perishable in the Philippines' sweltering hot tropical climate. Fresh *lumpia*, or spring rolls, which consist of vegetables rolled in edible wrappers, differ from their Chinese counterparts and take on a distinct Southeast Asian flavor because, for one, they are not fried (although there is also a fried version called *lumpiang Shanghai* that is closer to the Chinese spring roll). Second, the dipping sauce (*sawsawan*) is made with lots of garlic; and third, the vegetables that are sometimes used (e.g., heart of palm) are abundant only in the tropical climates of Southeast Asia and therefore hardly figure in traditional Chinese cuisine. Even fried chicken more or less takes on a different flavor when Filipinos make it. This is in part due to the use of only free-range and chemical-free poultry, but also because the chicken is often first marinated in (again) vinegar and garlic before it is fried.

Hardly anything takes place in the Philippines without food being consumed. It accompanies every social activity—from small, jovial affairs and informal get-togethers with only a handful of family members or friends shooting the breeze, to huge and lavish functions celebrating any of the important life-cycle events (birthdays, baptismal ceremonies, weddings, and funerals) and special occasions (job promotions, winning in the *hweteng* numbers game, store openings, etc.) Many individuals are said to dispense with looking at a clock and simply gauge the time of day with their stomachs and when they feel like they need to eat, which is quite frequent and generally number up to five meals on an ordinary day (breakfast, morning *merienda* or midmorning snack, lunch, afternoon *merienda*, and dinner), if one does not count happy hour with *pulutan* and *pica-pica* (assorted finger foods and appetizers somewhat similar to Spanish *tapas,* accompanied by beer and cocktail beverages) and the proverbial midnight snack.

Growing up in a society wherein food dominates life to such an extent that it is common to greet someone with the question of whether he or she has already eaten (*Kumain ka na?*), I was therefore quite shocked and disappointed to find almost nothing but alcoholic drinks served at the very first party that I attended after coming to the United States in 1985. American parties, I quickly found out, are not focused on communal food consumption but, rather, on mingling and socializing with other guests, hence the precedence of drinks over edibles, with the intention of loosening up inhibitions and drawing out the timid into participating in the conversation. When I related this incident to a friend back in Manila who is a great cook and prepared most of the meals in her extended family, she was aghast and scoffed, responding with a Chinese saying:

"Talk doesn't cook rice." This was like saying, "Talk is cheap." She was referring to the fact that in the Philippines, nobody would dream of throwing a party without offering the guests some kind of substantial fare to eat—it is unheard of and would be considered completely ungracious of the hosts and therefore embarrassing. Even among the less privileged, a Filipino meal would consist of at least one meat or fish dish, a cooked vegetable dish, and plenty of steamed white rice, or else people don't feel like they have eaten at all. Filipinos' legendary hospitality centers on feeding their guests and making sure the latter do not leave feeling hungry, even if it means that the hosts themselves might have to give up their last edible morsel and go without.

In the same way that Filipino social gatherings are unthinkable without food, they are also incomplete without some kind of music being played, whether it be live or from a recording. Filipino food critic, Edilberto Alegre, described the importance of the simultaneous presence of both food and music in any Filipino social event quite eloquently when he wrote: "We do not simply ingest our environment. We dance to it, dance with it, sing to it, caress it; we are in awe of it, and respectful towards it. Eating is not just ingestion. Eating is the occasion for the rites and rituals of our lives."[1] The quintessential Filipino social ritual is the fiesta, which refers to the festivities held in honor of a town's patron saint in parishes throughout the Christianized lowland areas of the country all through the year. Fiestas are held with much fanfare. Music is typically provided by marching bands as they parade on the streets of the town or district, along with the float carrying the image of the patron saint. An abundance of food and drink is consumed during these fiestas. Almost every household in a town gears up months in advance and prepares a feast to feed the constant flow of relatives, friends, and neighbors who drop by for a visit during this occasion. In the old days, well-to-do families may have hired a band, often a *rondalla* ensemble made up of instruments of the guitar family, to serenade their guests while they partook of the sumptuous feast. After sunset, the young people take over with open-air concerts or singing contests featuring the electronically amplified performance of Philippine language pop songs in the town plaza or a large school playground. Food is present and continuously consumed by the audience throughout these outdoor musical extravaganzas, provided by food vendors selling roasted peanuts, various kinds of rice cakes (*suman*, *kutsinta*, *bibingka*, and *palitao*), fried fishballs on a stick, roasted corn on the cob, and other finger foods. Inside the homes, the men gather to drink beer or hard liquor until the wee hours of the morning, accompanied by *pulutan* (like buffalo-style chicken drumsticks and wings), goat stew (*kaldereta*) or, sometimes, dog meat. If a karaoke machine is available, each person takes turns singing with the accompaniment, their inhibitions washed away as their friends ply them with more drink. If not, they sing unaccompanied anyway, their voices ringing into the night.

To experience what I have just described above, I recommend going to any of the towns and districts in and around Manila in the Tagalog region of Luzon during that town's patron saint's day to catch a fiesta and get yourself invited into the house of somebody in the area. For the dates of fiestas of various towns, consult a Catholic calendar with the saint's days clearly marked—the town is often named after a particular saint. But an easier way to find out this information would be to simply ask the townfolk or somebody connected with the parish church.

NOTES

1. Fernandez, Doreen, and Alegre, Edilberto. 1988. *Sarap: Essays on Philippine Food*. Aduana, Intramuros, Manila: Mr. & Ms. Publishing Co.

RECOMMENDED LISTENING

Find a Filipino grocery store, often found in many major urban areas with a large population of Filipino immigrants or overseas workers. It usually sells CDs and cassette recordings of "traditional" and popular Filipino music (*musikang Pinoy*).

FOR FURTHER INFORMATION

Dioquino, Corazon. 2002. *Philippine Music: A Historical Overview*. Available at: History of the Rondalla. Available at: http://www.likha.org/history/rondalla.asp

SURAKARTA, JAVA, INDONESIA

Marc Benamou

As long as you can gather together, who cares if you have enough to eat?
(Mangan ora mangan, angger ngumpul)

Menu: *Ayam Gorèng* (Fried Chicken), *Sambal Gorèng Jipan* (Chayote Stewed in Coconut Milk), *Nasi Putih* (White Rice), *Krupuk Udang* (Fried Shrimp Crackers), *Tahu Gorèng* (Fried Tofu), and *Wédang Jeruk* (Hot Citrus Drink). May be served, instead or additionally, with water or tea.
Preparation Time: 2–3 hours.
Cooking Process: Marinate the tofu and begin simmering the chicken. Fry the shrimp crackers and set aside. Then fry the tofu, and, finally, the chicken. Start the rice and make the chayote stew.

The Recipes

AYAM GORÈNG (FRIED CHICKEN)

1 large shallot
2–3 cloves garlic
12 chicken pieces
½ t. ground coriander

¼ t. ground cumin
2 slices fresh ginger
2 stalks fresh lemongrass (tie each stalk into a knot, if you like), bruised
2 c. (at least) vegetable oil for frying

If you have a stone mortar-and-pestle, grind 1 large shallot and several cloves of garlic in it to a paste (if your mortar is smooth you may wish to add some salt). You could also use a meat grinder with a fine blade or, in a pinch, a food processor (or else a blender, with a little water added). Cut the chicken into small pieces, leaving the skin on (divide legs into drumsticks and thighs; separate wings from breasts, and cut each breast into two or three smaller pieces, if possible). Place all ingredients (except the oil), with about ½ c. water in a wok or large skillet and simmer, covered, stirring occasionally, until tender and the mixture is dry (you may wish to uncover it toward the end). Add salt if necessary. Remove the chicken pieces, dry them, and fry in hot, deep oil until brown and crisp. May be served room temperature.

Sambal Gorèng Jipan (Chayote Stewed in Coconut Milk)

3 chayotes
salt
3 cloves garlic
5 small shallots
2 small, firm tomatoes
2–3 medium-hot red chili peppers (such as "cherry bomb")
3 *kemiri* nuts (optional)
1 nickel-sized slice of *terasi*
1 thin slice fresh or frozen galangal
2 *salam* leaves
1 small handful of tiny dried, salted shrimp
2–3 tiny green or yellow hot peppers, whole
1 (13.5-oz.) can coconut milk

Coat your hands with vegetable or mineral oil so chayote sap does not stick to them—or wear clean rubber gloves. Slice chayotes in half. Cut out and discard the soft, whitish center that contains the seed. Peel. Cut into 1" long julienne (slice into thin strips then slice again cross-wise), then toss with a bit of salt. Let stand. Rinse and drain before cooking. Slice thinly 3 cloves of garlic and 5 shallots lengthwise. Quarter, then slice the tomatoes. Slice off the caps of the chili peppers, gently roll them to loosen seeds, then knock out the seeds; slice into thin rounds. Pound the *kemiri* nuts to a paste in a mortar. Wrap the *terasi* (fermented shrimp paste, also called *blacan*) tightly in a small square of aluminum foil. Roast it briefly in a heated cast-iron pan, until "fragrant." In a thick-bottomed saucepan fry the garlic, the chopped shallots, the red peppers, 1 thin slice of galangal (look for this in a Vietnamese or Thai store), 2 *salam* leaves (look for these in an Asian grocery that caters to Indonesians), a handful of small dried shrimp, and several whole hot peppers, with some salt, in a bit of oil. Add the *kemiri* nuts and *terasi*, and fry some more, stirring constantly. Add the sliced tomatoes and the julienned chayote, and fry about a minute more. Add coconut milk and about ½ can of water (depending on how thick it is). Bring to a boil, stirring constantly. Cook, stirring, until chayote is translucent but still slightly crunchy. Taste for salt. Serve over plain, unsalted white rice with something crackly on the side (*krupuk* are ideal).

Nasi Putih (White Rice)

3 c. Thai jasmine rice

Rinse 3 c. Thai jasmine rice in a thick-bottomed saucepan, then drain. Cover with enough water to come to your first knuckle when you rest the tip of your index finger on the surface of the rice. Bring to a rapid boil, stirring occasionally. Let boil, uncovered, until water level is at the surface of the rice and you hear a gurgling sound coming up from the many small holes that will have formed. Cover and reduce heat to low. Cook another 20 minutes or so, stirring occasionally, until water is absorbed and rice is fluffy and tender. Fluff once with a fork and serve. If you let it sit, covered, for a few minutes before serving, you will be able to detach the chewy, slightly browned bottom layer, called the *intip* (it may be eaten with the rest of the rice, or removed in a single piece, dried in the sun or in a slow oven, then deep-fried).

KRUPUK UDANG (FRIED SHRIMP CRACKERS)

2 c. (or more) vegetable oil for frying

1 packet of Javanese *krupuk* (shrimp or prawn crackers; Vietnamese crackers are acceptable)

Pour enough vegetable oil into a deep saucepan to a depth of 2 inches. Heat the oil to 365°F. Anything below 355°F and above 375°F will produce disastrous results (once you're experienced there's no need to use a thermometer—just test with a little broken bit of *krupuk*). At the correct temperature, the *krupuk* will sink to the bottom, then rise to the top in 8–10 seconds. The whole process should take 15–20 seconds. You will need a couple of long-handled implements. Two barbecue or carving forks should work (I use a Chinese mesh frying strainer with a bamboo handle in my left hand and bamboo chopsticks in my right). As soon as the *krupuk* rises to the top, push it down so that it is completely submerged. It will unfurl rather quickly, making a hissing noise. As it unfurls, flatten it out, using the tools in both hands. As soon as it is flat and completely puffed, turn it over, give it a couple of dunks, lift it, give it a couple of shakes, then place on paper towel to drain and cool. A properly made *krupuk* is pale, perhaps tinged with tan in places, especially at the edges. Once cool it will stick to the tongue, and will be crackly but tender (the Javanese word for this is *renyah*). If the oil is too hot or too cold, it will look glossy, and will be small and hard rather than porous. The *krupuk* may be done several days in advance if kept airtight. Note: do not be tempted to throw several in the fryer at once. When cold, the *krupuk* can be transferred to large Tupperware bowls or to plastic bags.

TAHU GORÈNG (FRIED TOFU)

1 lb. very firm, coarse-textured tofu (not the smooth and soft Japanese style)

salt

5–6 cloves garlic

2 c. (or more) vegetable oil for frying

Make just enough brine to cover the tofu. For one pint of water add 1 t. salt. To this, add 5 or 6 cloves of raw garlic, sliced thinly lengthwise (this is enough for about 1–1½ lb.). If using the 1-lb. bricks of very firm tofu sold in health-food stores, slice into thin rectangles (about 1" x 3" x ¼", or a little larger, depending on the size of the cake). If using the smaller, Chinese-style squares sold in Asian markets, cut diagonally to make two isosceles triangles, then turn each triangle onto its hypotenuse and slice into four thin slices. In either case, make two shallow gashes on each side so that the garlic brine soaks in. Let the tofu sit in the brine for a few hours (a minimum of 2, for the best flavor). Heat the oil slowly until it reaches medium-hot temperature. Deep fry the tofu, moving it gently about the pan. For the firmest tofu, fry until an even tan color; for Chinese-style tofu, fry until surface is pock-marked and a mottled brown (tofu will swell and then shrink back); this may take as long as 30 minutes if the tofu is on the soft side. Turn tofu over at least once so that both sides fry evenly. The softer the tofu the less it will brown. Drain on brown paper or paper towels. Do not let it sit for too long on the absorbent paper, or the paper will soak up all of the water as well, and the tofu will be dry. Serve hot or room temperature (do not refrigerate), with small fresh green chilies (Javanese eaters often alternate bites of tofu with the searing little chilies called *cabé rawit*).

Wédang Jeruk (Hot Citrus Drink)

4 medium juice oranges
2 lemons
1 small lime
1 c. sugar

You will need to juice 4 medium juice oranges, 2 lemons, and 1 small lime. For 1 part citrus juice use about 3 parts boiling water. For an average-sized glass (an 8-oz. serving), use 2–3 t. sugar (a scant tablespoon is usually about right). Mix the sugar with the juice in the bottom of a glass, then stir in the hot water. The above quantity is enough for about eight servings. You may make *ès jeruk* (iced citrus drink) by using 2 parts water to 1 part juice, then pouring the mixture into another glass filled with ice.

Tasting the Music of Solo

The associations Javanese musicians make between food and music are not just incidental, they are profound. That is, music and food are intertwined not just indexically (in the sense of frequently being found in the same place, at the same sorts of events), but symbolically as well, primarily through language.

Music and food—the aural and the oral—are both objects of pleasure that are offered to guests and to the spirit world at ritual events. Since spirits eat only the fragrance, food offerings may be eaten by humans after their ritual purpose has been served. But the food that is offered to guests is usually prepared primarily for them; they need not wait for the spirits to have had their fill. Apparently it used to be that, in certain circles, musicians, who were considered of lower social status, would be served only inexpensive food; but nowadays they are fed the same dishes as the most honored guests (as is everyone else). For many professional or semi-professional gamelan musicians, being properly fed at a lengthy musical event, such as an all-night shadow play or an informal music-making session (*klenéngan*), is more important than getting paid immediately. Since music is, among other things, bodily work, the hosts are expected to fuel the bodies that create sonic delight for them. In fact, according to the Solonese musician Bapak Minarno, when the food served to the musicians is deemed insufficient, the drummer may play a pattern that sounds like and means *wis entèk* ("it's all gone")—a rare instance of Javanese drum language. (Although drum patterns often act as signals to other performers, they do not usually have lexical meaning.) Of course, only musicians, by and large, would get the joke, but it may be that publicly ridiculing their hosts—even cryptically—may be enough retribution to stave off more hostile forms of protest (such as refusing to play).

Many gamelan groups operate as social clubs, and so food is also expected at weekly rehearsals, which often go from about 8 pm to midnight. The all-women's groups, in particular, tend to have varied and ample snacks, which may range from assorted fried finger foods to steamed banana-leaf packets filled with banana slices and sweetened, congealed coconut milk (*någåsari*).

There are many ways in which food enters into the language that revolves around music. One rather obvious one is in the great number of songs and gamelan pieces whose titles are food related. The foods thus evoked tend toward the sweet, while the affect of the music tends toward the light-hearted. The link, here, it would seem, is hedonistic pleasure. But food also shows up in song lyrics, particularly in certain kinds of texts that are not specific to any one piece but rather are chosen for their syllable count and inserted at the singers' discretion into an appropriate piece. These include a set of texts called *rujak-rujakan*, so called because they describe, in the nonsense-like first line of each couplet, any one of a large number of spicy fruit salads or *rujak*; the main content of the couplet is then given in the second line, which is related to the first through elaborate word play.

As a metaphor, food is at the very heart of Javanese musical aesthetics. For example, in describing voice types, musicians place the singing voice along two continua, both derived from food textures. The first is from "hard" to "soft" (in English we would probably say "sharp" or "metallic" to "rounded" or "velvety," although these words don't quite conjure up typically Javanese vocal qualities). In the middle of this continuum is the word *renyah*, which means "crisp but tender." Such a voice is characterized mainly by its agility, whereas a representative food is a properly fried *krupuk* (see recipe). The second continuum is from "tough/elastic" to "tender/crumbly." I despair of ever finding even approximate English equivalents for a "tough" voice (as in a tough steak) or a "crumbly" one.

Still in the realm of musical performance, spiciness, saltiness, and their opposites are often used as metaphors for how interesting or satisfying a particular performance is or isn't. A player might say, for example, that another performer sounds "bland" (*cemplang, kembå, ampang, åntå, bumbuné kurang*).

More generally, all music may be divided into "hot" or "cold," according to its musical affect. This notion is borrowed from a way of categorizing foods—common throughout Asia—according to whether they heat up or cool down the body. Watermelon, for example is a "cold" food, even if it is eaten at room temperature, whereas goat meat is a "hot" food. Similarly, music that is flirtatious, humorous, exuberant, or tense is considered "hot," while music that is stately, sad, devotional, or spooky is "cool." Stylistically, this translates into performance techniques that are either excited (such as dance-style drumming) or calm (such as soft, sparse concert drumming), respectively.

At an even deeper, more general level, music and food are linked through the concept of *råså*, which is fundamental to Javanese aesthetics. This term, which is borrowed from ancient Sanskrit, can mean many things: mood, feeling, interpretation, deep knowledge, inner meaning, intuition, *inter alia*. These various meanings may be placed on a bodily continuum from outward sensation to innermost direct perception that bypasses the senses (*råså sejati*, or true feeling). Whereas both music and food are sensually pleasurable, and both can cause the body to feel hot or cold, in Javanese aesthetics only music engages the mind right down to its inner core of "pure feeling." The overlap, in other words, seems to occur only in the outer layers of sensation. But this overlap is considerable. For, if a literal meaning could be ascribed to *råså*, it would probably be "taste." Javanese music is not just heard, it is savored.

RECOMMENDED LISTENING

Chamber Music of Java. King World Music Library. KICC 5152.
Javanese Court Gamelan, Volume II. Nonesuch. WPCS-10711.
Klenéngan Session of Solonese Gamelan I. King World Music Library. KICC 5185.
Rebab and Female Singing of Central Javanese Gamelan. King World Music Library. KICC 5211.
Shadow Music of Java. Rounder. CD 5060.
Solonese Gamelan: A Garland of Moods. 4 CDs. Maison du Cultures du Monde. Inédit 260125.

FOR FURTHER INFORMATION

Lindsey, Jennifer. 1992. *Javanese Gamelan: Traditional Orchestra of Indonesia*, 2nd ed. Singapore; New York: Oxford University Press.

Sorrell, Neil. 1990. *A Guide to the Gamelan*. Portland, OR: Amadeus Press.

Spiller, Henry. 2004. *Gamelan: The Traditional Sounds of Indonesia*. Santa Barbara, CA: ABC-CLIO.

Sutton, R. Anderson. 2002. "Asia/Indonesia." In *Worlds of Music: An Introduction to the Music of the World's Peoples*, 4th ed. Edited by Jeff Todd Titon. Belmont, CA: Wadsworth Publishing.

SUNDA, INDONESIA
Sean Williams

> *If you haven't eaten rice, you haven't yet eaten.*

Menu: *Opor Ayam* (Chicken in Coconut Milk), *Nasi Putih* (White Rice), *Acar* (Pickled Vegetable Salad), *Krupuk Udang* (Shrimp Crackers), and *Buah-Buahan* (Fresh Fruit). Serve with water and weak black tea or sweetened coffee.

Preparation Time: Approximately 2½–3 hours.

Cooking Process: Place the sliced tropical fruits on an attractive platter and sprinkle with lemon or lime juice to keep the color looking nice. Start the *acar* first and chill; fry the *krupuk* and set aside. Begin the *opor ayam*, then start the rice 40 minutes before eating. For a vegan option, substitute 2 packages of *tempeh* (cubed) for the chicken and omit the *krupuk*. Serves six people.

The Recipes

Opor Ayam (Chicken in Coconut Milk)

2 lb. boned chicken meat, cut into bite-sized pieces
2 T vegetable oil
1 onion
2 cloves garlic
2" fresh ginger root
4 candlenuts
2 salam leaves
1½ t. coriander
1 t. cumin
2" piece of galangal
salt
pepper
4 c. coconut milk (or 3 14-oz. cans)
1 t. tamarind paste
2 stalks lemon grass, bruised, knotted, or chopped into 3" lengths
2 limes, juiced

Prepare all the items to go into the cooking pot before you start cooking. Using a large stainless steel pan, brown the cut-up chicken pieces for a few minutes in 1 T vegetable oil; set aside. Chop 1 onion, slice 2 cloves of garlic, and peel and crush or dice 2" fresh ginger root; mix and set aside. Crush 4 candlenuts (or blanched peeled almonds or macadamia nuts) until they are in very small pieces; set aside. Add 1 T vegetable oil to the pan in which you browned the chicken, then heat the oil. Fry 2 salam leaves (found in Asian food stores), 1½ t. coriander, 1 t. cumin, 2" sliced galangal (found in Asian food stores), 1 t. salt, and ½ t. black pepper for about a minute. Add the onion/garlic/ginger/nut mix, then fry for a few more minutes until they are tender and the onion is close to being translucent. Add 4 c. coconut milk, 1 t. tamarind paste, 2 lemon grass stalks (found in Asian food stores) and the chicken pieces; bring to a low boil. Cook, stirring, for about 5 minutes, then reduce heat to a simmer. Allow to cook, uncovered, for another half hour until the chicken is done and the sauce has reduced. Just before serving, add the juice of 2 limes to the sauce. Serve directly over warm white rice.

Nasi Putih (White Rice)

3 c. white rice

Bring 6 c. water to a boil. Carefully rinse and add 3 c. white rice; reduce heat to simmer, covered, until rice is tender (about 20 minutes). Remove from heat, fluff with fork, then allow to sit, covered, for another 10 minutes.

Acar (Pickled Vegetable Salad)

4 carrots
3 cucumbers
½ head of cabbage
½ medium yellow onion
1" fresh ginger root
1 c. rice vinegar
salt
pinch of red chili pepper flakes
1 T sugar

Peel and julienne carrots and cucumbers (seeded). Thinly slice ½ cabbage. Thinly slice ½ medium yellow onion. Peel and crush 1" fresh ginger root. Mix together. Make the marinade by combining 1 c. rice vinegar, 1 t. salt, 1 pinch red chili pepper flakes, and 1 T sugar. Chill until ready to serve.

Acar **(Sundanese pickled vegetables, Indonesia). Photo by Sean Williams.**

Krupuk Udang (Shrimp Crackers)

2 c. vegetable oil for frying
1 package shrimp crackers (*krupuk*)

Pour enough vegetable oil into a pan for deep frying (1½" deep). Heat the oil so that it appears wavy below the surface, but not smoking. (Note that some *krupuk* [found in Asian food stores] packages tell you to fry it at what seems to be a surprisingly low temperature: that's the Celsius measurement.) Test it with a tiny piece of *krupuk*; if it's hot enough, the *krupuk* should spin around in the oil and inflate to twice or three times its size. You may need to break the crackers in half prior to placing them in the oil, if the size of your frying pot is narrow. Place one shrimp cracker at a time in the hot oil, using tongs to turn and remove them. *Krupuk* take about 5–10 seconds at the most, per side, to fry. When cooked (very pale beige, neither brown nor white), place on a plate covered with a paper towel. Assume that you will need at least 30 krupuk for six people. Any that you do not eat can be stored in an airtight container for a day or two.

Buah-Buahan (Fresh Fruit)

Arrange an assortment of fresh fruits in season; ideally, bananas should be a centerpiece. If you can find them, mangoes, passion fruit, mangosteens, kiwis, or other strong-tasting fruits are ideal. Serve with sweetened black coffee.

The Concept of Ramé

Music is rarely performed without the accompaniment of food in the mountainous Sundanese region of Java. From 2,000-guest weddings in which the music is the background for a staggering buffet with its rows of stacked glass plates and steam tables to the all-night singing parties with fried bananas and boiled peanuts, food and its accompanying conversation are a must in most musical settings. In West Java, the buffet is a customary way of getting your food; you never know when friends and neighbors plan to drop in unannounced, so the more food available, the better! The Sundanese frequently speak about what it is that makes something *khas sunda* or genuinely and deeply Sundanese; the quality of *kasundaan* ("Sundanese-ness") can be imparted through the food as well as through the music.

Just as a musical performance is not nearly as enjoyable in the absence of food, food in the absence of music (or at least sound) is considered incomplete. As a result, when live music is unavailable, a radio or television is turned on to accompany the act of eating. Such close ties between food and music make successful rehearsals and performances very difficult during the month of Ramadan; as a result, they are often shifted to the late evening when food and drink can accompany sound, and vice versa. The sought-for situation in all of this joining of food and music is the quality of *ramé*, which means fun, busy, chaotic, and lively. Traffic jams, parties, markets, evening strolls downtown, music performances, and meals are all expected to be *ramé*. The opposite of *ramé* is *sepi*—quiet, lonely, and inherently sad. Unlike regions of the world where solitude is a welcome respite from the chaos of everyday life, solitude in Sundanese culture is strange and makes people ill at ease. Far preferable is the noisy, festive meal with music, group participation, lively conversation, and plenty of distraction.

Rice is the staple food of every Sundanese meal, and if one has not eaten rice, one has not eaten at all. Servants (many families employ helpers, not just the upper classes) cook a large container of rice in late morning for the noon meal, then everyone eats leftover rice in the evening and fried rice the next morning, before the cycle starts over again. A Sundanese meal comprises a considerable plateful of white rice; several cups or enough to fill a wide shallow bowl by an inch or two in depth. Small cut-up pieces of meat, *tempeh*, and raw vegetables are placed on top of the rice, followed by a large *krupuk* or cracker made from rice flour and shrimp. Most people eat with their right hand, or with a large spoon held in the right hand and a fork held in the left. The only purpose of the fork is to push the food onto the spoon. It is polite to leave a little food on the plate, and to turn the fork and spoon over in an x on the plate, upon finishing.

In addition to rice, Sundanese people enjoy a rich variety of fresh fruits and vegetables, exceptionally good tea, and a number of savory dishes. They are well known among other Indonesian ethnic groups for their marked preference for raw vegetables. Local culinary favorites include water buffalo jerky, deep fried *tempeh*, spicy carp steamed in banana leaf, baked freshwater fish, and hot ginger-coconut or ginger-coffee drinks served late at night. Beef, goat, and chicken meat (including various innards) are common at the dinner table. At all hours of the day and night you can hear local food hawkers walking up and down the street with their three-wheeled pushcarts (*kaki lima*, "five legs"). Each seller has a particular noisemaker associated with the type of food being sold, and Sundanese people and foreigners alike keep one ear cocked for the sound of one's favorite treat: *bakso* (meatball soup), *rujak* (spicy unripe mango salad), and my personal favorite, *sekoteng* (hot sweet ginger soup). The cacophony of "food sound" that fills the ears mixes with the call to prayer multiplied by the dozens of mosque loudspeakers within earshot, the honking of trucks and cars, and lively, *ramé* conversation.

I learned to cook during my time in the Sundanese region of Java by watching closely, eating well, and asking questions. Sundanese people jokingly judge outsiders by their preferences for certain foods and types of music, based on a continuum of "more Sundanese" or "less Sundanese." For example, the more searingly spicy food a foreigner can handle, the more approval (and uproarious teasing) one wins. Food is often used to elicit humorous and erotic comparisons either to body parts or bodily functions, particularly in terms of shape, size, smell, taste, and the reaction of one's body to the food. It is considered wildly inappropriate, for example, for women to openly consume either pineapple or young coconut (because their inherent "juiciness" is supposed to have a corresponding effect on women's bodies). The foreigner who enjoys local "folk" traditions and foods (music played on bamboo instruments, for example) garners mixed reactions, at least partly because of local mixed feelings about class issues surrounding rural traditions. I had several teachers, including the well-known singer Euis Komariah, who spoke often about food and cooking even as she taught me to sing and to become more effectively Sundanese. The woman I employed as my helper and the keeper-of-my-reputation, Tikah, fiercely guarded the kitchen from my husband who, like all men, was generally forbidden from entering the kitchen. The kitchen is considered the central "soul" of the home and—for many (devoutly Muslim) Sundanese—the sacred home of the (Hindu) rice goddess, Dewi Sri. The domains of women and men are clearly laid out: women work within the interior domain of the home (including the food and cooking activities), while men work in the exterior domain of the outer portions of the home and the outside world. This gender division plays out on the performance stage as well, in which women often serve as "hosts" for the male performing "guests." I was often told, by both men and women, that only when someone knows how to enjoy and appreciate the food (and the methods by which it is prepared) can that person understand the music...and, by extension, Sundanese culture.

RECOMMENDED LISTENING

Jugala Orchestra. *Jaipongan Java*. 1989. (A lively blend of singing, dance drumming, and fiery *gamelan salé-ndro* playing.)

Komariah, Euis, and Wiradiredja, Yus. *The Sound of Sunda*. Globestyle, 1989. CDORB 060. (Collection of Sundanese popular songs using extended *gamelan degung*.)

Permas, Imas, and Kosasih, Asep. *Tembang Sunda: Sundanese Classical Songs*. Nimbus, 1993. NI 5378. (Elite music for voice, 18 string zither, and bamboo flute.)

FOR FURTHER INFORMATION

http://www.sunda.org/sundanese/sundanese.htm

Spiller, Henry. 2004. *Gamelan: The Traditional Sounds of Indonesia*. Santa Barbara, CA: ABC-CLIO.

Weintraub, Andrew. 2004. *Power Plays: Wayang Golek Puppet Theater of West Java*. Athens, OH: Ohio University Press.

Williams, Sean. 2001. *The Sound of the Ancestral Ship: Highland Music of West Java*. New York; London: Oxford University Press.

BALI, INDONESIA
Ni Wayan Murni and Jonathan Copeland

Always different, but always delicious.

Menu: *Base Genep* (Complete Spice Paste), *Babi Kecap* (Pork in *Kecap* Sauce), *Lawar* (Spicy Green Beans), *Nasi Putih* (Steamed Rice), *Krupuk Udang* (Shrimp Crackers), *Tahu Goreng* (Fried Tofu), and *Pisang Goreng* (Banana Fritters).

Preparation Time: 3 hours.

Cooking Process: In Bali, you take a large bowl-like plate and fill it with rice, then place small portions of many different dishes around the edges. It would be smart to make some of these ingredients the day before (particularly the spice mix), then to label and store them in the refrigerator overnight. Once you have made the spice mix, make the *krupuk* and set them aside. Now prepare the *babi kecap*, the *lawar*, the *tahu goreng*, and the *nasi*. The *pisang goreng* should be done last. It is normal for Balinese food to be served at room temperature. Serves six people.

The Recipes

BASE GENEP (COMPLETE SPICE PASTE)

5 shallots
5 cloves garlic
⅓ c. lesser galangal
3½ T fresh turmeric
3½ T galangal
2 t. fresh peeled ginger root
5 candlenuts
1 t. coriander seeds
1 t. black peppercorns
1 t. grated nutmeg
1 t. shrimp paste
1 t. fresh lemongrass
vegetable oil

Prepare the spice mixture by placing all the following ingredients in a blender: 5 shallots, 5 cloves garlic, ⅓ c. lesser galangal, 3½ T fresh turmeric, 3½ T galangal, 2 t. fresh peeled ginger root, 5 candlenuts (or macadamia nuts), 1 t. coriander seeds, 1 t. black peppercorns, 1 t. grated nutmeg, 1 t. shrimp paste, and 1 t. fresh lemongrass. Add salt and pepper to taste, and a little water if the mix becomes too dry. Fry the mix in a little vegetable oil for a few minutes; do not scorch. This spice mix recipe (*base genep* or "complete spice") is the mainstay of many Balinese dishes. Every grandmother in Bali has her own secret recipe that is passed down to the next generation. It will keep in the fridge for up to one week.

Babi Kecap (Pork in Kecap Sauce)

2 lb. pork fillet, cubed

1 qt. chicken stock

⅔ c. of the *base genep* (see previous recipe)

2 red peppers

2 cubes chicken bouillon, crumbled

2 T vegetable oil

5 T sweet soy sauce (*kecap manis*)

5 T unsweetened tomato sauce

Set aside the pork fillet and chicken stock. Pulse the following ingredients in a blender into a smooth paste: half the *base genep*, 2 red peppers, crumbled bouillon cubes, 2 T vegetable oil, 5 T sweet soy sauce (*kecap manis*) (found in Asian food stores), and tomato sauce. In a heavy saucepan, brown small batches of the pork on all sides in some oil. Do not burn or overcook; set aside. Bring the chicken stock to a simmer and add the spice paste, together with salt and pepper to taste. Mix and add the browned pork, then gently simmer until the meat is tender.

Lawar (Spicy Green Beans)

2 lb. long green beans

15 shallots

5 cloves garlic

5 red chili peppers (to taste)

5 hot green chili peppers (to taste)

1 lime

¾ c. grated coconut

2 T vegetable oil

⅓ c. of the *base genep* (see recipe, above)

Cut 2 lb. green beans into short lengths (¼"–½") and boil or steam until done, about 3 minutes. Allow to cool and set aside. Finely chop 15 shallots, 5 cloves of garlic, 5 red chili peppers, and 5 hot green chili peppers, and mix together with the juice from 1 lime and ¾ c. grated coconut. Quickly fry for a few minutes in some vegetable oil; do not scorch. Cool. Combine the green beans with the remaining half of the *genep* to taste, then add the coconut.

Nasi Putih (Steamed Rice)

3 c. white rice
pinch of salt

Rinse 3 c. rice and place in a rice cooker (or pan with a tight-fitting lid) with 6 c. water and a pinch of salt. Press start or bring to a boil, then reduce heat to simmer, covered. Do not lift the lid until the rice is done, about 20 minutes. Turn off the heat. Let it stand for another 10 minutes before opening.

Krupuk Udang (Shrimp Crackers)

2 c. vegetable oil for frying
1 package shrimp crackers (*krupuk*)

Heat enough cooking oil to cover the bottom of a saucepan 1-inch deep. Place individual crackers in the hot oil one or two at a time, turning once as soon as they have "blown up" (increased dramatically in size), usually 5 seconds or so per side. Dry on a plate with paper towels to absorb the oil, or on a cooling rack. They do not need to be kept warm. Use the fry oil to fry the tofu for the *Tahu Goreng* at the last minute.

Tahu Goreng (Fried Tofu)

1 package of firm coarse tofu
2 c. vegetable oil for frying (use leftover from the *Krupuk Udang*)

Rinse the block of tofu and cut into cubes. In a saucepan pour enough oil to cover the bottom of the pan, heat the oil (not until smoking), then gently fry tofu until lightly browned.

Pisang Goreng (Banana Fritters)

1 c. plain white flour
1 egg
½ c. milk
1 t. vanilla
2 c. vegetable oil
6 large, ripe bananas (*pisang raja*, king bananas, are best)
⅓ c. sugar
2 T cinnamon

In a bowl, mix 1 c. flour, 1 egg, ½ c. milk, and 1 t. vanilla to a smooth batter. Allow to stand for 1 hour. Heat oil gently in a frying pan until almost smoking. Cut each banana into thirds. Dip banana pieces in the batter and carefully drop into the hot fry oil; fry until golden brown. If desired, roll the cooked fritter in a mixture of sugar and cinnamon.

Ingredients for *base genep* (Bali, Indonesia). Photo by Jonathan Copeland.

Eating in Bali

One of the most frequent comments I hear is that it's very hard to get Balinese food in Bali! Well, this is true, and it is partly explained by our strange eating habits. It is extremely rare for a Balinese family to sit down and eat together. The concept of "the family meal" is almost unknown. We rarely (if ever) give dinner parties. Most meals revolve around rice as the prime focus. For us, rice is "breakfast, lunch, and tea." Indeed the Balinese word "*ngajeng*" (in mid-level Balinese) means both "to eat" and "to eat rice," which gives you an idea of the central importance of rice. The Indonesian word "*nasi*" means both "food" and "rice."

We tend to serve food at room temperature. We add a small amount of whatever happens to be available that day to a plate of rice—perhaps steamed green vegetables, a bit of fish, some rice field eels, a little *tempe,* maybe *tofu,* and the like. Almost always a hot chili *sambel. Sambel* are small dishes served on the side, consisting of red chilies, sweet purple shallots, small garlic cloves, and shrimp paste. Even at formal gatherings, such as weddings, there is no set meal. Guests arrive at the family compound at different times. The food is ready and waiting buffet-style. They help themselves and usually eat quietly, sitting alone. The Balinese believe that food contains *amerta*, the life force, which is brought alive by cooking, and talking can disturb it.

Finger bowls of water are passed around, one per person. We prefer to eat with our hands. We never use knives, maybe a fork and spoon. The food tastes better by hand, untouched by metal. We only use our right hands. The left hand is unclean. We have no concept of three courses—or dessert for that matter (except possibly fresh fruit in season). In fact, guests visiting a Balinese family are almost always immediately presented with a selection of sweet cakes and a beverage before they partake of the main (savory) course.

Alcohol is almost never served. Normally, it's sweet tea or water. After eating, guests go home quickly. As we jokingly say *"Sudah makan, pulang!"* ("Eaten now, going home!") Oh, that Western dinner parties were more like this! So, for a Balinese to recreate an authentic dining experience risks offending his Western guests. It is quite possible to be invited to a friend's house in Bali and find your hosts have already eaten and you're on your own!

The recipes for this meal reflect important aspects of Balinese food and culture. Pork features heavily in the Balinese diet. Nearly all ceremonial dishes include pork, the most famous being *babi guling* (literally "turned meat"), a pit-roasted suckling pig. It is always eaten during the great Balinese festivals of *Nyepi* and *Galungan*. As this is a little difficult to recreate in the average Western kitchen, this recipe for *babi kecap* captures the flavor of Bali, whilst being much easier to prepare. This dish can be prepared ahead and refrigerated—the flavor improves and can easily be reheated. You can finish up with *pisang goreng,* fried bananas. Usually served as a dessert in the West, *pisang goreng,* served with a cup of Bali coffee, is a typical breakfast in Bali. Note that any time the recipe calls for grinding with a blender, the preferred method in Bali is with a mortar and pestle. The taste is noticeably better.

Music and food are both deeply integrated into Balinese daily life. Gamelan rehearsals take place in village meeting halls all over the island. As you walk through the villages, you hear their wonderful percussive sounds and are welcome to sit down and listen. Never very far away are ladies selling food in small stalls.

Music and offerings, which always contain food, are intended primarily to entertain the gods and ancestors during the hundreds of ceremonies staged throughout the Balinese calendar of 210 days. Private family ceremonies, such as the dedication of buildings, baby ceremonies, tooth-filings, weddings, and even cremations are normally accompanied by music.

I use recipes from my village; actually, from my family. If you go to the next village or the next family, the recipes will be different. Such is dining in Bali—*"Selalu lain tapi selalu enak!"* ("Always different, but always delicious!") Finally, when things go wrong in the kitchen, remember the old Balinese proverb, *"Nasi sudah menjadi bubur"* (literally "The rice has already become porridge" or "There's no use crying over spilt milk").

If you ever find yourself in Bali, you can try these dishes at my restaurant in Ubud, Murni's Warung.

Selamat makan! ("Happy eating!")

RECOMMENDED LISTENING

Baleganjur of Pande and Angklung of Sidan, Bali. World Music Library, 1995. KICC-5197.
Bali: Musique pour le Gong Gedé. Ocora, 1987. C559002.
Gamelan Batel Wayang Ramayana. Creative Music Productions, 1990. CMP CD 3003.
Golden Rain: Gong Kebyar of Gunung Sari, Bali. World Music Library, 1995. KICC-5195.
Music from the Morning of the World: The Balinese Gamelan. Nonesuch. 79196.

FOR FURTHER INFORMATION

http://www.murnis.com; e-mail murni@murnis.com
Bakan, Michael B. 1999. *Music of Death and New Creation: Experiences in the World of Balinese Gamelan Belegangur.* Chicago: University of Chicago Press.
Copeland, Jonathan. 2006. *Secrets of Bali.* Jakarta: Gateway Books International.
Gold, Lisa. 2005. *Music in Bali.* New York: Oxford University Press.
Tenzer, Michael. 2000. *Gamelan Gong Kebyar: The Art of Twentieth-Century Balinese Music.* Chicago: University of Chicago Press.

THAILAND
Andrew and Christina Shahriari and Terry Miller

Eat well, live well.

Menu: *Khao Soi* (Chiang Mai Curry Noodle Soup), *Kai Satay* (Chicken Satay with Peanut Sauce), *Khruang Prung Ajad* (Cucumber Salad), and *Khao Nieow Ma Muang* (Coconut Sticky Rice with Mango/Fresh Fruit). Serve with water or black tea.

Preparation Time: 3 hours, not including time for the marinade and soaking the rice.

Cooking Process: Start soaking the sticky rice 4 hours from when you would like to eat. Place the bamboo skewers in water for 30–60 minutes before using. For the coconut sticky rice, you will need a large pot with a steamer insert and some cheesecloth. Next, prepare the chicken satay marinade. Then prepare the cucumber salad and chill. One hour before eating, skewer the chicken satay and prepare the grill. Then make the soup. Serve the satay and peanut sauce with the cucumber salad first, then the soup, then the sticky rice. Serves six people.

The Recipes

(by Andrew and Christina Shahriari)

KHAO SOI (CHIANG MAI CURRY NOODLE SOUP)

2 T coconut milk
3 T Panang curry paste
3½ c. chicken stock
12 skinned chicken drumsticks
6 c. coconut milk
1 package pickled mustard greens
6 shallots
1 T vegetable oil
1 T crushed red pepper flakes
1 large package ¼"-thin Thai egg noodles (enough for six people)
1 lime

Heat stock pot on medium heat, add 2 T coconut milk, stir in 3 T Panang curry paste, and cook (stirring constantly) for 3 minutes, until fragrant. Add 3½ c. chicken stock; bring to a boil. Add 12 skinned chicken drumsticks and 6 c. coconut milk. Bring to a boil, reduce heat and let simmer for 90 minutes. Rinse 1 package pickled mustard greens and chop into 1– pieces; set aside. Peel and halve 6 shallots; set aside. In a small saucepan, heat 1 T vegetable oil and remove from heat. Mix in 1 T crushed red pepper flakes and pour into a bowl. Fill a cooking pot with enough water to cook noodles; bring to a boil, add noodles, and cook for 5 minutes. To serve, divide the noodles into 6 bowls equally, pour 1 c. broth over each one, and add a drumstick to the bowl. Serve the mustard greens, shallots, chunks of a single lime, and the oil/pepper mix in bowls for guests to season to taste.

Kai Satay (Chicken Satay with Peanut Sauce)

2 skinless, boneless chicken breasts
1½ t. fish sauce
1½ T dark soy sauce
2 cloves garlic, chopped
⅔ c. peanut butter
1 T curry powder
1 T coconut milk
2 T Panang curry paste

Place 12 bamboo skewers in cold water to soak for half an hour. Slice 2 skinless boneless chicken breasts into 12 strips. Combine 1 t. fish sauce, 1 T soy sauce, 2 cloves of garlic, 1 T peanut butter, 1 T curry powder, and marinate chicken for at least 2 hours. Make the peanut sauce by heating a saucepan over medium heat, adding 1 T coconut milk, adding 2 T Panang curry paste, and sautéing for 3 minutes, stirring constantly. Stir in ½ c. peanut butter, ½ t. fish sauce, and ½ t. soy sauce, and add just enough water to make a sauce. Skewer chicken pieces and grill 5 minutes on each side. Be careful not to overgrill, as the chicken will become tough. Pour the peanut sauce over the finished satay skewers and offer two to each person with the cucumber salad.

Khruang Prung Ajad (Cucumber Salad)

½ c. rice vinegar
½ c. sugar
3–4 *prikinu* chili peppers
dash of fish sauce
6 cucumbers

In saucepan bring ½ c. water to a boil, add ¼ c. rice vinegar and ¼ c. sugar stirring continuously for 5 minutes until it begins to thicken; remove from heat. Add 2–3 *prikinu* peppers and dash of fish sauce. Let cool, stir in 6 peeled, seeded, and chopped cucumbers. Serve chilled.

Khao Nieow Ma Muang (Coconut Sticky Rice with Mango/Fresh Fruit)

1 c. Thai sticky (or "sweet") rice
2 c. coconut milk
½ c. sugar
3 mangoes (or other fresh fruit), cubed

Rinse 1 c. Thai sticky rice with hot water 6–8 times, put in bowl and cover with hot water, leaving to soak for a minimum of 3 hours. In saucepan bring 2 c. coconut milk to a boil; add ½ c. sugar, let cool. Bring 4 c. water to a boil in large pot; line steamer pan with cheesecloth. Drain rice and add to steamer, cover with a lid and steam for 20 minutes, until rice begins to appear translucent and sticky. Spread rice out on a cutting board to cool. In a bowl, mix rice with all but ½ c. coconut milk/sugar mixture. Serve with fresh cubed mangoes, peaches, or berries with reserved sauce on top.

Prepared foods for sale (Thailand). Photo by Terry E. Miller.

Thai Food: Music for Human Stomachs/ Thai Music: Food for the Gods

(by Terry Miller)

Every time I return to Thailand I become even more convinced that the reason God created the Thai people was for them to create and consume food. It remains impossible for us even to sample a sizeable percentage of all the goodies available during a trip lasting even two months. Thai people eat whatever they wish whenever they wish, all day and all night. And until the rise of Western fast/ junk food in the 1990s (it seems no one now lives more than a kilometer from a 7-Eleven), obesity was not an issue. Similarly, the Thai are seldom without music. You hear it during rituals, while shopping, eating, riding in taxis, tour buses, and even in museums and at outdoor ruins.

It seems that no music event would be complete without some kind of food being consumed. The VIPs seated at the front are always treated with sweet coffee and small cakes. At less formal events, people bring their own, buy it from the food vendors that seem to appear out of thin air, or eat what their friends have brought. At Teacher Greeting (*wai khru*) ceremonies, the gods too are offered food. The altar area includes an amazing variety of fresh and cooked foods, including colorful fruit. For example, Totsakan, the demon king of Lanka from the Thai version of the Indian *Ramayana*, is said to enjoy pigs' heads, and consequently no Thai *wai khru* altar is complete without at least one of these noticeable offerings. Similarly, humans seldom eat in public without music. While modernity has brought forth the ubiquitous loudspeaker playing recordings of Thai, Chinese, or Western pop music in any and all venues, the "better" restaurants are more likely to provide an endless string of what we call "songbirds," colorfully dressed women and men who sing pop songs now accompanied by computer-driven sound systems. Since the demand for skilled singers exceeds the supply, one's digestion may sometimes be affected negatively by the out-of-tune songbirds. The larger restaurants also offer private dining rooms with karaoke machines.

While it is clear that food and music may occur in proximity, it is more of a challenge to demonstrate deeper relationships. But permit me to attempt it nonetheless. Thai food is primarily known for its spiciness and vivid colors, those pots of various curries with all sorts of things found within, such as lemongrass, bay leaves, chilies of many shapes and sizes, various meats, vegetables, ginger, garlic, etc. Many such dishes are indeed spicy, and the obligatory plates of rice that accompany them are a welcome relief from the culinary fires. But Thai people also eat a greater number of dishes that are not spicy at all. Indeed, some Thai actually cannot eat spicy food or, because of health problems, are no longer permitted to do so. They still have plenty of choices.

As distinctive as Thai cuisine is, the full range of foods is actually quite cosmopolitan. By far the greatest number of such dishes are of Chinese origin, for Chinese-Thai make up a high percentage of the population of most Thai cities and were the original business people. Over time, Chinese food has become Thai food, just as in the United States, Italian food has become American food. What do Thai eat for breakfast? If it's not Western (toast, eggs, bacon, coffee), then it's likely *khao tom* (literally, boiled rice), a soupy rice into which one places all sorts of condiments, including pickled vegetables, meat, egg, etc. Equally popular is *jok*, a thicker, more porridge-like rice soup whose condiments are typically pork and ginger. While these are normally pretty bland, one also has the option of adding all sorts of sauces, many of which have bits of chilies or chili seeds, as well as *nam pla* (fish sauce) or vinegar. For lunch, the most usual foods are rice or noodles. While many rice dishes are served with toppings of spicy Thai curry, virtually all noodle dishes are of Chinese origin and are bland unless altered with a sauce. When ordering a more formal meal, one is likely to select both spicy, colorful Thai-originated dishes as well as blander dishes of Chinese origin.

Modern Thailand, however, is far more eclectic than even this. No mall is complete without one or two *suki* restaurants, where one selects a set of foods that are cooked in a gas or charcoal-fired pot on the table. While the term comes from the Japanese *sukiyaki*, most Thai say the idea is from Korea. And of course, one can no longer omit the ubiquitous American chains, for they are now found throughout the country.

So, how does all this relate to Thai music? First, Thai music is as eclectic as the food choices. Not only are the pop and classical musics of the West well known, but pop music from Taiwan, Hong Kong, Japan, and Europe—along with Thai forms, which are often derivative—tends to dominate the soundscape. Within the world of Thai classical music, composers have shown the general Thai fascination with the exotic by creating pieces/songs written in "foreign accents" (called *samniang*): Lao, Khmer, Burmese, Malaysian, Javanese, Vietnamese, Chinese, Mon, and Western. Each *samniang* is usually expressed through the percussion instruments along with invocations of musical stereotype. Therefore, the Thai music spectrum, like the culinary one, is eclectic and international.

The sounds of Thai instruments for some takes some getting used to. Each instrument in the *piphat* percussion ensemble has a distinctive and colorful sound: the nasal oboe, the sharply percussive xylophones, the metallic and ringing gong circles, and beats strongly articulated by drums and cymbals. The total sound is a mixture of seemingly unrelated timbres, analogous to the seemingly unrelated mélange of meats, vegetables, and spices of a Thai curry. Just as with the food, some music is sweet to hear and other kinds are more piquant, spicy, or vinegary. The Thai music world offers many alternatives just as restaurants offer alternatives for souls of milder tastes, such as the noodle and soupy rice dishes. Musically these include less striking (no pun intended), more blended ensembles like the *mahori* (which mixes xylophones, gong circles, strings, and flute), or the subdued sound of the old-time *mahori*, which had only a fiddle, lute, and flute.

Anyone visiting Thailand, then, will be faced with endlessly wonderful decisions about which foods to consume and which musics to hear, but visitors will rarely encounter one without the other.

RECOMMENDED LISTENING

Chang Saw: Ensembles Si Nuan Thung Pong. PAN 2075CD
Fong, Naam. *The Sleeping Angel: Fong Naam.* Nimbus. NI 5319.
Fong, Naam. *Siamese Classical Music, Vol. 3: The String Ensemble.* Marco Polo. 8.223199.
Prasit Thawon Ensemble. *Thai Classical Music.* Nimbus. NI 5412.
Royal Court Music of Thailand. Smithsonian-Folkways. SFCD 40413.
Silk, Spirits, and Song: Music from North Thailand. Lyrichord LYRCD-7421.

FOR FURTHER INFORMATION

Miller, Terry E. 1998. "Thailand," in *The Garland Encyclopedia of World Music*, Vol. 4 (Southeast Asia). New York; London: Garland Publishing.
Rutherford, Scott. 2002. *Insight Guide: Thailand.* Munich: Langenscheidt Publishers.
Shahriari, Andrew C. 2006. *Khon Muang Music and Dance Traditions of North Thailand.* Bangkok: White Lotus Press, Inc.
Wong, Deborah. 2001. *Sounding the Center: History and Aesthetics in Thai Buddhist Performance.* Chicago: University of Chicago Press.
Wyatt, David K. 1982. *Thailand: A Short History.* New Haven, CT; London: Yale University Press.

VIETNAM
Phong T. Nguyen

Watch the rice pot to ensure equal shares; find your proper place at the table.

Menu: *Gỏi Cuốn* (Fresh Spring Noodle Rolls), *Canh Mồng Tơi* (Spinach Soup), *Gà Xào Sả* (Lemongrass Chicken), and *Cơm* (Steamed Rice). For dessert, serve a fresh tropical fruit (banana or mango).

Preparation Time: Approximately 3 hours.

Cooking Process: Prepare the spring rolls first, then the lemongrass chicken. Start the rice 30 minutes before you plan to eat, then make the spinach soup. Serves six people.

The Recipes

GỎI CUỐN (FRESH SPRING NOODLE ROLLS)

½ lb. pork or chicken
12 prawns
rice noodles (*bún*) (enough for six people)
1 jar of sweetened red bean "hoisin" sauce (*tương*)
1 large head Boston lettuce
½ lb. bean sprouts
1 bunch peppermint leaves
1 bunch scallions (*hẹ*)
12 rice sheets for wrapping (*bánh tráng*)
½ c. roughly crushed peanuts

Boil ½ lb. pork (or chicken breasts) in one saucepan for 30 minutes, 12 prawns in another for 5 minutes, and rice noodles in a third saucepan for 5 minutes. (Tip: To preserve the flavor and good texture of the meat and prawns, don't overcook them.) Slice meat thinly into 1– rectangles. Peel the prawns and cut into two halves. (Tip: Lay prawns down and slice horizontally while holding with your fingers.) Drain noodles in cold water. Wash 1 large head of Boston lettuce, ½ lb. bean sprouts, 1 bunch of peppermint leaves, and 1 bunch of scallions. Place meat, prawns, noodles, lettuce, bean sprouts, peppermint leaves, and scallions in separate bowls.

Rolling requires a little skill: quickly dip a rice sheet in a large bowl of warm water and place it on a clean surface. On the damp rice sheet, place the 2 prawn halves cut side up at the top center. Place 2 slices of meat below the prawns. Place a large lettuce leaf on top with the greener side facing down (vein facing up). Place some noodles, peppermint leaves, and bean sprouts on top. Fold the rice sheet in this order: right side, left side, and bottom. Place 1 or 2 scallions on top of the folded sheets allowing one end to extend beyond the edge. Roll the sheet up from the bottom. (Tip: After rolling up the sheet, the ingredients originally facing down will be visible through the wrap to please the eye. You can dip 2 rice sheets and assemble 2 rolls at once to save time.) Dip the spring rolls in sweet red bean sauce sprinkled with crushed peanuts to eat.

Canh Mồng Tơi (Spinach Soup)

3 T dried shrimp
3 scallion stalks
3 cloves garlic
½ small red onion
2 T olive oil
2 bouillon cubes
pinch of salt
pinch of sugar
2 large bunches of fresh spinach

Soak 3 T dried shrimp in lukewarm water for 10 minutes to clean and soften shrimp. Drain. Cut 3 scallions into 1– pieces. Press 3 cloves of garlic with flat side of knife blade and cut finely. Chop ½ small red onion into small pieces. Sauté in 2 T olive oil. When red onion and garlic are browned, add 10 cups of water and begin to boil. Add 2 bouillon cubes ("Maggie" brand preferred), dried shrimp, and a little salt and sugar. Season to taste. When the broth is boiling, add 2 large bunches of fresh spinach and the chopped scallions. Boil again and turn off the flame. The soup is ready to serve for six people.

Gà Xào Sả (Lemongrass Chicken)

2 lb. skinless boneless chicken breast
3 stalks lemongrass
3 garlic cloves
salt
pepper
2 T vegetable oil
2 T sugar
2 T fish sauce (*nước mắm*)

Cut 2 lb. chicken breast into bite-sized pieces. Slice 3 stalks of lemongrass and grind with 3 garlic cloves in vegetable chopper (or coffee grinder). Mix the chicken with 1 t. salt, ¼ t. black pepper, the garlic, and the lemongrass. Set aside for 20 minutes. Heat the frying pan, add 2 T oil and when oil is hot, add the chicken mixture. Stir-fry on medium heat for 10 minutes until chicken is cooked. Season with 2 T sugar, 2 T *nước mắm* sauce, and ½ t. pepper to taste. Stir well. Serve immediately with rice.

Cơm (Steamed Rice)

3 c. white rice

Bring 6 c. water to a boil. Rinse and add 3 c. white rice. Reduce heat to simmer, covered, until the rice is tender (about 20 minutes). Fluff gently with a fork, cover again, and allow to sit for another 10 minutes.

Music, Food, and the Natural World

Nature has an impact on all aspects of Vietnamese life, including music. The year-round warm climate and multiple river basins help keep the soils fertile. Though Vietnam was profoundly influenced by Chinese culture over a period exceeding a thousand years and its food appears superficially to be like that of the Chinese, in fact, Vietnamese cuisine has links to both East Asia and Southeast Asia, in terms of spices, methods of preparation, and the manner of eating. For example, Vietnamese use both chopsticks (East Asian) and their hands (Southeast Asian).

Fruits and rice grow to nourish everyone, including musicians, who have created a music richly described the same way that fruits and foods are. Some types of vibrato are described as the varied sizes of a *hạt* or seed. Decades ago I sat down with my first teacher, the man who initiated me into traditional Vietnamese music. In his first lessons I felt enlightened because his approach was based on foods and cooking. A well-ornamented melody is comparable to a dish well-seasoned called *đậm đà*. A sharp pitch is described as like a ripe fruit, or *già*; while a flat one is *non* (green, too young). A correct ornamentation is called *chín*, meaning well-cooked or ripe. An ornament which effectively moves the hearts of listeners is said to be *mùi*, or "flavorously ripe;" even more so, it is *mùi rệu* or "very ripe," so much so as to cause a ripe fruit to drop off the branch. A delicate voice being able to delight the audience is said to be *ngọt*, meaning sweet. Thus a substantial terminology in the traditional music of Vietnam shows relationships to cooking.

Although things are changing rapidly for city people, for traditional villagers music and cooking remain tightly bonded. Annual or seasonal festivals cannot happen without music and cooking. However, Vietnamese value music in a special way: music is preferred not to entertain the meals of the livings but is performed for the dead. In the latter case, a ritual repertoire is played during food offering rituals, i.e., offerings of food and music together. Even among common folks, music has a place of its own. Traditional songs and folk songs are performed before or after eating. Nevertheless, people also enjoy listening to and commenting on music while cooking.

Music and food have a great similarity in terms of cultural concepts. Visitors to Vietnam are first struck by how green herbal vegetables decorate the tops of most of Vietnamese dishes (usually, mint leaves, coriander, green onion, or basil leaves). This top layer may be compared to an introduction to the piece of music. It is arranged with skill and comparable to the concept of *rao* or *dạo* (pronounced "zao"), an improvised prelude. This flexible arrangement is like an improvised prelude to a musical composition. An experienced *phở* (beef noodle soup) eater, immediately aware of the combined flavor of the green vegetables and the steamy broth of the bowl, can determine whether the soup is good; just as a musical connoisseur can tell whether the musician is skilled in music by his *rao*.

Music reflects culture. In many ways, one can find similarities between eating or playing music. As a proverb says, "Watch the rice pot to ensure equal shares; find your proper place at the table," a hierarchy guides how a musician knows where to sit, what instrument to play, and who leads the music. As a sign of respect, a younger musician must give the *song lang* foot clapper or a drum to the more experienced (usually older) musician. With his strokes, musicians in the ensemble know when to start, when to slow down or accelerate, and when to end the piece. During the playing, the younger or less skilled musicians interchange phrases in a humble and considerate manner with the more experienced ones just as the musical scales themselves have hierarchical degrees (i.e., more or less frequent).

As far as Vietnamese cooking is concerned, I find that individual or family tastes are distinctive. Just as there is a high degree of flexibility in the measurement of ingredients, there is a corresponding flexibility in Vietnamese music seen in both the ornamentation and in the improvised sections.

RECOMMENDED LISTENING

Vietnamese music compact discs can be purchased at the Institute for Vietnamese Music. You can write to ivm@vietnamesemusic.us for information.

Eternal Voice: Traditional Vietnamese Music in the United States. New Alliance.
Mother Mountain, Father Sea. White Cliffs Media.
Music from the Lost Kingdom: Hue, Vietnam. Lyrichord.

FOR FURTHER INFORMATION

http://www.phamducthanh.com
http://www.phong-nguyen.com
http://www.vietnamesemusic.us
http://www.vietnamtourism.com
http://vn-style.com/vim/index.html
Nguyen, Phong T., and Campbell, Patricia Shehan. 2000. *From Rice Paddies and Temple Yards: Traditional Music from Vietnam.* New Haven, CT: World Music Press.
Ray, Nick, and Yanagihara, Wendy. 2005. *Lonely Planet Vietnam*, 8th ed. Footscray, Victoria, Australia: Lonely Planet Publications.

6
Middle East

MOROCCO

Philip Schuyler

God gives fava beans to the one who has no teeth.

Menu: *Harira* (Hearty Soup), Dates, Coffee, and Milk.
Preparation Time: Not counting the preparation of the sourdough starter and soaking the beans, approximately 2 hours.
Cooking Process: The night before, mix the "sponge" (sourdough starter) for the *harira*. At the same time, you could soak the garbanzo beans. Alternately, you could use regular sourdough starter and canned beans, and then just start cooking on the day you plan to eat. Serve with dates, coffee, and milk. Serves six people.

The Recipe

HARIRA (HEARTY SOUP)

¼ c. flour
½ oz. fresh yeast (or 1 t. active dry)
salt
1 14-oz. can chickpeas (or 1 c. dry chickpeas, soaked overnight)
1 lb. meat (lamb, beef, ground beef, chicken, or chicken livers), cut in bite-sized pieces
Soup bones (or add/substitute 4 c. broth)
2 T butter or *ghee*
2 T olive oil
1 c. finely chopped onion
1 c. parsley
1 t. turmeric
½ t. cinnamon
½ t. saffron
½ t. ground ginger
½ t. sweet red pepper/paprika
3 cinnamon sticks
1 c. lentils
2 T tomato paste (optional)
1½ lb. tomatoes, peeled, seeded, and chopped
½ c. vermicelli, broken into pieces
4 eggs
2 T cilantro
1–2 t. pepper
1 lemon, cut into wedges

Advance Preparation: 12–24 hours before cooking, mix ¼ c. flour, ½ oz. fresh yeast (or 1 teaspoon dry), ½ c. water, and a pinch of salt. Cover and let sit at room temperature. The resulting sponge helps produce a velvety texture and adds a yeasty tang to the soup. Sourdough starter, if you have it, works just as well. If using dried chickpeas/garbanzos, soak them overnight and remove skins. If using canned chickpeas, drain and rinse. Two hours before you are ready to begin eating, brown the meat and bones in 2 T butter or *ghee* and 2 T olive oil over high heat in a large pot. Add 1 c. finely chopped onion and cook, stirring frequently, over medium-low heat until wilted and lightly browned (about 5 minutes). Add ½ c. chopped fresh parsley, 1 T salt, 1 t. turmeric, ½ t. cinnamon, ½ t. saffron, ½ t. ground ginger, ½ t. red pepper, and 3 cinnamon sticks, and cook, stirring constantly, for 2 minutes. Add 1 c. lentils and 1 can rinsed or 1 c. soaked dry chickpeas and cook for 2 minutes, stirring to avoid burning and sticking. Add 4–6 c. of water or broth to cover mixture. Bring to a boil, cover and simmer for 45 minutes to 1 hour. Add yeast sponge or sourdough starter and 1½ c. water. Mix well. Add 2 T tomato paste (optional), 1½ lb. peeled, seeded and chopped tomatoes, and ½ c. broken vermicelli. Stir frequently for 45 minutes to 1 hour more. The liquid should be the consistency of a rich cream soup, thick but not pasty. Add water, if necessary, to achieve the proper texture. Remove soup bones. Add 4 eggs one at a time into the *harira*, stirring vigorously. Add 2 T fresh chopped cilantro, 1 t. (or more) black pepper, and salt to taste. Serve with lemon wedges or additional *ghee* to taste.

Bismillah!

Harira, a velvety Moroccan breakfast soup, comes in many forms and many flavors. In the countryside, *harira* may be a simple gruel of water and flour, flavored with salt, pepper, and a little oil or butter—a tangy cream of wheat with the appearance, if not the flavor, of library paste. The citified recipe reproduced here, on the other hand, uses a riot of different ingredients. It may, in fact, be the world's most perfect food, with a healthy balance of all the major food groups—grains, vegetables, fruit, legumes, meat, dairy, and oil—brought together in a combination that is filling, nutritious, and exceptionally tasty. Whether humble or rich, the thick, hot liquid goes down easily, instantly warming the body and providing the fuel to start the day. It's a wonderful way to wake up in the morning.

During the month of Ramadan, however, "breakfast" (called *ftur*) takes place at sunset. Ramadan, the ninth month of the Muslim calendar, commemorates a long fast and meditation by the Prophet Muhammad, at the end of which he received the first revelations of the Qur'an. Muslims reenact the fast by refraining from earthly pleasures between dawn and dusk for an entire lunar month. Believers may not eat, drink, smoke, or make love during daylight hours. In addition, women should forego jewelry, makeup, and other adornment, and everyone should maintain an even temper. The fast is one of the five pillars of Islam (along with the Testimony of Faith, Prayer, Charity, and the Pilgrimage to Mecca) and adherence to the discipline is a tangible demonstration of submission to the will of Allah. Ramadan is also said to encourage detachment from worldly concerns, meditation on the divine, and sympathy for the poor. Some even argue that it is good for your health.

The reward for following the strictures comes not only in the afterlife, but also during every evening of the month. Although believers are urged to maintain their normal daily activities throughout Ramadan, in practice the rhythm of life changes. The workday is shortened and many people take naps during the day. In the late afternoon, traffic in the cities grows chaotic, as half the population, slightly dazed by hunger, thirst, and nicotine-deprivation, rushes in different directions to the same destination—breaking the fast at home. Those who can't go home head to the nearest café, and soon the streets are deserted.

In the final minutes before sunset, people gather around the table staring at the steam rising from bowls of soup. Smokers sit at the ready, with a cigarette in one hand and a match in the other.

Finally, the end of the fast is signaled by the call to prayer, recited live by a *muezzin* from the minaret of a neighborhood mosque, but also broadcast on radio and television, and underlined in larger towns by a shot from a cannon or a blast from an air-raid siren.

Devout believers pray first and then eat, while the weaker in spirit give a quick *Bismillah* ("In the name of God") and dig right into their meal. The breakfast menu varies from one Muslim country to another, but in Morocco, the centerpiece of *ftur* is *harira*, accompanied by sweet warmed milk flavored with a splash of strong coffee. Dates, dried figs, and nuts are also at hand to provide energy. Lucky eaters get sugar bombs called *shebbakia* or *griush*—rosettes of deep-fried dough flavored with sesame seeds and orange water, and saturated with honey. After a full day of abstinence, the sudden infusion of so many smells and flavors is intoxicating. Under these circumstances, a bowl of soup and a handful of sweets—let alone the first cigarette—can be dizzying; sweat pours off your face and your digestion rumbles to life. Even for a nonbeliever, the culinary reward is enough to repay the rigors of fasting.

After *ftur*, guests relax, talk, and watch television. They also continue to snack, switching from coffee to mint tea while still picking at sweets. But before long new plates appear: cooked salads; round, flat loaves of bread; and a stew of chicken or meat (or perhaps both, one after the other). This is dinner, just half an hour after breakfast, and the main dishes arrive so quickly that one could be forgiven for thinking that it is all a single meal, very long and very rich.

Once dinner is done, the city comes alive. Friends get together to play cards and tell jokes well past midnight. The streets are brightly lit and the cafés are full of laughter. Some men, especially craftsmen and food vendors, keep their shops open far into the night. In the hours before dawn, when the city finally falls still, *muezzins* lead up to the call to prayer with long (and loud) hymns, prayers, and readings from the Qur'an. Different voices reciting different texts from different minarets serve as aural landmarks in the dark, and, taken together, give a sonic texture to the night sky. In cities like Fes, Marrakech, and Tangier, the same tunes are played in the minaret on the *ghaita*, a shawm, alternating with rhythmic passages on the *nfar*, a six-foot brass trumpet. In some neighborhoods, the local garbage collector goes from house to house with a large mallet, waking his clients with several thundering raps on the door. All of this is to remind people to pray or, at the very least, eat that last meal before another day of fasting begins.

No one knows on what day the angel first appeared to Muhammad, but by custom, that visit is celebrated on the 27th night of Ramadan, known as *Lailat al-Qadr*, or the Night of Destiny. On this night, every act is magnified 10,000 times, so many believers spend the entire night in prayer. *Lailat al-Qadr* also marks the beginning of the end of Ramadan. Even today, no one knows exactly how long the month will last; it ends, as it began, when an authorized observer spies the new moon. By the 27th night, however, everyone understands that Ramadan will soon be over, and they begin to make preparations to celebrate what Moroccans call Aid es-Saghir, the "little feast" that ends the fast for the year. Parents shop for gifts for their children, and whole families stroll through town in new clothes for the holiday. The joyful atmosphere that characterizes every night in Ramadan reaches its peak.

As breakfast food, *harira* has no particular connection to music, and Ramadan in general is a time when music making drops off dramatically. Still, there is one kind of music that many people associate with *ftur*. Tapes of Andalusian music, the classical style patronized by the royal court and the old bourgeois families of Fes and Tetouan, are broadcast on television in the last half hour before sunset, to distract people as they wait to break the fast. "I can't stand it, ever," a friend once said of Andalusian music. "It always reminds me of being hungry."

RECOMMENDED LISTENING

Anthology of World Music: The Music of Islam and Sufism in Morocco. Rounder, 1999. CD 5145.
Le Malhun de Meknes. Institut du Monde Arabe. 50305-2.
Morocco: Berber Music from the High Atlas and the Anti-Atlas. Le Chant du Monde, 1994. LDX 274 991.
Morocco Crossroads of Time. Ellipsis Arts, 1995. 4030.
Radio Casablanca at http://www.maroc.net/rc/

FOR FURTHER INFORMATION

Canetti, Elias. 1978. *The Voices of Marrakesh: A Record of a Visit.* London: M. Boyars.
Fernea, Elizabeth Warnock. 1976. *A Street in Marrakech.* Garden City, NY: Anchor Books.
Kramer, Jane. 1970. *Honor to the Bride like the Pigeon that Guards its Grain under the Clove Tree.* New York: Farrar, Straus & Giroux.

ANDALUSIAN MOROCCO
Julia Banzi

One bean does not make a whole meal.

Menu: *Miriam's Souk-su Bil Jodera* (Miriam's Vegetarian Couscous), *Sfuf Tetuani* (Sesame, Almond, and Honey Cone), and *Atey bil Na'ana* (Mint Tea or *A'te*).
Preparation Time: 1½ hours.
Cooking Process: You can prepare the dessert first. Scrub or peel (depending on your preference) the vegetables and half or quarter them. Leave them in large pieces. It takes about 15 minutes to wash/peel the vegetables for this dish. Once you've got everything ready, however, the process is easy. Make the basic vegetable dish for the couscous, and while it's cooking you can work on the topping for it. Once the vegetables are done, use 3 cups of the broth to make the couscous. Note that you can also add lamb, chicken, or beef (as noted below) to this dish. Add 45 minutes to cook time. Serves six people.

The Recipes

Miriam's Souk-su Bil Jodera (Miriam's Vegetarian Couscous)

3 onions
2 cloves garlic, peeled and sliced
2 stalks celery, with the leaves on
2 T olive oil
¼ c. parsley
¼ c. fresh cilantro
pepper
½ t. cinnamon
¼ t. nutmeg
1 c. cooked garbanzo beans
1 tomato (or diced canned tomato)
salt
¼ cabbage
2 zucchinis
A 5" x 4" chunk of pumpkin squash (or ½ acorn squash)
1 eggplant
1 white turnip
1 white potato
1 green bell pepper
2 carrots
¾ c. raisins
2–3 T rosewater (optional)
½ c. blanched slivered almonds
2–3 T sugar
2 c. dried couscous

Cut up 1 onion, slice 2 cloves of garlic, and chop 2 stalks of celery, and fry them in a large pot in 2 T olive oil at medium heat until almost translucent. Start bringing a full teapot of water to a boil. Chop up ¼ c. parsley and ¼ c. cilantro and add them to the onion. Keep frying. Add 1 t. pepper, ½ t. cinnamon, ¼ t. nutmeg, and 1 c. drained garbanzo beans. Add 1 tomato, cut up in big pieces. Add 1 t. salt and fry everything for about 10 minutes. Next you're going to add all the vegetables (add meat here if desired and cook until tender) to this mixture. Quarter, halve or leave whole the turnips, zucchini, carrots, pumpkin, cabbage, potato, and eggplant; cut the green peppers into big pieces and put them in the big pot to boil. Cook for 20–30 minutes. Meanwhile you can work on the topping: wash ¾ c. raisins and let them sit in water for about 20 minutes. Cut up 2 onions and fry in olive oil until transparent; add 1 t. black pepper and 1½ t. cinnamon. Stir for awhile, then cover and cook for about 10 minutes. Add 2–3 T rosewater (optional), drained raisins, ½ c. blanched slivered almonds, and 2–3 T sugar. Cook for about 2 minutes. Add 2 c. water. Cook until the onions are done and almost no liquid remains.

Last, make your couscous by adding 2 c. dried couscous to 3 c. of the vegetable water. Cover and let sit for 5 minutes, then fluff with a fork. To put it all together, place the couscous in a large platter in a big circle with a hole in the center. Fill the hole with meat (if adding meat) then cover with the cooked vegetables, then cover the vegetables with some of the couscous from the sides (they're hidden inside). To keep the "treasures" (the tastiest vegetables or the meat) modestly hidden inside the mound so that they are not immediately apparent is a very Moroccan way of doing things. Decorate the sides of the couscous with a few pieces of vegetables, then sprinkle cinnamon on the top. Serve from the one main platter, where everyone helps themselves to their own plates. Have some of the onion/raisin topping also as a side dish, and a separate bowl with some more of the broth for people to ladle over their couscous if they like it more moist or with more of the onion/raisin topping.

Miriam's *Souk-su Bil Jodera* (Andalusian-Moroccan vegetarian couscous). Photo by Julia Banzi.

SFUF TETUANI (SESAME, ALMOND, AND HONEY CONE)

3 c. flour
¾ c. sesame seeds
1 T butter
½ c. sugar
½ c. blanched almonds, finely ground
1 t. cinnamon
pinch of nutmeg
2 T honey
powdered sugar

Toast 3 c. flour in a frying pan, stirring constantly until it browns. Add ¾ c. sesame seeds, 1 oz. butter, and stir until the seeds turn gold. Add ½ c. sugar, almonds, 1 t. cinnamon, and a pinch of grated nutmeg and cook together for about 3 minutes, stirring constantly. Place the *sfuf* in small dessert dishes or in a communal serving plate to be eaten with dessert spoons. It is powdery and yummy! If you like, you can also shape it into a cone or other shapes by adding honey (once its cooled) enough to hold its shape. Decorate your finished sculpture with powdered sugar. If you have any left over, make paper cones and fill them with *sfuf* for your guest to take home. It makes a wonderful parting gift. It also keeps for a very long time in a sealed jar in the fridge.

ATEY BIL NA'ANA (MINT TEA OR A'TE)

1 T Chinese green jasmine tea
large bunch of fresh mint
sugar to taste

Take a large teapot and add 1 T Chinese green jasmine tea (or 1 T "gunpowder" tea, or 1 bag of plain black tea). Stuff the teapot with as much fresh mint as you can fit inside it. Bring the teawater to a boil, then remove from heat and let it cool for 1 minute. Add the hot water to the teapot, stir well, and serve in small glass cups. In Morocco, tea is served with about ½–1 cup sugar (or more); you may leave the choice of how much sugar to add up to your guests.

Remembering al-Andalus in Contemporary Morocco

Moroccan food and music are quite distinct from that of most other Arab countries. The late king of Morocco, Hassan II (d. 1999), had a famous saying: "Morocco is like a tree with its roots in Africa and its branches in Europe." This phrase voices a sentiment common among many Moroccans, that they are from both the East and the West. This concept is reflected in the culture through music, dress, language and, of course, the food!

While it is difficult to generalize for a whole country, Moroccan food tends to use spices and cooking techniques that guard the original flavors of the meats and vegetables. The manner of doing this for food, as with the music, could be described as a marriage of Occidental and African and Arab. Similar to the music, Moroccan cuisine encapsulates its own indigenous culture: the *Amazigh* (Berber), influenced by invasion of the Arabs (632), enriched by culinary secrets brought from its foreign exploits and the high court life of *al-Andalus* (Spain 711–1492), and later influenced by colonization of Spain and France (1912–1956). Morocco's two long coastlines (Mediterranean and Atlantic), fertile agricultural belt, desert regions, and five mountain ranges provide an abundance of fine ingredients for Moroccan cooks to explore and create a dizzying array of dishes for all tastes, from those of a pauper to those of a king and everything in between. Moroccans take great pride in their culinary richness, but it is not a restaurant culture; the best Moroccan food is to be found in people's homes and at special celebrations.

I have come to know Moroccan cuisine first through my in-laws (since 1986), and later through my many years of research (and now living) in Morocco. My research in Morocco has centered on Andalusian women musicians. Traditionally, they perform at exclusively female social gatherings in ensembles ranging from three to nine musicians. This women's music tradition remains vibrant in the northern regions of Morocco where festivities remain gender-segregated. Andalusian musical events go to great extremes to create what participants perceive as the courtly life of medieval *al-Andalus*. This recreation is accomplished not only through music, food, and dress, but also through the performance venues where women's Andalusian music takes place.

Women's celebrations occur throughout the entire year and are pivotal to many women's lives. Food and music are the centerpieces to these celebrations as each household strives to outdo the other in delicately prepared cuisine and beautiful presentations set against a backdrop of Andalusian music. Family, friends, and neighbors all help for big feasts, and this cross-fertilization further enriches the food as well as ensures the continued survival of complicated or rarely prepared delicacies. Traditionally, these celebrations are graced by female musicians and constitute occasions in which women share collective experiences with family, friends, neighbors, distant relatives, and even complete strangers.

There are nine celebrations, as well numerous religious events in which food and women's music play an essential role. There is even one festival, *el'ajeen* ("dough" or "to knead") that is the day they make sweets and pastries for the wedding. It has developed into a ceremony in itself for the benefit of family and close friends. Wealthier women employ female Andalusian ensembles for this event while others make their own music by singing and clapping, sometimes to the accompaniment of drums, ouds, or violins. Since so many people are invited to help, and these people also need sweets, there is also *el'ajeen* of the *el'ajeen*.

Special occasions are often accompanied with classical Andalusian music believed to be descended directly from the courtly music of Islamic Spain that continues today as an important echo of the past. As *al-Andalus* fell to the Catholic *reconquista*, the Muslims and Jews of *al-Andalus* emigrated from Spain to different cities in North Africa, leaving many treasures behind but transporting their music and culinary secrets with them as a living reminder of *al-Andalus*. This tradition is considered by many scholars to be one of the longest continuous traditions of art music in the world.

Esthetic principals that guide the music are also applicable to the food. It is emphasized in the culture that a good Andalusian musician is subtle and never stands out, and the entire ensemble should function as one unit "like the fingers of a hand." Likewise, there should be a harmony in the dish itself; one spice should not stand out, but should blend instead with the others into something new. Andalusian banquets are grandiose affairs lasting many hours where dish after dish is offered, each piled high. The accompanying Andalusian *Nawba* (song cycle) builds and falls in tempo, alternating instrumental with poetic sung texts extolling the pleasures of love, wine, piety, and Sufism. As in the music there must also be a harmony between dishes and to the meal as a whole. Sweet ingredients are often mixed with meats, providing a savory contrast and enhancing its flavor. It is the fluidity of the ensemble in its ability to navigate shifting tempos, dynamic shifts, key changes, starts and stops, and contrasts to create the proper mood that is highly prized both in the ensemble and in the individual musician. Likewise, the food preparation, presentation, and timing is judged on its ability to create the proper mood and feeling for the guest.

Souk-su (couscous) and *atey bil na'ana* (mint tea) are the quintessential Moroccan foods served throughout Morocco. *Sfuf* is an Andalusian aphrodisiac dessert. *Souk-su*, more commonly known as *couscous* (outside Morocco), is considered Moroccan's national dish. People often think of couscous as a grain, which of course it is! *Souk-su* is a form of pasta made from semolina flour. However, in Morocco, what really counts in the *souk-su* is what goes on top. Carefully prepared in a rich variety of ways, think of *souk-su* as a steaming mountain of vegetables (carrots, cabbage, squash, peppers often with a piece of lamb, beef, or chicken buried in the center)—all piled atop the steamed couscous grain and crowned with a delicious onion-raison-almond mixture, its broth doused over it, and a sparkle of cinnamon. Don't be intimidated; it's easy to do, but it is like three separate things put together (vegetables, *souk-su*, and topping). *Souk-su* is the traditional Friday lunch meal in Morocco. Friday is the holy day when people go to the mosque to pray and to the *hamman* to bathe. *Souk-su* is also served at many other special occasions. In cities, *souk-su* is eaten with spoons. Further south and in many parts of the countryside, it is eaten by shaping a small handful into a ball and popping it into your mouth (which takes a bit of practice!). There are scores of different recipes for *souk-su*; I've included this one because it can be made either vegetarian or with meat; it's fairly easy to make.

Sfuf is a healthy and easy to make fragrant dessert served at Andalusian weddings and during the holy month of fasting (Ramadan) where it becomes a favorite nutritive dessert. It is considered an aphrodisiac, said to increase both male and female libido and to fortify one's health in general. It is one of the living legacies of *al-Andalus* kept alive by Moroccan Andalusians who fled their homes in southern Spain over four centuries ago. *Atey bil na'ana* is traditionally served in small, jeweled glasses and drunk several times a day. It is an integral part of Moroccan hospitality. The recipes I've included here were taught to me by my dear friend Miriam, who always sings while we cook and laughs while we eat!

RECOMMENDED LISTENING

Al-Andalus. *Alchemy.* http://cdbaby.com/cd/alandalus4/ 2006.
Al-Rais, Haj Abdelkrim, and Orchestre al-Brihi de Fes. *Anthologie "'Al-Âla" Nouba Gharibat Al-Husayn 1 and 2.* Maison Des Cultures du Monde Paris and Royaume Du Maroc Ministere de la Culture, 1989. CD liner notes by Mohamed Ben Aissa, Minister of Culture of Morocco.
Chekarra, Abdessadek. *Al 'aila mulaati; B'nt Ya'laadi; Al Tuashe Alsaba.* 3 CDs.
Larbi-Temsamani, Mohammed, and Orchestre du Conservatoire de Tétouan. *Anthologie "Al-Âla," Musique Andaluci-Marocaine.* 2005.

FOR FURTHER INFORMATION

Bahrami, Beebe. 1995. The persistence of the Andalusian identity in Rabat, Morocco. Unpublished Ph.D. dissertation. University of Pennsylvania.
Banzi, Julia. 2002. Women's Andalusian ensembles of Tetuan, Morocco. Ph.D. thesis. University of California at Santa Barbara.
Beckwith, Stacey, ed. 2000. *Charting Memory: Recalling Medieval Spain.* New York: Garland.

Menocal, María Rosa, Raymond P. Scheindlin, and Michael Sells, eds. 2000. *The Literature of Al-Andalus*. New York: Cambridge University Press.

Wolfert, Paula. *Good Food from Morocco*. 1989. London: John Murray Publishers.

Zubaida, Sami, and Richard Tapper, eds. 2000. *A Taste of Thyme: Culinary Cultures of the Middle East*. London; New York: Tauris Parke Paperbacks.

JUDEO-SPANISH MOROCCO
Suzanne Benchimol and Judith Cohen

She went to buy cilantro and came back nine months pregnant.

Menu: *Ensalada de Zanahoria* (Carrot Salad), *Pollo con Aceitunas* (Chicken with Olives), *Sopa de Verduras* (Vegetable Soup), and *Datiles Rellenos de Almendra/Marzipan* (Dates Stuffed with Almond Paste).
Preparation Time: Approximately 3 hours.
Cooking Process: Start boiling the olives first, then prepare the chicken dish, then the vegetable soup. Make the carrot salad and arrange the dates. Serve with coffee. Serves six people.

The Recipes

Ensalada de Zanahoria (Carrot Salad)

1 lb. carrots
¼ c. olive oil
3–4 cloves garlic
½ t. cumin
½ t. paprika
1 lemon
salt
1 lemon, juiced
¼ c. parsley

Peel and cut 1 lb. carrots with a waffle cutter; boil them for several minutes until slightly tender, and drain well. Make the marinade: In a saucepan, heat ¼ c. olive oil and sauté 3–4 cloves of crushed garlic. Add ½ t. cumin, ½ t. paprika, ¼ t. salt, and the juice of 1 lemon. Bring the marinade to a quick boil. Add the carrots to the marinade and sauté for several minutes until the marinade has been absorbed. Add ¼ c. chopped parsley; serve hot or cold.

Pollo con Aceitunas (Chicken with Olives)

1 lb. pitted green olives
2 large onions
2 T olive oil
2–3 tomatoes
4–5 cloves garlic
1 t. ginger
pinch of saffron
1 t. paprika
1 t. cumin
12 chicken pieces (enough for six people)
¼ c. parsley
1 lemon, juiced

Poyo con Azeitunas **(chicken with olives, Judeo-Spanish Morocco). Courtesy of Suzanne Benchimol.**

Boil 1 lb. of pitted green olives (or 2 cans) three times, changing the water each time, to remove the excess salt. Drain and set aside. In a large casserole, fry 2 large finely chopped onions in 2 T olive oil at medium-high heat. Add 2–3 fresh chopped tomatoes and sauté with the onions. Add 4–5 cloves of pressed garlic, 1 t. ginger, a pinch of saffron, 1 t. paprika, 1 t. cumin, 1 c. water, and bring to a boil. Wash and drain the chicken pieces, then add to the casserole. Reduce the heat to medium. Add the olives and cover the pot; cook for 30 minutes. Reduce the heat to simmer; add about ¼ c. fresh parsley and the juice of 1 lemon. Let it simmer for another 30 minutes to 1 hour. Serve hot.

SOPA DE VERDURAS (VEGETABLE SOUP)

2 carrots
2 parsnips
2 onions
2 tomatoes
2 large potatoes
2 celery stalks
1 large piece of meat (or beef bones)
salt
pepper
¼ t. turmeric
2 T vegetable oil

¼ c. parsley

¼ c. cilantro

Wash and cut 2 each of the following vegetables into pieces: carrots, parsnips, onions, tomatoes, large potatoes, celery stalks, and any other available vegetables (yams, zucchini, broccoli, leeks, etc.). Bring 6 c. water to boil in a large casserole. Add a large piece of meat or beef bones and all the vegetables. Add ½ t. salt, ¼ t. pepper, ¼ t. turmeric, and 2 T vegetable oil. Allow it to cook, uncovered, for 1 hour, then add ¼ c. each of fresh parsley and fresh cilantro. Simmer for a few more minutes, then serve hot.

DATILES RELLENOS DE ALMENDRA/MARZIPAN (DATES STUFFED WITH ALMOND PASTE)

2 lbs. dates

1 14-oz. package of almond paste or marzipan

food coloring

liqueur (any type you prefer)

1 lemon, zested

¼ c. sugar

Slit the dates along one side, remove the pit and wipe the dates. Open 1 14-oz. package of almond paste or marzipan, and divide it into two parts. Flavor and color the almond paste to your taste (for example, pale green or pink), sprinkle with liqueur to your taste, or add lemon zest. Place small chunks of the paste in the hollow place of each date half, allowing the almond paste to show from within the slit. Decorate the top of the almond paste with a knife or fork, dip each one in sugar, and place them in small paper cups. Serve with tea or coffee.

Getting Married in Sephardic Morocco

One of the most compelling ways to understand the context of food and music in the Sephardic community is through seeing a wedding celebration through the eyes of contributor Suzanne Benchimol. This wedding ceremony actually took place in France, yet its food, its music, and virtually everything about it speaks of the Sephardic community in Morocco. Judith Cohen translated the following description with Suzanne's permission.

> The wedding took three days. It was a civil marriage of the sort where perhaps 20 or 30 guests might show up, but here there were more than 100. The mayor himself was Jewish, and instead of a quick city hall ceremony, he took a full hour, talking to the bride and groom as if they were family. He even got the groom to perform the traditional Jewish ritual of breaking a glass, and then the "you-you's" (traditional ululations) broke out, and the music began. We went out to look for a glass of water and were astonished to find a beautiful buffet sweets table, with champagne; the wedding party had taken over city hall. Everyone was beautifully dressed, the decorations were splendid, and the *petit fours* were an immediate addition to the newlyweds' happiness.

The next night was the henna night. The hall was decorated as if it were part of the Thousand and One Nights. There was a tent-like *huppa* (ritual bridal canopy) for the bride to have her hands painted with henna designs. A group of Gnaouis greeted us with tambourines, and we walked through to the cocktail room. Along one wall was a selection of all kinds of Moroccan spices, in small jute bags, as if we were back in the old markets; the enticing smell of the spices, of orange blossoms. ... Together with the women dressed in kaftans, and Andalusian music, it brought me a wave of nostalgia for the Morocco I had left as a child.

The decorated tables were covered with delicious small Moroccan salads, the chicken with olives dish which is a favorite of so many of us, the "couscous royal" with vegetables and dried fruits, and more. There was lamb and tagine, with all the different flavors of the dishes matched by the flavor of the music. The young newlyweds had left the room, and reappeared borne aloft on litters (*ambarias*) carried by their friends, who moved them so the couple was dancing above us all. It went on until about 1 am.

On Sunday, it was time for the religious marriage ceremony at the synagogue. And that evening yet another party: a long cocktail hour followed by the wedding supper. While the henna party meal was Moroccan, this one was more French; the music was loud, not the Arab-Andalusian music of my childhood. The tables were adorned with sweet-smelling flowers, beautiful cakes, pyramids of cream puffs, ice swans, and later, fine coffee and tea. It went on until about 2 am and we were exhausted but happy after three days of dashing around from part of the celebration to another.

Weddings are on Sundays because Saturdays, the Sabbath, are devoted to going to synagogue, eating a leisurely meal, and spending the afternoon quietly with family and friends, often singing around the table. Because one is not supposed to work on the Sabbath, including cooking or lighting a fire, the midday meal (called the *adafina* from 'ada fina,' fine custom) was prepared on Friday and left to cook slowly in the baker's oven all evening and night. The next day, someone, usually a Muslim boy, would bring the *adafinas* to each home.

For a typical Moroccan *adafina*—the Eastern European Ashkenazi Jewish equivalent is called a *cholent*—you take a generous casserole dish and put some dates on the bottom, then add meat (beef) and marrow or foot bones for the gelatin. Then add chickpeas, small red or white potatoes, and a few hard-boiled eggs. Next, add a stuffing of ground meat with raisins and fried onions, nutmeg, mace, ginger, salt and pepper, and sugared potatoes cut in lengthwise strips. Cover with water, cover with a lid, and bring to the baker's oven. On Saturday when you return from the synagogue a delicious meal is all ready, perfectly slow-cooked, without anyone having to desecrate Shabbat, the Sabbath, by working.

For Orthodox Jews, instruments cannot be played on Shabbat, but many songs are heard around the table, especially in Hebrew. Keeping rhythm by tapping on the table does not count as playing an instrument!

RECOMMENDED LISTENING

Bowles/Seroussi. *Sacred Music of the Moroccan Jews*. Collected by Paul Bowles, edited with notes by Edwin Seroussi. Rounder Records, 2000. 82161-5087-2.

Cohen, Judith R. *Canciones de Sefarad*. Pneuma, 2000. PN230.

Gerineldo. *Cantos judeo-españoles*. Tecnosaga. KPD 10.201.

Weich-Shahak. *Susana, Judeo-Spanish Moroccan Songs for the Life Cycle*. Jerusalem, Jewish Music Resource Center, 2001. AMTI 5 CD0101.

FOR FURTHER INFORMATION

http://www.cryptojews.com/clearing_up_ladino.htm
http://www.wzo.org.il/en/resources/view.asp?id=1596
http://rickgold.home.mindspring.com/links1.htm

Cohen, Judith R. 1989. "Ya Salió de la Mar": Judeo-Spanish wedding songs among Moroccan Jews in Canada. In *Women and Music in Cross-Cultural Perspective*. Edited by Ellen Koskoff. Urbana: University of Illinois.

EGYPT
Mina Girgis

An onion from a dear one is worth more than a goat.

Menu: *Karkade* (Hibiscus Iced Tea), *Falafel* (Fried Garbanzo Beans), *Babaghanoush* (Eggplant Dip), *Koshary* (Lentil/Pasta/Rice/Vegetable Dish with Sauces), *Salata Baladi* (Fresh Vegetable Salad with Dressing), *Um Ali* (Sweet Coconut/Nut/Raisin Dessert), and *Shay Bel Neenaa* (Mint Tea).
Preparation Time: 3–4 hours, not counting soaking the beans and chickpeas.
Cooking Process: Read through the recipes carefully; soak the chickpeas for the *koshary* and the broken beans for the *falafel* overnight or use canned versions. Put the eggplant in the oven for the *babaghanoush*; start the chickpeas (2 hours) and the lentils (1 hour) for the *koshary*; then make and chill the hibiscus tea; then do the dessert and the *babaghanoush*. Put the rice and macaroni on for the *koshary* 40 minutes before eating so that they are ready when you are to do the layers. Make the *falafel* mix. Fry the onions for the *koshary*, keeping the oil ready, then fry the *falafel*. Make the sauces and salsa for the *koshary*; then layer the *koshary* in a large casserole dish with rice, macaroni, lentils, salsa, fried onions, and chickpeas. Make the vegetable salad, then serve everything except the dessert and mint tea. The *falafel* should be served on a large tray, the *babaghanoush* served as a dip, and the *koshary*, salad, and *um ali* are all served in big bowls on table so that the guests may help themselves. Serves six people.

The Recipes

KARKADE (HIBISCUS ICED TEA)

1 c. dried hibiscus leaves
1 c. sugar
1 lemon, juiced

Rinse 1 c. dried hibiscus leaves by quickly passing them under cold water. In a large container, add the leaves to 8 c. water and heat until boiling. Once the water is boiled, cover and let simmer for 5 minutes, then add 1 c. sugar and stir until all sugar is dissolved. Turn off the heat and let the leaves steep until the water turns a dark burgundy color. Pour the liquid through a strainer to remove the hibiscus leaves. Add the juice of 1 lemon, stir, and cool. Store in the refrigerator.

FALAFEL (FRIED GARBANZO BEANS)

2 c. garbanzo beans
½ c. parsley
¼ c. cilantro
¼ c. dill
1 c. scallions
½ medium yellow onion
3 cloves garlic

2 t. salt
½ t. pepper
1 t. ground coriander
1 t. baking soda
1 qt. vegetable oil for frying
½ c. sesame seeds

Rinse 2 c. garbanzo beans thoroughly, then soak in 6 c. water for 2 days in a cool place, changing the water regularly. Finely chop ½ c. parsley, ¼ c. cilantro, ¼ c. dill, 1 c. scallions (using both white and green parts), ½ c. onion, and 3 cloves of garlic. Drain the beans, then grind them until their texture is fine. In a food processor, blend the greens, the onion and garlic, then add the beans. After processing, the mixture must be a green homogenous batter. In a bowl, mix the batter with 2 t. salt, ½ t. black pepper, 1 t. ground coriander, and 1 t. baking soda. Let the mix sit in the refrigerator for 1 hour. In a deep frying pan, heat 1 qt. of vegetable oil. The oil must be 1-inch deep. Make sure the oil is neither too hot (to avoid burning the *falafel*) nor too cool (to avoid the falafel becoming too oily). Once the oil starts to have a wavy appearance, you may test it by dropping in a small amount of the *falafel* batter; the batter should immediately be covered with small bubbles when it hits the oil. Using a large spoon, scoop the batter, pressing firmly into the spoon. Sprinkle the top with sesame seeds, and push into the frying oil. When the *falafel* patties turn golden brown, turn them around in the oil. Remove from the oil, and dry on a paper towel.

BABAGHANOUSH (EGGPLANT DIP)

1 large eggplant
5 T lemon juice
½ c. tahine
4 cloves garlic
1 t. salt
1 pinch pepper

Pierce 1 large eggplant in several places. Bake the eggplant at 350°F for 45 minutes, turning it over every 15 minutes. After the eggplant is cooled down, peel it and extract the pulp. In a food processor, mix the eggplant pulp with 5 T lemon juice, ½ c. tahine, 4 cloves garlic, 1 t. salt, and a pinch of pepper. Process until texture is smooth.

KOSHARY (LENTIL/PASTA/RICE/VEGETABLE DISH WITH SAUCES)

The word *koshary* comes from the Hindi *kishri*, meaning an unlikely mixture. In Egypt, *koshary* is a fast food served in stores and street carts.

2 c. white rice
5 c. vegetable oil
3 t. salt
1 lb. elbow macaroni
2 T butter

7 large onions
1 c. brown lentils
½ t. black pepper
3 t. cumin
4 t. white vinegar
2 c. tomato puree
1 c. chickpeas
1 medium tomato
1 small carrot

Garlic and Vinegar Sauce

1 t. crushed garlic
4 T white vinegar
2 T lemon juice
1 t. cumin
½ t. salt

Hot Sauce

1 t. crushed garlic
½ c. vegetable oil
½ t. chili flakes
1 red hot chili pepper

Layer 1: Rice
Wash rice in a large bowl, then drain the water. Add 2 T oil to a hot saucepan, then add the rice and cook on high heat for 5 minutes. Pour 2 c. hot water into the saucepan. Stir and cover. Cook on high heat until the water boils. Lower the heat to low and cook for 20 minutes. Let sit for 10 minutes, then stir with a fork.

Layer 2: Macaroni
Bring a large pot of water to a boil, then add a pinch of salt. Add the macaroni, and let cook until tender, stirring occasionally. When cooked (about 15 minutes), drain the water. Add 2 T butter and toss the macaroni until it is well coated.

Layer 3: Lentils
Cut one onion into thin slices. Wash the lentils, then drain the water. Heat ½ c. oil in saucepan. Add the onion slices, and sauté until golden, stirring frequently. To the saucepan, add 2 c. water, a pinch of salt and the lentils. Bring to a boil then lower the heat and simmer for 1 hour, making sure the lentils are constantly covered with water. When the lentils are cooked, drain the water. Add a pinch of black pepper and a pinch of cumin.

Layer 4: Salsa
Chop 2 onions thinly. Heat 4 T oil in a saucepan. Add the chopped onions, and sauté until golden, stirring frequently. Add 4 T white vinegar, and cook for 1 minute. Add 2 c. tomato puree, 1 t. cumin, a pinch of salt, and a pinch of black pepper. Cook until the tomato sauce's texture is thick.

Layer 5: Onions
Cut 3 onions into thin slices. Heat 2 c. oil in a saucepan until it appears wavy (about 365°F). Add the sliced onions, and sauté until golden, stirring frequently. When crispy, remove the onions and drain on a paper towel.

Layer 6: Chickpeas
Wash the chickpeas and drain the water. In a saucepan, soak the peas in 3 c. water overnight. To the peas and soaking water, add 1 whole tomato, 1 whole carrot, and 1 whole onion. The water should be covering the peas. Simmer for 2 hours. When tender, drain the liquid and reserve it aside.

Garlic and Vinegar Sauce

Mash 1 t. crushed garlic with a pinch of salt. Add 4 T white vinegar, ½ c. water, 2 T lemon juice, and 1 t. cumin to the garlic, and mix well.

Hot Sauce

Mash 1 t. crushed garlic with a pinch of salt. Heat ½ vegetable oil, and add ½ t. chili flakes and stir. Add 1 chili pepper and garlic, and stir.

In a large casserole dish, spread out each layer one by one; serve with garlic/vinegar and hot sauces on the side.

SALATA BALADI (FRESH VEGETABLE SALAD WITH DRESSING)

1 c. cucumber
1 c. tomato
1 c. green peppers
1 c. lettuce
1 c. onions
½ c. parsley

Dressing

1 T lemon juice
1 T white vinegar
2 T olive oil
1 pinch salt
1 pinch pepper
1 pinch cumin

Finely chop and mix 1 c. each of cucumber, tomato, green bell peppers, lettuce, and onions, and ½ c. parsley. Mix together 1 T lemon juice, 1 T white vinegar, 2 T olive oil, and 1 pinch each of salt, black pepper, and cumin. Toss the salad with the dressing immediately before serving.

Um Ali (Sweet Coconut/Nut/Raisin Dessert)

1 lb. phyllo dough
1 c. melted butter
2 c. whole milk
½ c. sugar
1 c. walnuts
1 c. raisins
1 c. dried coconut

Place a single layer of phyllo dough on an ungreased cookie sheet. Place in a 350°F oven to brown for 2 minutes, then remove and place on a rack to cool. Repeat procedure until all dough has been browned. Heat 2 c. milk and ½ c. sugar in a medium saucepan, and mix until the milk is hot and the sugar is dissolved. Mix together 1 c. each walnuts, raisins, and dried coconut. Slightly butter a 9"-square pan. Break half of the browned dough and place in the bottom of the pan. Sprinkle with ⅔ of the nuts and ½ of the milk. Break the rest of the dough and put on top of the milk. Sprinkle the remaining nuts and the pour the remaining milk. Sprinkle the top with butter. Bake in the oven at 400°F until the top is golden and most of the milk is absorbed.

Shay Bel Neenaa (Mint Tea)

1½ T dry mint leaves
2 T sugar
2 T black tea leaves

Pour 6 c. cold water into a teapot; add the mint leaves and the sugar. Bring to a boil, lower the heat and simmer for 2 minutes then turn off. Add the black tea and let it steep for 2 to 3 minutes, then serve.

Hospitality in Egypt

Sharing is the first concept that comes to my mind when I think of food and music in Egypt. Whether in the processes of making food and making music, or in the rituals of eating and listening, Egyptians have extremely acute sensors for generosity and hospitality. In this sense, sharing is not a positive quality to be adorned on a selected few, but a cultural standard expected of everyone. Most of my non-Egyptian friends make fun of how overly generous Egyptians are. They laugh when I offer them my own sandwich, and remind me of all the instances when they were invited into a stranger's house to find a huge heavy meal waiting for them. What's worse is that they couldn't leave before finishing all the dishes they were served. For Egyptians, however, no one can be too generous. During the holy month of Ramadan, Cairo's streets are filled with tables where the wealthy are expected to furnish dinners for the poor. Anyone is invited to eat for free for 30 days.

Having studied both music and cooking (hospitality administration) in Egypt, I find that the two traditions are transmitted in equally nonsystematic ways. One can learn Egyptian cooking nowhere but at home. Children learn from older family members by watching them every day.

Because Egyptian cooking lacks a rigorous pedagogy, it is considered an art mastered by the gifted ones, not a common body of knowledge accessible to any person. When someone is a good cook, Egyptians usually say that this person has "good breath," as if the success of a person's cooking relates to something as personal as their breathing. Along the same lines, an Egyptian proverb goes: "not everyone who blows (meaning cooks) can be a cook."

Similarly, Egyptian musical skills are transmitted mainly by osmosis. Unlike other world traditions, there are no rigid structures in Egypt for becoming a musician. Candidates cannot join the conservatory without a certain level of musicality that they have to achieve on their own (as the Egyptian educational system lacks any early musical pedagogy). Beyond casual singing and drumming, musical practice is mostly limited to professional musicians. A person interested in becoming a professional musician must venture into the stigmatized entertainment world; it is an adventurous step often taken to the dismay of family members due to the relatively negative connotation of the profession. Even if a professional musician puts considerable time and effort into practicing, his or her musical proficiency is often justified as pure talent. This person is said to have a good voice—a quality, again, as personal as someone's cooking breath.

Similarities in treating food and music transcend the pedagogical customs circumscribed to the production sphere (of both food and music). As I mentioned earlier, sharing food and sharing music obey a cultural understanding common among all Egyptians. In the same way that a diner is not meant to take more food than his commonsensical share, a musician should not take more time than he/she is supposed to during an improvisation (taqsim) to show off musical chops. In both cases, these cultural faux pas cause a clear change in the mood of the dinner/performance. Therefore, the diner/musician should refrain from these greedy behaviors not because of the scarcity of available resources (food or time), but rather to maintain a healthy, generous, and hospitable atmosphere at the gathering. When such behavior takes place, it is rarely brought into the conversation. On the other hand, one can notice how it fouls the communal mood of the gathering through the unspoken body language of the attendees.

Meanwhile, eating and listening occur in different contexts, and music is not necessarily an intangible food. Egyptians cherish social time. They take their time to eat and drink while telling stories and jokes. Social dining is one of the most common familial activities in Egypt. I do not know of many families who do not share at least one meal a day (be it lunch or dinner) when all members are present and eating in no hurry. Even in today's fast-paced world, Egyptians still manage to spend enough time socializing with family and friends. Of course, a communal meal where no one is talking is considered awkward, and someone usually jumps in to fill the silence.

Live musical performances usually involve similar social interaction. If it is a house concert, then everyone is expected to pay attention and listen actively. However, in many stage performances, one has to keep asking neighbors to shut up and listen. Egyptians like to talk all the time. ... Of course, the audience behaves differently depending on the context of the musical performance. In a loud cabaret or nightclub, everyone is drinking, talking, and dancing, and the music is merely the accompaniment to a dancer or a singer. On the other hand, an evening of classical Arabic music is treated differently. Everyone is there to listen to the music and pay attention to the performance. These contexts are often confused, and it is up to the musicians or the producers to draw the line. My violin teacher, for instance, refuses to perform if the audience is sitting at tables (cabaret style) or when food is served during the performance. He knows that Egyptians need no excuse to start talking, and he is not willing to ask the audience to remain quiet while his group is performing. Of course, few musicians adopt this attitude in Egypt. Whether private or public, Egyptian musical concerts are usually followed with a late night dinner.

Contemporary Egyptian food and music suffer from a similar degeneration. While home cooking is alive and well, and Egyptians never fail to cook and eat extravagantly when they can, they often complain about rising prices and the falling quality (in both taste and aroma) of gastronomic products; vegetables, fruits, and bread are on top of the list. My mother often jumps into nostalgic recollections of the good old days. Back then, she would say, one could smell the aroma of strawberries when the fruit vendor was barely around the block. Discourse on the current state of Egyptian music is even more prevalent. Everyone complains that there are no more Umm Kulthums, Abdel Wahabs, and Abdel Halims, and that most of today's hits rely on a catchy phrase devoid of the complex poetics of bygone eras. To use chords for guitar riffs, contemporary Egyptian pop singers stay within just a few Arabic musical modes that are easily adapted to Western harmony.

Egypt is rich with food, music, and proverbs about both. for example, both "cook your beans in your own pot" and "our oil is in our flour" mean "we keep our issues to ourselves." Similarly, "like salt, he inserts himself everywhere" refers to someone who doesn't keep to his own business. Our eagerness to share and be hospitable is reflected in "greed diminishes what is shared," "who asks for more gets less," and "a good cook can feed the whole party with one goose." "Our barley rather than other people's wheat" is an important statement of our independence. Lastly, "If you like your food, eat it all" refers to the idea of thoroughly enjoying what you have, rather than hoarding it.

RECOMMENDED LISTENING

Charcoal Gypsies. *Musicians of the Nile*. Real World, 1997. 62366.
Fadl, Mahmoud. *The Drummers of the Nile in Town: Cairosonic*. Piranha. CD-PIR 1791.

FOR FURTHER INFORMATION

Abu-Lughod, Lila. 2000. *Veiled Sentiments: Honor and Poetry in a Bedouin Society*. Berkeley: University of California Press.
Danielson, Virginia. 1998. *The Voice of Egypt*: *Umm Kulthum, Arabic Song, and Egyptian Society in the Twentieth Century*. Chicago: University of Chicago Press.
Lagrange, Frederic. 2001. *Musiques D'Egypte*. Paris: Cite de La Musique/Actes Sud.
Roden, Claudia. 2000. *The New Book of Middle Eastern Food*. New York: Knopf.
Wright, Clifford. 1999. *A Mediterranean Feast: The Story of the Birth of the Celebrated Cuisines of the Mediterranean from the Merchants of Venice to the Barbary of Corsairs, with More than 500 Recipes*. New York: Morrow Cookbooks.

PALESTINE
David McDonald

Between us is only bread and salt.

Menu: *Masâkhân* (Baked Chicken), *Mlukhîya* (Collard Greens), *Arz* (Rice), *Khadar* (Fresh Raw Vegetables), *Lebneh* (Unsweetened Plain Yogurt), and *Ba'lawa* (Layered Honey-Nut Dessert).
Preparation Time: 3 hours.
Cooking Process: Make the *ba'lawa* first, then start baking the chicken, then the rice, then the collard greens, then prepare the fresh vegetables. Serve with a variety of sliced cheeses (white and yellow as well as goat cheese), plain unsweetened yogurt, and the beverages. Before serving the dessert, slice some fresh fruit. Serve this meal with soft drinks, water, or tea. Serves six people.

The Recipes

Masâkhân (Baked Chicken)

1 t. ground ginger
1 t. garlic powder
1 t. cinnamon
1 t. white pepper
1 t. red pepper
1 t. coriander
1 t. cardamom
1 t. ground cloves
1 t. paprika
salt
1 whole chicken
1 c. olive oil
5 medium onions
⅓ c. ground sumac
6 large flat bread rounds

In a small bowl mix 1 t. each of ground ginger, garlic powder, cinnamon, white pepper, red pepper, coriander, cardamom, ground cloves, paprika, and salt. Rub the whole chicken generously with olive oil and season with the spice mixture. Bake, covered with foil, in roasting pan at 450°F for 5 minutes, then reduce heat to 350°F and continue baking for 1 hour or until done. Remove foil and brown for another 5 minutes. While the chicken is baking, chop 5 medium onions into fine strips, sauté in olive oil until translucent, and salt to taste. Drain oil from the onions into a medium bowl and mix with juices from the roasted chicken. In separate large bowl mix the onions with ⅓ c. ground sumac (can be found online and at Middle Eastern food stores). Lay out 6 to 8 flat bread rounds on cookie sheets. Glaze generously with onion oil/chicken juice mixture, cover rounds with thick layer of the seasoned onions, and heat in the oven for 5 minutes. Place a piece of chicken on each round and heat for 3 minutes. Serve hot, eaten without utensils by pulling chicken apart with pieces of the flat bread.

Mlukhîya (Collard Greens)

1 t. cinnamon
salt
1 t. cardamom
black pepper
2–3 large bunches collard greens
6 cloves garlic
2 T corn oil
1 lemon

In large saucepan mix 3½ c. water with 1 t. each of cinnamon, salt, cardamom, and black pepper. Wash and boil 2–3 large bunches of collard greens for 10–15 minutes. Slice and fry 6 garlic cloves in corn oil, then add to the greens and let stand for 2 minutes. Serve in its own bowl garnished with slices of lemon.

Arz (Rice)

3 c. white rice

Bring 6 c. water to a boil. Add 3 c. white rice (rinsed), cover and reduce heat to simmer for 20 minutes, until done. Fluff with a fork and let stand, covered, another 10 minutes.

Khadar (Fresh Raw Vegetables)

2 tomatoes
2 cucumbers
2 green bell peppers
2 T olive oil
salt

Wash and slice 2 tomatoes, 2 cucumbers, and 2 green bell peppers. Serve raw in a bowl with olive oil and salt.

Lebneh (Unsweetened Plain Yogurt)

1 qt. plain yogurt

Serve 1 qt. of plain unsweetened yogurt in a bowl with dinner.

BA'LAWA (LAYERED HONEY-NUT DESSERT)

1⅓ c. sugar
1 t. cinnamon
2 c. walnuts
1 4-oz. stick butter
1 package phyllo dough
¼ c. honey
1 T lemon juice

Mix ⅓ c. sugar with 1 t. cinnamon; set aside. Chop 2 c. walnuts. Melt 1 stick of butter. Take out a cookie sheet and lay out your phyllo dough, placing a lightly dampened dishcloth over it to keep it from drying out. In a 9" x 9" buttered baking pan, lay several sheets of buttered phyllo dough on top of one another (you do not have to butter every sheet). Sprinkle 1 c. chopped walnuts and half the sugar/cinnamon mix. Add 4 more layers of buttered phyllo on top. Cover with another c. chopped walnuts and the rest of the sugar/cinnamon mix. Cover with 4 more buttered layers of phyllo. Cut sharply through the layers in a diamond pattern. Bake in a 300°F oven for 45 minutes until the top layer looks gently browned. Mix 1 c. water with 1 c. sugar, ¼ c. honey, and 1 T lemon juice. Bring it to a boil and simmer for about 10 minutes until it is syrupy. Pour it over the *ba'lawa* and let it cool.

A meal with friends (Palestine). Photo by David McDonald.

"Living History" in Palestine

For many Palestinian refugees cultural practices passed down through the generations are believed to be sacred. Styles of music, dance, embroidery, and especially food are guarded treasures capable of linking families and communities across space and time. Flora Khoury, my Palestinian teacher in all things culinary, felt that when she prepared her mother's recipes she was, in essence, "living history." Assembling exact ingredients and following painstaking steps was one way in which she was able to impart on her children one small aspect of the Palestinian life she knew as a young girl in Bir Zeit. The pride she felt placing a large platter of *masâkhân* or *mlukhîya* in front of her three insatiably hungry sons (four if we count equally hungry ethnomusicologists) was evident by her loving smile and repeated offerings, "*Sahtain habibi*" (*bon appétit*, sweetheart).

We each possess talents capable of "living history." How we choose to express them is one of the great fascinations of ethnomusicology. For this Palestinian family, and millions like them, a simple meal, a song, a poem, or an embroidered dress, can serve to signify a time, a place, and a homeland unknown for over 50 years. Flora Khoury's three sons have never crossed the Jordan River to experience Palestine and Palestinian life for themselves. However, thanks to the loving efforts of their mother, they can know how life in Bir Zeit once tasted. If only in one small way, they can know the smells and tastes of their grandmothers' kitchens. For this reason, families will preserve with incredible detail many of the recipes (culinary and cultural) that govern their daily lives. Recipes for singing and dancing, for courtship, getting married, raising a family, and ultimately for preserving a common past are all treated with the same attention to detail. Following the words of Flora Khoury, these recipes are each formulas for "living history" that, when prepared correctly, coalesce into the building blocks of a distinct Palestinian delicacy.

As researchers we seek to understand these recipes for daily life. We hope to sample the cultural dish and determine its constitutive ingredients. Yet, awash in the busy streets of Amman it can be at times difficult to discern the Palestinian character (ingredients) of this cosmopolitan city. Over time, refugees and even their camps have been absorbed into the cityscape, leaving few remnants of the years spent in tents and shantytowns. As such, the polished public face of Amman rarely reveals its inner cultural diversity and history. Even after one has learned to read the Palestinian signs of family names, accents, styles of dress, and/or certain physical features, it can be near impossible to see this inner Palestinian character. Yet, in the home, the ingredients for Palestinian life are both preserved and displayed freely. Opinions widen, faces relax, and the cultural dynamics of a life spent in exile are revealed. Not unlike the architecture of the common Arab home, where a detached formal parlor or salon receives guests and hence protects and shields the inner family rooms, so too, the city streets act as the public domain of formal business separate from the inner sanctuary of the home and family. It is here, away from the politics of the street, where one can watch as Palestinian recipes are assembled and prepared. Here, one can sample their ingredients and savor the nuances of flavor which define Palestinian life in Jordan.

In this inner space food acts as one of the primary means by which families come together. In the camps, where families are notoriously large and apartments alarmingly small, a family will eat in a tight circle kneeling on a large tablecloth spread out on the floor. Hovering over a heaping platter of rice and baked chicken, a flurry of arms competes for each bite. The meat will then be pulled from the bones with one's right hand or with a pinched piece of flatbread (*khubz arak*). Smaller side dishes of *hummus, foûl, taboûleh, falâfil*, and assorted vegetables, cheeses, and yogurts (collectively called *mezze*), will be served in small bowls surrounding the main platter shared and dipped into by everyone. Of these *mezze*, olives, tomatoes, sliced cucumbers, goat cheese, freshly baked flat bread, and copious amounts of olive oil are obligatory. The olive tree, a symbol of strength, history, and steadfastness for Palestinians, is an important component to any Palestinian home or plaza. Many such olive trees have been transplanted, much like their caretakers, from villages in the fertile hills of the West Bank and have had to adjust to the harsh arid climate of Jordan. To broach the subject of olives at the dinner table will likely elicit a story of origins, history, and flavor. One begins to wonder if the story is of the olive tree, or of the family tree; each growing in new soil.

In a Palestinian home rarely will people have their own plates, their own portions, their own silverware. Rather, food, like music, is a participatory dish collectively eaten and savored in large quantities. Meals, like performances, last well into the night bringing family members together in one of the most routine celebrations of "living history." My lessons in the kitchen with Flora Khoury were no different than my lessons on the patio with her sons playing music. We all had the same goal of bringing people together into a communal moment. To eat with family, much the same in music, is to savor life, to remember a common history, and to affirm a shared future. Upon finishing a great meal there is no greater sign of respect in Palestinian life than the proverb, "*Bainna khubz wa malah*" ("Between us is only bread and salt"). Those who have broken bread together share a bond known and defined within the inner sanctity of the family, and hence share in the preparation of a great recipe for "living history."

"*Sahtain!*" Traditional Arabic toast before eating, "To your health!"
"*'Ala 'Albek!*" Traditional Arabic response, "Upon your heart!"

RECOMMENDED LISTENING

El-Funoun. *Zaghareed: Music from the Palestinian Holy Land*. Sounds True Direct, 1999. 109.

FOR FURTHER INFORMATION

Barghouti, Mourid. 2000. *I Saw Ramallah*. New York: Anchor Books.
Kaschl, Elke. 2003. *Dance and Authenticity in Israel and Palestine: Performing the Nation*. Leiden: Brill.
http://www.el-funoun.org

SUWAYDA PROVINCE, SYRIA
Kathleen Hood

A dinner for guests feeds the whole village.

Menu: *Tabikh 'ala Banadura* (Cracked Wheat with Lamb and Tomatoes), *Salatit Laban wa Khiyar* (Yogurt and Cucumber Salad), *Salatit Khass* (Lettuce Salad), *Zaytun* (Green or Black Olives), *Khubz 'Arabi* (Arab Bread), and *Shay Aswad* (Black Tea).

Preparation Time: Approximately 1½ hours.

Cooking Process: For this meal you will need a Dutch oven or 6 qt. pot with lid and a 3 qt. saucepan or a large frying pan. Make the *Tabikh 'ala Banadura* first, then make the two salads. Put the olives in a shallow bowl on the table. Just before serving, heat some Arab bread for a few minutes in the oven or over the flames of a gas stove. Serves six people.

The Recipes

TABIKH 'ALA BANADURA (CRACKED WHEAT WITH LAMB AND TOMATOES)

2½ t. salt

4 c. *burghul* #3 (cracked wheat)

2 c. chopped onions

4 c. diced or chopped fresh tomatoes

¼ c. olive oil

1 lb. ground or minced meat, preferably lamb

½ t. black pepper

½–1 t. Aleppo red pepper (more or less to taste)

¾ t. cinnamon

3 T melted *samni/samn* (*ghee* or clarified butter)

Add ¾ t. salt to 6 c. water and bring to a boil in the 6 qt. pot or Dutch oven. Rinse and drain 4 c. *burghul* and add to boiling water. Bring back to a boil, then turn heat to the lowest possible setting and cover. Cook for about 25–30 minutes, or until done. (This process is similar to cooking rice; the cooked grains should be fluffy and cooked through. In Syria, the cooking process is somewhat different, but does not lend itself to measurements. The end result is basically the same.) While heating the water, chop 2 c. onions, and dice 4 c. tomatoes. Heat ¼ c. olive oil in the 3-qt. saucepan or large frying pan, add onions, and cook over medium heat for about 2–3 minutes, or until they start becoming translucent. Add 1 lb. ground meat and brown. Add diced tomatoes, 1¾ t. salt, ½ t. black pepper, ½–1 t. red pepper, and ¾ t. cinnamon, and cook until the meat is done. Add the meat and tomato mixture to the *burghul* and heat through. Adjust seasonings and just before serving, mix in 3 T *samni*. (Note: Meat is rather expensive in Syria and is used in this dish primarily as a flavoring. The recipe can also be made meatless, substituting 2 c. cooked garbanzo beans [*hummus* in Arabic] for the meat. In fact, it is often served this way.)

**Close-up of *Salatit Laban wa Khiyar* (shredded cucumbers for Syrian cucumber/yogurt salad).
Photo by Sean Williams.**

Salatit Laban wa Khiyar (Yogurt and Cucumber Salad)

1–2 hothouse cucumbers (3–5 Persian cucumbers)

32 oz. (2 lb.) yogurt

2–4 cloves garlic, depending on size and your preference

¾ to 1 t. salt

1–2 t. dried mint (more or less, to taste)

2 T olive oil (more or less, to taste)

Grate 1½ c. of unpeeled cucumbers (preferably Persian cucumbers) on the large-holed part of the grater and place in a large salad bowl. Add 32 oz. yogurt and mix well. Grind 2–4 cloves of garlic in a mortar (you can also mince garlic or use a garlic press) with ¾–1 t. salt and add with 1–2 t. dried mint and 2 T olive oil to the cucumber/yogurt mixture. Blend thoroughly.

Salatit Khass (Lettuce Salad)

1 large head romaine lettuce
2 garlic cloves
¼ t. salt
⅓ c. lemon juice
¼ c. olive oil
pepper to taste

Wash, dry, and dice lettuce (into ½" squares). For the dressing, grind 2 cloves of garlic in a mortar (you can also mince garlic or use a garlic press) with ¼ t. salt and mix with ⅓ c. lemon juice and ¼ c. olive oil. Add pepper to taste. Toss dressing with the lettuce before serving.

Zaytun (Green or Black Olives)

½ lb. green or black olives

Arrange an array of green or black olives on a plate so that the dinner guests may select the number of olives they prefer.

Khubz ʿArabi (Arab Bread)

1 12-piece package of Arab bread

Slice the individual pieces of Arab bread in half and arrange on a plate on two sides of the table.

Shay Aswad (Black Tea)

After the meal, serve hot black tea sweetened with sugar. (In Syria, tea is served in clear tea glasses.)

Eating and Singing in Suwayda, Syria

Food in Syria varies somewhat by region, although many dishes are common all over and indeed are found throughout the entire Levant region, since the food cultures are not necessarily defined by national boundaries. The recipes above are from Suwayda Province in southern Syria, but the main dish is also eaten in some of the mountain villages of Lebanon. The meatless version can be found in northern Jordan. The *burghul* featured in the main dish is commonly eaten in rural wheat-growing areas; but in the urban centers of Syria, rice, an imported product, is the preferred grain. *Burghul* is versatile: it is used in simple, everyday dishes, but it is also the main ingredient of the *mansaf*, the principal dish for weddings and other festive occasions (*mansaf* is also served in northern Jordan, but is made with rice instead of *burghul*). A dish of Bedouin origin, the *mansaf* consists of a large platter of *burghul* cooked in a yogurt sauce and topped with lamb and *kibbi* (oval-shaped balls of a *burghul* and meat dough filled with ground lamb). Versions of the *salatit laban wa khiyar* (yogurt and cucumber salad) can be found throughout the Middle East. People eat it as a side dish, or sometimes spoon it over the *tabikh ʻala banadura* as a sauce. The *salatit khass* (lettuce salad) is very simple, and makes use of romaine lettuce, which is commonly found in the markets in Suwayda.

The flat Arab bread made from wheat is a staple at every meal throughout Syria, whether it be the urban Arab flatbread made with refined white flour or the very large (about 2 feet in diameter), paper-thin loaves of wholewheat bread (*mulawwah*) found in rural areas. Pieces of bread are used to scoop up food during meals—the only other utensils found on a typical village table would be spoons. Dishes of black or green olives accompany most meals, and there is even a saying that "the olive is the king of the dining table." Finally, heavily sweetened hot black tea is served at the end of the meal. Although there are many varieties of sweets in Syria, dessert is not typically served following a meal.

In Suwayda Province, there is a Druze majority, with small minorities of Christians and Muslim Bedouin. While conducting field research for my dissertation on the Druze wedding song repertoire, I lived in Suwayda Province with Dr. Naʻim Abu ʻAssaf and his family. His wife, Hind, taught me how to cook the typical dishes eaten in the area. I watched, took notes, and often helped her prepare meals for their family. Breakfast may be a quick sandwich of *labni* (yogurt cheese, available in Middle Eastern grocery stores in the United States) rolled up in Arab bread. Another quick (and high calorie) breakfast may be a sandwich of sesame *halwa* rolled up in bread spread with butter. A more leisurely breakfast may include eggs (boiled or scrambled), tomatoes, cucumbers, and olives. The recipes above represent a typical lunch meal, and indeed we ate this combination of items various times during my stay. Later in the evening, a little meal is eaten that may consist of leftovers from lunch, some hard-boiled eggs, or possibly a potato salad moistened with yogurt and olive oil instead of mayonnaise. Of course, no meal in Syria is complete without the flat loaves of Arab bread.

Music is part of daily, public life in Syria, particularly in the form of commercial urban recordings that are blared from stores and heard on buses. The advent of satellite television in the area has opened the region to a wide variety of music from around the world. During my stay there, the family's television viewing included a Handel opera, a taped performance of Umm Kulthum singing "al-Atlal," and music videos from the United States and the Middle East. The range of available videos is quite remarkable. For example, a video by the Red Hot Chili Peppers might be followed by one from Egyptian superstar ʻAmr Diab. Daily meals, however, are often rather silent, since people generally do not listen to music while eating and even conversation is limited to some degree. I noticed a somewhat austere attitude toward eating, and men in particular tend to eat very quickly and leave the table as soon as they finish. On the other hand, socializing with one's friends and neighbors after work is one of the main pastimes in Suwayda, and combines eating, drinking, and conversation.

Although men and women now will often get together in mixed groups, segregation of the sexes was, and still is, common in many areas of life. Women entertain other women in one room of the house, while men generally receive their visitors in the *madafa*, or reception room. A man serves his visitors *qahwa murra*—bitter, unsweetened Arab coffee flavored with cardamom. The ritual preparation and serving of this coffee by men is one of the main symbols of hospitality in much of the Levant. Originally a Bedouin custom, both Christians and Druzes in Suwayda Province have adopted this practice. Men prepare the coffee in a ritual fashion that involves roasting the beans and then grinding them in a mortar called *mihbaj* that doubles as a percussion instrument. While grinding the coffee, the long pestle is struck against the side of the mortar in a rhythmic pattern. Coffee is such an integral part of Druze life that *qasa'id*, sung or recited poems, have been written about it. Music is connected to the *madafa* in another way: evening poetry parties are often held in the *madafa*, and poets and poet-singers accompanying themselves on the one-stringed fiddle (*rababa*) participate. Music, coffee, and the *madafa* are thus inextricably linked to one another (see Racy 1996 and Hood 2006).

Since the latter part of the twentieth century, houses are often built without a *madafa*, so couples may entertain guests in their living room. In this case, the wife does the serving. She first offers small cups of Turkish coffee, which may be accompanied by cookies or various other sweets, such as *baqlawa* (commonly known in the United States as baklava). After a while, she may serve dishes of watermelon, pears, or grapes or, in the winter, biscuits or mixed nuts. One of the main beverages served in Suwayda province and parts of Lebanon is *maté*, a tea-like, Argentinean beverage (brought back by visiting emigrant family members who resettled in South America). Finally, toward the end of the visit, another round of Turkish coffee may be served. Turkish coffee is also known as *qahwa hilwa* (sweet coffee), as opposed to the bitter Arab coffee discussed above. Not a traditional part of Suwayda culture, it has become popular since the latter part of the twentieth century because it is quick and easy to prepare.

Food is combined with music mainly at weddings, and each is an indispensable part of the festivities. There are few instruments in Suwayda, and performative traditions in the area generally combine unaccompanied communal singing with dancing. Although in the past the various events relating to the wedding lasted several days, now the festivities generally are compressed into one or two days. At a typical traditional wedding ceremony, the groom and his entourage arrive singing at the bride's home where her friends and family are singing and playing frame drums. The groom then "takes" his new bride in a procession (*zaffa*) to his parents' home. This procession is characterized by singing and dancing, the men singing one song and the women another. Shortly after arrival at the groom's home, the main meal, the *mansaf*, is served. Multitudes of large platters are carried to the eating area by groups of men who may sing a *hida'* (a very ancient type of song, originally used to drive camels). Since the men and women eat separately, each group can continue singing and dancing while the other eats. After this meal, people go to visit their friends and families. During the evening, they return to the wedding to sing and dance traditional songs.

RECOMMENDED LISTENING

Diab, 'Amr. 2000. *Tamally Maak*. EMI Music Arabic. 07243 528264 21.
Fairuz. *The Very Best of Fairuz, Vol. 1*. VDL CD 501.
Umm Kulthum. *al-Atlal*. Sono Cairo. SONO 101.

FOR FURTHER INFORMATION

Betts, Robert Brenton. 1988. *The Druze*. New Haven, CT; London: Yale University Press.
Hood, Kathleen. 2006. *Music in Druze Life: Ritual Values and Performance Practice*. London: Druze Heritage Foundation (including CD).
Racy, Ali Jihad. 1996. Heroes, Lovers, and poet-singers: The Bedouin ethos in music of the Arab Near-East. *Journal of American Folklore* 109(434):404–424.

IRAN
Niloofar Mina

In the garden of life there is honey and there are also sour grapes.

Menu: *Mast u Khyar* (Cucumber and Yogurt), *Kashk u Bademjoon* (Whey and Eggplant), *Noon-u Panir u Sabri* (Feta, Mint, Walnuts, and Bread), *Chicken Tah Chin* (Saffroned Yogurt Rice and Chicken), *Shirazi Salad* (Cucumber, Tomatoes, and Onions with Lemon/Olive Oil Dressing), *Khyar Shoor* (Sour Pickles), *Dooq* (Salty Yogurt and Sparkling Water), *Bastani-ye Irani* (Rosewater Ice Cream with Pistachios), Cookies, and Fruit. Serve with *dooq*, Shiraz wine, and tea.

Preparation Time: 3 hours, not counting the time to soak the rice.

Cooking Process: Start soaking the rice approximately 6 hours before you would like to eat. Then prepare the eggplant dish, the chicken, and the cucumber dishes. Arrange the sour pickles and cheese/mint/walnut appetizer before your guests arrive. Freeze the ice cream before you start eating. Serves six people.

The Recipes

MAST U KHYAR (CUCUMBER AND YOGURT)—APPETIZER

2 large cucumbers
1 bunch scallions
½ c. fresh mint
1 qt. yogurt
salt
½ c. walnuts
⅓ c. raisins

Mince 2 large cucumbers with 1 bunch of scallions, and finely chop ½ c. fresh mint. Mix together in a bowl with 1 qt. of yogurt. Add salt to taste. Add ½ c. walnuts and ⅓ c. raisins, and more salt if necessary.

KASHK U BADEMJOON (WHEY AND EGGPLANT)—APPETIZER

salt
2 large eggplants
3 T olive oil
5 cloves garlic
1 c. mint
1 c. *kashk* (whey)

Peel, cube, and salt 2 large eggplants and set aside for 30 minutes. Drain the eggplants and steam them until they are semicooked. (Note: To steam in a medium-size pot bring 2 c. water to boil, place a metal steamer in the bottom of the pot, and place the eggplants on top.) Drain the eggplants and fry them in olive oil until they are brown. Mince and brown 5 cloves of garlic

146

in olive oil. Brown 1 cup finely minced mint, then mix all the ingredients together in a bowl. To the mixture add a cup of *kashk* (whey) to taste. (Note: You can replace *kashk* with *lebneh* [Arab yogurt]). Brown 2 T dried mint and two cloves of garlic to decorate the top of the *kashk u bademjoon*.

Noon-u Panir u Sabri (Feta, Mint, Walnuts, and Bread)—Appetizer

½ lb. feta cheese
2 c. fresh mint
¼ c. walnuts
Barbari bread

Arrange ½ lb. feta cheese, 2 c. fresh mint and ¼ c. walnuts on a dinner plate. Serve with Barbari bread (also known as Afqan bread) or Lavash bread.

Chicken Tah Chin (Saffroned Yogurt Rice and Chicken)

5 c. basmati rice
pinch of saffron
1 large onion, chopped
4 T olive oil
1½ lb. boneless chicken pieces
4 egg yolks
1½ c. yogurt

Soak 5 c. basmati rice in salted water for 5 hours. Grind a large pinch of saffron and mix with 4 T boiling water in a small bowl; set aside. Drain the rice and then boil it until the rice is semicooked. Drain again and rinse the rice. In a medium-size pot, fry a large onion in olive oil, place boneless cubed chicken at the center of the pot and allow it to brown on medium heat. Add 2 c. boiling water and 2 T saffron water. Allow the chicken to cook. Take the chicken out and discard the onions. Set aside 3 c. semicooked rice. Mix the rest of the semicooked rice in a bowl with 4 egg yolks, 1½ c. yogurt and saffron/water mixture. Pour 2 T olive oil at the bottom of a nonstick pot. Add ¼ c. water. Add the rice/egg mixture, cover the pot with a towel, and place the lid on top of it, letting it cook over low-medium heat for 10 minutes. Then open the pot and place the chicken inside the rice. Add ½ c. water. Cover the pot and let it steam for an additional 20 minutes or until a thick brown layer of *tah dig* (crunchy golden brown rice) is formed at the bottom of the pot. In a different (nonstick) pot, steam the rest of the semicooked rice with oil and ½ c. water; cover it with a towel and then place the lid over it. Let it steam for 20 minutes on medium heat. The towel will absorb the moisture and create a dry steamed rice. To serve: place a large platter on top of the pot containing the rice/chicken mixture and slowly drop the rice cake on it, upside down. You will have a large yellow cake shaped rice, topped with golden *tah dig*. Place the steamed white rice on a separate large serving dish, then carefully place the rice cake on top of it.

SHIRAZI SALAD (CUCUMBER, TOMATOES, AND ONIONS WITH LEMON/OLIVE OIL DRESSING)

2 large cucumbers
3 medium tomatoes
1 small onion
2 T olive oil
1 lemon, juiced
salt

Dice 2 large cucumbers, 3 medium tomatoes, and 1 small onion. Mix the ingredients in bowl. Add 2 T olive oil and the juice of 1 lemon to taste, then chill for a couple of hours. Add salt to taste before serving with the main meal.

KHYAR SHOOR (SOUR PICKLES)

2 c. small sour pickles

Arrange 2 c. small sour pickles in 2 bowls and make them accessible to all the guests.

DOOQ (SALTY YOGURT AND SPARKLING WATER)

3 c. yogurt
½ c. fresh mint
salt
2 qt. sparkling water

Mix 3 c. yogurt, ½ c. fresh mint and salt to taste in a pitcher, then add a small amount of sparkling water to make a smooth mixture. Add more sparkling water to reach your desired consistency. Chill and serve over ice, topped with a sprig of fresh mint.

BASTANI-YE IRANI (ROSEWATER ICE CREAM WITH PISTACHIOS)

½ c. heavy cream
3 t. Persian rosewater
1 qt. vanilla ice cream
¼ c. roughly crushed unsalted pistachios

Pour a small layer of heavy cream on a flat surface and freeze for 2 hours. Mix 3 t. Persian rosewater with 1 qt. vanilla ice cream. Remove the frozen cream from the freezer and smash it, adding it to the ice cream mixture with ¼ c. crushed pistachios.

CHAY AND SWEETS (TEA WITH NABAT, GAZ, OR SUGAR CUBES)

Make an attractive arrangement of cookies on one platter and place fresh fruits in a bowl. A typical Persian fruit bowl always contains thin Persian cucumbers as well as apples and oranges. Additionally, seasonal fruits are added to the bowl; these may include pomegranates, persimmons, sour cherries, peaches, and apricots. Serve tea in small tea gold-rimmed hourglass-shaped tea glasses (*kamar barik*) with china saucers. Serve *nabat* (hard candy), *gaz*, or sugar cubes on the side.

Cooking from the Heart

I started cooking Iranian food a couple of months after I moved to the United States. Although I was 22 years old, I had never been allowed to cook in my mother's kitchen and had no cooking skills. But here I was in New York, in charge of my own life, and I had to eat! Thus, I began experimenting with Iranian cooking and happily noticed that I already knew a good deal about Iranian food preparation. For example, I knew all about the significance of *piyaz daq* (fried onions). My mother and grandmother always cooked meat and chicken in a bed of crispy fried onions as they believed *piyaz daq* removes the fleshy smell (*booye zokhm*) of meats.

I also knew about the significance of *polo* (steamed rice) in Iranian diet. Almost all Iranian dishes include rice. When served with *khoresht* (stew) or *kabab* (barbequed meat), *polo* has to be

Spices at Tehran's bazaar (Tehran, Iran). Photo by Niloofar Mina.

Women on their lunch break (Iran). Photo by Niloofar Mina.

fluffy and dry. If overcooked or understeamed the rice becomes sticky (*shefte*) and is no longer deemed fit to be served in public. *Polo* is always accompanied with *tah dig*, a crunchy layer of rice that is formed at the bottom of the cooking pot as a result of the steaming process. As a lifelong consumer of *tah dig*, I knew it should be prepared in nonstick pots while the semicooked rice is steamed over very low heat for a long period. Dedicated cooks often place a thin layer of bread or potatoes to enhance the quantity and quality of *tah diq*. I noticed that while in the Iran of my youth most families did not ordinarily bother with this extra effort, immigrant Iranians frequently serve their *polo* with extra crispy potato *tah dig*.

One my favorite activities in Iranian cooking is the preparation of herbs and vegetables. Iranian women usually perform the ritual as they select, buy, wash, cut, chop, and fry large quantities of cilantro, parsley, dill, mint, and basil. These are the basic ingredients of many Iranian dishes, and preparing them is among periodic tasks of most Iranian women. They usually sit on the floor of their kitchens or family rooms, with a large pile of herbs spread in front of them. They then pick the herbs, separate their stems from the leaves, one by one, before they can wash and ultimately chop them. Herb cleaning sessions are warm and intimate affairs as women sit together and chat about their lives.

In my family, dinner parties (*mehmooni*) are usually held for family and close friends. Upon arrival, the daughter of the family serves tea along with cookies and fruits. Guests sit in the living room and quietly chat. Once everyone has gathered, cold drinks are brought in along with a large array of side dishes. Iranians tend to overload the table with an abundance of small foods to make everyone feel welcome. After dinner, guests usually separate along gender and generational lines.

Women usually help the host clear the table and wash the dishes. After serving dessert they usually sit down and sip their tea and chat about family and friends. Men gather on a different corner. Some play *takhte nard* (backgammon) while shouting and screaming. Others speak animatedly about politics and social issues. If the topic is of interest to women, a loud and lively discussion ensues.

Outside good conversation, poetry recitation is one of the most prestigious recreational activities enjoyed by Iranians. Among poetic recreational activities is Fal-e Hafez (alt. spelling, Hafiz): the use of Hafez's poems to predict or interpret an individual's fortunes. Fal-e Hafez is taken as the master of the ceremony makes a wish on behalf of an individual and then opens the book of Hafez's poetry at random to read the poem printed on the page. The guests then try to interpret the poem to shed light on the individual's fortune. Fal-e Hafez in translation is available online at http://www.falehafez.com.

During my recent trip to Iran I noticed that these days a musical segment is often included in family gatherings. In my aunts' house I noticed that the older generation often takes turns singing nostalgic songs while invited guests bring their instruments and play. I also noticed that mediated music was played back during and after dinner. It was especially intriguing to observe middle aged women laughing and dancing to Arabic and Iranian pop songs while the younger generation looked on with a bit of embarrassment, and men had their serious conversations.

RECOMMENDED LISTENING

Below is a list of music I used in our family gatherings last winter in Tehran. You will notice CDs of popular music produced in Iran as well as in the diaspora. Also included are recordings of Kurdish music, as my mother's side of the family is entirely Kurdish. To order the CDs, a quick search of the recording company will yield the Web address.

Popular Music

Arian. *Va Amma Eshq*. Tehran: Taraneh Sharghee Co.
Assar, Alireza. *Molaye Eshgh*. Tehran: Iran Gam Co., 2004.
Helen. *Your Eyes*. Encino, CA: Avang Music Company, 2003.
Mohammad Esfahani. *Barakat*. Tehran: Iran Seda, 2005.
Rahnama, Mani. *The Song Is Over*. Tehran: Avangtar, 2004.

Traditional and Regional Musics

Bahmani, M., A. Qorbani, and A. Nabiollahi. *Kurdish Dances*. Tehran: Mahoor Institute of Culture and Art, 2003.
Ebrahimi, Amirullah Shah. *Sama: Tanbur Music of Kermanshah*. Tehran: Mahoor Institute of Culture and Art, 1999.
Margiri, Qolam Ali. *Zar Songs*. Tehran: Mahoor Institute of Culture and Art, 2004.
Shahriyari, Arash. *Elegies for the Sun*. Tehran: Hozeye Honari, 2004.
Shahriyari, Mohammad Reza, and Kalhor, Keyhan. *Desert, Silence, Night*. Vancouver, Canada: Rayan.

FOR FURTHER INFORMATION

http://www.gooya.com (A popular portal to cultural and political site on Iran and its diaspora).
http://iranian.com (Voicing the Iranian Diaspora).
http://www.tavoosmag.com/english/index.asp (A bilingual art quarterly published in Iran).
http://www.iranartists.org/en/ (Iranian Artists organization).

7

South and Central America

BOLIVIA

Thalia Rios

The angrier the cook, the spicier the dish.

Menu: *Palta con Llajua* (Avocado with Uncooked Salsa), *Sopa de Quinoa* (Quinoa Soup), *Picante de Lengua* (Beef Tongue in Chili Sauce), *Arroz* (Steamed Rice), and *Empanadas de Lacayote* (Squash Turnovers). Serve dinner with soft drinks or fruit juice.

Preparation Time: 3 hours (plus 4 hours in advance to simmer the beef tongue).

Cooking Process: Start preparing the beef tongue early, as it will need to simmer for 4 hours, cool, and be added to cooking vegetables. Prepare the vegetables for the other dishes. Prepare the empanadas but do not place in the oven until you are ready to eat. One hour before you would like to eat, start the soup, then the vegetables for the beef tongue, then the rice. Finally, make the avocados and salsa. When you sit down to eat, place the empanadas in the oven. Serve the dessert with tea or coffee. Serves six people.

The Recipes

Palta con Llajua (Avocado with Uncooked Salsa)

3 large roma tomatoes
1 serrano (or jalapeño) chili pepper
½ c. cilantro
3 garlic cloves
⅛ c. diced onion
salt
3 ripe Haas avocados

For the *llajua*: cut 3 large, ripe roma tomatoes into chunks and place in a blender with 1 serrano (or jalapeño) chili pepper, ½ c. cilantro (if desired), 3 garlic cloves, and ⅛ c. diced onion. Blend until it becomes a sauce; salt to taste. Cut 3 ripe Haas avocados in half and remove the pits. Carefully scoop out each entire half avocado and place each half on individual plates. Spoon *llajua* over each half avocado. Use the remaining *llajua* to serve with the soup and main dish.

Sopa de Quinoa (Quinoa Soup)

½ c. diced onion
½ medium acorn squash
½ small green pepper, diced
1 T vegetable oil
1 t. ground *aji colorado*
½ t. black pepper
1½ t. ground cumin
1 t. dried oregano
¾ c. quinoa
salt

154

Llajua (Bolivian salsa). Photo by Cary Black.

Sopa de quinoa (quinoa soup, Bolivia). Photo by Sean Williams.

In a large pot, toast ½ c. diced onions, ½ of a medium green acorn squash (keep the other half for dessert) that has been peeled and cut into small chunks, and the diced green bell pepper in 1 T vegetable oil with 1 t. ground *aji colorado* (ground *chili guajillo* is a good substitute), ½ t. black pepper, 1½ t. ground cumin, and 1 t. dried oregano leaves. Add 7 c. of water and ¾ c. quinoa to the pot and bring to a boil. Reduce heat to medium-low, cover, and simmer until the grains swell and are soft (about 20 minutes). Add salt only after the grains have softened; otherwise they will remain hard. Adjust the seasonings to taste. Serve the soup with *llajua* (see recipe, above).

PICANTE DE LENGUA (BEEF TONGUE IN CHILI SAUCE)

3–4 lb. fresh beef tongue
4 t. ground *aji colorado* (dried red chili)
2 t. ground cumin
1 t. dried oregano
black pepper
½ c. vegetable oil
1 medium red onion, thinly sliced
½ c. fresh or frozen peas
1 medium carrot, diced
1 medium ripe tomato
4 new potatoes, quartered
5 cloves garlic, sliced
salt

After rinsing, place beef tongue in a large pot. Cover tongue with cold water and bring to a boil, then reduce heat and simmer, covered, until very tender (about 4 hours on a stovetop, or 5–6 hours in a crock pot on high). Once tender, remove tongue from pot and allow to cool, reserving 2–3 cups of the resulting broth to use for the sauce. Peel the tough outer covering of the tongue (it should peel easily) and slice the tongue into thin pieces, then set aside. In another large pot, fry 4 t. ground *aji colorado* (or ground *chili guajillo*), 2 t. ground cumin, 1 t. dried oregano leaves, and ½ t. black pepper until fragrant. Add ½ c. vegetable oil and fry the red onion, ½ c. fresh or frozen peas, diced carrot, tomato, potatoes, and sliced garlic. Fry, stirring, until the vegetables are soft (about 15 minutes). Add the reserved broth and the pieces of sliced tongue and simmer for another 15–20 minutes. Adjust spices and add salt to taste. Serve with white rice and *llajua* (see recipe, above).

ARROZ (STEAMED RICE)

3 c. white rice
bouillon cube (optional)

Bring 6 c. water to a boil; rinse 3 cups of white rice and add to the water. You can add a bouillon cube to the cooking water, or you can add salt to taste. Reduce heat and simmer, covered, until the rice is done (about 20 minutes). Fluff with a fork, then let sit, covered, for another 10 minutes.

EMPANADAS DE LACAYOTE (SQUASH TURNOVERS)

2 c. powdered sugar
½ medium acorn squash
1½ c. sugar
1½ t. ground cinnamon
1 t. ground clove
2 c. flour
½ c. butter
salt
2 t. baking powder
1 egg

In a bowl, mix 2 c. powdered sugar with 4–5 T water (tablespoon by tablespoon) until you have a thick glaze; set aside. Take the second half of the green acorn squash (leftover from the soup) and cut it into small chunks. Cook squash in a saucepan covered with water on medium heat until soft (about 15 minutes). Drain squash and (in the same saucepan) combine with 1½ c. sugar, 1½ t. ground cinnamon, and 1 t. ground clove. Cook mixture another 15–20 minutes until soft and thick. Remove squash filling from heat and transfer to a bowl to cool. In a large bowl, cut together 2 c. flour with ½ c. butter or margarine until the mixture is crumbly (like making a pie crust). Add 1 t. salt, 2 t. baking powder, and 1 egg. Slowly mix in ½ c. warm water, little by little, until you can form a rough dough. Transfer the dough to a floured surface and knead briefly until smooth. Roll dough out with a rolling pin until it is about ⅛" thick. Cut dough out into rounds; depending on the size of the cutting tool, the quantity of the empanadas will vary. Stretch out each round slightly and fill with the squash mixture, making sure not to overfill. Fold each round in half and crimp the edges of the pastry tightly to prevent the mixture from flowing out during baking. Bake the empanadas at 350°F until golden (about 20–25 minutes). Cool and bathe the empanadas with the sugar glaze. Serve with tea or coffee.

Buen Provecho!

This menu includes dishes typically associated with the highland and valley regions of Bolivia. The use of *llajua* is ubiquitous, whether served as a dip for bread or spooned over salads, soups, and main dishes. Quinoa, a nutritious grain full of protein, minerals, and fiber, is a popular addition to soups. Special Sunday lunches, which are usually more extravagant than daily fare, often feature *picantes* (spicy dishes made with *aji colorado*, a flavorful, dried red chili) as the main attraction. *Picante de lengua* is a good example. Finally, the *empanadas de lacayote*, with a sweet squash filling, are normally served for teatime (between lunch and dinner), but work well as a dessert course. *Buen provecho!* ("Good appetite!")

La Paz, the capital city of Bolivia, is where we spent one year during my husband Fernando Rios's fieldwork. We looked forward to sampling local dishes and were fortunate to have experienced food and music in a variety of colorful contexts. A common urban meal pattern consists of a light breakfast of coffee and bread, a midmorning *salteña* (meat pie snack), a heavy multicourse lunch, teatime pastries in the late afternoon, and a light dinner. While having a "set lunch" of *entrada* (appetizer), *sopa* (soup), *segundo* (main dish), and *postre* (dessert) at a local restaurant, we would hear the latest Latin hits and Bolivian folkloric music, which blared from speakers and often drowned out our conversation. The other patrons, who were savoring the heavily meat-and-starch-centered main plates, didn't appear to be bothered by the volume, which seemed to enhance the animated lunchtime chatter. Radio or recorded music constantly played at eateries, just like at many American restaurants.

The main stretch of tourist shops are located on the steep Calle Sagárnaga where vendors sell items like beautiful textiles, silver jewelry, Andean folkloric music CDs, and instruments. There are a few music *peñas* on this street that offer dinner shows where patrons can dine on Bolivian fare, such as *chairo* soup (with lamb meat and dehydrated potato), *picante de pollo* (spicy chili pepper chicken dish) and, at one place: llama steaks! Live Andean folkloric groups, with their characteristic panpipes and alpaca wool ponchos, entertain diners with "classic" tunes such as *"El Cóndor Pasa"* and *"Dos Palomitas."*

When I think about shopping at the popular Mercado Uyustus, food and music always come to mind. This vast, open-air market, located away from the tourist area, staggers the mind with its incredible variety of goods for sale and its incessant throng of visitors and vendors. I remember holding a newly purchased bedspread over my head, patiently inching down the street, while being pressed in all directions by the multitude of shoppers. I tried to avoid knocking over the towering glasses of *mocochinchi* (dried peach drink) and other *refrescos* that vendors had so artfully arranged in a way that, to me, looked like I. M. Pei's glass pyramid at the Louvre. Food vendors sold snacks on foot, in stalls, on the ground, and even perched in the middle of the already narrow pedestrian path! The sights and smells of sizzling *chorizo* sausages, red, spicy, greasy and nestled in a large silver pan of boiling oil, grabbed the attention of worn shoppers who then willingly stopped for a taste. Meander through another section of the market and you could take in the fresh aroma of papayas, sweet mangos, and dusty potatoes that mingled with the musty odor of recently slaughtered animal parts. Swirling around the entire sensuous experience of the market were the competing strains and pulsing rhythms of Bolivian *cumbias* (the *cumbia* is a Colombian genre), folkloric music, and international pop hits that battled from nearby stalls full of CDs and cassette tapes.

Food and music were always present during holidays and *fiestas*. *Carnaval* in February with its *coplas* (song duels) and parades coincides with the season for *choclo* (starchy, large-grained, white corn). Local teatime shops would begin selling *humintas,* and we savored every bite of this cornhusk-wrapped corn casserole, which could be steamed or baked, but was usually filled with *quesillo* (fresh cheese) and studded with raisins and licorice-scented anise seeds. Wandering the streets near a *presterio* (neighborhood *fiesta*) where dancers and musicians were practicing for the big festival of *Gran Poder*, a stranger might hand you a beer and a *salteña*. The Bolivian version of the *empanada*, the juicy *salteña* drips its delectable contents of beef or chicken, potato, oregano, olive, egg, raisin, and chili pepper all down the front of your shirt as brass bands belting out the jerking rhythms of the *morenada* dance mesmerize you with their powerful energy. I will always remember the spectacle of the masks and hundreds of shiny costumed dancers who swayed to the sounds of voices, brass bands, and noisy *matracas* (idiophones) during the *Gran Poder* festival in May. I'll also never forget the tempting smell wafting from rows of charcoal pits that vendors had pitched along the parade route to entice spectators with *chorizos, anticuchos* (marinated slices of beef heart), and *chicharrones* (chicha [alcoholic corn drink]-dipped, pan-fried pieces of pork or chicken). Makeshift tables held plastic bowls of yellow, green, and red *salsas* that people eagerly slathered on the glistening, grilled meat. The aromatic, thick gray smoke filled the air and provided an otherworldly backdrop to the devil-masked dancers and smartly dressed musicians who paraded by. For the *Fiesta de Todos Los Santos* (All Saints Day) in November, we traveled to the nearby rural town of Patacamaya where we listened to musicians playing *pinkillos*, cane duct flutes associated with the rainy season. With the high-pitched music in the background, we wandered through the cemetery where we saw *tanta-wawas* ("bread babies") placed on gravestones. Inside the tents, elaborately decorated altars displayed pictures of the deceased as well as plates of the departed person's favorite food. Mourners passed around little, figure-shaped breads made of corn, while saying a blessing to the spirits of their loved ones.

Back in the city, we would occasionally attend a soccer match at the Hernando Siles Stadium. Before a late afternoon game, we liked to pick up some teatime snacks of *llauchas* (spicy, cheese-filled bread) and *api morado* (sweet, purple corn beverage). As we entered the stadium, dozens of snack vendors greeted us with cauldrons of the ubiquitous *chorizos*, crispy-skinned *chicharrones*, and *pasankalla* (caramel-coated corn puffs). Sitting on the cold, hard stone benches, luckily having just bought styrofoam pads that feel okay for about half an hour, the momentum of hundreds of fellow spectators leaping to their feet swept us out of our seats as we listened to the crowd begin singing the Bolivian National Anthem. Vendors, weighed down by baskets, yelled out guttural groans of "sandwich, sandwich, sandwich" to advertise the cold roast pork and pickled vegetable *sandwich de chola*, while others screamed "*empanada!*" in a nasally singsong fashion. Insults, cheers, chewing sounds, and conversation mixed with boisterous renditions of team songs and of the *cueca Viva mi Patria Bolivia* ("Long Live My Country Bolivia"), the unofficial national anthem, which never failed to rejuvenate the crowd.

From the spicy dishes of the *altiplano* to the distinctive corn pastries of the eastern lowlands, Bolivia has a richness of regional cuisine that we love to prepare and enjoy. We hope this menu set provides you with a glimpse into the wonderful food of Bolivia.

RECOMMENDED LISTENING

Bolivia Manta. *Wiñayataqui*, Auvidis. (France). AV 6504. (This Paris-based ensemble has made several fine recordings of their interpretations of rural Andean mestizo and indigenous musical traditions from Bolivia, Peru, and Ecuador.)

Kolla Marka. *Lo mejor*. Discolandia (Bolivia). TLDCD13885. (Based in La Paz, this group performs similar repertoire as Bolivia Manta.)

Sacambaya de Bolivia. *En el Alma de los Andes*. ARC (Germany). EUCD 1808. (This ensemble performs cosmopolitan versions of Andean music of the type most popular in the transnational "world music" milieu. Proceeds from Sacambaya's CD sales fund various humanitarian projects in rural Bolivia [Cochabamba].)

FOR FURTHER INFORMATION

http://www.boliviaweb.com

http://www.lonelyplanet.com/destinations/south_america/bolivia/

Buechler, Hans. 1980. *The Masked Media: Aymara Fiestas and Social Interaction in the Bolivian Highlands*. The Hague; New York; Paris: Mouton Publishers.

Klein, Herbert. 2003. *A Concise History of Bolivia*. Cambridge, UK: Cambridge University Press.

Sánchez, Walter. 2001. *Luzmila Patiño Festival: 30 Years of Cross-Cultural Encounters Through Music*. Geneva: Simon I. Patiño Foundation.

Stobart, Henry. 2000. "Bolivia." In *The Garland Handbook of Latin American Music*. Edited by Dale A. Olsen and Daniel E. Sheehy. New York: Garland Publishing: 326–343.

BRASÍLIA, BRAZIL
Jesse Samba Wheeler and Rosa Virgínia Melo

He who counts on the pan of another, risks not having dinner.

Menu: *Creme de Abóbora* (Creamy Squash Soup), *Salada* (Salad), *Couve* (Collard Greens), *Arroz Integral com Alga e Gergelim* (Brown Rice with Seaweed and Sesame), *Barquinhos de Beringela* (Eggplant Dinghies), *Creme de Papaya* (Papaya Mousse), and *Maçãs Recheadas com Tahine* (Tahine Apples).

Preparation Time: 2½ hours.

Cooking Process: If you are interested in an entirely vegan meal, you could either make the *maçãs recheadas* instead of the *creme de papaya*, or substitute soy- or rice-based "ice cream" for dairy-based ice cream in the *creme de papaya*. Prepare the *maçãs recheadas* early. Then begin preparing the rice, then the eggplant, then the soup, the collard greens, and the salad. Prepare the *creme de papaya* after dinner so that it is very fresh. Serve with cold, fresh pineapple juice that has been blended with mint and chilled. Serve hot *ban-cha* (toasted green tea) or *genmai-cha* (toasted rice green tea) after dinner. Serves six people.

The Recipes

CREME DE ABÓBORA (CREAMY SQUASH SOUP)

1 whole Japanese squash
2 c. vegetable stock
salt
½ t. nutmeg

Cut 1 whole, unpeeled Japanese squash (round with longitudinal furrows, green skin with orange spots, yellow-orange flesh—*abóbora japonesa*) in large chunks; discard seeds and steam until tender. Peel and discard skin. Blend with 2 c. vegetable stock. Place in saucepan over low heat. Add salt and nutmeg to taste. Add more stock if too thick. Serve hot.

SALADA (SALAD)

1 beet
2–3 carrots
1 turnip
½ lb. alfalfa sprouts
1 T tamari
2 T olive oil
1 lime (optional)

Grate 1 beet, 2–3 carrots, and 1 turnip. Place root vegetables and sprouts in four separate bowls. Dressing suggestion: Tamari and olive oil with optional lime. Serve cold.

Couve (Collard Greens)

1 large bunch fresh tender collard greens
1 lime, juiced
2 T olive oil
salt

Remove stems from 1 bunch of collard greens. Place leaves flat, one on top of the other, the largest on the bottom. Roll the pile up and beginning at the top (the leaves' tips) slice across, shaving strips as fine as possible. The delicacy of the leaves is necessary to avoid a chewy, bitter dish. Toss with juice from 1 lime, enough olive oil to lightly coat everything, and salt to taste. Serve cold. This salad can also be cooked with butter and garlic and omitting the lime juice, in which case it becomes the "national side dish" served with *feijoada* (see recipe for *feijoada* in Southeastern Brazil).

Arroz Integral com Alga e Gergelim (Brown Rice with Seaweed and Sesame)

3 c. rice
2 sheets of *nori* (tender, dried Japanese seaweed)
3 t. sesame seeds
salt

Bring 6 c. water to a boil. Rinse and add 3 c. rice; cover and simmer until tender (about 20 minutes). Fluff with a fork; let sit for another 10 minutes, covered. Cut 2 sheets of *nori* into 1"-square pieces. When rice is ready, let cool slightly, then add 3 t. sesame seeds, *nori*, and salt to taste. Mix well. (Note: If *nori* is added to hot rice, it shrinks.)

Barquinhos de Beringela (Eggplant Dinghies)

3 large eggplants
salt
1 large yellow onion, chopped
2 T olive oil
3 cloves garlic
10 roma tomatoes
12 scallions, chopped
1 bunch parsley, chopped
pepper

Slice 3 large eggplants in half vertically. Scoop out center of each half, making 6 "dinghies." Reserve the insides of the eggplants. Salt dinghies and reserved eggplant. Set aside. Sauté onion in 2 T olive oil, and when nearly clear, add 3 cloves of pressed garlic and sauté until transparent. In a separate saucepan, boil 10 whole ripe roma tomatoes. When their peels begin to wrinkle, remove tomatoes from water and peel. Chop tomatoes, return to pan and simmer for 10 minutes. Dry dinghies and their reserved filling with paper towel. Cut filling into cubes and add to tomatoes. Add onions and garlic to this mixture and simmer for 5 minutes. Add scallions, parsley, and pepper and salt to taste. Simmer for 5 more minutes. Remove from heat. In a large frying pan, sauté dinghies, covered, on both sides until soft; 2 minutes each side should be enough. Fill with tomato mixture and simmer, covered, for 3 minutes. Let stand for 20 minutes, keeping warm. Serve warm.

CREME DE PAPAYA (PAPAYA MOUSSE)

6 papayas
6 scoops vanilla ice cream
3 t. liqueur de cassis

Peel 6 papayas; remove and discard seeds. Blend papayas in blender with 6 scoops of vanilla ice cream. Serve in 6 small white or transparent bowls. Pour liqueur de cassis over mousse, perhaps ½ t. per person. Serve immediately.

MAÇÃS RECHEADAS COM TAHINE (TAHINE APPLES)

6 apples
4 T light tahine
2 T honey
⅜ t. cinnamon
salt

Wash 6 apples well. Remove tops by digging out with a paring knife; save tops. Core each apple with knife, but do not remove the bottom—you want an apple that can be filled. Dig out the seeds, etc. and a little extra as well, so as to make the space a little more generous. Mix 4 T light tahine, 2 T honey, ⅜ t. cinnamon, and ⅜ t. salt. Fill each apple with about 2 t. of the mixture, replace tops, wrap in foil, place on baking tray, and bake at 350°F for 30–40 minutes or until the apples are soft. They can be served either hot or at room temperature. I think the latter is tastier. Oven does not need to be preheated.

Hardcore Healthy on Brazil's Central Plateau

These recipes are from the capital city Brasília. It is a completely vegetarian meal, even vegan, except for the dessert (though we have included a vegan option). Inland and in the south, beef has been the center of Brazilian cuisine, served simply, as in the famous *churrasco* barbeque style, or in elaborate dishes from the state of Minas Gerais. In the north and all along the coast fish and seafood have been staples. Vegan and vegetarian food is still uncommon in many parts of the country and is often viewed as odd. Vegetarians are thought of as sacrificing pleasure by excluding meat, rather than enhancing it through a healthier, more varied approach to eating.

In Brasília, however, things are different. Located in the country's middle west, it is influenced by both the traditional meat and dairy culture of the surrounding, largely rural state of Goiás, and the cosmopolitan culinary diversity of a big city. Brasília is a new city (it was inaugurated in 1960) and, as such, does not have a long-standing culinary tradition like other regions. But, as it was settled by people from all over the country, as well as diplomats and scholars from other countries, the variety available is as great as that of São Paulo or Rio de Janeiro. Thus far the city's main contribution to the country's cuisine has been its vegetarian innovations and adaptations to favorite foods, such as the pork-beef-black-bean *feijoada*. What we have presented here are items that are readily available in vegetarian restaurants, and even in some standard ones.

The city's youth is reflected in the lack of long-standing musical traditions, too. But as with culinary traditions, settlers brought music from just about every part of the country. Thus, it is possible to hear performances of *chorinho* from Rio, *música caipira* from rural São Paulo, *axé music* from Bahia, *maracatu* from Pernambuco, *forró* and *repente* from the northeast, *calypso* from the north, and nationally popular styles like *samba, pagode, sertaneja*, jazz, reggae, blues, electronica, orchestral music, and *MPB* (*música popular brasileira*).Undoubtedly, Brasília is best known for its rock scene, which began shortly after the city's inauguration. The two are about the same age: in 1955, as the future site of the city was selected, Little Richard was recording "Tutti Frutti"; the inauguration of the city five years later coincided with the beginning of U.S. congressional investigations into payola. Besides being "the new thing" in the 1960s, rock'n'roll provided a neutral musical language for the city's early inhabitants, making collaboration easier. The first rock'n'roll band to have recorded seems to be the aptly named Os Primitivos, "The Primitives."

It was in the 1980s that the national rock scene boomed, and Brasília launched some of the era's most important bands, earning it the title "The Capital of Rock." Those early bands included Legião Urbana, Plebe Rude, Capital Inicial, and Os Paralamas do Sucesso. In the 1990s, Os Raimundos, Little Quail and the Mad Birds, and Cássia Eller succeeded in solidifying Brasília's fame.

Whereas punk rock was fierce in the 1980s and into the 1990s, the strongest wing of the rock scene these days is hardcore, including such variants as grindcore, prog metal, death metal, black metal, crossover, sludge, crust, metalcore, nü metal, and thrash metal (pronounced here as "trash"). What may shock people as much as the music itself is the "straight edge" discourse associated with much of hardcore music. The straight edge movement, like the music, is international, and wherever found, its members eschew drugs, alcohol, cigarettes, and behavior motivated by hate. Furthermore, they are often vegetarians or vegans. In South America generally, straight edge bands tend to be more engaged in the animal liberation movement than their counterparts in the northern hemisphere.

The lyrics of many of these bands, though difficult to understand because of the vocal techniques utilized (delivery is generally gutteral and/or screamed), frequently address social, political, and environmental issues. To get the message across, bands often precede each song with a short commentary when performing live, and print the lyrics on websites and in CD liner notes. The look, sound, message and lifestyle are consistent in the straight edge philosophy, and things are urgent!

> Libertação animal e humana caminham lado ao lado
> Realizar uma sem realizar a outra é uma tarefa impossível
> Por isso cada dia que eu vejo só existe um caminho
> Veganismo.

> (Animal and human liberation go side by side
> Realizing one without realizing the other is an impossible task
> Because of this everyday I see that there exists but one way
> Veganism.)

From "Desculpas" ("Excuses"), by xLINHA DE FRENTEx, lyrics by xmanekox. (The x before and after names—and drawn or tattooed on the body, especially on the back of the hand—indicates allegiance to the straight edge movement.)

Vegan- and vegetarianism are gaining ground in Brazil. Some of its greatest proponents are hardcore musicians. One of the biggest punk/hardcore music festivals is the semiannual *Verdurada* in São Paulo, whose name roughly translates as "derived from vegetables" and features workshops and lectures on vegan/vegetarian living. A completely vegetarian meal is served at the end of the festival.

RECOMMENDED LISTENING

Since many rock bands operate independently of the mainstream music industry, they offer songs for download on their websites. Note that the x's below are a form of "straight edge" code.

ARD (punk/harcore). http://www.myspace.com/ardhc
xLINHA DE FRENTEx (veganstraightedge). http://www.purevolume.com/xlinhadefrentex
Peixa (alt rock). http://www.tramavirtual.com.br/peixa
Poena (crossover). http://www.poena.com.br

FOR FURTHER INFORMATION

Hardly anything has been written on music (and even less, if anything, on hardcore) in Brasília, though the city has been the subject of other interesting works; most are in Portuguese.

Behr, Nicolas. 2004. *Eu engoli Brasília*. Ed. do Autor, Brasília. (Poetry collection)
Holston, James. 1989. *The Modernist City: An Anthropological Critique of Brasília*. Chicago: University of Chicago Press.
Marchetti, Paulo. 2001. *O diário da turma 1976-1986: a história do rock de Brasília*. Conrad. São Paulo: Conrad.
Vieira, Evandro. 2005. *Esfolando ouvidos: memórias do hardcore em Brasília*. Brasília: Evandro Vieira (esfolando@pop.com.br).

MINAS GERAIS, BRAZIL
Suzel A. Reily

Not even a dog will eat that; there won't be any left for him.

Menu: *Feijão Tropeiro* (Mule Train Operators' Beans), *Costelinha de Porco da Dona Maria* (Dona Maria's Pork Ribs), *Quibebe* (Pumpkin), *Angu* (Corn Porridge), and *Arroz* (Rice). For dessert, serve *Doce de Leite* (Milk Fudge) with cheese. Serve with cold beer, *guaraná*, or any tropical fruit juice.
Preparation Time: 2½ hours, not counting soaking the beans overnight.
Cooking Process: Soak 1 lb. brown beans overnight in water. Start the bean dish, then make the milk fudge while the beans are simmering. Now start the pork ribs while the beans continue to cook. Once the ribs start to cook, turn your attention to the pumpkin. Start the rice, then whip up the corn porridge at the last minute. Place everything in bowls in the center of the table and allow guests to serve themselves. Serves six people.

The Recipes

FEIJÃO TROPEIRO (MULE TRAIN OPERATORS' BEANS)

1 lb. small brown beans
3 bay leaves
2 thin salami-type sausages, sliced and quartered
salt
½ lb. fresh bacon
1 large onion, finely chopped
3 cloves garlic
10 or more collard green leaves, chopped into thin strips
a few leaves of fresh parsley, chopped
several shoots of spring onion or scallions, chopped
1 or 2 hard boiled eggs, chopped
1 c. manioc (or cassava) flour
black pepper

Leave 1 lb. beans soaking in water overnight. Simmer them with 3 bay leaves and 2 thin salami-type sausages. When the beans are almost ready (after about 1 hour), add salt. Drain the beans, getting them as dry as possible. (You can save the bean juice for soup, if you like.) Cut ½ lb. bacon into small cubes and fry. Remove the bacon and use the excess fat to fry the onion and 3 cloves of garlic. When they are golden brown, add the collard greens (can substitute kale or cabbage) and allow it to cook down. Then add the parsley, spring onions, beans, sausages, bacon, eggs, and the manioc flour. Sprinkle with pepper to taste. Mix well and place in a serving dish. (Note: For a lighter version, omit the sausage, the bacon, and/or the eggs.)

Costelinha de Porco da Dona Maria (Dona Maria's Pork Ribs)

1 T vegetable oil
1 onion, finely chopped
3 cloves garlic, crushed
2¼ lb. pork ribs (cut in pairs of ribs 3" long)
salt
black pepper
½ c. dry white vine
3 spring onion or scallion stalks

In a large saucepan heat 1 T vegetable oil and add the onion and garlic. Stir until golden brown. Rub the pork ribs with salt and pepper, then add to the pan and fry lightly. When the ribs have browned, add ½ c. dry white wine a bit at a time. Cover and cook until they are done. If necessary, add a bit of water from time to time. To check if the ribs are ready, pierce them with a fork. Chop up 3 spring onion or scallion stalks. Just before they are done, add the spring onions and leave the ribs on the heat until most of the water has dried. Transfer to a serving dish.

Quibebe (Pumpkin)

2 t. vegetable oil
1 small onion, chopped
2 garlic cloves, pressed
salt
pepper
1 medium pumpkin or other type of orange squash, cubed
¼ c. parsley, finely chopped

Heat 2 t. vegetable oil in a pan and brown 1 small onion and 2 cloves of garlic. Add ½ t. salt and pepper to taste. Add the chunks of pumpkin, stir, and cover. Let the pumpkin cook on low heat until it disintegrates. (Note: Avoid adding water, as the pumpkin produces sufficient water while it cooks.) Just before serving, add chopped parsley.

Angu (Corn Porridge)

1½ c. cornmeal
salt (optional)

Whisk 1½ c. cornmeal into 6 c. water; bring to a boil, stirring constantly. *Angu* is made just like Italian *polenta*, except that it is much thinner, so add a bit more water and remove from heat before the porridge thickens too much. If you want to be "authentic," don't add salt. However, since even many *mineiros* find this too unsavory, go ahead and salt your *angu* to taste.

Arroz (Rice)

1 medium onion, finely chopped
2 cloves garlic, sliced
2 c. white rice
salt

To make Brazilian rice, begin by browning the onion and garlic. Wash rice and add it to the pan. Let the rice fry for a few minutes with the onion and garlic, until it begins to stick to the pan. Add 4 c. water and 1 t. salt. Bring to a boil, cover, leaving a slight opening for the steam, and reduce the heat. When the rice is almost dry, cover completely until the rice has finished cooking.

Doce de Leite (Milk Fudge)

6 c. milk
4 c. sugar
1 t. baking soda

Mix all the ingredients and cook over a low heat, stirring from time to time. When the mixture begins to thicken, stir continuously, cooking until it's so thick you can see the bottom of the pan when you stir. Remove from heat and beat the mixture. Before it hardens, pour it on a stone or ceramic surface. When it has cooled, cut into squares and serve with a mild cheese.

Complete meal (Minas Gerais, Brazil). Photo by Marina Roseman.

The Legacy of Gold in the Music and Food of Minas Gerais

Minas Gerais was a large wilderness until gold was discovered around Ouro Preto in the late 17th century. The gold rush that followed attracted thousands of prospectors from all over the colony as well as from Portugal and further afield. Towns and settlements sprang up overnight wherever traces of the precious metal were found. Within a century, though, there was very little gold left. Yet the legacy of the gold era has remained strong through Minas Gerais, and it defines the emblems of identity. Food, music, the arts, architecture, and religiosity bear witness to the region's glorious past.

The cuisine in Minas is closely linked to circumstances of the mines. The state is associated with dairy products and pork and its derivatives, even though they were not the staple diet. Red meat was the staple, but because it had to be brought in from the coastal settlements by mule train operators and cattle herdsmen, it was always in short supply. This meant that people often had to rely on cheese for their protein, and they also took to keeping pigs anywhere they could build a pen. Even in towns many *mineiros* were still keeping pigs up until the late 1960s. My mother-in-law, Dona Maria, only gave up her pigs when it became illegal to keep them within the city limits. Her pork ribs, above, are still a family favorite. It was also because of the requirements of the miners that *feijão tropeiro*, or mule train operators' beans, became a regional specialty. This dish was convenient for the traveler because it could all be made in a single pot. Mule train operators were a lifeline for the mining communities.

The gold era also had a significant impact on the development of the region's musical traditions. In particular it allowed the mining communities to support large numbers of professional musicians, whose main activities were directed toward indulging the rich in their displays of wealth. Throughout the urban areas of colonial Brazil the privileged classes demonstrated their social position through a life of idleness and conspicuous consumption, and in the mining areas this tendency became even stronger. Important arenas for flamboyant displays of wealth were religious festivals, which were promoted through lay confraternities (*irmandades*), which also became the institutions through which Brazilian colonial society was organized. Each confraternity was dedicated to a different Catholic saint and patronized by a particular racial group: there were separate brotherhoods for whites, people of mixed descent (*pardos*), and blacks. It was only during festivals that greater integration of the segregated social sectors took place, temporarily bridging the racial divides.

The confraternities competed with one another, each hoping to outdo the others in their annual displays of grandeur. Each year a composer would be commissioned to generate new music for the confraternity's main festival, and to perform it he contracted singers and instrumentalists for the orchestra. In the latter half of the 18th century there were nearly a thousand active musicians associated with the confraternities of Minas Gerais. The overwhelming majority of them were mulattoes, often the sons of Portuguese immigrants and African slave women. The music of the period has often been referred to as *mineiro baroque*, but it actually has more to do with the preclassical homophonic style. Many of the compositions involve one or two four-part mixed choruses with an orchestral accompaniment of two violins, viola, bass, and two French horns, and occasionally oboes, flutes, and keyboard.

Among the lower classes of Minas Gerais music and food have always been intricately linked, and this is most evident in the world of popular Catholicism. For example, the *folia de reis*, a rural mumming tradition that is especially strong in Minas, involves a group of musicians who reenact the journey of the Wise Men during the Christmas season. These ensembles roam from house to house singing to bless the families they visit in exchange for food and money. The donations they collect are then used to promote a large festival on the 6th of January, or Kings' Day, to which all the families that have been visited are invited. In their songs the musicians proclaim the message of the Wise Men, or moral truths, and in return they receive donations that are then distributed equally at the end of the journey. During the final festival, hundreds of people are fed, the menu generally consisting of rice, beans, meat, macaroni, potatoes, lettuce, and manioc flour. This grand event is a concrete expression of the community's generosity and it confirms the power of the Wise Men to ensure the continuity of life.

Among *congados*, which are African-Brazilian, drum-based dance ensembles with roots in the black confraternities of Our Lady of the Rosary, there is also an exchange of symbolic goods in the form of music and dance for material goods, or food. During the Festival of Our Lady of the Rosary all the *congados* of the town, as well as a few from neighboring towns, congregate around the Church of the Rosary—and every town in Minas has a Church of the Rosary. All the ensembles beat their drums as loudly as possible, competing with one another for dominance over the sound space. A successful festival is linked to the number of *congados* that attend it, so the festival host does his best to attract the groups by indicating his intent to feed them during the festival. At a large festival the host may serve several hundred people every day for three days or more. While it is generally only the dancers who receive full meals, everyone who goes to the Festival of Our Lady of the Rosary is offered the saint's fruit preserve. Many people think it's very important to eat at least a spoon full of this sweet, as it is meant to protect one, especially children, against illness throughout the coming year.

RECOMMENDED LISTENING

The link between music and gold in Minas Gerais is most directly embodied in the colonial music commissioned by the confraternities. Up until recently recording of this repertoire were very difficult to come by. Now, however, numerous projects have emerged to make this repertoire accessible. But there are other suggestions if you prefer to hear something more recent.

All these CDs can be ordered on the Internet.

Acervo da Música Brasileira—Restauração e Difusão de Partituras (Archives of Brazilian Music—Restoration and Dissemination of Sheet Music), coordinated by Paulo Castagna. (Nine CDs with full scores.)

Mestres da Música Colonial Mineira (Masters of Colonial Music from Minas Gerais), with Ars Nova, choir of the Federal University of Minas Gerais, directed by Carlos Alberto Pinto Fonseca.

Música do Brasil Colonial: Compositores Mineiros (Brazilian Colonial Music: Composers from Minas Gerais), with the Brasilessentia Grupo Vocal e Orquestra, directed by Vitor Gabriel.

Nascimento, Milton. *Minas, Pietá, Travessia* (all recommended). (See also Wagner Tiso, Tavinho Moura, Toninho Horta, Lô Borges, Sá & Guarabira, or Flávio Venturini.)

Rezende, Alda. *Samba Solto* (Loose Samba).

Silva, Kristoff, Makely Ka, and Pablo Castro. *A Outra Cidade* (The Other City).

Uakiti. *Mulungu do Cerrado*. (Uakiti produce a unique sound by performing on instruments they have made and adapted themselves.)

FOR FURTHER INFORMATION

http://www.pacificislandtravel.com/south_america/brazil/about_destin/minasgerais.html
http://www.brazilmax.com/news1.cfm/tborigem/pl_southcentral/id/17
http://darkwing.uoregon.edu/~sergiok/brasil/ouropreto.html#start
http://www.qub.ac.uk/sa-old/resources/HolyWeek/index.html

SOUTHEASTERN BRAZIL
Carla Brunet

An empty sack does not stay upright.

Menu: *Feijoada* (Bean and Pork Stew) with *Molho Vinagrete* (Vinaigrette Sauce), *Arroz* (Rice), *Couve* (Sautéed Collard Greens), *Farofa* (Manioc Flour with Butter and Onion), and *Pudim de Leite* (Flan). Serve with *Caipirinha* (Brazilian National Drink).

Preparation Time: Approximately 4½ hours, not including the beans (which need to soak overnight).

Cooking Process: Soak the beans overnight. Make the *feijoada* first, then prepare the other menu items while it is in its final cooking stage. *Farofa* is a mixture of toasted manioc flour with other ingredients. It can include fruits, olives, nuts, sausages, and bacon, but normally, when served with *feijoada* it is simply toasted with butter, onion, and salt. Note that although the *feijoada* appears to be rich with meat, some of that weight is in the bones. Serve in large containers in the table and allow people to serve themselves. Serves six people.

The Recipes

Feijoada (Bean and Pork Stew)

1½ lb. black beans
3 bay leaves
2 T olive oil
½ lb. salt pork, cubed
½ lb. lean smoked bacon, cubed
1½ lb. pork ribs, separated
½ lb. smoked ham hocks
2 large Portuguese sausages (*linguiça*)
1 large onion, chopped
4 cloves garlic, finely chopped
sprig of thyme

Soak 1½ lb. black beans in cold water overnight, making sure they are completely covered. Drain the beans and place them into a saucepan with 6 cups of cold water and 3 bay leaves. Bring it all to a boil over high heat, cover and reduce heat to a simmer. Cook until tender but not too soft. Reserve. Coat a large pot with olive oil and place over high heat. When hot, add ½ lb. cubed salt pork. Every 2 minutes, pour ⅛ cup of water until cubes are browned. Add ½ lb. cubed lean smoked bacon, 1½ lb. separated pork ribs, ½ lb. smoked ham hocks, and 2 large Portuguese sausages (*linguiça*), and let it cook, stirring for 5 minutes to render out the pork fat. Add onion, garlic, and a sprig of thyme. Continue cooking until onion is translucent. Pour in the cooked beans with their liquid. If there is not enough liquid to just cover all the ingredients, add more cold water. Bring it to a boil and then reduce the heat to medium-low. Let it cook, stirring now and again, for about 1 hour or until meat is falling off the bone. Remove ham hocks from the pot. After discarding the rind, shred the meat and return it to the pot. Taste and check for seasoning.

Arroz (Rice)

3 T olive oil
½ onion, finely chopped
2 cloves garlic, chopped
2½ c. long grain white rice
salt

In a pot, heat 3 T olive oil over high heat. Add onion and garlic and sauté until golden. Rinse and drain 2½ c. long grain white rice, then add it to pot, stirring constantly, until slightly toasted (2–3 minutes). Add 5 c. water and 1 t. salt and bring to a boil. Cover and reduce the heat to low. At this point, let the rice cook without stirring until tender. Remove rice from heat, fluff it quickly with a fork and then let it rest for 10 minutes.

Couve (Sautéed Collard Greens)

3 large bunches of collard greens
3 T olive oil
3 cloves garlic

Cut leaves of 3 bunches of collard greens in half lengthwise, removing and discarding the center stems. Stack half of the collard leaves and roll into a cigar like shape. With a sharp knife, cut the leaves crosswise into very thin strips. Repeat with remaining leaves. Heat 3 T olive oil in a heavy skillet over medium-high heat. Add 3 cloves of thinly sliced garlic and cook, stirring, until light golden. Add the collard greens, tossing, until tender. Season with salt and pepper to taste.

Molho Vinagrete (Vinaigrette Sauce)

3 large tomatoes, chopped
1 small onion, finely chopped
½ c. parsley, finely chopped
1 small jalapeño pepper, chopped
½ c. white vinegar
½ c. olive oil
1 lime, juiced
salt

Combine tomatoes, onion, parsley, jalapeño pepper (or to taste), white vinegar, olive oil, and the juice of 1 lime in a large bowl. Stir well and season to taste with salt. Serve over meat and beans.

Farofa (Manioc Flour with Butter and Onion)

4 T butter
1 small onion, finely chopped
2 c. manioc flour
salt

Melt 4 T butter in a heavy skillet. Add the onion and cook until tender. Add 2 c. manioc flour and cook over low heat stirring constantly until golden. Season with salt.

Pudim de Leite (Flan)

1 c. sugar
2 c. canned, sweetened condensed milk
1 can full milk (use the can to measure the milk)
½ can full orange juice (optional; if using juice, use the can to measure half milk and half orange juice)
5 eggs

Preheat oven to 325°F. Have ready a shallow baking pan, which can accommodate a 2-quart flan mold. The flan should be cooked in a water bath. Place the sugar in a heavy saucepan, set over moderately low heat. Allow it to melt and caramelize to a rich golden brown. Do not stir the sugar as it melts but do shake the saucepan from time to time. Add ½ cup of boiling water, stirring with a wooden spoon to dissolve the caramelized sugar. Simmer uncovered until mixture reaches the consistency of maple syrup (around 8 minutes). Pour caramel into a shallow fluted 2-quart mold, coating bottom and sides. Set it aside. In a large bowl, whisk together condensed milk, milk, orange juice (if using it), and eggs until smooth. Pour it into prepared mold and cover it tightly with aluminum foil. Place flan mold in a shallow baking dish on the middle rack in the oven. Pour in enough hot water to reach halfway up the sides of the mold and bake it for 90 minutes, or until a toothpick inserted near the center of the flan comes out clean. Remove from the oven and the water bath; cool for 1 hour before removing from mold. To loosen flan from mold run a knife around the inside of the mold or using a finger, gently press down the edges of the flan. Place a dessert plate on top of the flan and invert to pop it out. Refrigerate it for at least 2–3 hours before serving it.

Caipirinha (Brazilian National Drink)

6 limes
6 T sugar
8–12 oz. *cachaça* liqueur (alcohol made from sugar cane; may be replaced by vodka)

Wash the limes and roll them firmly on a cutting board to loosen the juice inside. Peel each lime, removing as much of the white underflesh (pith) as possible so that the drink does not turn bitter. Cut each lime in several pieces, placing the pieces inside 6 short glasses and crushing them with a pestle together with 1 T sugar each. Add 1–2 oz. *cachaça*, water, and ice to each glass, and mix well.

Cooking and Music Making at Home in Southeastern Brazil

Most of Jundiaí's longtime residents knew the "house of the grotto." Situated in downtown, not far from the town's cathedral and the social club, my grandparents' two-story, colonial home built at the turn of the twentieth century was a notable site, notwithstanding its size or architectural aesthetics. Naturally, the grotto, built on the frontside of the home to house my grandmother's image of the Virgin of Lourdes, compelled attention. But even if one grew accustomed to the unusual structure, there was no getting used to the many sounds coming from the home of the couple who had ten children, scores of grandchildren, and many friends. As enthusiastic amateur musicians, my grandparents encouraged music making at their home and hosted almost weekly informal gatherings. And it seemed only natural that such gatherings would also include a meal, if not two. After all, it is safe to say that in Brazil any gathering requires that some food be present, be it a simple afternoon pastry and coffee or a full meal.

At their house, not unlike many other Brazilian families' homes, adults and children of both genders would partake in music making. By observing adults playing, some children learned their instruments, while others used the event to practice in front of an audience what they had learned in private music lessons. From other rooms in the house, people would sing along and clap as each song came to an end. For some, these interactions were merely a part of social life; after all, solitude and quietness are generally not regarded as desirable states in Brazilian culture. For others, however, it provided an exclusive outlet for performance. The home functioned as a prudent place for the performance of music, especially popular music. At the time I was growing up in the 1970s, professional musicians, or musicians performing outside of family homes or the church, were perceived as "bohemians," not serious individuals. And for women, the implications were even more negative, as professional women musicians were considered to be promiscuous, "loose" women. As soon as my mother entered puberty, she was prohibited by her father from singing at the radio station as she had done before. It was no longer appropriate or socially acceptable for her, who had then become a "woman," to be singing outside of the home or the church. It was only at her home, under the gaze of the family, that Mom had the opportunity to compose and perform for an attentive audience without the stigmas associated with the music profession. Presently, some of these notions are no longer prevalent, yet for many Brazilians, the home continues to be an important place for music making.

While men and women equally participated in music making, most of the cooking was, and still is, primarily left in the hands of women. While the cuisine of this region of the country (southeast) is very diverse and shows the influence of many immigrant cultures, most meals revolve around meat. At these gatherings, it was not uncommon for my grandmother, mother, and aunts to prepare several different types of meat: usually pork, chicken, and beef, served with the usual accompaniments of rice, beans, manioc flour, and greens. Two of the most popular meals prepared at the house of the grotto were *feijoada* and *churrasco*. Particularly favored during the summer and spring seasons, *churrasco*, or grilled meats, were an all-day event at my grandparents' home. Guests were not expected to gather at a table at a specific time to eat together. Rather, people would come and go, helping themselves to servings of different meats as they wished, drinking beer or *caipirinha*, a sweet drink made with lime juice and sugar cane alcohol. Since the grilling was done in the backyard, the men were usually in charge of it, while in the kitchen, the women would marinate the meats, cook rice and manioc flour, and prepare different types of salads. But my personal favorite was Mom's *feijoada*. Considered the national dish, *feijoada* is similar to a *cassoulet*, a stew of black beans and a variety of pork meats, served with white rice, collard greens, manioc flour, salsa, and orange slices. I began learning how to cook this dish while still a young girl. I would watch my grandmother and mother in the kitchen and was guided on how to perform small tasks like washing the greens or toasting the manioc flour, between performing a waltz and a *modinha* on the piano. Since moving to California, I have had to modify the recipe to an extent, substituting the original pork tongue, feet, tail, ears, and snout with other more readily available pork cuts. But I have cooked my version of *feijoada* for my mom and she approves!

RECOMMENDED LISTENING

The following is a short list including some of the artists I enjoy listening to: Os Ingênuos, Elis Regina, Luiz Melodia, Djavan, Chico Buarque, and Sepultura.

FOR FURTHER INFORMATION

Levine, Robert M. and John J. Crocitti, eds. 1999. *The Brazil Reader: History, Culture, Politics*. Durham, NC: Duke University Press.

Levine, Robert M. 1997. *Brazilian Legacies*. Armonk, NY: M. E. Sharpe.

Veloso, Caetano. 2002. *Tropical Truth: A Story of Music and Revolution in Brazil*. Trans. by Isabel de Sena. New York: Alfred A. Knopf. Originally published in Brazil as *Verdade tropical*. São Paulo: Companhia das Letras, 1997.

Vianna, Hermano. 1999. *The Mystery of Samba: Popular Music & National Identity in Brazil*. Edited and trans. by John Charles Chasteen. Chapel Hill: University of North Carolina Press.

OAXACA, MEXICO
Mark Brill

Él que come y canta, loco se levanta.
He who sings while eating will wake up crazy.

Menu: *Mole Oaxaqueño* (Oaxacan *Mole*) and *Arroz con Crema y Queso Oaxaqueño* (Creamy Rice with Oaxaca Cheese). Serve with cold dark beer or sweet cold tropical fruit drinks (*aguas frescas*).
Preparation Time: 2–3 hours.
Cooking Process: Prepare the *mole* first, then the rice. Serve the turkey or chicken, covered in *mole*, and with the rice on the side. As with most Mexican food, corn tortillas should be plentiful. Oaxaca meals are usually accompanied by *aguas frescas*, sweet cold drinks made from tropical fruits such as lime, strawberries, melon, watermelon, or zapote, or the sweet *horchata* drink made from rice. Purists wanting to honor the Aztec roots of the dish will opt for the emperor's drink of choice: a thick *atóle*, made with cornmeal, chocolate, cinnamon, almonds, and water. (The Aztecs had no dairy products). But on a hot day, a Oaxacan *mole* is best accompanied by ice-cold dark beer. After the meal, one can have the traditional *café de olla*, coffee with a spiced brown sugar called *piloncillo* (available at any Mexican market) or sip on a high-end mezcal or tequila, which can be as smooth and satisfying as a fine French brandy or a 25-year-old single-malt scotch. Note: Look for the chilis in specialty/Mexican markets. Serves six people.

The Recipes

Mole Oaxaqueño (Oaxacan Mole)

4–6 turkey (or 8–12 chicken) parts
2 large onions
1½ heads of garlic
1 bunch of cilantro
salt
½ t. anise seed
½ t. coriander
½ t. cumin seed
½ t. thyme
1 t. allspice
10–15 peppercorns
1" stick of cinnamon
2–4 avocado leaves
2 T dry oregano
3–6 whole cloves
3 *guajillo* chilis
3 *chilhuacle negro* chilis
3 *mulatto* chilis
3 *pasilla* chilis
3 *ancho* chilis

½ c. sesame seeds
2 T *manteca* pig lard (or vegetable oil)
1 c. fresh pineapple chunks
1 ripe plantain, peeled and sliced
1 c. raisins
2 c. sherry or brandy
2 tomatoes, peeled, seeded, and chopped
4–6 *tomatillos* (green tomatoes), chopped
½ c. almonds
½ c. walnuts
½ c. peanuts
36 corn tortillas
4 c. chicken broth
4 oz. Mexican chocolate
2–4 sprigs mint
1 t. sugar
salt

Prepare the poultry first. Boil 4 quarts of water in large pot. Add enough poultry parts for six people, 1 large onion, quartered, 5–10 cloves of peeled garlic, 6–8 sprigs of cilantro, and salt to taste. Reduce heat to medium-low, simmer for 30 minutes. Remove and reserve. You will be making several separate elements for the sauce. First, toast the spices. In a dry pan, lightly toast over medium heat ½ t. each anise seed, coriander, cumin seed, and thyme, then 1 t. allspice, 10–15 peppercorns, a 1" stick of cinnamon, 2–4 avocado (or bay) leaves, 2 T dried oregano, and 3–6 cloves to release the flavor. Remove from heat. Reserve the avocado leaves. After they have cooled, grind the remaining spices together with a mortar and pestle or spice grinder. Reserve. Put on a pair of kitchen gloves. Remove the stems and seeds from the chilis (3 each of *guajillo*, *chilhuacle negro*, *mulatto*, *pasilla*, and *ancho*). Toast the chili seeds and ½ c. sesame seeds in ½ T lard or oil over high heat, stirring constantly, for about 2 minutes, until they begin to darken, but before they burn. They will smoke, so this step is best done outdoors or with plenty of ventilation. Remove from heat, and grind in the mortar and pestle or spice grinder. Reserve. Discard kitchen gloves and wash hands.

The following steps can be done in the same large pan. Start with 1 T lard or oil, then add more as necessary. Sauté the seedless chilis over high heat, stirring constantly, for about 3 minutes, or until they begin to brown. Remove from heat, place them in a bowl, cover with boiling water, and let them soak for about 30 minutes. Sauté 1 c. fresh pineapple chunks, 1 ripe peeled and sliced plantain (or banana), and 1 c. raisins over high heat, stirring constantly, for about 3 minutes, or until they begin to brown. Remove from heat, place them in a bowl, cover with 2 c. heated (but not boiled) sherry or brandy, and let them soak for about 30 minutes. Sauté 1 peeled and quartered onion; 6–10 cloves of peeled garlic; 2 peeled, seeded, and chopped tomatoes; and 4–6 chopped tomatillos over high heat, stirring constantly, for about 3 minutes, or until they begin to brown. Reserve. Sauté ½ c. each almonds, walnuts, and peanuts over high heat, stirring constantly, for about 3 minutes, or until they begin to brown. Reserve. Now drain the chilis and purée the chilis, fruits, and vegetables in a blender, in small batches, until a paste is formed, adding a little of the sherry or brandy to smooth the texture. Set aside. Purée the sautéed nuts, ground chili seeds, sesame seeds, and 2 crumbled tortillas in a blender, in small batches, until a paste is formed, adding a little more of the sherry or brandy to smooth the texture. At this point you should have three different mixtures: (1) spices, (2) chilis, fruits, and vegetables, and (3) nuts and seeds. Combine all in a large pot. Add 4 c. chicken broth and the rest of the sherry or brandy. Bring to a boil, then reduce heat to medium-low. Add 4 oz. ground Mexican chocolate (Ibarra or Abuelita), 2–4 sprigs of mint, 6–8 sprigs of cilantro, the 2 avocado leaves, 1 t. sugar, and salt to taste, stirring constantly until chocolate is completely melted. Cover and simmer for 30 minutes, stirring occasionally, and adding broth as necessary to preserve desired thickness. Add reserved turkey or chicken pieces and cook on medium for another 15–20 minutes, or until meat is completely cooked.

ARROZ CON CREMA Y QUESO OAXAQUEÑO
(CREAMY RICE WITH OAXACA CHEESE)

5 T vegetable oil
2 c. white rice
2 large onions, sliced
2 cloves garlic, minced
2 c. frozen corn
2 c. chicken broth
2 c. milk
1 c. Oaxaca or Chihuahua cheese, grated
4 sprigs cilantro
salt
½ c. sour cream

Heat 5 T vegetable oil over medium-high heat. Sauté 2 c. rice, stirring constantly, about 3 minutes. Add onions, garlic, and 2 c. frozen corn. Cook another 5 minutes, stirring constantly. Add 2 c. chicken broth, 2 c. milk, 1 c. Oaxaca or Chihuahua cheese, 4 sprigs cilantro, and salt to taste. Cover and reduce heat to low. Cook another 15 minutes. Turn off heat, pour ½ c. sour cream on top, replace cover, and let sit for 5 minutes.

Music and Food in Oaxaca

Oaxaca (pronounced Hua-HA-ka) in southern Mexico is a land of mountains and valleys, of sunshine and rain, of ancient mystery, myth, and ritual. It is also a land of food and song, as attested by the myriad feasts and fairs that mark the calendar, each with its own individual tradition, but all linked by culinary and melodious delights. These religious *fiestas* can be traced to Mexico's multifaceted past, with roots in pre-encounter days, bolstered by post-*Conquista* Catholic feasts. Since every day is a saint's day, there are always *fiestas* somewhere in Oaxaca. Sometimes, they become week- or month-long regional affairs and are called *ferias*, such as the summer Guelaguetza festival or the ubiquitous Day-of-the-Dead, when the dearly departed are invited to share in the drink, food, and music. *Fiestas* and *ferias* are a time to commune with your neighbors and with the saints, who are always guests of honor. The saints are human; thus, the celebrations are always lively, rarely solemn, and never restrained. Festivals have become elaborate colorful rituals where fun and courtship abound, with dances, costumes, decorations, drama, and fireworks. At the center of everything lay music and food and drink, inexorably intertwined.

Virtually any get-together—whether a formal *fiesta*, an extended Sunday afternoon meal, or a light evening supper—is an opportunity for Oaxacans to delve into their love of food and music. Evening strolls in town squares invariably lead to encounters with guitar trios or marimba ensembles entertaining jovial diners and amorous couples. One still finds wooing serenaders with guitars, crooning romantic renditions of *"Las Mañanitas,"* though much of the town youth will flock to the disco to hear the latest *techno* offerings from Europe or the United States. In the villages where Spanish is rarely spoken, mothers and grandmothers sing ancient Zapotec and Mixtec tunes, prepare mouth-watering dishes, and teach their daughters the intricacies of tortilla-making and pentatonic singing. Oaxacans have long developed a culinary sensitivity and sophistication that set them apart from other Mexican cooks. They have mastered difficult preparation techniques and the art of ingredient selection. In the capital city, lavish colonial restaurants and unassuming eateries named after the family matriarch serve wide varieties of exotic fare. Markets offer local delicacies such as *chapulines* (grasshoppers), *tunas* (prickly pears), rose-petal ices, *tamales*, and *empanadas*. It is in these Oaxacan restaurants, markets, villages, and homes that one can find the culinary delights that have made the region famous, and particularly one dish that has come to define Oaxaca: *mole*.

If carefully prepared with quality ingredients, this recipe will yield a black sauce—a *mole*—with a deep, shiny veneer and a complexity of flavor that will not be soon forgotten. Those who have never had good Mexican—and specifically Oaxacan—*mole* will be immediately besieged by a combination of flavors that will stimulate their taste buds like few things they have ever eaten.

Mole (pronounced MO-leh) is derived from *molli*, which means "sauce" in the Aztec language. Many legends exist regarding the origin of *mole*, with variations of time and place. One of the most popular can be boiled down to this: Chocolate was bequeathed by the gods to the Aztecs, who reserved it for the emperor, the nobility, and the clergy. It was altogether forbidden from women, whose job was to prepare chocolate-based sauces and beverages without ever tasting them. Not long after the Conquest, the Convent of Santa Rosa in Puebla was to receive the visit of the viceroy and the archbishop. The old Aztec servant women at the convent, hearing that royal dignitaries were coming, remembered a chocolate-based dish that they had prepared for the emperor in their youth. The *mole* was prepared, and the visitors, wholly impressed, demanded the recipe, which has since become popular throughout Mexico. Had the viceroy not visited the convent, and had the Aztec women not had the presence of mind to prepare this wonderful dish, it most certainly would have been lost.

In fact, while pre-encounter Mexicans unquestionably had complex chocolate-based sauces, contemporary *moles* result from the same syncretic process that affected virtually every other aspect of Mesoamerican life. Like Mexicans themselves, most of whom are Mestizo, *mole* combines native and European elements to create a new dish not present in either source culture. It resulted from the melding of Old World (cinnamon, cloves, black pepper, almonds) and New World (chilis, tomatoes, turkey and, of course, chocolate) ingredients.

A good *mole* is a perfect triad of spicy, sweet, and tangy, and will balance four distinct elements: a solid vegetable base (provided by onions, tomatoes, and *tomatillos*), exotic tastes (myriad herbs and spices), heat (chilis), and sweetness (chocolate or fruit). Some delicious *moles* are thin and watery, though typically *mole* has a thicker texture achieved with ground sesame or pumpkin seeds, corn meal, or a wide variety of ground nuts. *Moles* can also include sherry or dry white wine.

Chocolate has become the most famous ingredient in *mole*, and non-Mexicans often pause at the thought of a chocolate hot sauce, but are invariably delighted when they first taste it. As a result, chocolate has almost come to define *mole*, but many *moles* do not, in fact, call for it. The chocolate stores in downtown Oaxaca and other towns do not sell candies and confections. Rather, they are busy factory-like mills where cocoa beans are roasted and ground into a paste, which can then be purchased by the kilo. This is the best ingredient for *mole*, though commercial brands such as Abuelita and Ibarra are perfectly acceptable.

Mole can be served with pork, beef, venison, and fish. There is even a vegetarian version, served over beans and *nopal* cactus. But the most popular *moles* involve turkey or chicken. For a true pre-encounter meal, *guajolote* (wild turkey) is the meat of choice, since chicken, beef, and pork were unknown to the Aztecs. The chili selection is essential, not only for degree of heat, but also because chilis have distinct tastes that will affect the *mole*. There are over 30 varieties of chilis found in Oaxaca alone, some dried, others fresh, still others smoked. They come in a veritable rainbow of colors which affects their aroma, flavor and degree of heat. Adventuresome cooks can experiment widely in the realm of the chili.

Moles themselves come in a variety of colors, reflecting the color of the chilis used: *verde* (green), *rojo* (red), *amarillo* (yellow), and *negro* (black). Though many regional *moles* exist, the states best known for *moles* are Puebla and Oaxaca. Mexican restaurants in Europe or the United States will typically serve *mole poblano* ("from Puebla"). Oaxaca is known as the Land of Seven *Moles*, where local variations change from village to village, even from family to family. Women crouching over cast iron *comal* pans will argue in their native language as to which combination of chilis or spices is more appropriate for this or that *mole*. The recipe presented here combines important elements of the seven traditional moles, injecting the fruitiness of the *manchamanteles* with the robustness of the *negro*. The dried fruit marinated in sherry gives it a sweet tangy undercurrent which combines well with the chilis.

RECOMMENDED LISTENING

Brisas Del Grijalba. *Asi Canta Mexico, Vol. 3: Musica de Chiapas, Oaxaca Y Guerrero*. Asi Canta Mexico, 1995. (Traditional marimba music.)
Explorer Series: Mexico—Fiestas of Chiapas and Oaxaca. Nonesuch Records, 2003. (Traditional folk and indigenous music.)
Trio Fantasia. *Linda Oaxaca*. I.M. Records, 2000. (Romantic popular songs.)
Trio Mexico. *Song of the Oaxaca*. Agave Records, 1998. (Romantic popular songs.)

FOR FURTHER INFORMATION

On the history, culture, music, and food of Oaxaca, see the following websites:

http://www.mexconnect.com/mex_/oaxaca/oaxacaindex.html
http://www.allaboutoaxaca.com

8
North America

NEWFOUNDLAND AND LABRADOR

Beverley Diamond

Save your breath to cool your porridge.

Menu: Pan-Fried Cod Cheeks with Scruncheons, Jiggs Dinner, Peas Pudding, Bannock, and Figgy Duff or Frozen Partridgeberry Soufflé. Serve with Quidi Vidi 1892 Beer and Bakeapple Icewine (Rodriguez Winery) for dessert.

Preparation Time: 3–4 hours on the day of cooking, and 1 hour the night before. Note: There isn't so much active cooking time as watching things simmer slowly.

Cooking Process: You will need to find two "cotton pudding bags" or make them yourself. Soak 2 lb. salt beef (for the Jiggs Dinner) and 2 c. yellow split peas (for the peas pudding) overnight. Also, the night before your dinner, make the frozen partridgeberry soufflé. Gather the peas into one bag and place them in the pot with the salt beef for Jiggs Dinner. Start making the figgy duff and place into the second bag, stowing in the same pot as the Jiggs Dinner. While the Jiggs Dinner, peas pudding, and figgy duff are cooking, make and fry the cod cheeks and the bannock. Serves six people.

The Recipes

Pan-Fried Cod Cheeks with Scruncheons

¾ c. flour
1 t. lemon zest
salt
pepper
18 cod cheeks
¼ c. lard or olive oil
small amount of pork fat cut into ¼" cubes ("scruncheons")
8 oz. mixed greens

Combine ¾ c. flour with 1 t. lemon zest, ½ t. salt, and a dash of pepper in a plastic bag. Dredge cod cheeks in the flour mixture while heating ¼ c. lard or olive oil in a frying pan. Fry until golden brown, adding the pork fat scruncheons for flavor and additional fat. A lower fat (but nontraditional) alternative to scruncheons is a garnish of avocado slices. Serve on a bed of greens.

Jiggs Dinner

2 lb. salt beef
peas pudding (see recipe, below)
6 carrots
6 potatoes
1 head of cabbage
1 medium turnip

Cut 2 lb. salt beef into pieces and soak in cold water overnight. Drain off water. Re-cover with water. Add peas pudding in cotton pudding bag. Bring to boil and then cook slowly for 2 hours until tender. Clean and halve 6 carrots and 6 potatoes, clean 1 head of cabbage and 1 medium turnip and cut each into 6 chunks. Add turnip, potatoes, carrots, and cabbage (in that order), then cook another 30–40 minutes before serving. (Recipe courtesy of Janice Tulk.)

PEAS PUDDING

2 c. yellow split peas
⅓ c. butter
1 t. salt
1 t. pepper

Soak 2 c. yellow split peas in pudding bag overnight. Leave peas in bag. Tie top of bag and boil in the same pot as Jiggs Dinner. Turn peas out into bowl and mash with ⅓ c. butter, 1 t. salt, and 1 t. pepper. (Recipe courtesy of Janice Tulk.)

FIGGY DUFF

3 c. bread crumbs
2 c. raisins
½ c. brown sugar
salt
1 t. ginger
1 t. allspice
1 t. cinnamon
3 T molasses
¾ c. melted butter
1 t. baking soda
½ c. flour

Soak 3 c. bread crumbs in water for a few minutes. Squeeze out water (measure without tamping down). Combine bread with 1 c. raisins, ½ c. brown sugar, ½ t. salt, 1 t. each ginger, allspice, and cinnamon; mix with a fork. Add 3 T molasses, ¾ c. melted butter, and 1 t. baking soda which has been dissolved in 1 T hot water. Add ½ c. flour and mix well. Pour into dampened pudding bag. Cook in same pot with Jiggs Dinner for 1½ hours. (Recipe courtesy of Bridget Murphy.)

BANNOCK

3 c. flour
2 T baking powder
1 c. molasses
½ c. sugar
1 c. raisins
lard or vegetable oil

Mix 3 c. flour, 2 T baking powder, 1 c. molasses, ½ c. sugar, and 1 c. raisins with spoon or hands. Add more flour until it is no longer sticky or add more water if it is too dry. Take a bit of dough and pat it flat. Arrange in a circle, doughnut shaped, and fry in hot (but not smoking)

Frying bannock (Newfoundland, Canada). Photo by Sean Williams.

lard or oil until done. If you would prefer not to fry the bannock, you can take the same dough and bake it on a non-stick baking sheet for 15 or more minutes until it is done. Check to test its doneness by seeing if it springs lightly back when you touch the center.

Frozen Partridgeberry Soufflé

2½ c. partridgeberries
2 c. sugar
4 large eggs
pinch of salt
2½ c. whipping cream
⅓ c. light corn syrup (optional)

To make the partridgeberry mixture: In a heavy saucepan combine 2½ c. partridgeberries (or lingonberries or cranberries), ⅔ c. sugar, and ⅔ c. water, and bring mixture to a boil, stirring until the sugar is dissolved. Simmer, stirring occasionally, for 5 minutes or until thickened. Let cool completely. To make the meringue: In a small heavy saucepan combine ¾ c. sugar and ⅓ c. water and bring the mixture to a boil, stirring until the sugar is dissolved. Boil the syrup, washing down any sugar crystals clinging to the side of the pan with a brush dipped in cold water, until it registers 248°F on a candy thermometer. Remove pan from heat. While the syrup is boiling, beat 4 large egg whites with a pinch of salt until they hold soft peaks. With the motor of the mixer running, add the hot syrup in a stream, beating at medium speed for 8 minutes or until the mixture cools to room temperature. Fold the partridgeberry mixture into the meringue gently but thoroughly. In another bowl with clean beaters, beat 2½ c. whipping cream until it holds stiff peaks and fold it into the partridgeberry mixture until just blended. Spoon the soufflé into a 2½ quart (8" diameter), freezer-proof, glass serving bowl, smoothing the top; and freeze the soufflé, its surface covered with plastic wrap, overnight (or up to 3 days in advance). Optional garnish: Combine ⅓ c. light corn syrup and ¼ c. sugar. Bring to a boil over moderate heat, stirring until sugar is dissolved. Boil until syrup registers 320°F on a candy thermometer. Oil lightly a 12"-square sheet of foil and arrange ½ c. partridgeberries in an 8"-wide wreath shape. Let syrup cool for about 30 seconds and then drizzle the syrup over the berries. Let cool completely. Arrange on soufflé and garnish with mint.

Kitchen Parties in Newfoundland and Labrador

One night I came home from evening school and found the family as usual waiting up in the glow of the little wood-burning stove, with its low fire-box and its round oven up above in the chimney. Aunt Fanny Jane brought me a delicious pork bun and a glass of milk. While I was eating, Uncle Dan Endacott offered to sing me a song. I listened with particular interest, until it suddenly dawned upon me that he was singing a real folk-song, one handed down by oral tradition.

Elisabeth Greenleaf 1965, xix

It's no accident that "kitchen parties" are primary events for music making in Newfoundland and Labrador. The warmth of good company, food, and song described above by Elisabeth Greenleaf clearly combined to become something of an epiphanal moment in the early 1920s for her. She would return a few years later with Vassar friend Grace Yarrow Mansfield to make one of many significant folk song collections in Newfoundland. While the life of outport Newfoundland has changed dramatically, particularly with the demise of the North Atlantic cod fishery that had sustained it for centuries, community music making and food sharing remains strong at the beginning of the twenty-first century. Kitchen parties now also take new forms. Newfoundland expatriates and anyone else can participate in the Downhomer Internet Kitchen Party at www.downhomer. com. (The Downhomer company has also published three Newfoundland cookbooks.)

Stories of food and song texts both recount hardship, cooperation, and resilience, arguably qualities that still constitute the public perception of Newfoundland identity, whether one's ancestry is English, Irish, French, or Scottish, Mi'kmaq, Innu, Inuit, or Metis, or any of the dozens of new ethnocultural groups that now comprise the approximately half million who reside in Canada's "far east." Consider the story of "Newfoundland stone soup" for instance. It was said that the recipe developed at a point where people were desperately short of food. One person boasted that she would make a stone soup that would satisfy their needs. So she put a stone and some water in the pot and invited all the neighbors. Well, one had a single onion left in the cupboard and another a bit of salt beef; a third found a carrot and potato to add to the pot and so on. They declared that stone soup was the most delicious meal they could remember.

Food has clearly inspired a lot of local music. The most famous band of the folk revival of the 1970s and 1980s was Figgy Duff, named for the pudding that is described above. More recently, the ensemble Trimmed Naval Beef has come on the scene, choosing their name from the buckets of salt beef that every family used for Jiggs Dinner. For several decades, the percussion ensemble at the School of Music at Memorial University has been the Scruncheons, named after those tasty bits of pork fat that adorn many a Newfoundland dish. There's also many a song that narrates the pleasure of food. From Buddy Wasisname and the Other Fellers' "Salt Beef Junkie" and the "Chocolate Song," Simani's "Bottle of Wine" or "All for me Grog" to Lem Snow's song "The Great Lobster Boil" and Dick Nolan's greatest hit "Aunt Martha's Sheep," food has inspired laughter and camaraderie.

The Newfoundland menu in this cookbook is typical in that it uses local ingredients, prepared relatively simply. The recipes above range from traditional (Jiggs Dinner, Figgy Duff) to somewhat newer ways of using those local ingredients (the Partridgeberry Soufflé, for instance). Despite the commercial scarcity, cod remains a staple and is available in local restaurants. Other seafood, Atlantic salmon, sole, trout, mussels, or scallops, for instance, are enjoyed fresh from the sea. There are many distinctive moose recipes, although moose is not generally sold commercially. Rabbit ravioli is equally a local favorite. At the right season you can buy seal flippers on the waterfront in St. John's. My personal favorite, among local food stuffs, are the berries. From July through most of the fall, one can pick bakeapples (called cloudberries in Scandinavia) but don't let anyone know "your" spot or you're not a true Newfoundlander. Blueberries, partridgeberries (much like lingon-berries), chuckley pears (or Saskatoons), dogberries (Mountain Ash berries)—all are deliciously available on the rocky hillsides. The berries have also contributed to a fledgling wine industry. For many, however, the beverages of choice are "Screech," a rough-flavored rum, and the local beers—"1892" (the date commemorates one of the worst sealing disasters and also a major fire that devastated St. John's) from a microbrewery in St. John's is on the menu in this cookbook.

RECOMMENDED LISTENING

Bartlett, Lloyd. *Reflections: Newfoundland Classics*. Landwash, 2001. V11CD. (Favourite traditional songs arranged for solo guitar.)

Crooked Stovepipe. *Pickin' On the Rock*. Third Wave Productions, 1997. TWPCD104. (Bluegrass, one of Newfoundland's popular genres.)

Figgy Duff. *Figgy Duff. A Retrospective 1974–1993*. Amber, 1995. 02 50325. (Internationally acclaimed folk revival band.)

The Janet Cull Band. *The Janet Cull Band*. Landwash, 2004. 7-75020 566422-0. (Jazz and R&B influenced album.)

The Newfoundland Symphony Youth Choir. *Reaching from the Rock*. St. John's: NSYC, 1998.

Various artists. *Our Labrador*. (Innu, Métis, and other artists.)

FOR FURTHER INFORMATION

There are two journals devoted to the province's culture: *Newfoundland and Labrador Studies* and *Newfoundland Quarterly*. And we have our very own dictionary and a five-volume encyclopedia. A useful website with 400 audio clips, song texts, and extensive documentation regarding the earliest recorded collections made in the province may be found at http://www.mun.ca/folklore/leach/

Harp, Elmer Jr., Renouf, M. A. P., and Elain Groves Harp, eds. 2003. *Lives and Landscapes: A Photographic Memoir of Outport Newfoundland and Labrador, 1949–1963*. Montreal: McGill Queen's University Press.

Major, Kevin. 2001. *As Near to Heaven by Sea. A History of Newfoundland & Labrador*. Toronto: Penguin.

Pocius, Gerald. 2000. *A Place to Belong: Community Order and Everyday Space in Calvert, Newfoundland*. Montreal: McGill Queen's University Press.

Story, George, et al., eds. 1982. *Dictionary of Newfoundland English*. Toronto: University of Toronto Press.

ROMANIAN JEWISH NEW YORK
Jeffrey A. Summit

If you prolong your stay at table, you prolong your life.

Babylonian Talmud, Tractate Berachot 54b

Menu: Nanny's Chicken Soup, Nanny's Glazed Brisket, Kasha, and Honey Cake.
Preparation Time: 2½ hours, not including the brisket preparation the night before.
Cooking Process: Start the brisket the night before so that it has the chance to cool and be cut up. Start the cake. While the cake is baking, start the chicken soup. Once the soup starts boiling, prepare the brisket and place in the oven. When the soup is almost done, start the kasha. Serves six people.

The Recipes

NANNY'S CHICKEN SOUP

1 3–4-lb. whole chicken
1 medium yellow onion, chopped
2 stalks celery, chopped
4 carrots, sliced
1 parsnip, peeled and chopped
½ bunch of parsley, chopped
¼ bunch of dill, chopped
4 packets chicken bouillon
salt
pepper

Cover 1 whole chicken with 6–8 c. of water. (We take off the skin, but that's not how they did it in Romania.) Add onion, celery, carrots, parsnip, half a bunch of parsley, and half of the dill (you'll need the other half later). Bring to boil, spooning off the scum as soup boils. Cover and simmer until chicken is soft, about 90 minutes. Strain, take chicken off bones and add back to soup, add 4 packets of chicken bouillon (George Washington brand is preferred), and salt and pepper to taste. Nanny's secrets: grate a half a carrot into soup when soup starts to boil for "lovely golden color." Add the remainder of the chopped fresh dill to soup during the last 15–20 minutes. The key to making this correctly is not to use too much water. You will want to put in more water. Don't.

Nanny's Glazed Brisket

3–4 lb. first-cut beef brisket, cut flat
salt
pepper
½ t. oregano
½ t. basil
1 bay leaf
1 8-oz. bottle of Red Russian salad dressing
1 10-oz. jar of apricot jam
1 package onion soup mix

In a pot, place 3–4 lb. beef brisket in enough water to almost cover meat. Add salt, pepper, a little basil, oregano, and a bay leaf. The spices are optional except for salt and pepper. Bring water and brisket to a boil on top of stove then cover and place in 350°F oven to cook until "fork tender" for 3–4 hours. Drain water and refrigerate brisket until cold. This may be done 1 or 2 days ahead. When ready, slice brisket on the diagonal, against the grain and place thin slices in shallow serving dish. An oblong glass baking dish works well. To make the glaze, cook dressing, jam, and soup mix (Lipton preferred) on top of stove for 20 minutes. Cover sliced brisket with glaze and let it drizzle a bit between meat slices. Thirty minutes before serving, place dish in oven uncovered at 350°F, continue to baste the meat and keep checking to be sure it doesn't burn.

Kasha

1 egg
2 c. kasha (buckwheat)
2 packets chicken bouillon powder
1–2 T margarine or butter
1 onion
1 lb. mushrooms
vegetable oil

Beat 1 egg. Mix it into 2 c. kasha. Make 4 c. chicken bouillon with 2 packets of bouillon powder (George Washington brand is preferred) and 4 c. water. Heat pot so that broth dances. Brown the kasha and egg mixture in a pan over high heat, cooking the egg and separating the grains as they heat while constantly stirring until they're dry; about 5 minutes. Pour in bouillon broth carefully. Put in 1–2 T margarine or butter. Cover and turn to low for 15–20 minutes. Peel and chop 1 onion; wash and slice 1 lb. mushrooms. Sauté these two items in vegetable oil and mix them in with the kasha when it is finished. You can also add cooked peas and cooked bow tie noodles to make kasha *varnishkas*.

Kasha ingredients (Romanian Jewish, New York). Photo by Morgan Black.

Honey Cake

3½ c. flour

2½ t. baking powder

1 t. baking soda

salt

1 t. cinnamon

½ t. ground cloves

¼ t. ground ginger

1 c. sugar

½ c. chopped walnuts

½ c. raisins

3 eggs

¼ c. canola or vegetable oil

1⅓ c. honey

1 c. strong coffee

Sift together 3½ c. flour, 2½ t. baking powder, 1 t. baking soda, ½ t. salt, 1 t. cinnamon, ½ t. cloves, ¼ t. ginger, and 1 c. sugar. Add ½ c. chopped walnuts and ½ c. raisins. Separate 3 eggs; beat the yolks and whites separately. Make a well in the dry mixture and add the beaten egg yolks, ¼ c. oil, 1⅓ c. honey, and 1 c. warm strong coffee. Mix on medium speed until well mixed. Fold in stiffly beaten egg whites. Bake in tube pan at 350°F for 1 hour. Invert onto serving plate.

It's Shabbas. Eat Slowly

These recipes, typical of a *Shabbat* (Sabbath) or holiday dinner, are from my Romanian grandmother, Fanny Slomowitz. As the family moved from the Lower East Side of New York to the Bronx and finally to Waterbury, Connecticut, these recipes have been altered by my mother, Elsie Summit. In their current form, they are the product of Jewish suburbia in the late 1940s and 1950s. My grandmother would say, "In the old country, when a Jew would eat a chicken, one of them was probably sick." Not so in Connecticut. Food was plentiful and love was measured in the amount one could put on the table and the amount one could consume in return. On Shabbat and holidays, *challah*, braided egg bread, is also traditional. The honey cake is special for Rosh Hashanah, the New Year, symbolic of wishes for a sweet year.

Music frames the traditional Friday night Shabbat meal. Women light Shabbat candles and either sing or softly chant the blessings in Hebrew. The family sings *Shalom Aleichem* (peace be upon you). The leader begins chanting the *Kiddush*, Sabbath blessing over wine, and at set points all join in to sing the blessing. The husband sings a selection from the book of Proverbs praising his wife, and parents place their hands on the heads of their children, offering a blessing of peace. All of this is done in song and it is almost impossible to imagine "making Shabbas" without music. After the meal, one of the guests or family members leads the *Birkat Hamazon*, the blessing after meals. Some parts of this prayer are chanted in an undertone recitative. At other passages, group singing turns raucous and guests pound on the table.

While the food in our home has gotten less traditional (read: more vegetarian) over the years, the music has grown more so. Much of our family's "traditional" music is reclaimed, as our own practice has become more ritually observant over time. While many of these blessings were always a part of our family's practice, singing around the table was truncated in the 1950s. When I was a rabbinical student in Jerusalem in the early 1970s, I consciously set out to change that, and much of my friends' social and religious life was organized around music. We would prowl the alleys of the Yemenite, Hasidic, or Syrian sections of town, looking for the synagogue with the best music. We would gather in student apartments for potluck dinners, packing tape recorders and bottles of cheap Israeli brandy for *zemir*-ins (after "sing-ins," from the Hebrew *zemirot* [Sabbath table songs]). A few years before, we had organized and participated in "sit-ins" as we occupied campus buildings during the late 1960s; now we came together with a different purpose. Wanting to learn more about our history and traditions, we met to trade and record as many melodies as we could collectively assemble, looking to expand and broaden our repertoires. I searched out my Romanian relatives who had settled on a kibbutz in Israel and spent Shabbat with them. The tunes that I and many other American Jews learned at that time still make up the staple of our favorite liturgical and para-liturgical repertoires. Our *zemirot* come mostly from that time, as we set about to re-learn the music that our parents had chosen not to sing.

While Jewish liturgical music is the performance of sacred text, these Sabbath table hymns are valued less for their Hebrew poetry than for their melodies, often drawn from both Jewish and non-Jewish folk songs. Influenced by Jewish mystical teachings, many of these texts developed between the eleventh and sixteenth centuries. Their strophic form and use of refrains encourages group participation. While a good Shabbat guest will bring a nice bottle of kosher wine to dinner, a *really* good guest will bring some wonderful, unfamiliar melody for one of the *zemirot* and teach it as these hymns are sung around the table after the meal.

The Jewish tradition has been talking about food for the past 3,000 years and history is referenced and reexperienced at the table. On Passover, *matzah* is both the "bread of affliction" eaten by slaves and the "bread of liberation" sustaining the Jews on their flight to freedom. *Latkes* (potato pancakes) or *sufganiot* (doughnuts fried in oil) mark the miracle of Hanukah when according to legend, a small flask of oil burned for eight days in the liberated temple. Ideally, the laws of keeping kosher are meant to deepen one's awareness of the sacredness of life and bring careful, sober consideration to the act of slaughtering a living creature. When the twelfth-century sage Maimonides wrote about the importance of moderation and balance in diet he was not only approaching this as a doctor but also as a rabbi who taught the value of the *shviel hazahav*, the golden path of moderation.

In the Jewish tradition, eating requires focus and concentration. One says a different blessing over an apple than over a potato. Before eating, you have to stop and ask, "Where does this food come from? Does it grow on a tree or in the ground?" For that matter, you are not allowed to eat anything until you thank and acknowledge the Holy One who created the food. In the Talmud, the rabbis state that eating something without saying a blessing is akin to stealing! Yet once you have focused on the food, said the appropriate blessing, and expressed your thanks, it is yours to enjoy. Furthermore, over a meal, one is obligated to exchange words of Torah: good, deep, meaningful conversation should be part of every meal.

The Blessing after Meals contains the line "you will eat, be satisfied and bless..." The tradition underscores that satisfaction with food comes from much more than the quantity, or even the quality, of the food one eats. Satisfaction comes from the full experience of the table; eating mindfully, being actively thankful, engaging in deep conversation over food. At the Shabbat table, from the beginning of the meal to its formal close, these elements are bound together with song.

RECOMMENDED LISTENING

Ben Zion Shenker. *Modzitz Classics, Volume One and Two: A Selection of the Finest in Chassidic Neginah Composed by the Famous Rabbis of Modzits.* Mosdos Modzitz, 1992.
Open the Gates! New American Jewish Music for Prayer. Compiled and annotated by Robert Cohen. Sterling Media Productions, 2002.
Shabbos in Shomayim: The Final Album. Composed and sung by Shlomo Carlebach. Aderet, 2000.
With Every Breath: The Music of Shabbat at BJ. Produced and arranged by Anthony Coleman. Congregation B'nai Jeshurun, New York, 1999.

FOR FURTHER INFORMATION

Kligman, Mark. 2000. Music in Judaism. In *The Encyclopaedia of Judaism*, edited by Jacob Neusner, Alan J. Avery-Peck, and William Scott Green, vol. 2. Leiden: Museum of Jewish Heritage; Brill, 905–924.
Schleifer, Eliyahu. 1992. Jewish liturgical music from the Bible to Hasidism. In *Sacred Sound and Social Change: Liturgical Music in Jewish and Christian Experience.* Edited by Lawrence A. Hoffman and Janet R. Walton. Notre Dame, IN: University of Notre Dame Press, 59–83.
Summit, Jeffrey A. 2000. *The Lord's Song in a Strange Land: Music and Identity in Contemporary Jewish Worship.* New York: Oxford University Press. (CD included.)

SOUTHERN APPALACHIA (WESTERN NORTH CAROLINA)
Lucy M. Long

The beans they are half done, the bread is not so well.
The meat it is burnt up, and the coffee's black as heck.
But when you get your task done, you're glad to come to call,
For anything you get to eat, it tastes good done or raw.

From "Buddy, Won't You Roll Down the Line"
(*Old-Time String Band Songbook*, 204)

Menu: Country Ham, Soup Beans, Cornbread with Molasses and Homemade Jams, Leather Britches, Greens, Fried Hominy, Sauerkraut, Fried Irish Potatoes, Fried Apples, and Corn on the Cob. For dessert, serve Blackberry Cobbler. Serve dinner with sweet milk and water.

Preparation Time: Approximately 3 hours.

Cooking Process: The night before, start soaking the "leather britches" (dried green beans) and dried navy or pinto beans. In the morning fry 1 lb. bacon or fat back in order to get some grease. A spoonful of grease adds flavor to all these dishes. A cast iron frying pan is a necessity. If possible, use several—one for baking; the others for the cooking. Time the cooking so that the cornbread and corn on the cob go straight from cooking to the table. The cobbler can be put in the oven when the cornbread comes out. This traditionally would be a midday meal (dinner). Evening meal (supper) would be leftovers or buttermilk poured over crumbled cornbread. Serves six people.

The Recipes

COUNTRY HAM

3 lb. salt- or smoke-cured country ham
1 T bacon grease

Cut 3 lb. salt- or smoke-cured country ham into ¼" slices. Fry in a cast iron skillet, preferably with high slanted sides, in about 1 T of bacon grease at medium-high heat until it smells and looks done. It should be a reddish color with a fairly chewy texture. Save the grease.

SOUP BEANS

½ lb. navy or pinto beans, field or black-eyed peas
1 ham hock (optional)
1 T bacon grease (optional)
1 medium yellow onion, chopped
1 medium green bell pepper (optional), chopped
salt
pepper

Rinse, sort, and soak the beans overnight. Drain, place in large pot, cover with cold water and bring to a boil. Add ham hocks or bacon grease. Simmer for 3 hours. Add onion (and green peppers if you want to be fancy) and simmer for another hour. Add salt and pepper to taste. (Optional variation—season with hot sauce.)

Cornbread with Molasses and Homemade Jams

2 c. cornmeal (or 1 c. cornmeal and 1 c. flour)
1 t. salt
3 t. baking powder
2 eggs, beaten
1 c. buttermilk (or 1 egg and 1¼ c. milk)
¼ c. oil, melted shortening or butter, grease from bacon or ham

Mix dry ingredients. Make a well and stir in liquid ingredients. Stir only until mixed and pour into hot greased cast iron skillet (or 9" x 9" cake pan). Bake for 20–25 minutes at 400°F. Remove from heat; slather with butter and honey, molasses, or homemade jam.

Leather Britches

1 lb. green beans, dried (or fresh)
1 ham hock
1 T bacon grease
salt
pepper

Leather britches are green beans that have been strung on a long thread and dried in a cool dark place. They're picked after the seed has matured (word is that the mature beans have more protein). Prepare beans by washing and soaking overnight (fresh ones can simply be washed and trimmed). Cover with water, add 1 ham hock, bacon grease, salt, and pepper, and simmer for about 6 hours for the britches and about 3 hours for fresh.

Greens

3 lb. mixed greens
½ lb. bacon
2 ham hocks (optional)
1 medium yellow onion (optional), chopped
¼ c. white vinegar
2 hard boiled eggs, sliced

Wash mixed greens (turnip, collards, mustard, kale, chard, poke sallet, or dandelion) several times in cold water and trim. Method I: Cover with water. Bring to a boil, add fried bacon or ham or a spoonful of grease with salt and pepper to taste (optional chopped onion). Simmer for about 30 minutes or until tender. Method II: Boil 2 ham hocks in 2 quarts of water for 1 hour; add greens with salt and pepper. Serve with vinegar or top with sliced hard boiled eggs. Save the "pot likker" for dunking cornbread or for broth for soup or gravy.

Fried Hominy

1 14-oz. can yellow hominy
1 14-oz. can white hominy
1 T bacon grease
salt
pepper
1 medium yellow onion (optional), sliced
1 medium green bell pepper (optional), sliced

Fry the hominy in bacon grease with salt and pepper. Optional: add sliced onions and green pepper when frying.

Sauerkraut

2 14-oz. cans of sauerkraut (or homemade)

If you don't have the good fortune to have access to homemade sauerkraut, open 2 cans of sauerkraut and heat, either on top of stove or bake in oven. Optional: cook with pork for flavoring, or mix with fried apples.

Fried Irish Potatoes

2 large potatoes
1 T bacon grease
salt
pepper

Wash and boil 2 potatoes. Drain. Keep skins on. Slice and fry in bacon grease until brown. Add salt and pepper to taste. For variation, mash the boiled potatoes and add salt and pepper. Form into patties and fry.

Fried Apples

6 medium apples
1 T bacon grease
salt
lemon juice

Wash and core apples (don't peel). Slice into ¼"-thick pieces and fry in grease. Sprinkle with a pinch of salt and lemon juice (to keep the color from turning brown). If desired, add molasses, honey, or sugar while cooking. (Reconstituted dried apples can be used instead of fresh ones.)

CORN ON THE COB

6 ears corn
butter
salt

Start boiling enough water in a large pan to cover corn. Shuck 6 ears of corn. Drop into boiling water for 2–3 minutes or when it smells ready. Don't let boil too long—the kernels will get tough. Roll in butter and salt if desired.

BLACKBERRY COBBLER

2 c. fresh blackberries
½ c. sugar
6 T butter
¾ c. flour
1 c. sugar
2 t. baking powder
½ t. salt
¾ c. milk

Preheat oven to 350°F. Wash and sort blackberries. Sprinkle with ½ c. sugar and set aside. Melt 6 T butter in baking pan. Mix together dry ingredients; stir in ¾ c. milk. Pour batter over melted butter. Pour blackberries over batter. Bake 50 minutes.

Homemade Food and Music in Western North Carolina

It is almost impossible to do music fieldwork without encountering food—especially in the southern Appalachian mountains where food represents hospitality, generosity, belonging, and an appreciation for the culture as a whole. It is not surprising then that some of my most memorable and insightful moments in researching dulcimer traditions in western North Carolina were situated around food. It was while stringing beans on a front porch that I learned that a dulcimer player who had just received a national award was considered just plain lazy by his wife; it was while eating pieces of Spam fried on a wood stove that I heard about how one of the few women fiddle players had neglected cooking for her own children in favor of making music; and it was at a kitchen table that I discovered that banjo heads were made from groundhog skin; and that, with enough boiling and gravy, the rest of the groundhog made tasty steaks and stews. It was over food that "informants" related to me as a guest and potential friend; that they "interviewed" me to see if I was the kind of person they could trust with their traditions. If I turned my nose up at their food, failed to understand the generosity symbolized in it, or failed to understand the importance of taking time to socialize, not just to "collect," they had no interest in sharing themselves with me.

While I did not realize it at the time, music and food in Appalachia share a number of similarities, embodying and presenting a distinctive aesthetic and ethos. Food tends to be simple, straightforward, and plain, adjectives frequently applied to the music. Structurally, tunes tend to involve two parts of 16 bars each. These are each repeated; and then the entirety is repeated as many times as desired according to context (9–12 times for a dance; 4 times for a performance; 25 times to put the children to sleep or to teach the tune). Meals, likewise, tend to involve the same basic ingredients: cornbread and milk with pork or beans—repeated daily. Variations occur on both, but tend to be subtle to the point that they are not recognized except by those steeped in the tradition. For example, a fiddler may add a melodic ornament or shift the bowing rhythm, a guitarist might put in a double strum or hold a chord longer than usual. Similarly, the food can be varied in subtle ways—sugar or white flour used in the cornbread; green peppers cooked with the beans; different varieties of greens used; bacon rather than salt pork used for flavoring.

Both the music and the food traditionally were homemade and handmade, drawing from local and usually natural resources. Both cooks and musicians had to make do with whatever was available, adapting resources and adapting themselves. Historically, food was either grown, gathered, or hunted. Procuring (hunting, gathering, gardening), preserving (canning, smoking, drying), and preparing food took up the bulk of both adults' and children's lives. Stores brought in some necessities and niceties (baking powder, salt, sugar, coffee), but were almost more important socially, offering a site for gathering, gossiping, storytelling, and music making. Above all, both food and music were social, a way to bring people together and to create community (especially at dances and church events). Sharing food was a way to ensure survival during times of hardship; sharing music was a way to affirm relationships, to entertain and pass the time, and occasionally, to bring in extra cash.

The importance of food is reflected in tune titles and lyrics referring to food or the activities surrounding it. Wild game was an important staple of the mountain diet ("Squirrel Heads and Gravy," "Groundhog," "Possum Up a Gum Stump," "Rabbit Ain't Got No Tail At All," "Forked Deer"), along with nuts and berries that grew wild ("Blackberry Blossom," "Chinquapin Hunting"). Almost every family kept some chickens ("Cluck Old Hen," "Crow Black Chicken") and pigs ("I've got a pig at home in a pen, corn to feed him on"), and some were let loose to forage for acorns ("Wild Hog in the Woods"). Kitchen gardens and orchards supplied most of the fresh and preserved produce ("Cabbage Head," "June Apple"—a sweet yellow apple that ripened earlier than most varieties). Corn was another staple of the Appalachian diet, usually as corn bread, hominy, fresh on the cob. The best-known and most stereotypical use of corn was for "moonshine." This liquor was used for medicinal purposes as well as recreational ones, and for many farmers provided a convenient way to ship their corn to market. It also provided the subject of many songs, both celebratory of its qualities ("Hot Corn, Cold Corn," "Stillhouse") or condemnatory ("Likes Likker Than Me," "Goodbye Booze").

RECOMMENDED LISTENING

Contemporary performers of old-time music: any recordings by Dan Gellert, Brad Leftwich, Bruce Green, Ida Red, Rhythm Rats, The Rockinghams, Tom, Brad, and Alice, Highwoods String Band ("Feed Your Baby's Onions"), Rayna Gellert. Re-issues include: *Times Ain't Like They Used to Be*, 9 volumes (Yazoo); *The Cornshucker's Frolic*, 2 volumes (Yazoo); *Music from the Lost Provinces* (Old Hat Enterprises); *The Bristol Sessions*. Documentary recordings: Mike Seeger, Melvin Wine, American fiddle tunes, High Atmosphere, Library of Congress Field Recordings.

FOR FURTHER INFORMATION

Old-Time Music Homepage at http://www.oldtimemusic.com

Page, Linda Garland, and Eliot Wigginton, eds. 1992. *The Foxfire Book of Appalachian Cookery*. Chapel Hill: University of North Carolina Press.

CANOE NATIONS OF THE PACIFIC NORTHWEST

Pauline "Isumatta" Tuttle

You can't sing with a full stomach.

Menu: Red Raspberry Juice and Rose Hip Tea; Prelude: Coastal Fry Bread with Venison and Saskatoon Berry (or Wild Blueberry) Soup; Main Meal: Baked Salmon, White Rice, Steamed Vegetables (Fiddleheads and Asparagus); Dessert: Candied Salmon with Berry Cup.

Preparation Time: 4 days (beverage); 24 hours (appetizer and dessert); 1½ hours (other).

Cooking Process: Prepare red raspberry juice and rose hip syrup for tea 4 days prior to meal. Marinate the candied salmon, soak the venison, and prepare the dessert berries the night before. Rinse and scrape the venison the next morning. Take ½ c. butter out to soften early in the day. When ready to prepare and cook meal, prep vegetables for soup. Put berries in dessert cups and place in fridge. Prepare venison for soup and once it is simmering, preheat oven to 375°F and then prepare salmon for baking. Prepare vegetables for main dish. Prepare dough for fry bread. While dough is rising, put salmon in the oven to bake, prepare rice, and heat oil for fry bread. Once oil is almost at the right temperature for deep frying, add vegetables to soup and bring to a boil. Cook fry bread, turning soup to a simmer once it boils. Bring rice and vegetables to a boil, turn down to simmer and serve soup and fry bread with red raspberry juice. Clear soup dishes, turn rice and vegetables off, take salmon out of oven. Turn oven down to 350°F and prepare salmon and vegetables to serve. Put candied salmon in the oven. Serve the main course. After dinner, take candied salmon out, prepare rose hip tea, and serve dessert with tea. Note: To serve, place salmon on platter, arranging rice and vegetables around the salmon. If you don't have a large enough platter, serve each dish individually. Serves six people.

The Recipes

RED RASPBERRY JUICE

1 c. fresh, unpasteurized apple vinegar
4 c. wild raspberries
2 c. sugar (more or less)
2 qt. sparkling water

This is one of several Aboriginal precursors to the Slushy, which has become a core part of the diet of coastal youth in recent years. Pour 1 c. fresh apple vinegar (unpasteurized apple vinegar can be homemade or bought in health food stores) over four cups wild raspberries and let stand for 4 days. Drain off juice and add 1 c. sugar to each cup of juice. Boil gently for 15 minutes. Cool. To serve, dilute 1 part syrup to 3 parts sparkling water and pour into tumblers filled with crushed ice.

Rose Hip Tea

2 c. rose hips
1½ c. sugar

When in season, pick rose hips and remove stems. Wash in warm water. Bring 1½ c. water to a boil in large saucepan. Add rose hips and boil for 20 minutes. Strain into a large measuring cup through a jelly bag overnight. Place juice in saucepan and add 1½ c. sugar. Stir until dissolved and bring to a boil. Boil for 5 minutes. Let cool and store in fridge or preserve in sealed sterilized jars until ready to use. To make tea, simply add syrup to hot water according to taste. For a cold drink, dilute with sparkling water.

Coastal Fry Bread

1 package yeast
2 T white sugar
5 c. flour
salt
3 c. vegetable oil for frying

Dissolve 1 package of yeast and 2 T white sugar in ½ cup of warm water (should be about 110°F or lukewarm when dropped on your wrist). Once dissolved, add another 1½ cups of warm water. Mix together. Add 5 c. flour, mixed with 1 t. salt, a cup at a time until the dough no longer sticks to the bowl. Turn the dough out onto a floured counter and knead for about 10 minutes, or until the dough is satiny. Add more flour as needed until it no longer sticks to your hands. Oil the original bowl. Shape the dough into a round ball and place in oiled bowl. Cover with a warm damp tea towel and place in a warm spot to rise for about 20–30 minutes.

When finished rising, pinch chunks off the ball to make the individual fry breads. For a generous portion, pinch off a piece of dough the size of an orange and for smaller portions, pinch off a piece the size of a small kiwi. Slowly heat 3 c. vegetable oil (this should take 15–20 minutes) to the point that it appears wavy (not smoking); it should be about 365°F. I just use a candy thermometer and a heavy skillet but you could also use a deep fryer or an electric frying pan to ensure an even heat. This seals the dough immediately and does not let the oil in, keeping the fry bread light and fluffy inside. Test the oil with a tiny piece of dough; the dough should rise to the surface. Gently pull and stretch the ball out into a thin circle with your hands. Place it in the hot oil and let it cook until a rich golden brown. In a large skillet, you can comfortably place about 4 or 5 large pieces of fry bread. Once the bread floats to the top of the oil you can easily check the underside to see if it's ready to be flipped over but once you've flipped it, don't flip it back to the other side or it will get tough. When both sides are brown, take it out and drain any excess oil on a piece of paper towel. Allow 20 minutes to make three rounds; this will give you 12 pieces—2 for each person. Fry bread is best served hot with butter, so you will need to time your dinner prep so that the bread is finished just as the soup is ready to be served. This is not something that you can leave alone while doing other prep work as you really need to keep an eye on the browning process or they will burn.

Venison and Saskatoon Berry (or Wild Blueberry) Soup

1 lb. venison loin
1 c. white vinegar
2 c. potatoes
4–6 carrots
4 celery stalks
1 medium yellow onion
2 T olive oil
½ c. flour
1 t. celery salt
1 T soy sauce
1 c. Saskatoon berries (or wild blueberries)

Prepare 1 lb. of venison; the loin and ribs are the most tender cuts but round is fine for a soup if properly tenderized. To reduce the gamey flavor of the venison, cut all fat off and place in a large pot or bowl filled with water and 1 c. of vinegar. Soak overnight in the fridge. In the morning, rinse extremely well. Lay out flat on the counter and scrape off the thin layer of tallow on both sides of the venison. Pound the meat to tenderize and cut into small chunks, about ¾" cubes. You can either return the meat to the fridge until ready to make the soup or prepare the meat and cook in the slow cooker for the day, adding the vegetables about 30 minutes before you want to serve the soup. When you are ready to make the soup, dice 2 cups of potatoes, slice 4–6 carrots into thick rounds, slice 4 stalks of celery into thin semirounds, and finely chop 1 medium onion. Separate onion and celery from potatoes and carrots and set aside. Heat a thin layer (about 2 T) of olive oil in large saucepan.

While the oil is heating, put the venison chunks into a small brown paper bag with ½ c. flour and shake until they are coated. Drop the coated venison chunks into the oil and brown on all sides. Venison tends to be very dry so this helps seal the fats in. Add the celery and onions, sautéing until onions are clear. Add 2 c. water a little a time, stirring as you go each time. As you add the water, the texture should gradually change from a smooth gravy to a thick cream-like texture to a thinner soup-like texture (if you add it too quickly, you'll end up with lumps). Add 1 t. celery salt and 1 T soy sauce. Add 4 more cups of water and bring to a boil. Immediately turn heat down and simmer for about 1 hour (you can simmer it as long as you like; the longer you simmer the meat the more tender it will be). Add prepared vegetables and 1 c. Saskatoon berries (or wild blueberries if you can't find Saskatoons) and bring to a boil, reducing to a simmer immediately. Simmer for about 30 minutes or until all ingredients are tender. Serve with fry bread and butter.

BAKED SALMON

6 lb. fresh wild (Pacific) salmon
3 T butter
½ medium yellow onion, diced
1 lemon
1 bunch fresh thyme (optional)
1 bunch fresh sage (optional)

Preheat oven to 375°F. Wash, scale, and clean 6 lb. fresh wild salmon as soon as you bring it home. Traditionally the head and tail are removed and used in the coastal delicacy, Fish Head Soup. If you prefer, leave the head and tail on and bake the salmon whole. Dot the inside of the salmon generously with butter and sprinkle the inside with about 2 T diced onions. Squeeze ¼–½ of a lemon on top of salmon. Some like to fill a cotton seasoning pouch with minced onion, thyme, and sage and place it inside the salmon while it bakes (just take a piece of cotton and wrap the seasonings inside). Cover cookie sheet with foil and oil it so the salmon doesn't stick. Place salmon on foil and bake at 375°F for about 30 minutes on each side, 1 hour in total.

WHITE RICE

3 c. white rice (preferably long grain)
butter to taste

Boil 3 c. long grain white rice with 5 c. water (covered) until tender, about 20 minutes. Serve with butter.

STEAMED FIDDLEHEADS AND ASPARAGUS

24 fiddleheads
24 young asparagus shoots
1 lemon, juiced

If using fresh vegetables, wash first. Place 24 fiddleheads (sword fern shoots—just the young and tender curled part) and 24 young asparagus shoots in steamer and steam for about 15–20 minutes. If using frozen fiddleheads, cook according to directions on package. Squeeze fresh lemon juice on vegetables before serving.

Candied Salmon with Berry Cup

6 c. mixed berries
1 c. white sugar
2 6–8 oz. salmon fillets
⅛ c. butter
⅔ c. dark brown sugar
2 T soy sauce
1 t. finely grated ginger root
⅔ c. apple cider vinegar
2 medium cloves garlic, finely chopped
1 small can condensed milk

Mix berries (blackberries, blueberries, huckleberries, gooseberries, raspberries, thimbleberries, elderberries, or whatever is in season and available) and sprinkle with 1 c. white sugar the night before the meal. Cover and let sit overnight in fridge (the sugar causes the juice to extract from the berries and serves as a sauce for the dessert). Also the night before, skin and debone 2 6–8 oz. salmon fillets, slice into strips about ¾" wide and 1½" long or finger food-sized. Caramelize ⅛ c. butter and ⅔ c. dark brown sugar in saucepan, stirring constantly, cook over medium heat until sugar melts and bubbles. Let it bubble for a couple of minutes and then add 2 T soy sauce, 1 t. finely grated ginger, ⅔ c. apple cider vinegar, and 2 medium cloves of garlic; heat until it boils; let mixture simmer and caramelize for about 5 minutes before taking off heat. Cool and place your salmon fingers and the marinade in a plastic baggie. Lay flat in fridge and turn often. Marinate for 12–24 hours.

Prior to cooking main dishes and fry bread, place berries in sherbet cups or small glass bowls. Just before you serve dinner, drain salmon fingers and place on oiled foil laid on a cookie sheet. While your guests are enjoying dinner, bake candied salmon at 350°F for 10–15 minutes, turn over and bake for another 10 minutes. When ready to serve, top berries with a light swirl of condensed milk (Eagle brand is preferred) and place 1–2 pieces of candied salmon diagonally on side, like a stir stick. Place remainder of candied salmon on the plate the sherbet bowl is sitting on.

To Share a Table of Food and Song: Canoe Nations of the Pacific Northwest

The relationship between the peoples of the Northwest Coast and their food resources permeates all aspects of life in the Canoe Nations, where the principle that any action has a reaction is key to the rationale for food-resource protocols. Here, "the land" is much more than just landscapes—mountains, forests, rivers, lakes, coastlines—that support an abundance of wildlife, fish, and medicinal and food plants. "The land," rather, refers to all life inhabiting the lands. The importance of the relationship with the land is expressed through spoken prayers before dinner, prayers in which all aspects of creation are addressed as peoples and thanked: the finned-ones, the four-leggeds, the two-leggeds, the rooted-ones, the winged-ones, the crawling-ones—all said to be living beings, ancestors who walked this earth in the time before Transformer separated the species, turning some into humans, others into stone, and leaving some to continue as animals. Expressed through dinner songs, dances, and stories reenacted at potlatches, winter dances, canoe festivals, and life-cycle ceremonies, this relationship is protected and nurtured by protocols that teach one how to interact with the environment and with food resources, providing a sense of identity and defining who the Coastal Canoe peoples are.

Key to the ongoing survival of those who dwell in the Canoe Nations are the finned-ones, especially the Salmon People who, it is said, at the time of transition, consciously chose to sacrifice their lives every year so that the transformed humans might survive. It is said that Transformer taught the new humans how to maintain a proper relationship with the Salmon People, how to show respect for each of the five Chiefs in the diverse Salmon Nations–Coho, Sockeye, Pink, Chinook, Dog Salmon—by holding a First Salmon Ceremony annually for each ancestral Salmon Chief. Although community-specific protocols change, the basic traditions remain constant. When the First Salmon of the year is caught, it is welcomed as an honored royal guest. In some areas, it is ceremonially given a name that is validated through feasting, songs, dance, and gift-giving. The head, bones, and entrails of the First Salmon are ceremonially returned to the water, sometimes sprinkled with eagle down, to rest on a bundle of cedar—in other areas it may be wrapped in a woven cedar mat—to return home to the Salmon People and tell of the dignity and respect they were shown, thus ensuring a plentiful harvest next year.

Particularly important on the Northwest Coast are ceremonies linked to the first harvest of the year, such as the First Root and First Berry ceremonies, in which the harvest is thanked and welcomed as a new relative would be. Always, the plant from which the berry is taken is thanked, either through a sung or spoken prayer or by offering a pinch of tobacco to the roots of the plant. Songs are a crucial part of these ceremonies for it is known that when words are intoned and given life by the drum, their efficacy is enhanced. Rarely do you hear a song that is about the geography of the land. Rather, songs embody the relationship of people to particular sites and aspects of the land. Hundreds of songs are linked to all of the living resources that come from the land, that live on the land and in the waters and provide for the needs of the people, such as whale songs, bear songs, salmon songs, root songs, potlatch songs, and more.

Cooking, like music, is taught through example and passed down along familial lines. Young women learn to cook by assisting their mothers and aunts, while the young men learn their roles from their fathers and uncles. Typically, women prepare the meals, with the exception of barbecuing the salmon on cedar spits, which is the prerogative of the men. While men procure and clean the wildlife and large species of fish, the women often clean the salmon and collect shellfish. Everyone learns to participate in food gathering and preparation in one way or another. Likewise, almost everyone learns to sing and dance. Yet, there are those who go on to specialize in cooking or creating music. Unlike cooking, music is passed on through structured interaction between those who carry family songs and those who need to learn family songs. While only the men traditionally sing and drum songs linked to hunting and dinner songs sung in potlatch contexts, the singing and sharing of food-gathering songs are the perogative of women.

Dinnertime at a potlatch is a time when food for hundreds of people is served with breathtaking efficiency to the rhythm of the drum and the vocal strains of a wide array of dinner songs. Throughout the meal, dinner songs are sung and accompanied on the frame drum by a group of local singers from the family who is hosting the potlatch. There is not a unique body of dinner songs. Rather, they are drawn from the repertoire of the group singing. Sometimes, the plates, cups, and silverware are presented to the guests as gifts, thus serving to raise the prestige of the host family and also saving the time involved in washing the dishes after such a large meal. During the songs, teams of youth begin by bringing plates of food to the elders, then the children, and finally to those in their middle years. These same youths take away the dirty plates, quickly replacing them with dessert and tea or coffee, and just as quickly doing the rounds with large garbage bags. Singers come and go, joining in the dinner songs intermittently so that others can eat and tend to the needs of their guests. At various times in the evening, during masked dances and breaks, box after box of fresh fruit are passed out to the guests: oranges, apples, bananas. Leftover food goes home with the guests and can just as easily come in the form of sacks of flour, sugar, or potatoes that weren't used, or bowls/plates of prepared food.

Tastes on the Northwest Coast are simple; the simpler, the better. The use of spices is pretty much limited to salt, onion, and, for special treats such as some candied salmon recipes, wild ginger. The taste is in the rich flavors of the local foods, locked in through the processes by which they are preserved and cooked, rather then with the addition of condiments and spices. Nowhere is this more true than with smoked salmon, which gleans its full-bodied flavor from the type of wood used in the smoker. Today, rice is a staple here and people prefer it plain and simple. White rice with butter is much preferred to the wild rices so typically featured on the menus of restaurants catering to tourists in search of a Northwest Coast experience. Wild rice is seen as foreign food, imported from the eastern First Nations.

Powwow fare differs from potlatch and feast fare in significant ways. While all are considered sacred activities, there is much more of a carnival type of atmosphere at most powwows on the Northwest Coast, and this is reflected in the foods sold by the vendors surrounding the dance circle. The one food that is common to both is fry bread, a delicious fried bread that accompanies every feast. While I have not met a First Nations woman who does not know how to make a mean batch of fry bread, there are professional fry bread makers in every community who make several hundred pieces of fry bread for potlatches, cultural festivals, memorials, and large gatherings. A favorite food at any powwow or festival is Indian Tacos, a syncretized version of the Sloppy Joe using fry bread, Sloppy Joe filling, and cheese topping. Another favorite food at powwows is Indian ice cream, made from soapberries, a sticky translucent orange-red berry. These berries are too bitter to be eaten fresh but when mixed with a little sugar and water they foam up like a meringue and make a wonderful ice cream. All you need to do is whip 1 qt. berries with about ½–1 c. water and about 2 c. sugar to taste; then freeze. Traditionally, the berries would be beaten into a pulp and dried in flat cakes or loaves for storage during the winter months and then beaten together with fish oil, often oolichan, and snow for a winter treat.

The menu I have chosen for you offers both a sample of everyday cuisine, which is very simple on the Northwest Coast, and a special treat of candied salmon. While I have offered only two ways of preparing salmon, when invited to the home of a coastal chief for dinner once, we were offered salmon prepared in about twenty different ways, from several types of candied salmon to barbecued salmon to wind-dried salmon to salmon chips, and much more. A family rich in food resources is indeed a rich family on the Northwest Coast and it is their honor to display this wealth for guests and to share it with those in the community whose stores are less plentiful. When resources are low, the old ones suggest that singing makes you forget your hunger. Hence, the proverb, "you can't sing with a full stomach," cautions us to always remember to set a table for our friends and relatives and to welcome our guests with song.

RECOMMENDED LISTENING

George, Len, and Rick Peter. *Share Our Pride: The Original Soundtrack from "Great Deeds."* Cowichan Native Village. CNVCD98-01.

Halpern, Ida, collector. *Indian Music of the Pacific Northwest Coast.* Folkways Ethnic Library: Folkways Records & Service Corp., 1967. FE 4523.

Wakatush (Carlo Anne Hilton). *Mother and Child.* LWMS, 2000.

Wasden, William Jr., Dorothy Alfred, and Caroline Rufus. *One Nation One Voice: Songs of the Kwakwaka'wakw.* U'mista Cultural Society. UCCCD-8802.

FOR FURTHER INFORMATION

Batdorf, Carol. 1980. *The Feast is Rich: A Guide to Traditional Coast Salish Indian Food Gathering and Preparation*. Bellingham, WA: Whatcom Museum of History & Art.

Bouchard, Randy, and Dorothy Kennedy, eds. 2002. *Indian Myths & Legends from the North Pacific Coast of America: A Translation of Franz Boas' 1895 Edition of Indianische Sagen von der Nord-Pacifischen Küste Amerikas*. Trans. Dietrich Bertz. Vancouver, BC: Talonbooks.

Ryan, Esmé, and Willie Smyth, eds. 1997. *Spirit of the First People: Native American Music Traditions of Washington State* (with accompanying CD). Seattle: University of Washington Press.

Turner, Nancy. 2005. *The Earth's Blanket. Traditional Teachings for Sustainable Living*. Seattle: University of Washington Press.

9
Oceania

AUSTRALIA

Jennifer Gall

To cook a galah [Australian parrot], put it in the pot with a stone, boil the lot for a day, throw away the galah, and eat the stone.

Menu: Outdoor Bush Dinner: Macadamia Nuts and Cold Beer; Longmore's Snake Patties, Jacket Potatoes, Pumpkin, and Parsnip, Damper, Garden Salad, and Bananas in the Fire (with melted chocolate and marshmallows) served with Mango Ice Cream. Enjoy this meal with cold beer. Finish up with Boiled Fruit Cake and Billy Tea.

Preparation Time: 1 hour for the fruit cake prepared before the meal; 30 minutes for the ice cream; for the main meal, 2–3 hours, depending on the size of the snake and the heat of the fire.

Cooking Process: Make the mango ice cream and bake the fruit cake the night before. The vegetables are simply wrapped in aluminum foil and buried in the coals of the fire for about an hour—it's a bit unpredictable. This is what we call a laid-back evening, when you are in the bush camping, or with rural-dwelling friends, in the middle of nowhere, and time doesn't matter. Half the fun is in fiddling with the fire, pulling things out, and testing them. For indigenous and nonindigenous Australians, eating outside, celebrating the mild climate and the spaciousness of our country, is a fundamental part of our lifestyle. This meal should be cooked in an open fire outdoors on a balmy summer night. Serves six people.

The Recipes

LONGMORE'S SNAKE PATTIES

1 c. lentils
1 large potato
1 medium (about 3 c. meat) carpet or other fat snake (or fish for the squeamish)
1 egg
1 medium yellow onion, diced
½ t. cardamom
½ t. cumin
½ t. coriander
½ t. salt
chili powder to taste
1 T vegetable oil
1 jar store-bought tomato chutney

Cover 1 c. brown lentils in water and bring to a boil. Simmer, covered, until lentils are tender (up to an hour). Peel and cut the potato, then place pieces in a medium pot of boiling water. When the potato is tender (about 15 minutes), drain the water and mash the potato. Reserve the mashed potato and the cooked lentils. Peel off the skin of the snake with pliers. Remove all the flesh from the bones with your fingers. (Removing the bones takes ages as there are zillions of bones. If you are lazy, simply throw the whole snake on the fire; this recipe is for gourmet snake!). Mix the flesh of the snake (or fish) with one egg, the lentils, the potato, diced onion, and seasoning. Form into patties and cook on hot plate with 1 T oil, set on hot coals of the fire, turning until golden brown. Serve with sauce or chutney. (Note: You do have to live in the country to acquire your own snake for this recipe; it's not usual dinner fare.)

JACKET POTATOES, PUMPKIN, AND PARSNIP

6 medium baking potatoes
¼ pumpkin, cut into 6 pieces
6 medium parsnips

Wrap the individual vegetables in aluminum foil and place in the coals for an hour, more or less.

DAMPER

4 c. self-raising flour
½ t. salt

Mix 4 cups of self-raising flour (or 2 T baking powder, 1½ t. salt, and 4 c. flour) and a scant ½ t. salt to make soft dough, adding water gradually. Grease (using a butter wrapper) and flour the inside of a camp oven (heavy cast-iron pot with a wire handle), cover and leave the dough inside to rise for 15–20 minutes or so. Then place the camp oven on hot coals and cover the lid and surround the oven with more coals. Check it in about 30 minutes: knock it, as if testing bread, to see if it sounds hollow and therefore cooked. Eat with butter or golden syrup, jam, or honey. Damper is a bit of a novelty made in this way, but it is often commemorated in folk songs as itself or as its variant: Johnny Cakes.

With my little round flour-bag sitting on a stump
My little tea-and-sugar bag looking nice and plump
A little fat cod-fish just off the hook
And four little johnny-cakes, I'm proud to be the cook!

"Four Little Johnny Cakes," traditional

GARDEN SALAD

1 head of lettuce
1 head of arugula (rocket)
2 tomatoes, cut into ⅛
1 c. sugar or snow peas
nasturtium, comfrey, or borage flowers
¼ bunch of cilantro
4 T olive oil
2½ T white vinegar
1 t. honey
1 t. wholegrain mustard
1 clove garlic, crushed

Wash and mix the salad together in a large bowl. Mix up the vinaigrette by whisking 4 T olive oil with 2½ T white vinegar, 1 t. honey, 1 t. wholegrain mustard, and 1 crushed clove of garlic. Pour on just before serving. Allow guests to serve themselves.

BANANAS IN THE FIRE

6 bananas
18 squares of chocolate (about 3–4 bars)
18 marshmallows

Take as many bananas as you have guests and split them in half. Alternate 3 squares of chocolate with 3 marshmallows down the middle. Squash them closed and wrap in aluminum foil, then cook carefully in the coals until soft and signs of oozing chocolate appear.

MANGO ICE CREAM

3 medium ripe mangoes
2 eggs
1 c. sugar
1 lemon, juiced
1 c. cream

Peel and puree the mangoes in a blender. Separate the eggs; beat the yolks and the cream until they are thick and creamy. Beat egg whites until they hold stiff peaks, then gradually add 1 c. sugar to form soft peaks. Fold in yolks, then mango puree and lemon juice. Pour into a suitable mold or bowl and freeze overnight. Mangoes are a delicacy, and on the North Coast of New South Wales they grow wild abundantly. As kids we'd go out in search of mangoes on horseback, stand on the horses' backs and knock them down with the riding crop.

BOILED FRUIT CAKE

1 lb. dried currants
1 lb. mixed dried fruit
1 c. fresh orange juice
1 bar melted cooking chocolate
3 (heaping) T treacle (molasses)
3 T olive oil
1 c. plain wholemeal flour
2 large free-range eggs, beaten
1 t. baking soda
½ c. almonds, slivered, for decoration
1 c. whiskey for pouring over the cooked cake

Place all ingredients except the flour, eggs, almonds, and whiskey in a large saucepan and heat until the juice begins to bubble. Keep stirring occasionally so that the chocolate and treacle melt and don't burn. When bubbling well, turn off the stove and remove the saucepan from the heat to let the fruit mixture cool. Add the flour and the eggs and mix well. Pour into a medium-sized, round cake tin lined with 2 layers of brown paper (you may use brown paper bags or baking paper) and decorate with slivered almonds. Bake at 350°F oven for roughly 1 hour. Leave the cake to cool in the tin and tip whiskey over it a couple of times.

BILLY TEA

Fill a large Billy (tin can with a wire handle) with rainwater from the tank (traditionally galvanized iron, fed by a pipe attached to roof gutters) and place on hot coals. When the water boils throw in a scant handful of tea, remove from the coals, but keep it near the fire's warmth, and let it draw for 5 minutes. You can either bang the side of the Billy with a stout stick to make the tea leaves settle, or be really authentic and swing the Billy around your head (the centrifugal force keeps the tea in the Billy), pour out into mugs and add milk and sugar if desired. As the song tells us:

You can talk of your whisky, and talk of your beer
There's something much nicer that's waiting me here
It sits on the fire, beneath a gum tree,
There's nothing much nicer than a Billy of tea!

"Billy of Tea," traditional

Dinner Cooked on the Fire and Music under the Stars

Indigenous Australians have centuries of expertise in managing their food supplies through nomadic land usage. Each different population group of aboriginal people had or has different migration patterns and allegiances with particular territories which have shaped complex ways of managing, hunting, and gathering their food, just as the relationship with the land has shaped the distinctive kind of music and rituals practiced by each group of people. As my field of research relates to Australian folk music after white settlement, this essay will be focused on these aspects of our food and music. Interaction between indigenous and nonindigenous Australians often results in unexpected musical and food stories. My father, as a boy, was taken swan shooting on the Coorong (a system of salt lagoons in South Australia) by old Alf Watson, an aboriginal man whom he was fond of. His memory of the event was crowned by the smell of roasting swan wafting from Alf's hut on the evening air along with the strains of 78-RPM records of opera, which Alf and his wife played regularly on their wind-up record player.

Australia has had a multicultural population from the earliest days of white settlement. Our early foodways were determined by serious food shortages as colonists struggled to clear the land and encourage plants and animals to survive in a climate of extremes. Early white settlers were dependent on food supplies brought by ship while the farms were being established. The resourcefulness necessary to survive this deprivation and the harsh climatic conditions has become a hallmark of our domestic cuisine, our music, and indeed our national character. Improvisation around recipe ingredients is still important for people who may live on remote cattle stations, a day's drive away from a store, just as a Norwegian immigrant here will have to search the delicatessens for a substitute for fermented shark. This freedom to improvise is reflected in the eclectic nature of our folk music. Nineteenth-century musicians—hungry for new tunes—learned an amazing variety of tunes by ear, to entertain people who traveled on horseback from remote farms to attend dances and balls. In addition, new publications of sheet music reached many remote locations by mail delivery, and again, the oral tradition spread versions of these tunes.

The teaching of both cooking and traditional music in Australia occurs in the family and through a network of family friends, or within the folk community belonging to particular ethnic groups. Our folk festivals are the place where many of these groups intersect, and so provide the opportunity to learn and exchange music, songs, and dances. Many Australian children study classical music or are introduced to music through school band programs. They branch into folk music as an alternative to these mainstream genres and see it as an opportunity to explore their cultural roots and the music of other cultures in Australia. The inclusive character of folk music is also valued as an alternative to more regimented forms of music-making, and is very much part of the Australian tradition of the home as a center for musical entertainment. One stream of Bush music is associated with the lifestyle of male itinerant rural workers: drovers, shearers, fencers, rabbiters, and so forth, although songs that deal with this lifestyle are sung freely by both men and women. The other stream preserves variants of old songs and ballads from the old European cultures, e.g., "Barbara Allen," and again, these are sung by men and women.

The menu above includes food that comes from both spheres of the Australian experience: bush and domestic. I have had this kind of meal with different groups of friends and both the food preparation and the music are communal. Preparing food seems to evoke shanty singing among those who are doing things together like peeling snakeskin or pulling flesh from bones. Shanties like "Paddy Lay Back" and "Haul Away Jo," "Ranzo," and "Liverpool Town" present rich opportunities to make up new and ridiculous verses, and can easily be learned by anyone in the party who is unfamiliar with the song.

Music tends to cease while the serious business of eating is underway, but where there is a gap in courses, like the time required for slitting, stuffing, and wrapping bananas, those guests with fiddles, concertinas, flutes, and so on, will fit in a tune or two. The shared repertoire is eclectic, spanning Australian dance tunes (schottisches, mazurkas, varsoviennas, and waltzes), Scandinavian, French, English, and Scottish tunes. Most participating musicians have traveled widely and play the tunes they have learned in other countries from musicians met at festivals, but Irish music provides the broadest common ground. Musicians learn by blending ear learning with reference to printed music. Items are mainly selected by hearing an appealing song or tune, then tracking it down to the source to learn; which might mean a person or a recording. Visiting musicians are always welcome and are invited to play their favorite party pieces. The fire is the focus of these gatherings, as you will see at folk festivals or at a party.

People tend to drink freely. I've named beer on the menu; a favorite is Cascade Premium Lager from Tasmania, but in reality, people "bring their own poison" which will include cider, wine, whiskey, and Guinness as well as beer. In fact, sharing is an essential part of these gatherings. Usually guests offer to bring a course like the salad or provide the makings of the banana dessert, while the snake patties would be the specialty of the host. Guests from different cultural backgrounds will contribute their specialties, so the menu will always have an element of surprise.

Traditionally, boiled fruitcake was a farmhouse favorite, and it goes down well with a good strong cup of Billy tea. Boiled fruitcake, sponge cakes, Anzac biscuits, and slices (flat frosted bars) were and are a staple part of the suppers served at bush dances. Traditionally, these would be baked at home and transported to the dance hall in suitcases, or "ports" (from *portmanteau*) as they are called on the North Coast of New South Wales. Fruitcake also has great "keeping" properties, and traditionally a couple will keep one tier of their wedding cake (a rich dark fruit cake, covered with marzipan and sugar icing) to eat on their first wedding anniversary.

Australia's wildlife, like the landscape, is colorful and can be tough! The adage, "To cook a *galah*, put it in the pot with a stone, boil the lot for a day, throw away the *galah* and eat the stone," is characteristic of Australian "wisdom" in that it really is not a conventional proverb at all. In fact, proverbs are usually from other cultures when they are quoted here. In a situation where other nationalities would offer a proverb, Australians mostly revert to humor. We like to parody our cultural heritage by playing with inherited sayings and rearranging the words; for example, the mother of a friend of mine comforted her daughter after the collapse of a romance with the advice, "Don't worry, Love, time wounds all heels." Likewise, a "new chum" (someone newly arrived in

Australia) response to the prospect of preparing unappealing food might be "waste not, want not"; an Australian would send up this thrifty sentiment with the warning about the *galah*.

Whether the musical occasion is a group of friends playing together round a campfire, or a bush dance in a tiny country hall, there is always a sense of continuing the tradition of music and food bringing together people from diverse backgrounds to celebrate a special occasion.

RECOMMENDED LISTENING

Jacques, Judy. *Making Wings*. Wild Dog Hill Studio, 2002.
Skedaddle. *Take Me Down the Harbour*. 1992. Available from: David.Game@anu.edu.au
Tiddas. *Inside My Kitchen*. 1991. Available from: tiddagirl90@hotmail.com
Where the Sunlight on the Dew-Drops Shine: Barry Macdonald and Marulan, Folk Music from New England. Harbour Town, 1998. (Featuring Aboriginal Contact songs.)

FOR FURTHER INFORMATION

Davey, Gwenda Beed, and Graham Seal, eds. 1993. *The Oxford Companion to Australian Folklore*, Melbourne: Oxford University Press.
Gollan, Anne. 1978. *The Tradition of Australian Cooking*. Canberra: ANU Press.
http://www.loreoftheland.com.au/index.html (website for *Lore of the Land*, indigenous information).
http://www.musicaustralia.org (website for *Music Australia*, the online music archive of the National Library of Australia).
http://www.wongawillicolonialdance.org.au/
http://en.wikipedia.org/wiki/Galah

NEW ZEALAND
David G. Hebert

The early arrivals get food, the late ones can but swallow their spittle.

Menu: Green-Lipped Mussels, Manuka Honey Kumara (Sweet Potatoes), Aotearoa Salad, Black Tea with Cream, and Port Kiwis. Serve the dinner with white wine and the port kiwis with Black tea.

Preparation Time: Approximately 1 hour.

Cooking Process: Buy a loaf of fresh bread. Select only live mussels with fully closed and undamaged shells. It is common for a few barnacles to be attached and for "beards" to be hanging out of the shells—not a problem. Begin by carefully rinsing and scrubbing the mussels in a sink. Do not expect the mussels to ever become perfect physical specimens as a result of your scrubbing, but the point is to at least remove any sand or other loose bits. Once the mussels are scrubbed, it is best to prepare the side dishes, and leave the mussels for last since they cook quickly and are best served immediately after cooking. You will need two very large pots with lids. The *kumara*, bread, and salad are served along with the mussels, and the remainder of the white wine may also be served at this time. Mussels are served in their opened shell, along with the broth. It is best to set one or more extra large bowl(s) on the table, so guests may immediately deposit empty shells as they eat individual mussels. It is important to serve the broth along with the mussels and fresh bread on each plate. Guests are encouraged to soak up their broth with large pieces of fresh bread, alternating with roasted garlic. The port kiwis and tea with cream are best served after dinner. Serves six people.

The Recipes

GREEN-LIPPED MUSSELS

2 T olive oil
2 heads garlic, chopped
1 bunch Italian parsley
1 bunch fresh chives
1 lemon
2 c. white wine
pepper
salt
60 live green-lipped mussels, scrubbed and de-bearded

When you are ready to cook the entrée, begin by placing both large pots on the stove, over gentle heat. Add at least 1 T olive oil into each of the large pots, and brush it around to cover the entire bottom surface. Slice one of the 2 garlic heads in half, horizontally, and place the two halves cut end down onto the warm oil, one in each pot. Sauté the garlic until it becomes golden brown. This must be done rather slowly on gentle heat in order for the garlic to be fully cooked and not burnt. As the two garlic halves are being sautéed, finely chop at least half the bulbs from each remaining head. Remove the sautéed garlic halves and set aside for use as a garnish. Now turn the heat up to medium-high and toss the chopped garlic into the olive oil, evenly divided between the two pots. Finely chop 1 bunch each of Italian parsley and chives, cut 1 lemon in half, and set these ingredients aside for later use. After 1–2 minutes, the chopped garlic will have become a bit browned, and now 1 c. white wine should be added to each pot. Toss in plenty of black pepper and just a bit of salt. Give one brisk stir, and pile in all the mussels, evenly divided between pots. Cover immediately with lids and check the time.

Now comes the fun part: lots of stirring and shaking of each large pot. Over the next 5–6 minutes, all of the mussels will pop open within a glorious steamy garlic and wine sauna. It is important to stir and shake the pots to ensure that the mussels are evenly cooked, but do keep the lids on as much as possible since lids also contribute to this process. Once all the mussels appear to have opened (about 5–6 minutes), toss in the parsley and chives and squeeze a lemon half into the mussel broth (evenly divided between the two pots). Once these final ingredients have been added, stir the mixture in each pot, allow the mussels to cook for one more minute, and then remove from the heat. Discard any mussels that did not fully open, as these may not have been fresh. Serve immediately.

Manuka Honey Kumara (Sweet Potatoes)

6 sweet potatoes (*kumara*)
½ c. honey
salt
pepper

Preheat oven to 400°F. Peel and slice 6 *kumara* (sweet potatoes) into large chunks, generously dab honey onto each, and bake in a lightly greased oven pan for about 20–25 minutes. Finish with a dash of salt and pepper.

Aotearoa Salad

1–2 packages mixed greens
1 c. snow pea shoots (or alfalfa sprouts)
1 lemon, halved
1 T olive oil

Rinse and drain 1–2 packages of mixed leafy greens and 1 package of snow pea shoots (or alfalfa sprouts). Place in a large salad bowl. Kiwis tend to use minimal dressing, if at all. The following light treatment is recommended: squeeze a few drops of lemon juice onto the salad, and drip 1 T olive oil across it before lightly tossing all the ingredients.

Black Tea with Cream

7 t. black tea leaves

Bring 6 c. water to a boil; heat a large teapot with hot water, then drain. Add 1 t. black tea leaves for each person, plus 1 "for the pot." Add the boiling water and allow tea leaves to steep for several minutes until the water has reached the desired color. Pour into cups and allow each guest to add cream and/or sugar, as desired.

Port Kiwis

6 kiwi fruits
1–2 c. port wine
2 T cornstarch
1 c. fresh cream
6 sprigs of mint

Peel and cut 6 kiwi fruits into attractive shapes and arrange on 6 small dessert saucers. Heat 1–2 c. port wine in a saucepan over medium heat. Gradually add a few spoonfuls of cornstarch, while constantly stirring. When the mixture thickens into a dense liquid, remove from the heat and ladle across each of the kiwi fruit plates. Drip some fresh cream across each plate for added color and texture, and finish each with a sprig of mint.

Before Your Kai

Maori are the native people of *Aotearoa* ("land of the long white cloud"), a nation known to outsiders as New Zealand. Despite the mass immigration of Europeans and other Polynesians over the last 150 years, Maori language and culture are alive and well in Aotearoa, and continue to influence the lifestyle of all Kiwis. This recipe is based on Maori custom, and represents the kind of cuisine often served on a traditional Maori *marae* overnight stay.

Green-lipped mussels (*Perna canaliculus*) have been a staple of the Maori diet for centuries, and play an important role in the folklore. Mussels are commonly served throughout Polynesia, regarded as an unusually attractive and nutritious entrée. *Kumara*, or sweet potatoes, are a popular side dish with historic importance to Maori. Traditionally, they were slow-roasted between layered leaves in smoky barbecue pits. Manuka honey is made by bees from pollen gathered off a manuka bush. A dab of honey on each *kumara* slice enhances its flavor during the roasting process. Fresh bread and salad are served with many Kiwi meals. Most Kiwi salads are rather simple, with lots of leafy greens and only a light dressing, if at all. The tradition of tea with cream was adapted from *Pakeha* (European) culture during the late nineteenth century, and is common throughout Aotearoa. Tea is often served with a dessert.

What does the phrase "mussel mana" mean? Surely readers are familiar with the notion of "muscle power," but the concept of mussel *mana* ("power" in Maori) may be entirely unfamiliar. Since 1973, numerous research studies have concluded that green-lipped mussels may have unique healing powers to alleviate the symptoms of arthritis. This is because the mussels contain a glycoprotein with powerful anti-inflammatory properties. Scientists have long noted the low incidence of arthritis among Maori, and findings from recent experiments among arthritic dogs are also promising. According to Dr. Linh Bui, "they improved amazingly." Hence, this delightful meal is uniquely powerful (heaps of *mana*!), and should be shared with elderly family members, and remember to leave some scraps for the dog as well.

Key Terminology: *Maori* (natives of New Zealand), *Pakeha* (European resident of New Zealand), *Kiwi* (any New Zealander, Maori, or Pakeha—don't worry, it's a polite term), *mana* (power/greatness), *Aotearoa* (New Zealand, lit. "land of the long white cloud"), *kai* (food), *whanau* (familial community), *hongi* (greeting by pressing noses), *marae* (traditional Maori community house).

Two of the key themes of Maoridom are *mana* (power and greatness) and *whanau* (familial community). Hence, it is important for hosts and guests at a meal to take turns speaking in confidence about his or her background and the purpose of the occasion, and to welcome everyone present into the *whanau*. Guests are welcomed with the generic "*Kia ora*" and "*tena koutou*" ("welcome, everyone"). The traditional *hongi* greeting entails the slow pressing of noses and inhaling of another's scent (and spirit). Maori men tend to greet in this fashion, although women usually prefer to deliver a brief kiss on the cheek. In cases where men have not met for a long time, contact is made simultaneously between both noses and foreheads, and deliberately held for more than a few seconds. Before eating, remember to welcome each of your guests with a *hongi*, take turns introducing yourselves, discussing where you are from and why you have gathered together, and end with a prayer or song. Now it's time to enjoy the *kai* (food).

RECOMMENDED LISTENING

Moana Maniapoto. *Toru*. Pirate/Sony, 2002.
Whirimako Black. *Tangihaku*. Mai Music, 2004.

FOR FURTHER INFORMATION

http://www.aucklandmuseum.com
http://www.manukahoney.co.uk/
http://www.maori.org.nz

TONGA
Adrienne L. Kaeppler

Living in a fruitful land [where none ever suffer want].

Menu: *'Otai* (Coconut Fruit Drink), *Ota Ika* (Raw Fish), *Lupulu* and Coconut Milk (corned beef in taro leaves), *Puaka Ta'o* (Roast Pork), *Kumala/Ufi/Talo* (Sweet Potatoes/Yam/Taro), *Fo'i 'Akau* (Fruit—Papaya, Mango, Pineapple), and Ice Cream or *Keke Fuamelie* (Fruitcake).
Preparation Time: 3 hours.
Cooking Process: About 3½ hours before you wish to eat, marinate the raw fish and start the roast pork. Then make the coconut fruit drink and place in the refrigerator to chill. Start the corned beef in taro leaves. Bake the sweet potatoes. Half an hour before eating, finish making the raw fish and cut up the fresh fruit for dessert. Serves six people.

The Recipes

'OTAI (COCONUT FRUIT DRINK)

4 c. coconut milk
1 T sugar
4 c. fruit pulp

Combine 4 c. coconut milk, 2 c. water, 1 T sugar, and 4 c. fruit pulp (watermelon, mango, or pineapple) in a blender. Chill.

OTA IKA (RAW FISH)

1 lb. raw fish
1 lime, juiced
⅛ onion, finely chopped
1 clove garlic, finely chopped
1 chili pepper, finely chopped
salt
1 green bell pepper, chopped
1 tomato, chopped
½ c. coconut milk

Cut 1 lb. raw fish into 1" cubes. Mix together with the juice of 1 lime, 1 T onion, garlic, chili pepper, and a little salt. Marinate for about 3 hours, then discard the marinade. Then mix the fish with the green bell pepper and the tomato. Add ½ c. coconut milk and mix well.

Lupulu (Lu, Made with Taro Leaves; Pulu, Corned Beef) and Coconut Milk

24 taro leaves
1 lb. corned beef
3 medium yellow onions, chopped
1 c. coconut milk

You will want to make 6 packets. First, wash 24 taro leaves (or large spinach leaves) thoroughly, removing the large stems. Now gather the ingredients to go into each of the packets, dividing them into six. Slice 1 lb. corned beef, the onions, and ½ c. coconut milk. Arrange 4 of the large taro or spinach leaves in the shape of a cross, with the smaller ends overlapping in the center. Place a slice of corned beef in the center, then pile ½ of a chopped onion and pour some coconut milk over the top. Carefully fold the leaves, wrapping them entirely around the contents. Wrap the packet in a piece of aluminum foil. Repeat this procedure 5 more times until you have 6 packets total. Bake the stuffed leaves for 90 minutes in a 350°F oven. Make sure the leaves are well cooked (if undercooked, a chemical substance in the leaves can cause an itchy throat). If you use spinach leaves cook for only about an hour. Fish or chicken can be substituted for corned beef, but Tongans far prefer the corned beef. These leaf packages can also be made vegetarian by simply omitting the meat.

Puaka Ta'o (Roast Pork)

2 lb. pork butt
2 T liquid smoke
2 T "Hawaiian" salt (or other rock salt)
ti leaves, if available

Score pork butt and rub with liquid smoke and salt. Place on *ti* leaves and fold into a package. Place on aluminum foil and wrap as a bundle. If you have no *ti* leaves, just wrap in foil. Bake in a 325°F oven for 2–3 hours or until very done. Shred the meat and serve. This can also be cooked in a crock pot on low for 10-12 hours. If using a crock pot, no *ti* leaves or foil is needed.

Kumala/Ufi/Talo (Sweet Potatoes/Yam/Taro)

3 large or 6 small sweet potatoes
2 T vegetable oil

Wash and lightly coat 3 large or 6 small sweet potatoes (or yams or peeled taro) with vegetable oil; bake in the oven on a cookie sheet (or wrapped in aluminum foil) at 400°F for 1 hour, or until soft. Or place them in the oven with the roast pork and turn the heat up once the pork has finished cooking to complete cooking the sweet potatoes. Note: Tongans would simply cook these in the oven without the vegetable oil or the cookie sheet, but sweet potatoes can drip.

FO'I 'AKAU (FRUIT—PAPAYA, MANGO, PINEAPPLE)

Various fresh tropical fruits
1 qt. ice cream
1 storebought fruitcake

Wash and dice a number of various tropical fruits (mango, kiwi, passion fruit, pineapple, etc.); it should be enough for 6 cups of fruit. Serve on ice cream with fruitcake (the Tongans' favorite dessert) with thick icing.

Food and Music in Tonga

On Sundays Tongans cook in the traditional manner, that is, in the underground oven. A large hole is dug (or reopened) by men, and special stones are heated. *Lupulu, ufi, talo*, and *kumala* are placed on the stones and covered with leaves and soil and left to cook for a few hours. Small pigs are roasted over an open fire (*tunu*) until the skin is crisp and the meat is done. Meanwhile, women prepare the table setting, fruit, and dessert.

For special occasions feasts are held on the village green. Each family or group of families from various villages contributes a *pola*, coconut leaf tray or long stretcher, filled with food; it is actually completely covered with food. The roasted pigs are placed in the center of the *pola*, and surrounded with *lupulu, luika* (*lu*, "made with fish"), fish cooked in various ways, the root vegetables, a pudding called *faikakai*, fresh fruit, and fresh coconuts. These *pola* are placed end-to-end on mats placed on the ground, so that several hundred may eat. The only condiment is salt, as Tongans do not enjoy spices or spicy food.

At large public feasts the king and/or members of the royal family sit at the head "table." At a large feast several hundred individuals may eat in "sittings." Traditionally food was eaten with fingers and pieces might be placed on a banana leaf "plate." After the high-status individuals of the first sitting have eaten their fill, the next in rank sit down to partake. This procedure is followed until all have shared in the feast. The rest of the food is given away or taken back to the village and distributed.

Tonga is a hierarchical society with a complicated ranking system. The father is the head of the family and sisters outrank brothers. At feasts brother-sister avoidance is strictly observed by sitting separately or at different sittings. Food is also ranked, pork being the most prestigious. Even parts of the animal are ranked; the highest part is the pig's back. *Ufi*, yams, are the highest ranking root vegetable.

On ceremonial occasions, called *kātoanga*, (usually during days before a large scale feast) food (most of it uncooked) and valuables (such as mats and barkcloth) are presented. In the court of the Tu'i Kanokupolu, of which the present King Tāufa'āhau is the 22nd, the last and largest pig is presented in conjunction with a ritual song. Food and valuables are counted in a most ceremonious manner, and the final offering is a music and dance performance. Today, the performance might be by a brass band (a special favorite of the present king), a string band, or even an "electric band" with amplified rock'n'roll music. But most highly regarded is the presentation of a traditional *lakalaka*, sung speech with choreographed movements.

During the associated feast speeches are given, and shortly after eating everyone moves to the side of the village green where chairs have been set up to watch hours of dancing, especially *lakalaka*. No important event is complete without music and dance, and what is often remembered about an event is the music that was performed. Music often defines the event by giving voice to the event's purpose and a composer or patron's official reaction to it.

In 2003, the *lakalaka* was proclaimed a "Masterpiece of the Oral and Intangible Heritage of Humanity" by UNESCO, and their most important performances are after a feast on the village green. *Lakalaka* are keys to understanding Tongan cultural and social values. Here, history, mythology, and genealogy are brought to bear on contemporary events, imparting values that deal primarily with the overall societal structure and the people of rank through whom it operates. The performers are both men and women, often 200 or more, arranged in two or more rows facing the audience. The men stand on the right side (from the observer's point of view), and the women stand on the left. Men and women perform different sets of movements that are consistent with the Tongan view of what is suitable and appropriate for that sex. The arm movements allude to words of the poetry, which often are themselves allusions, thereby creating the double abstraction so admired in Tongan performing arts. As this is a sung speech, it is necessary to listen to every word and watch every movement. Many of the references are common knowledge, but the association must be made instantaneously in order to proceed to an understanding of the next allusion. The figurative language and allusive movements elevate the king and chiefs, paying them the highest honor, while at the same time honoring the dancers and their villages.

The importance of food and music is enhanced by the manner of their presentations. As Vason noted in the early nineteenth century, "the manner of doing it rendered the present doubly valuable" (Orange 1840: 160). All the niceties and etiquette of presentation continue today, especially in the performance of *lakalaka* and the presentation of food and eating. Music remains an important element in the sociopolitical life of the Tongan people.

RECOMMENDED LISTENING

Afo 'O E 'Ofa. *Strings of Love: Tongan Stringband Music*. Pan Records, 1998. PAN CD 2088.
Ifi Palasa. *Tongan Brass*. Anthology of Pacific Music #4. PAN records (P.O. Box 155, 2300 AD Leiden, The Netherlands).
Music from the Kingdom of Tonga, Vols. 1 and 2. Olinda Road, 1997. 7112 and 7122.

FOR FURTHER INFORMATION

http://www.tongatapu.net.to
http://www.planet-tonga.com
Kaeppler, Adrienne L. 1993. *Poetry in Motion: Studies in Tongan Dance*. Nuku'alofa: Vava'u Press.
Kaeppler, Adrienne L., and J. W. Love. 1998. Australia and the Pacific Islands. *The Garland Encyclopedia of World Music*, Vol. 9. New York: Garland Publishing.
Moyle, Richard. 1987. *Tongan Music*. Auckland: Auckland University Press.
Shumway, Larry V. 1981. The Tongan Lakalaka: Music composition and style. *Ethnomusicology* 25:467–479.
Vason, George [James Orange]. 1840. *Life of the Late George Vason of Nottingham. One of the Troop of Missionaries First Sent to the South Sea Islands by the London Missionary Society in the Ship Duff Captian Wilson, 1796*. London.
Wood-Ellem, Elizabeth, ed. 2004. *Songs and Poems of Queen Salote*. Trans. Melenaite Taumoefolau, with essays by H.R.H. Princess Nanasipau'u Tuku'aho, Adrienne L. Kaeppler, Elizabeth Wood-Ellem, and Melenaite Taumoefolau. Nuku'alofa, Tonga.

10
Europe

ANDALUSIAN SPAIN

Julia Banzi

Love enters through the kitchen.

Menu: *Gazpacho de Mercedes* (Mercedes' Chilled Tomato Soup), *Paella de Mercedes* (Mercedes' Rice and Vegetable/Seafood Dish), *Arroz con Leche de Juan* (Juan's Rice Pudding), and *Tinto de Verano* (Summer Wine).
Preparation Time: Approximately 3 hours.
Cooking Process: Make the *arroz con leche* first, then start the *gazpacho*. Once you have begun to chill the *gazpacho*, start on the *paella*. Note: This recipe for *paella* is vegetarian; if you would like to add shellfish, it is common to add about 3 lb. assorted shellfish. You may even add a can of tuna at the very end instead of or with the seafood, or simply leave it vegetarian. Either way it is yummy! Serves six people.

The Recipes

GAZPACHO DE MERCEDES (MERCEDES' CHILLED TOMATO SOUP)

4 tomatoes
1 cucumber
1 small onion
1 small green bell pepper
1 clove garlic
3 T olive oil
2 T red wine vinegar
salt

Peel 4 tomatoes by scoring an x about ½" into the ends, then place them in a bowl and pour boiling water over them. Let them sit for 2 minutes, then rinse under cold water and slide the skins off. Chop the tomatoes into a blender with some water, then blend to make a liquid soup. Chop and add 1 cucumber, 1 small onion, 1 small green bell pepper, and 1 clove of garlic. Add some water and begin blending to make a liquid soup. Add 3 T olive oil, 2 T red wine vinegar, and ½ t. salt. Chill for 1 hour.

PAELLA DE MERCEDES (MERCEDES' RICE AND VEGETABLE/SEAFOOD DISH)

2 tomatoes
1 small onion
2 cloves garlic
1 bunch parsley
2 T olive oil

1 green bell bepper
8 mushrooms
1 small cauliflower
2 c. green beans
½ t. saffron
1½ c. canned artichoke hearts
3 c. white rice
3 lb. shellfish (optional)
salt

You will need a large, flat covered bowl that you can cook with over the stove and transfer to the table when it is finished. Chop 2 tomatoes, 1 small onion, and 2 cloves of garlic together with 1 bunch of parsley, then fry lightly in olive oil. Remove from pan and set aside. Chop and sauté 1 green bell pepper, 8 mushrooms, 1 small cauliflower, and 2 c. green beans for 5 minutes. Heat a teapot full of water. Add ½ t. saffron (or paprika), 1½ c. artichoke hearts (sliced in half), and 2 c. water to cook them in. Cook for just 3 minutes, then add the tomato/onion mix and cook for another 3 minutes. Add 3 c. rice (rinsed) and stir it around a bit. Add enough boiling water so that the rice is submerged. Cover and cook, but check periodically and stir, adding enough water to keep the rice submerged until the rice starts to get tender. Now would be the time to add about 3 pounds of shellfish, if you plan to use them. Add 2 t. salt as well. Cover and cook until the water is almost gone and little bubbles appear in the surface. Remove from heat and let sit for 5–10 minutes.

Arroz con leche de Juan (Juan's Andalusian rice pudding). Photo by Sean Williams.

Arroz con Leche de Juan (Juan's Rice Pudding)

⅓ c. seedless raisins
1 c. basmati rice
5 c. milk
2–3 pinches saffron
½ c. sugar
1 stick cinnamon
½ t. cinnamon
pinch of nutmeg
1 T slivered almonds

Soak ⅓ c. seedless raisins in a cup of boiling water and let sit for 15 minutes. Rinse 1 c. basmati rice, then cook it with 2 c. water for 15 minutes to allow the rice to soften. In a large, nonstick pan, bring 5 c. milk and several pinches of saffron to a boil. When the rice is done, add it to the milk with ⅓ c. raisins, ½ c. sugar, 1 stick of cinnamon, ½ t. cinnamon, and a pinch of nutmeg. Stir well, and simmer gently, uncovered, for about 30 minutes (stir periodically) until the milk is almost completely absorbed by the rice. Cover tightly and let sit for another 15 minutes. Transfer to serving bowls and sprinkle with cinnamon and nutmeg, and a few slivered almonds.

Tinto de Verano (Summer Wine)

assorted summer fruits
1 bottle chilled red house wine
1 bottle chilled *gaseosa* (sparkling water)

Cut the fruits (watermelon, honeydew melon, pineapple, apples, oranges, etc.) into bite-sized slices. Mix 1 bottle of chilled red house wine with a bottle of sparkling water 50/50 (or to taste) in a pitcher and add various cut-up fruits and ice. Let sit in the refrigerator for 30 minutes to 1 hour. The fruit soaks up the wine/sparkling water mixture and are delicious to eat; likewise, the fruit adds flavors to the wine. You can dilute the wine to varying degrees (even 25/75 or more) depending on your preferences. Serve in large wine glasses. *Tinto de verano* is a wonderfully refreshing drink in summer and is the perfect accompaniment for your Spanish Andalusian meal!

Wine for Its Color, Bread for Its Smell, and Everything for Its Taste

One might think of bullfighting, hand clapping, foot tapping, Jerez sherry, Picasso, and polka dots as being quintessentially Spanish, but it is Andalucia that claims them. Andalucia is the southern province of Spain. Andalusians are known for their vibrancy, strong spirit, humor, and relaxed approach to life—all of which are encapsulated in the food and music of Andalucia.

The gastronomy and music of Andalucia are very site specific. Each pueblo prides itself in its specific dishes as well as its specific contributions to the rich culture of Andalucia. My experience is rooted in *flamenco*, a type (but not the only type) of Andalusian folk music. I spent 10 years living in Spain throughout the 1980s, mostly in Andalucia, where I studied flamenco guitar and also learned to love, and eventually create, some of the dishes that Andalusians pride themselves on.

In my experience, both flamenco and cooking are taught informally from an early age through observation and active participation. Measuring spoons aren't used and rhythms aren't counted, notes aren't notated (or recorded), and recipes aren't written. It is somehow in that process of remembering, forgetting, and recreating again that the music and the dish gain both depth and personality. *Duende* (soul) is what one seeks in flamenco, while it is the *guiso* or sauce to dip bread in that is especially relished when eating.

Andalusian gastronomy may be divided into two main branches: coastal and interior. Foods of the interior or *serrana* includes dishes such as *potajes* (soups) of legumes, vegetables, and *guisos* (stews) of wild game. Defining Andalusian coastal regions are the myriad of ways in which seafood is prepared. No meal is complete without *pan, postre y vino* (bread, dessert, and wine) while olive oil, garlic, tomatoes, and lemon seem to make their way into virtually every meal: *El vino por el color, el pan por el olor y todo por el sabor* ("wine for its color, bread for its smell, and everything for its taste").

Exquisite cheeses, wines, and delicious desserts are shared by both interior and coastal regions. Andalusian desserts are unique not only for their taste, but also for their mode of fabrication. Many sweets continue to be made by nuns in convents and churches. Their names reflect Andalusian *guasa* or humor, such as *suspiros de monja* (nun sighs), *huesos de santo* (saint bones), *tocino de cielo* (heaven's lard), *borrachos* (drunks), or *las yemas de San Leandro* (the yolks of San Leandro). Ordering a half kilo of fragrantly scented and delicately wrapped *borrachos* (drunks) from cloistered nuns of Sanlucar de Barrameda always made me smile!

While the main meal is lunchtime (often followed by a *siesta* or nap), lots of eating goes on at night in the form of *tapas* (appetizers). Going out for dinner often means going out for *tapas* and rounds of drinks (mostly wine and beer, though sodas for the kids) in bars where people of all ages congregate. Each drink is served with an appetizer or *tapa* (from the word *tapar* or cover, hence to "cover" the hunger). Nightlife in Andalusian cities and flamenco circles often lasts until the sun rises, when one wanders home and on the way stops to pick up *pan caliente* (hot bread) from the bakery or *chocolate y churros* (hot chocolate and freshly made tube doughnuts).

After a "dinner" of *tapas* when flamencos are warmed up and fed, the *juerga* (party) begins. There are specific (often closed-door or private) bars or *peñas* (flamenco clubs) where flamencos go to play, listen to, and learn flamenco. The guitar is passed around as guitarists show off their new pieces, trade licks and accompany different singers who offer their own improvised *letras* (verses) or their versions of famous *letras*. Others in the *juerga* participate with *jaleo* (words or shouts of encouragement), *palmas* (rhythmic clapping), and sometimes with *baile* (dancing). There is usually a lot of joking going on, but there are also moments of profound stillness when a collective sigh seems to pass through the room. If participants get hungry again, or liked a particular *tapa*, they order *raciones* or full plates of what they might have liked. These *raciones* are shared by everyone at the table.

There are over 50 different flamenco *palos* (forms) defined by their *toques* (the art of flamenco guitar playing is collectively referred to as *el toque*, the touch, while the hundreds of different types of pieces within flamenco are collectively known as *los toques*, touches), *cantes* (songs), *bailes* (dances), *compás* (rhythmic patterns), and *aires* (moods; serious or light). Practically every pueblo in Andalucia has made its unique contribution to flamenco or other Andalusian folk music. These contributions are collectively remembered by the pueblo through naming, such as *Malagueñas* (from Malaga), *Granaina* (from Granada), *Buleria de Jerez* (Bulerias from Jerez de la Frontera), and *Tangos de Cádiz* (Tangos of Cádiz). The same follows in the gastronomy as illustrated with such *platos* (plates) as *riñones al Jerez* (kidneys of Jerez), *espinacas jiennense of Jaén* (spinach of Jaén), *la cazuela de fideos a la Malagueña* (pot of noodles of Málaga), *las habas a la Granadina* (the lima beans of Granada), *fino and vino de Jerez* (sherries and wines of Jerez), or the *paella Valenciana* (paella of Valencia).

Flamenco often explores dualities and stark contrasts; this is noted in the emblematic colors associated with flamenco (red and black). Contrasting dualities such male/female, sound/silence, rhythmic/free-meter, serious/light, and treating themes of love, loss, and wanting, offer a fertile ground for artistic expression. Food presentation is likewise colorful and full of contrasts with bright reds (tomatoes, red bell peppers, shrimps), yellows (lemons, saffron rice) contrasting with blacks (olives, dark meats). Andalusian food, however, does not tend to be spicy. Instead spices such as cumin, paprika, saffron, cilantro, parsley, and black pepper are subtly blended together and presented colorfully. These recipes were taught to me by my dear friends Mercedes *y* Pepe who fell in love while cooking!

RECOMMENDED LISTENING

The Alan Lomax Collection: World Library of Folk and Primitive Music, Volume 4—Spain. Rounder CD. 1744.
Duende. New York: Ellipsis Arts, 1994.
Festival Flamenco Gitano 3. Just A Memory Records, 1994.
Flamenco: Son Del Sur. Spain: EMI-Odeón, 1998.
Grandes Figures. In *Flamenco Disque catalogue*. France: Le Chant du Monde, 1992.
The Masters of the Guitar. Murray Hill, 1973.
The Young Flamencos Los Jovenes Flamencos. London: Hannibal Records, 1991.
Voice of Spain: Regional Music (1927–1931). Heritage, 1997. HT CD 38.

FOR FURTHER INFORMATION

García Lorca, Federico. 1975. *Deep Song and Other Prose*. New York: New Directions.
Malefyt, T. D. 1998. "Inside" and "Outside" Spanish flamenco: Gender constructions in Andalusian concepts of flamenco tradition. *Anthropological Quarterly* 57/1:63–73.
Manuel, Peter. 1988. Evolution and Structure in Flamenco Harmony. *Current Musicology* 42:46-57.
Noble, John, Susan Forsyth, Paula Hardy. 2005. *Lonely Planet Andalucia*, 4th ed. Footscray, Victoria, Australia: Lonely Planet Publications.
Steingress, Gerhard. 1998. *Social Theory and the Comparative History of Flamenco, Tango, and Rebetika*. Oxford, UK: Berg.
Washabaugh, William. 1996. *Flamenco: Passion, Politics, and Popular Culture*. Oxford, UK: Berg.
———. 1998. *The Passion of Music and Dance: Body, Gender, and Sexuality*. Oxford, UK: Berg.
Woodall, James. 1992. *In Search of the Firedance: Spain through Flamenco*. London: Sinclair-Stevenson.

IBIZA AND FORMENTERA (THE PITYUSIC ISLANDS)

Esperança Bonet Roig and Judith Cohen

On Christmas Day we'll kill a rooster...
And on Christmas Day, each sheep in its own yard.

Menu for Christmas Day Midday Meal: *Sopa Amb Arròs* or *Sopa Amb Fideos* (Rice or Noodle Soup), *Sofrit (Bollit) Pagès* (Countryside Stew), *Salsa de Nadal* (Christmas Pudding), *Bescuit* (Sweet Loaves), and optional dessert of fresh fruit and *turrón* (nougat).

Preparation Time: One evening (in advance of the day on which you plan to serve it).

Cooking Process: Preparing the *Salsa de Nadal* ideally takes three people working together. It is prepared at least 1 day before the Christmas Day meal. Usually the other dishes are also prepared the night before, to have everything ready for Christmas Day. You will need a large (10-quart) cooking pot to prepare the broth used in all the recipes. Once you have prepared the broth, assembling the *sopa*, *sofrit*, and *bescuit* are relatively easy. Ask for help to make the *salsa*, as you will need at least a couple of pairs of extra hands. Serves six people.

To make the broth: The recipes for all three stages of the meal depend on this broth or stock. Bring 1 gallon (16 cups) of water to a boil in a large cooking pot to produce needed amount of broth. Cut 2 lb. lamb and 4 lb. chicken (bone in) into large pieces, place in the water, and leave to boil gently about 1 hour. When it is done, remove the meat from the broth, reserving both the meat and the broth. Tear the chicken from the bone and mix with the lamb, then set aside for the *sofrit*.

The Recipes

SOPA AMB ARRÒS (RICE SOUP)

6 c. meat broth (see instructions, above)
2 c. white rice or dry pasta

Measure out 6 c. meat broth and bring to a boil. Either rinse and add 2 c. rice, or add dry pasta if preferred. Cook, covered, until the rice is tender (about 20 minutes).

Sopa, sofrit, y salsa de Nadal **(Christmas dinner, Ibiza, Spain). Photo by Judith Cohen.**

Sofrit (Bollit) Pagès (Countryside Stew)

cooked lamb and chicken pieces from making the broth (see above)
4 lb. potatoes, cubed
1 red pepper (*nyora*)
pinch of saffron
1 bunch parsley, chopped
3 cloves garlic, sliced
2 bay leaves
salt
pepper
2 T olive oil
3 c. meat broth (see above)
sausage (optional)

Assemble the cooked lamb and chicken pieces, potatoes, 1 *nyora* (red pepper) or equivalent, a pinch of saffron, parsley, garlic, 2 bay leaves, salt and pepper; and sausage (optional). Fry the potatoes in 2 T olive oil; set aside to add to the meat later. Lightly fry together *nyora*, saffron, parsley, garlic, bay leaves, salt and pepper; and (optional) sausage meat(s). Add about 3 c. of the meat broth. Transfer to a large cooking pot, then add meats and the fried cubed potatoes. Cover pot and cook on low heat for approximately 8 minutes. Keep the pot covered, and move it frequently to ensure that ingredients are evenly distributed, and making sure enough broth will remain for the soup. Do not stir with spoon or other utensil, as this will result in the ingredients becoming too separated.

Salsa de Nadal (Christmas Pudding)

3 c. meat broth (see above)
5 c. freshly ground almonds
2 eggs
1 c. sugar
1 T ground cinnamon
1½ t. ground cloves
½ t. black pepper

Use the lamb-chicken broth from the *sofrito* (or the meatless mixture of oil and water). Take 5 c. freshly ground almonds (see traditional method in the notes, below) and mix with 2 eggs and 1 c. sugar to make a paste. Place the colander over a cooking pot. Pass this paste slowly through a colander through which several cups of the hot broth is also poured, pushing all ingredients through with a wooden spoon, so that the harder paste is softened by the broth. This takes two or three people: one to pour the broth, one to push the almond paste through, and one to keep stirring with the special long wooden spoon so the ingredients go through together. Turn the heat under the cooking pot to medium. Add 1 T ground cinnamon, 1½ t. ground cloves, and ½ t. freshly ground black pepper; stir with the wooden spoon until the mixture is boiling. It should be relatively thick.

Bescuit (Sweet Loaves)

1 lb. flour
1 T anise seeds
1 package yeast
2 eggs
3 T butter
1¾ c. sugar

Mix 1 lb. flour, warm water, 1 T anise seeds, 1 package of yeast, 2 eggs, 3 T butter, and 1¾ c. sugar. Knead well, until dough is just a little hard. Form into small loaves (*cócs*), about 1 foot long. Let rise about 15 minutes. Bake in slow oven, about 15 minutes.

Extra Notes on Food for This Feast

The *Salsa de Nadal* is a very traditional dish, the emblematic Christmas Day offering. There are two varieties: one with a meat-based broth, usually a mixture of lamb and chicken, and the other on a base of water boiled with oil. The latter was used mostly for people who were ill, or on a special diet, and the almonds and spices were the same as for the more common, meat-based salsa. Traditionally, families prepared far more than enough for the household, to be able to bring some to households where for various reasons it couldn't be made that year, or to offer to guests.

This recipe was explained in the context of Dalt Vila, the old walled town of Ibiza perched high on a hill overlooking the port; it is also prepared everywhere else in the Pityusic Islands, including the typical *cases pagèses*, the isolated, self-sufficient houses in the wooded hills of Ibiza. Preparing the salsa is a festive occasion, and was even more so before modern heating, cooking and lighting appliances, and utilities were available to all: it is impossible to separate the instructions from this social context. Most houses had no gas, only coal, and families took care to store up some good coal which burned well and with little smoke, because the fire had to be kept going for several hours at just the right temperature under the huge clay cooking pot. Experienced people were needed to make sure the sauce was neither too thin nor too thick. Each house had its own secrets, adding spices so that the flavor of its sauce was unique. Salt, usually from the 3,000-year-old Ibizan salt pans, can be tossed on the coals to further reduce smoke.

Most houses had no refrigerators, so the salsa was kept in the coldest part of the house, and had to be reboiled every couple of days so it wouldn't go bad. Today it is often divided into small glass bowls and kept refrigerated or even frozen in case a visitor wanted to taste it at another time of year. After New Year's Day (*cap d'any*) and Epiphany (Three Kings' Day, *reis*, January 6), there was little left and this was consumed with special pleasure, everyone aware that it was the last time *fins l'any que ve si Déu vol* ("till next year, God willing"). Because enough must be made to last for the Christmas season, and for families who couldn't prepare their own, the pot might hold 10, 15, or sometimes even 20 liters, which meant several hours of stirring and boiling, with people taking turns as they tired.

For the salsa, use peeled, slightly toasted, ground almonds if necessary but ideally, hand-prepare the almonds ahead of time, as follows. Today, this almond paste may be bought specially prepared at some bakeries. Of the various types of almonds that grow in Ibiza, the ones known as *bessones*, with a softer, smoother texture are selected and carefully saved from the almond harvest. A festive evening, usually on a weekend, for young and old, is devoted to peeling the almonds, *esclovar ses metlles*, which were placed just a little while in previously boiled water to remove the skin easily. Through the 1960s, few houses in Dalt Vila had ovens, and most people used the baker's oven. The almonds were placed in the oven to toast for just a very few minutes, when the bread had been removed and the oven was still hot but not too hot. It was a time to enjoy chatting with neighbors, enjoying the welcome heat of the fire in the damp chill of the winter, with all the women watching over their almonds, and the young boys and girls milling around. The almonds were then ground with small hand grinders; not every family had one, and so either those who did brought it around to other houses, or those from other houses came to use a neighbor's; small children enjoyed turning the handle and being a central part of the activity. Families in mourning did not participate in these festive preparations or even prepare the sauce, but each family would bring a little of theirs and a house in mourning often ended up with more salsa than they had when they made it in other years.

Food and Song and Music and Dance in Ibiza and Formentera

What goes on in the famous (and sometimes infamous) discotheques of Ibiza is in many ways the antithesis of how music and food go together in traditional island life; in many ways, it is the antithesis of contemporary island life as well. Judith's daughter reports that in most of the clubs, a small bottle of water can cost €10 and that smuggling one's own water in is a valued skill. Anything other than water is even more expensive. Whether or not one is a fan of house music and the dancing that accompanies it, festive eating and drinking is not a part of that world—at least, not festively.

But if you go to a traditional dance—or the modern revival version of a "traditional" ball, a dance evening, out in the wooded hills of Ibiza, near a fountain or a well, there are tables laden with food. How can you choose from among the various types of *coques*? They're a kind of flat, straight-sided pizza, with peppers, tomatoes, onion, and spices, or a sweet variety...and then there's the island specialty of *sobrasada*, a sort of soft sausage prepared with red peppers, and *botifarrón* sausage grilled on the spot—all prepared at home by the women and sometimes men, who smilingly sit behind the tables and explain the ingredients of each mouthwatering variety, which they sell at more than reasonable prices. The drinks are likely to be the ubiquitous soft drinks in cans, but there's also wine, which you can buy by the glass or demonstrate your expertise drinking from the tilted flask, the *porrón*. ... All this food is a worthy rival to the fun of trying to learn the endlessly energetic bounds and leaps of the men's dance or the intricate, demure circles of the women's...and of course all that energy revives the appetite you'd thought had been quieted for hours.

When dances are not held because it's too cold, other activities bring their own mixture of music and food, especially the *matançes*, now seldom if ever held in Ibiza and Formentera. In the old days, a *matança*, a pig-killing session, was both a festival and a ritual. People arrived very early in the morning, and fortified themselves for the tasks with marinated fish and a type of doughnut with coffee, and by midday it was time to tase the ground meat mixture that would become the sausages, and a bit of fried pork, and get the real party ready. Anywhere from 50 to 100 people would show up, to slaughter poultry and make the special rice and stew for the occasion, with the freshly killed meat, fried potatoes, peppers, onions, garlic...the rice with green beans and bits of the fresh meat...then the doughnuts again. The women would divide into two groups, one to prepare the food and the other to clean the intestines to fill them with the sausage mixture. The children would bring water, and help out generally, but found time to affix a pig's tail to someone without their realizing it, or play with balloons they made from blown-up *vejigas*, bladder skins—Esperança's father was a designated *matancero*, butcher, and would always save her good *vejigas*. ... All the while, bits of songs flew about—"*Ton pare no te nas, ta mare es xata, i es teu germá petit cara de rata*" ("your father has no nose, your mother's nose is flat, and your little brother has a face like a rat's")...or longer songs, or people would sing their own new compositions full of satire and wicked double meanings.

These songs are rarely heard today, just as the preparation of the sauce has been simplified and shortened. During the long stages of preparing the *salsa de Nadal*, and the dark nights lit by flickering oil lamps, you might hear long narrative ballads (*romançcos*) or stories of elves and other mythical creatures, stories which made events in the films shown at the one cinema down in the lower town seem quite unremarkable by comparison. Or songs only heard at this time of year: "*es dia de Nadal, matarem un gall el poserem dins s'olla i que via si xirimolla*" ("On Christmas day one kills a rooster, and puts it in a pot, hurray for the holiday!"), or, following the old saying that this was not the time to keep anything stored away, but use it up happily: "*Toni mengemos sa truja, que la fi del mon vendrá, i naltros mos emportará i sa truja quedará*" ("Toni, let's eat the sow, for the end of the world is coming, and we'll stay and the sow will stay too").

At Carnival time, on Lard Thursday people would get together in the main square of Dalt Vila, the old walled city high up on a hill overlooking the port, to eat specially prepared *truita de potates* or *de esparces* (potato or asparagus) omelets. Even the most respectable adults would appear disguised and the children would run behind them, making jokes about them with impunity and singing nonsense rhymes or rhymes making fun of local characters. On the Sunday of Carnival there were no *truites*, but on the Tuesday there was thick, rich hot chocolate (*xocolatada*) with the local pastry specialty, *ensaimada*. Preparing the *salsa de Nadal*, the Christmas sauce whose recipe is provided here, involved all kinds of singing, already described.

Esperança Bonet Roig, writing to Judith about the salsa, and her memories of growing up in Dalt Vila, wrote: "*Tot aixó ha quedat com una boira que es perd en sa matinada, i queden es records, que estaran sempra com es caliu des foc que mantenien per coure sa salsa, sempra dins es nostros cors.*" ("All this has stayed, but like the fog lost in the early morning, and the memories remain;

they will always be there, like the warmth of the fire which we kept going to cook the salsa, always, in our hearts." [Translated from Spanish and Ibicenco by Judith Cohen.])

RECOMMENDED LISTENING

Ibiza and Formentera: the Pityusic Islands. Alan Lomax Collection. Rounder Records, 2006, edited by Espe-rança Bonet Roig and Judith Cohen.

FOR FURTHER INFORMATION

http://www.liveibiza.com
http://www.provincia.venezia.it/levi/ma/index/number9/cohen/coh_1.htm
http://www.ibizaholidays.com/history/ibiza_history.asp

CAMPANIA, ITALY
Jennifer Caputo

Place the bread under your teeth so that you will feel hungry.

Menu: *Salame, Olive, Formaggio e Pane* (Salami, Olives, Cheese, and Bread), *Prosciutto e Melone* (Ham and Melon), *Pasta e Ceci* (Pasta with Chickpeas), *Pane* (Bread), *Costolette di Maiale (o Manzo) al Pepe* (Pork or Beef Chops with Pepper), *Melanzane a Funghetto* (Eggplants Prepared like Mushrooms), *Insalata Mista* (Mixed Salad), *Frutta Mista* (Mixed Fruit), *Baba* (Neapolitan Sponge Cake Soaked in Rum), *Caffè* (Espresso), and *Limoncello* (Lemon Liqueur) or *Grappa* (Brandy Distilled from Wine). Serve dinner with dry red wine (from the region of Campania, Italy, if possible), and sparkling water.

Preparation Time: 3–4 hours, plus soaking the chickpeas overnight.

Cooking Process: Buy 2 loaves of fresh Italian bread; one for the appetizers and one for the second course. Prepare the dessert ahead of time (or purchase fresh pastries or tiramisu from a local Italian bakery). Soak chickpeas in water overnight (canned chickpeas or garbanzo beans may be used instead). Make the dessert and wash the fruit first and set aside. Allow 1 hour for the eggplant to sit covered in salt; make the eggplant dish next, while cooking the chickpeas. Make the pork chops, salad, and appetizers. You will need an espresso machine, or stovetop espresso maker. Serves six people.

The Recipes

ANTIPASTI (APPETIZERS)

SALAME, OLIVE, FORMAGGIO E PANE (SALAMI, OLIVES, CHEESE, AND BREAD)

1 loaf Italian bread
1 salami or other cured sausage
1 c. olives (green or black)
½ lb. fresh mozzarella cheese
½ lb. parmesan cheese (solid)

Cut one loaf of Italian bread into moderately thin slices and place in a basket. Do the same with the salami (or other cured sausage) and arrange on a small serving plate. Place the olives in a small bowl. (If the olives have pits you can remove the pits ahead of time or provide an empty plate for guests to leave the pits.) The cheese can be a soft, fresh mozzarella or a harder cheese such as *parmigiano* (parmesan) cut into small cubes and placed on a small serving plate. You can provide napkins and toothpicks so people can help themselves. This appetizer can be served buffet style before everyone sits at the table for the meal.

Prosciutto e Melone (Ham and Melon)

1 ripe cantaloupe
6 large, thin slices of *prosciutto di Parma*

Cut a ripe cantaloupe in half and remove the seeds and loose pulp. Cut the cantaloupe into long wedges (the length of the fruit) and remove the tough outer skin. You should be able to get about 12 wedges from one average size cantaloupe. Cut each piece of *prosciutto di Parma* (a type of ham from Parma, Italy) in half, lengthwise so you will have 12 long, thin slices. Loosely wrap one slice of prosciutto around one melon wedge until all 12 are complete. Once everyone is seated, serve on small plates (2 per person).

Primo Piatto (First Course)

Pasta e Ceci (Pasta with Chickpeas)

¾ lb. chickpeas
1 c. olive oil
1 clove garlic, finely chopped
pinch of dried oregano
1 t. chopped fresh parsley
salt
pepper
1 lb. *canneroni* pasta (or other small, tube-shaped pasta)
½ lb. parmesan cheese for grating

Soak the chickpeas in water overnight. When you are ready to cook, place them in a large pot of water (without salt) and bring to a boil. Simmer on low heat (allow the water to continue to bubble). After about 45 minutes the chickpeas should be about to break (or split). If the chickpeas are still hard after 45 minutes, remove most of them from the pot with a slotted spoon and place them in another bowl. Mash the chickpeas into a paste and return them to the pot with the rest of the chickpeas and liquid. Add approximately 1 c. olive oil, 1 clove of finely chopped garlic, a pinch of dried oregano, and/or 1 t. chopped fresh parsley, salt and pepper to taste. Before adding the pasta, be sure that there is enough water in the pot. If not, add more water (warm or room temperature is best, do not add cold water). Once the water has returned to a boil, add the pasta to the pot. When the pasta is almost *al dente*, turn off the heat and let it stand for about 10 minutes then serve into bowls. (Do not drain the pasta and chickpeas. Serve directly from the pot). Sprinkle with freshly grated Parmesan cheese. Add more oil, salt, pepper, and fresh parsley if desired.

Secondo Piatto (Second Course)

Pane (Bread)

Use the second loaf of Italian bread for the meal. Slice the bread and place it in a basket or bowl on the table so each person can help him/herself during the meal.

Costolette di Maiale (o Manzo) al Pepe (Pork or Beef Chops with Pepper)

6 thin pork chops or 3–6 small, thin beefsteaks (3 lb. total)
2 T crushed black peppercorns
2–3 T olive oil
4 cloves garlic, coarsely chopped
salt
½ c. dry red wine or beef broth

For this recipe, you can use any thin cut of pork or beef you prefer, with or without the bone. In Italy, the cuts of meat are generally thinner than in the United States (about ½"–¾" maximum). Before cooking, press crushed black peppercorns into both sides of the meat. Heat 2–3 T olive oil in a pan over medium-high heat. Add garlic and the meat. Brown both sides of the meat for about 2–2½ minutes per side. Add a pinch of salt and ½ c. dry red wine or beef broth. Reduce the heat and simmer for about 10 minutes, or until the meat is no longer pink when cut near the bone. Turn the meat occasionally. Serve with the liquid and garlic from the pan.

Verdure (Vegetables)

Melanzane a Funghetto (Eggplants Prepared like Mushrooms)

1½ lb. eggplant (about 2 medium-sized eggplants)
salt
3 T olive oil
1 14-oz. can chopped and peeled plum tomatoes (or 4–5 fresh plum tomatoes) (optional)
1–2 cloves garlic (optional)
¼ c. fresh parsley (optional)
pinch of dried basil (optional)
pinch of dried oregano (optional)
pepper

Remove the stems of the eggplants and wash them. Cut them into cubes and place them on a plate. Cover with salt and let stand for 1 hour. Drain the eggplant and soak up the extra liquid with paper towels. Fry the eggplant with 1–2 T olive oil in a pan over medium-high heat. Once the eggplant is tender (or to the desired softness), drain the excess oil from the pan and turn off the heat. If you would like to add tomatoes and garlic to this recipe, at this point remove the eggplant from the pan with a slotted spoon and in the remaining oil add 1 or more cloves of minced garlic and fresh parsley. Sauté the garlic for a few minutes until golden, then add 1 14-oz can of chopped/peeled plum tomatoes. You can also use 5–6 fresh plum tomatoes, chopped and peeled with the seeds removed. Sauté the tomatoes and garlic for another 4–5 minutes and return the eggplant to the pan. You may also add a pinch of dried basil or oregano. If you prefer, add salt and pepper to taste. Toss everything together and serve either with or after the second course.

Insalata (Salad)

Insalata Mista (Mixed salad)

Mixed salad greens
2 T extra virgin olive oil
salt
pepper
1 T balsamic vinegar
parmesan cheese (optional)

Rinse and spin or pat dry mixed salad greens (enough for six people). When ready to serve, toss with olive oil and salt. Sprinkle with pepper, balsamic vinegar, and Parmesan cheese if desired. (Many Italians only add salt and olive oil to their salad.) The salad may also be served with or after the second course.

Frutta (Fruit)

Frutta Mista (Mixed Fruit)

Selection of fresh fruits

Set a bowl of fresh fruit (enough for six people) on the table after the meal for guests to help themselves. Any fruit that is in season is fine (peaches, apples, oranges, slices of watermelon, tangerines, strawberries, etc.).

Dolce (**Dessert**)

Baba (Neapolitan Sponge Cake Soaked in Rum)

2½ c. flour

½ c. milk

2¼ t. dry yeast

3 eggs

1 c. sugar

salt

½ c. butter, melted

1 c. rum

1 T lemon juice

Grease a 12-muffin tin, dust with flour and set aside. In a small pot over low heat, warm ½ c. milk. Pour the milk into a large bowl, gradually adding 2¼ t. dry yeast, stirring until the yeast dissolves. Whisk in ½ c. plus 3 T flour and cover the bowl with a cloth or plastic wrap. Let rise in a warm place until it has doubled in size, about 30 minutes to 1 hour. Once the yeast mixture has risen, beat in 3 eggs, 1 T sugar, ½ t. salt, and the remaining 1½ c. flour until smooth. Gradually add ½ c. melted butter and mix until smooth. Spoon the dough into the muffin tin, filling each one halfway. Grease a piece of plastic wrap or waxed paper and cover the muffin tin. Let the dough rise until it has risen just above the level of the muffin tin, about 1 hour. Meanwhile, preheat the oven to 350°F. Remove the cover from the muffin tin and bake until the tops are a dark golden brown and a toothpick inserted into the center of the *baba* comes out clean (about 20–25 minutes). Let the tin cool on a wire rack. Remove the *babas* from the tin and slice them in half vertically. Place them on a plate and cover with plastic wrap to retain moisture until you are ready to serve them. When ready to serve, prepare the syrup. Bring 1 c. water and ¾ c. sugar to a boil. Stir to dissolve the sugar and remove from heat before the mixture changes color. Stir in 1 c. rum and about 1 T lemon juice. Let the syrup cool. Submerge each piece of *baba* in the syrup for 10–15 seconds. Place 2–4 pieces on each person's plate, cut side up. Drizzle with more of the syrup and serve.

Caffè (Espresso)

dark ground espresso beans (enough for six people)

½ c. sugar

In Italy, coffee is usually served after the dessert (not with the dessert). It is always a simple shot of espresso with sugar, served in a demitasse cup (*tazzina da caffè*).

Limoncello (Lemon Liqueur) or Grappa (Brandy Distilled from Wine)

This is optional and may be reserved for special occasions. After the entire meal is finished, while guests are still sitting and talking around the table, you can offer shots of *limoncello* or *grappa*.

Buon Appetito! (Good Appetite!)

In southern Italy, food and music are inseparable. An Italian friend from Caserta once said, "In order to study Italian music you must study and eat Italian food. A *festa* [feast/festival] is not a *festa* without food, and it is not a *festa* without music." He was absolutely right. While conducting fieldwork in the region of Campania, Italy, I learned almost as much about the cuisine as I did about the music. Italians are quite proud of their food and musical traditions and certainly enjoy sharing them with others. Both the cuisine and musical styles vary greatly from one region to another. Many people love to talk about the specific differences between the food and music of each region and most will happily explain what makes a certain dish or song from their hometown unique.

Usually, Italians eat a small pastry or some biscotti and drink an espresso or cappuccino for *colazione* (breakfast). The main meal, *pranzo* (lunch) begins around 1 or 2 o'clock in the afternoon and continues well into the late afternoon on Sundays and holidays. In most southern Italian towns, businesses close from 1 to 4 o'clock and children arrive home from school in time for lunch. For those who work through the entire day or far from home, lunch is brief and dinner becomes the main meal. On the weekends, however, lunch is still the largest meal. Many people do not eat *cena* (dinner) until 9 o'clock in the evening or later. Dinner often consists of pizza or a light dish such as a *frittata* (omelet). The menu included with this essay should be served in the afternoon, but may be served as a dinner in places where a three-hour, multicourse lunch is not possible.

Pasta and bread are the staple foods in southern Italian meals. Even with food as basic as pasta, Italians are rather particular when it comes to its preparation. For example, for each type of pasta, there is a specific sauce that accompanies it. Also, certain first course dishes are only to be served when meat is the second course, while others may be served with fish. For this meal I chose *pasta e ceci* (pasta and chickpeas) because it is one of the lesser-known pasta dishes outside of Italy. There are numerous pasta and bean dishes from Campania and other parts of Italy, called *pasta e fagioli*, so you can experiment with different bean and pasta combinations, just be sure to consult a native Italian or at least a cookbook to be sure you are using the correct type of pasta with the correct type of bean. In Italy, most people will undoubtedly voice their opinion if they think the pasta has been prepared incorrectly or if it is not *al dente* ("to the bite"). If they have enjoyed the meal, they will wipe their plate clean with a piece of bread to absorb any last bit of sauce or extra oil and eat the bread. It is best to eat everything on your plate to show you have truly enjoyed the meal.

When an entire family sits down to eat the main meal, music or the television may be left on, but only in the background. The main meal is a time for the entire family to talk about politics, sports, travel, parties, and events in everyday life. During the meal, conversation prevails and music is secondary. Conversation, especially in southern Italy, may actually be viewed as a form of music. Many people claim that the Neapolitan dialect is melodic when spoken. Others believe that even when Neapolitans speak Italian, it is melodious. Also, in Naples and the surrounding area, the hand gestures southern Italians use while speaking are just as significant as the dialogue. Even if you do not know a single word in the Neapolitan dialect, you can understand most of what is being said by carefully observing the gestures and listening to the vocal inflections of the language.

As I studied the *tammurriata/ballo sul tamburo* (music and dance with a tambourine) I discovered several parallels between musical traditions and eating habits. Dancers hold castanets in their hands, which are played along with the steady pulse of the tambourine. There are various hand and arm movements that accompany the steps and one woman stated that the arm movements for the dance are related to the hand gestures people use while speaking. Another parallel exists in the ways music making and cooking are transmitted from one person to another. Traditionally, young people learn to dance, sing, or play the *tammurriata* by participating at the festivals and carefully observing and listening to their elders. The same is true for cooking.

Women in Italy learn to cook by watching and helping their mothers and grandmothers. While I was living with Anna Carafa, a graduate student, she taught me how to prepare several traditional meals. I often asked her questions while she cooked and she wrote down a few recipes for me to bring back to Amercia. In general, men do not cook in southern Italy. However, everyone knows how to prepare a few simple pasta dishes and can quickly fry some meat or fish.

Finally, I must mention what is perhaps the most important component of Italian music and food: the people and their wonderful hospitality. Southern Italians take great pride in being excellent hosts. A meeting with friends or family is never without food or drink, even if it is only a *caffè* (espresso) or glass of wine. Whenever I met with friends and informants, it almost always began or ended with a meal or at least a pastry and an espresso. Of course, everyone insisted that I try a little bit of everything even if I was not hungry. Claiming that you do not have an appetite in Italy is simply unacceptable. If you ever visit southern Italy, be prepared to eat well, enjoy leisurely midafternoon conversations, and listen to beautiful music.

The meaning of the proverb ("place the bread under your teeth so that you will feel hungry") is that when a person sits down for a meal and claims that he or she is not hungry or has lost his or her appetite, the taste of the bread will revive one's appetite.

RECOMMENDED LISTENING

Cantica Popularia. *Doce Doce*. 2004. (This group performs unique arrangements of tammurriate and other traditional songs from Campania and Puglia. Available at: www.casertamusica.com/archivio/Cantica-Popularia/cantica_popularia.htm)

Canzone Napoletana [Neapolitan Songs]. (Try to locate recordings of Italian vocalists such as Enrico Caruso or Renato Carosone. If you are unable to find recordings of Italian vocalists, Italian-American vocalists who sing classical Neapolitan songs will do, e.g., Frank Sinatra, Jerry Vale, Dean Martin, and Tony Bennett.)

Nuova Compagnia di Canto Populare. *Antologia*. EMI Music Italy, 1999. 7243 4 98404 2 3. (This is a two-CD set of songs from one of the earliest musical groups of the folk music revival in Italy. This ensemble is based in Campania and has been performing traditional music from the region for almost forty years.)

Tammurriata/Ballo sul tamburo [Song and Dance with a Tambourine]: *Feste e Tamburi. Vol. 1—Balli sul tamburo, balli intrecciati, canti rituali*. Taranta, 1999. TA014. (Edited by Giuseppe Michele Gala. Collection of field recordings from various festivals throughout the region of Campania, Italy.)

FOR FURTHER INFORMATION

http://www.lonelyplanet.com/destinations/europe/italy/
http://www.angelfire.com/la3/campaniafelix/

GREECE
Maria Hnaraki

> *A hungry bear does not dance.*

Menu: *Avgolemono* (Egg-Lemon Soup), *Melitzanosalata* (Eggplant Salad), *Maroulosalata* (Lettuce, Dill, and Cucumber Salad), *Kotopoulo Sto Fourno Me Patates* (Chicken and Baked Potatoes), and *Halva* (Sweet Nut Dessert). Serve with bread. To drink, try a white wine, such as Kritikos by Boutari, Moshofilero by Boutari, or Retsina (such as Kourtaki, Boutari, Demestica), and water.
Preparation Time: 2 hours, not including the *halva*.
Cooking Process: Buy a loaf of rough, "peasant-style" bread. Prepare the *halva* the day before or before everything else. Put the eggplants in the oven to bake. Get the chicken in the oven, then prepare the soup and do all the preparation work for the *melitzanosalata*. Make the salad, but don't dress it until ready to serve. When the eggplants are done, remove from the oven and cut open immediately to cool faster. Serves six people.

The Recipes

AVGOLEMONO (EGG-LEMON SOUP)

1 medium yellow onion, chopped
salt
pepper
1 c. rice
2 eggs
1½ lemons, juiced

In a saucepan, bring 10 c. water to a boil with the chopped onion. Add 1 t. salt and ½ t. pepper. Add 1 c. rice, cover the pan, reduce heat to simmer and cook it until tender, for about 18 minutes. In a separate bowl, beat the eggs, while adding the lemon juice from 1½ lemons. Slowly add (in parts) the boiling soup and continue beating. Remove the saucepan from the heat and stir in the egg mixture. The rice will absorb most of the water. Taste, adding more water and lemon juice, if necessary, to keep it as a soup. Stir for a few more minutes; the soup will look frothy.

MELITZANOSALATA (EGGPLANT SALAD)

2 eggplants
2 cloves garlic
¼ c. parsley
2 tomatoes
1–2 T olive oil
salt
pepper
1 T lemon juice

Cut deeply into 2 eggplants (4" long scores on all sides), then wrap them in aluminum foil and bake for 30–40 minutes at 350°F until soft. Remove from oven and allow them to cool, then mash with a fork in a bowl or pulse briefly in a food processor. Chop two cloves of garlic and ¼ c. parsley into small pieces. Finally, chop 2 tomatoes. Add the eggplant, garlic, parsley, tomatoes, some olive oil (enough to lightly coat the mixture), salt and pepper to taste, and 1 T lemon juice. Garnish the spread with fresh parsley and olives. Chill and serve with slices of bread.

Maroulosalata (Lettuce, Dill, and Cucumber Salad)

1 head lettuce
2 cucumbers
½ bunch fresh dill
2 T olive oil
1 T red wine vinegar
salt
pepper

Wash, slice, and mix 1 head of lettuce, peel and slice 2 cucumbers, and ½ bunch of fresh dill (to taste). Add olive oil, red wine vinegar, salt and pepper to taste.

Kotopoulo Sto Fourno Me Patates (Chicken and Baked Potatoes)

5 cloves garlic
4 potatoes
¾ c. olive oil
2 T fresh or dried oregano
salt
pepper
2 lemons, juiced
12 chicken pieces

Chop 5 cloves of garlic into small pieces. Peel and slice 4 potatoes (½" thick), then place them in a roasting pan with the garlic. Add ¾ c. olive oil and 2 T oregano (enough to lightly coat everything), salt and pepper. Add the juice of 2 lemons and enough water to cover the bottom of the pan. Wash and place the 12 raw chicken pieces on top. Bake them at 350°F until tender (approximately 90 minutes). Broil for the last few minutes, turning once so that the chicken is nicely browned.

Kotopoulo (roasted Greek chicken). Photo by Cary Black.

HALVA (SWEET NUT DESSERT)

⅛ c. walnuts or almonds

½ c. sugar

1 lemon or orange, peeled

2 cinnamon sticks

4 whole cloves

¼ c. olive oil

⅓ c. semolina (⅔ coarse and ⅓ finely ground)

⅛ c. raisins

1 t. ground cinnamon

Make the syrup first. Chop ⅛ c. walnuts or almonds (blanched and peeled) into small pieces. Heat ¾ c. water in a saucepan. Add ½ c. sugar, peel of 1 lemon or orange, 2 cinnamon sticks, and 4 cloves. Bring to a boil. Remove syrup from heat and cool to room temperature. In a deep saucepan, place ¼ c. olive oil and cook until it begins to smoke, then add a little over ⅓ c. semolina (preferably ⅔ coarse and ⅓ fine). The mix may appear to swell; keep stirring. When the semolina turns brown, add the syrup slowly while continuing to stir. Add the chopped nuts and ⅛ c. raisins. Continue adding as much syrup as it needs to become a jellied mixture. Place in a bowl, sprinkling cinnamon powder on the top. Let it cool at room temperature.

Olive market (Greece). Photo by Terry E. Miller.

A Hungry Bear Does Not Dance

Imagine a gypsy wandering around with a bear. He would ask it to stand on its two hind feet and perform dancing movements. Today, although that type of entertainment at local fairs is—thank God for the poor bears—almost extinct, the old Greek proverb is very alive confirming the idea that for a dance event to be accomplished, food is necessary. In the same spirit, Greek folk music lyrics ask "the lords" to "eat and drink," because dancing won't start before everyone's stomach is well fed.

Greek cooking mostly relies on the produce of Greece: fresh seasonal fruits, vegetables, grains, pulses, legumes, goats, and sheep, fresh fish, and, of course, the ever present olive oil. Cheeses and yogurts are also fundamental. All of this is enhanced with fresh young wine from the patchwork of vineyards that quilt the Greek landscape, and digested with the ubiquitous presence of other "white" spirits (such as *ouzo, tsipouro, raki*). Most Greeks in rural areas have their own olive grove and vineyard, even a pergola of hanging grapes shading their porch, with fruit trees, gardens for vegetables, wild berries covering the property fences on their land, and a profusion of flowers.

Greeks need few excuses for social gatherings and *gledia* (feasts), which include not only dancing, but also drinking, singing, eating, talking, and, more generally, people in *kefi* (high spirits), who are willing to celebrate the event and share these moments with people in their community, their relatives and friends, and other guests. The distinctiveness of the Greek community, as well as that of Greece as a country, is reproduced in the pride of the individual performer. For instance, one who is "good at being a man" must know, among other things, how to eat (especially meat) and drink a lot. Serving massive amounts of meat and food at feasts signifies health and prosperity. Honey and walnuts are served to all unmarried women at a Cretan wedding after the religious ceremony.

Musicians all over Greece perform live music in combination with freshly made local variations of traditional foods at various events, which take place outdoors during the summer, and indoors during the winter. Festivals and celebrations may also be wine feasts. At the sounds of traditional music, Greeks open their wine barrels to festively honor saints (such as Saint George the Inebriant, the *Methistis*) or merely to socialize and have fun. Women from the village offer foods of the Greek cuisine, and specialists talk about wine and its history, one that has ancient roots in Greece, as the wine *patitiria* (presses) found in many places demonstrate.

Specific foods such as bread (a strong symbol of continuity and healthy life in Greek society) can mark certain events. Specific sweet breads are made during Easter (*tsoureki*) and at Christmas (*vasilopita*). At weddings in Crete, the round bread (*koulouri*) is "embroidered" to look like a traditional piece of cloth; it is important and as necessary for life as weddings are. Boiled wheat with sugar, several herbs, and spices (*kolyva*) are prepared for funerals and memorial services.

The Greek language itself borrows expressions from food. Greeks, for instance, talk of colors as those of the carrot (*karoti*), the eggplant (*melitzani*), the cabbage (*lahani*). They do not spend but "eat" time (Zeus was almost eaten by his father Time, thus Kronos), Greek clocks do not waste but "eat" minutes, whereas in Greece too much work doesn't harm but "eats" you, you are not being scolded but "eaten," you are not getting a boot but being "eaten," your head is not itching but "eating," and you are not searching thoroughly but you are "eating the world." Not only do you have to be aware of even "eating" someone with your eyes, meaning staring at someone, but also do not forget that getting older you are actually "eating your own bread"!

It is in Greece where one becomes the beneficiary of Zeus's virtue, the lavish and frequent *filoxenia* (hospitality). Village rules deem that one who enters the coffeehouse must treat those already present. Treating (*kerasma*) with drinks and nuts is still common in most of the public places of the Greek villages, but also among neighbors in the tiny side streets. Several times in a week, neighbors will share some of their cooking, bringing a plate of their day's lunch. You may often have to secretly empty your glass in order not to get drunk and, at the same time, be able to have it refilled when a "must" follows. Denying any food or drink that people may offer you may offend traditional rules and even get you into trouble.

CNN promoted the Greek diet through documentaries, showing how Greeks, and especially those from the island of Crete, hold records for longevity (the well-known "Mediterranean diet"). Researchers have discovered that Cretans have the lowest rate of heart diseases and cancer. They describe it as "the miracle of Cretan diet," where olive oil plays perhaps the biggest role.

The recipes I chose take a reasonable amount of time to prepare. As a Greek in America, I was many times asked to prepare a Greek meal. For these recipes I was able to find all the ingredients needed in the United States. So, after a while, the combination of all these dishes became, more or less, a standard meal for guests or parties. The advantage of these dishes is that they can please vegetarians too, and that they contain lots of variety for people with different tastes. I added bread, cheese, and olives, because these three things almost always exist on the traditional Greek table and accompany every Greek meal. (Bread and water are offered for free at restaurants.)

Greek cookbooks have been and are still being published in many languages. The roots of Greek cooking, as it is still practiced in the villages, are believed to stem from the Homeric, Minoan, and Hellenistic times of several millennia ago. Enriched with Mediterranean and Oriental recipes, Greek cooking presents a very varied and plentiful fare. Culture continuing through cooking is a widespread belief. Greek wine, for instance, is believed to be the nectar of gods. The word "*nostimo*" (tasty) itself shares the same root with the word "nostalgia." "*Nostos*" means "the return," "the journey," while "*a-nostos*" means "without taste." "*Nostimos*," thus, is the one who has journeyed and arrived, has matured, ripened, and is, therefore, tasty (useful). All in all, Greek food, like everything Greek, is certainly "big" and "fat."

RECOMMENDED LISTENING

Taste of Greek Music—Traditional Greek Food (includes 20 songs and 20 recipes). (Available at: http://www.greekmusic.com. There is also a vegetarian version of this CD/recipe set.)

FOR FURTHER INFORMATION

Kochilas, Diane. 2001. *Herbs, Greens, Fruit: The Key to the Mediterranean Diet.* Iraklio: MKS Metaxaraki Advertising.
Psilakis, Maria, and Nikos. 1995. *Cretan Cooking: The Miracle of the Cretan Diet.* Iraklio: Karmanor.
http://cretashop.gr/br/productsbr/booksbr/9607448073br.htm
http://www.aerakis.net
http://www.greecefoods.com/cookbooks.html
http://www.greekmusic.com

BULGARIA
Timothy Rice (based on instruction by Tzvetanka Varimezova)

Do not travel in winter time without some food, and in summer time without a coat.

Menu: *Shopska Salata* (Salad from the Shop Region near Sofia) with *Hlyab* (Bread), *Yahniya* (Chicken and Vegetable Stew) with *Hlyab* (Bread), and *Tikvenik* (Sweet Layered Squash Dessert).
Preparation Time: 3 hours.
Cooking Process: Make the stew and the dessert the evening before. On the day of the meal, buy a loaf of European or Italian-style peasant bread (preferably not sourdough); the classic Bulgarian shape is oblong but a round loaf is fine. An hour before eating, reheat the stew and make the salad. Serve the meal in three courses: salad, stew, and dessert, with the bread available for the salad and stew. Serves six people.

The Recipes

SHOPSKA SALATA (SALAD FROM THE SHOP REGION NEAR SOFIA)

2 large tomatoes, diced
1 cucumber (seedless English ones are convenient), diced
1 red onion, diced
1 green bell pepper (optional), diced
2 T vegetable oil
salt
6 sprigs English parsley
⅓ lb. feta cheese (preferably Bulgarian but Greek or French are fine)

In a large salad bowl, combine the vegetables. Add 2 T vegetable oil and 1 T salt and mix. Chop 6 sprigs of English parsley and sprinkle over the top. Grate or finely crumble ⅓ lb. feta cheese and sprinkle over the top. Serve immediately with bread for dipping in the salad dressing.

YAHNIYA (CHICKEN AND VEGETABLE STEW)

1 chicken or 3–4 lb. of chicken pieces (white and/or dark meat, as you prefer)
4 T vegetable oil
salt
4 large white onions
4 c. fresh or canned crushed tomatoes
1 red bell pepper (optional)
8 baby carrots (or 2 medium carrots)
1 T paprika
4 bay leaves
10 whole allspice berries
pepper
5 cloves garlic

1 bottle white wine
4 T flour (if necessary, for thickening)

Cut the chicken in pieces: legs, thighs, breasts, wings. Cut the breasts in half or even in thirds if they are large. Wash the chicken carefully, pull out any excess fat, and remove any loose bits from the skin. (Tzvetanka then held each piece over a gas burner and singed the skin to a light tan color the way her grandmother taught her. She regarded this as a hygienic step, but acknowledged that it probably was no longer necessary.) In a large pot, place 4 T vegetable oil, 1½ T salt, and the chicken pieces. Rub the oil and salt over the chicken and turn the heat up to high. Brown the chicken, turning occasionally, about 10 minutes. Add 1½ c. water, 4 large white onions, chopped into medium-to-large dice, and 4 c. crushed tomatoes. (Tzvetanka cut each tomato in half and, holding them by the skin, grated them until all the juice and pulp was released into the bowl, and she was left with only the skin in her hand. I would use crushed tomatoes from a can.) Then add 1 skinned and chopped bell pepper (I regard this as optional; the usual way to skin the bell pepper involves charring the skin, placing it in a closed plastic bag to steam and cool, and then slipping off the skin), 8 baby carrots (coarsely chopped), 1 T paprika, 4 whole bay leaves, 10 whole allspice berries, and 20 grinds of black pepper. Bring to a boil and simmer for about 10 minutes. Taste and add salt and pepper, if necessary. Add 5 gloves of garlic, peeled and cut in half. Simmer another 10 minutes. Add ⅔ c. white wine and simmer another 5 minutes. If the soup is watery, in a small bowl mix 4 T flour with a bit of water into a smooth paste. Add the paste to the soup and turn off the heat and let stand for a few minutes to thicken the soup into a stew. This stew can be made a day in advance and heated up when needed.

TIKVENIK (SWEET LAYERED SQUASH DESSERT)

2 pieces of banana squash or pumpkin (enough to make 8 cups of grated squash)
2 c. sugar
1 c. crushed walnuts
1½ T cinnamon
1 package of phyllo dough, defrosted
½ c. vegetable oil

Peel the skin off the squash or pumpkin and grate by hand, using a cheese grater, or using the grater blade in a food processor. Combine the grated squash in a bowl with 2 c. sugar, 1 c. crushed walnuts, and 1½ T cinnamon. Remove the defrosted phyllo dough from the package and open out onto a table. Lightly grease a 9" x 13" baking pan with vegetable oil. One by one take each sheet of the phyllo dough off the stack and cover the bottom of the pan with several layers, overlapping them as necessary (if they tear, don't worry). Drizzle with vegetable oil. Spread ¼ of the squash mixture over the layers. One by one, add 4 more layers of phyllo dough over the top, lightly drizzling the layers with oil, and cover with ¼ more of the squash mixture. Repeat 2 more times to create 4 layers of squash. Top with 4 layers of phyllo dough, which should just about use up the whole package of dough. Cut the *tikvenik* into 3" long diamond shapes (think *baklava*) by cutting parallel lines diagonally at a 45° angle to the edges of the pan. Then cut parallel lines along the long edge of the pan and *voilà*: diamond-shaped bars. Drizzle the top layer generously with oil so that some goes down into the cuts. Bake in an oven preheated to 400°F for about 30 minutes. Check for doneness and take it out when the top layer has turned a nice golden-brown color. Let cool and serve at room temperature or, if you can't wait, slightly warm. This may be made in advance.

When Guests Gather Together in Bulgaria

When I first went to Bulgaria in the summer of 1969, my senses were assaulted by new tastes unknown to the impossibly bland middle American diet of the time: sparkling mineral water, yogurt, and flavorful tomatoes. Though hardly the stuff of ethnomusicological culinary legend, Bulgarian food experiences have always been at or near the center of my fieldwork on music, song, and dance.

The connection of food and drink to music making and dancing was evident in the many weddings I was fortunate to attend during that first summer. Guests sat around one long table, as long as was necessary to accommodate all of us. At each place stood a soda bottle full of strong grape brandy (*rakiya*), a 24-oz. bottle of beer, and a bottle of wine. The meal started with a salad accompanied by the clinking of *rakiya*-filled glasses and periodic toasts to our health (*na zdrave*). I learned quickly that people don't toast just once and then proceed to drink randomly and privately on their own. Any time anyone wants to take a sip (or a gulp), they have to enlist the aid of all those nearby through a call for a toast (*a sega na zdrave*), the clinking of glasses, and only then the sip or gulp in a great show of comradely unison. After the salad, the bride's family typically served a meat stew with bread, and, if you made the mistake of cleaning your plate, as my mother taught me, another bowl would instantly appear until finally you couldn't eat any more and realized that the etiquette was the opposite of what your mother taught you. The toasting continued, now with wine and beer, and it is probably a measure of how much alcohol I consumed at these festive meals that I have no memory of any dessert ever being served.

The food seemed, at one level, very plain: cooked or soaked in sunflower oil, seasoned with salt and, from a post Julia Child culinary perspective, employing a limited palette of spices. But it was wonderfully tasty, based as it was on fresh ingredients and recently living animals from people's yards and gardens. It was also enlivened by the music that I had first heard and admired on recordings in the United States, the music that had drawn me to Bulgaria in the first place. In the middle of my first meal at a Bulgarian wedding, a female village singer sitting across from me at the table, with a voice of unmatched power, broke into a historical ballad about Krali (King) Marko. Suddenly, nonmetrical melodies that you couldn't dance to made perfect sense. Sitting and listening to and admiring her beautiful voice and rich ornamentation were as satisfying aesthetically as the food was gastronomically. And after everyone was sated with food and drink, we all jumped up to dance enthusiastically in long lines around the table, perfect for working up an appetite for yet more food and drink.

Many of the songs still sung in Bulgaria today carry labels describing a function in the ancient agrarian cycle of work and ritual: Christmas song, Easter song, harvest song, working-bee song. But most of these contexts for singing songs and playing music have disappeared since World War II with urbanization and industrialization. The main context for music making outside the mass media are gatherings of friends and family, either in informal settings around the kitchen table or at a restaurant or more formal celebrations, especially weddings. "When guests gather together," as they say, all sing together or enjoy music and song presented by a hired band. And dancing is a central and pleasant activity for all present. One can imagine that as long as Bulgarians continue to socialize together, there will be a natural place for singing, dancing, and playing a bit of music.

During my time in Bulgaria, I was happy enough to eat Bulgarian food, but my wife Ann, a skilled cook, made a point of learning some of the basic dishes. Perhaps the most fundamental homecooked item in Bulgarian cuisine and a dish that traditionally every girl learned to make is *banitsa*. *Banitsa* is made from thin phyllo dough like that used in baklava. Traditionally phyllo dough was not bought at the store but was homemade and, because of the difficulty of rolling out such thin dough, it acted as a measure of a bride's homemaking skills and thus her suitability as a wife. For *banitsa*, the phyllo is filled with a mixture of eggs and feta cheese and baked in the oven.

A variant that we frequently encounter in the United States is Greek *spanakopita*, in which spinach is added to the cheese-and-egg mixture. Ann asked our hosts in the village where we lived if she could learn how to roll out the dough and make *banitsa*. They directed her to a grandmother next door who made it every Sunday and was an acknowledged expert.

Ann secured the grandmother's agreement for a lesson the following Sunday and arrived with pencil and notebook in hand, ready to take notes and ask questions. After some time the grandmother said, "Can I ask you a question?" Ann said, "Of course." The grandmother asked, "Why didn't your mother teach you to make this?" Ann responded, "In America we don't eat *banitsa*." The grandmother, wide-eyed, exclaimed, "Then what do you eat?!"

After leaving Bulgaria, I became much more interested in learning the other skills associated with the Bulgarian home beyond singing, playing music, and dancing. I learned to make wine, which every Bulgarian village man can do. And I became more interested in cooking. I learned these recipes from Tzvetanka Varimezova, a wonderful singer, professionally trained folk musician, and cook. She has taught, along with her husband Ivan, Bulgarian music at UCLA for four years. I asked her to show me a simple meal of the sort that I had been served at those Bulgarian weddings I attended in 1969: the classic Bulgarian salad consisting of a mix of diced vegetables, salt, vegetable oil, and feta cheese; a chicken-and-onion stew; and a dessert made with phyllo dough, squash, walnuts, sugar, and cinnamon. I hope you enjoy trying it as much as I enjoyed learning how to make it.

Shopska salata (SHOWP-ska sa-LA-ta) is first, served with bread and traditionally a distilled fruit-based brandy like Italian *grappa* or Yugoslav *slivovica* or French-California-Oregon Pear William, poured in small glasses and served neat. The Bulgarian variety is called *rakiya* (ra-KEY-ya) and is a grape brandy like grappa, not a plum or pear brandy, but it is not readily available on the market. Any of these would be a fine choice, but of course can be omitted if you prefer. The juice from the tomatoes, the oil, and the salt fall to the bottom of the salad bowl to create a perfect dipping sauce for the bread. Do not miss this part of the meal. The next course is *yahniya* (yach-NEE-ya). Serve in soup bowls with bread as an accompaniment, again excellent for swabbing up the juices. Bulgarians traditionally drank homemade wine, either white or red, with the main meal. Drink whatever you like. The last course is *tikvenik*. Enjoy the Bulgarian version of pumpkin pie, eaten with the fingers.

During dinner I asked Tzvetanka about Bulgarian proverbs related to food, and this is what we came up with. "*Nyama po goliam ot hlyaba.*" ("There is nothing greater than bread.") This testifies to the central role of bread in the Bulgarian diet. "*Da kazhe hlyaba che tsar go e yal.*" ("May the bread say that a king has eaten it.") Said as an expression of satisfaction after a meal, it indicates again the central importance of bread conceptually in Bulgarian foodways. "*Ne hodi zimno vreme bez hranicka, I lyatno vreme bez abichka.*" ("Do not travel in winter time without some food, and in summer time without a coat.") In the summer, food was plentiful and could be picked from fields and trees, but not in winter. On the other hand, while it is obvious that you need a coat in winter, even in summer good weather can change unpredictably. "*Tikvenik sus tikvenik.*" ("Squash with squash.") When I expressed my concern that working with phyllo dough was difficult, Tzvetanka answered that it was really easy and indeed it is. In fact, it's so simple that when Bulgarians want to refer to a particularly simple or stupid person, they refer to this dish and to the person with the mild curse, "*tikvenik* with *tikvenik*."

RECOMMENDED LISTENING

Boyd, Joe. *Ivo Papazov and his Orchestra: Balkanology*. Hannibal, 1991. HNCD 1363.
Boyd, Joe, and Rumyana Tzintzarska. *Balkana: The Music of Bulgaria*. Hannibal, 1987. HNCD 1363.
Cellier, Marcel. *Le mystere des voix bulgares*, Vols. 1, 2. Nonesuch, 1987, 1988. 79165, 79201.

FOR FURTHER INFORMATION

For more on Bulgarian music and culture, see two books by Tim Rice: *Music in Bulgaria: Expressing Music, Expressing Culture* (New York: Oxford University Press, 2004) and *May It Fill Your Soul: Experiencing Bulgarian Music* (Chicago: University of Chicago Press, 1994). For more on Bulgarian cooking, try Atanas Slavov, *Traditional Bulgarian Cooking* (New York: Hippocrene Books, 1998), which contains some good writing on Bulgarian food culture as well as recipes. For more recordings and videos, check the website http://www.balkanfolk.com

ESTONIA
Ramona Holmes

One who is eating a lot is doing a lot.

Menu: *Kurgi Salat* (Cucumber Salad), *Rosolje* (Beet and Herring Salad), *Hapukapsa* (Sauerkraut), *Verivorst* (Blood Sausage), and *Bubert Ehk Mannapuder Munaga* (Creamed Semolina on Fruit Soup). Serve with Saku brand beer and juniper berry soda.
Preparation Time: Not counting the several hours involved in soaking the herring, making the blood sausage, and preparing the salad and sauerkraut, which you do the night before, approximately 2 hours on the day of the meal.
Cooking Process: Set the herring to soak, then make the sausage. Boil the beets and potatoes for the salad and make the sauerkraut the night before; everything else could be started a couple of hours before dinner. Serves six people.

The Recipes

KURGI SALAT (CUCUMBER SALAD)

3 cucumbers
½ c. sour cream
1 t. fresh dill
2 T white wine vinegar
salt

Peel and slice 3 cucumbers. Add ½ c. sour cream, 1 t. fresh dill, 2 T white wine vinegar, and salt to taste.

ROSOLJE (BEET AND HERRING SALAD)

2 eggs
3 beets (or 1 16-oz. can)
5–6 potatoes
1 c. sour cream
½ c. mayonnaise
1 T mustard
salt
pepper
pinch of sugar
1 salt herring soaked overnight in cold water or tea
4 pickles
1 apple
¾ c. cold lean meat
½ medium yellow onion

Hard boil 2 eggs. Cut 3 beets and 5–6 potatoes into cubes and boil until tender, about 20 minutes. Make the dressing by combining 1 c. sour cream, ½ c. mayonnaise, 1 T mustard, salt, pepper, and a little sugar to taste. Chop 1 salt herring and 4 pickles finer than other ingredients. Cube and mix in 3 cooked beets (or a 16-oz. can), 5–6 cooked potatoes, 1 apple, 2 hardboiled eggs, ¾ c. cold lean meat (usually leftover roast beef), and ½ onion. Mix the dressing into salad. Refrigerate 3–5 hours before serving.

Hapukapsa (Sauerkraut)

2 lb. sauerkraut
1 lb. pork loin
½ c. barley
salt
sugar
1–2 medium yellow onions, chopped
1 T vegetable oil

Put 2 lb. sauerkraut and 1 lb. pork in pot and cover with ½ c. barley (groats or pearl). Add water to cover and cook until tender, about 2 hours. Season with salt and sugar to taste. The onions may be sautéed in vegetable oil and added either in the beginning or at the end.

Verivorst (Blood Sausage)

1 lb. pearl barley
2 large onions
1½ lb. side of pork
1 qt. beef or pork blood
3 t. marjoram
½ lb. sausage casing

Boil 1 lb. pearl barley in 6¾ c. of water for 20 minutes. Chop 2 large onions, cut up 1½ lb. side of pork and fry at low heat for about 20 minutes. Strain 1 qt. blood. Mix cooked barley with onions, pork, blood, and 3 t. marjoram. You may test flavorings by frying small amounts in a pan. Soak ½ lb. sausage casing in cold water and rinse well. Fill a large pot ¾ full of water and set to boil. Fill loosely with mixture as it will expand. Make 2 sausage rings and tie ends. Place in boiling water and simmer 15 minutes. Poke sausages with large needle. Hang on wooden stick to cool and dry.

Bubert Ehk Mannapuder Munaga (Creamed Semolina on Fruit Soup)

5 eggs
¾ c. sugar
2 t. vanilla
4 c. milk
¾ c. semolina
6 c. berry soup (see instructions, below)

Beat 5 egg yolks, ¾ c. sugar, and 2 t. vanilla until creamy. Beat 5 egg whites until firm. Boil 4 c. milk. Add ¾ c. semolina while stirring. Lower heat and cook until thick. Quickly add egg whites and yolk mixture. Put a cup of berry soup in each bowl and add ½ c. of semolina mixture. (Note: If you can't find berry soup in a Scandinavian specialty store, you can make it yourself by mixing 6 c. berries with enough sugar to taste, and cook until the sugar dissolves but the berries are still firm.)

Food and Music in Estonia

Estonian food is based on peasant living in a Baltic Sea country with many small islands. Anything that can be prepared with herring is traditional. You will find recipes for herring soup, stewed herring, herring with potatoes, herring casserole, herring sauce, herring rolls, herring salad, and herring pancakes.

If you are not fond of herring, don't worry, since hearty wheat and rye bread are common. It is said that bread is sacred. One Estonian proverb says, "Have respect for bread; bread is older than us." In some parts of Estonia when a child dropped a slice of bread, they were told they should pick it up and kiss it for luck. In some communities, giving the heel of the bread to a young woman in the family was said to ensure her having larger breasts. When guests were at dinner, the housewife didn't give out the heel of the bread because that would mean she would lose her bread luck.

Estonians say, "meat will bring you closer, and cabbage will scare you away" ("*liha toob ligidale, kapsad viivad kaugele*"). However, cabbage is used in many Estonian dishes such as the *kapsapirukas* (cabbage-filled pastry). Estonian wedding feasts often go for many days with a wide variety of food and music. People sing songs and play bagpipes, violins, *kannels* (zithers), and various percussion instruments for dancers. The end of the wedding festivities is signaled by the bride's family serving cabbage soup, the sign to leave.

A common Estonian drink is barley malt beer served in wooden mugs and tankards. The handcarved wooden mugs sometimes have a wooden rattle in the bottom of the mug so the wife can hear when the mug is being emptied. Juniper berries are sometimes added to beer and are also used to make a soft drink or tea.

The recipes in this section are representative of meals I shared with friends and family at many events in the Estonian-American community over the past 50 years. Most of the Estonians in exile were originally immigrants who came to America after WWII and kept the traditions alive through food, music, and dance. The community now includes many recent emigrants from Estonia. Estonian-Americans celebrate together in big song festivals combined by regions, such as the "West Coast Estonian Days" held every other summer. There is always a celebration of Estonian independence in February (even held in the years when Estonian was under Soviet control.) Almost any gathering includes herring in many forms. Blood sausage is most likely to appear at Christmas.

My first fieldwork to Estonia took place in 1978 while the area was still controlled by the Soviet Union. Food was scarce and meals were based on the item available that day—often cabbage or rhubarb would be a key ingredient. There were very few restaurants, though coffee houses served delicious coffee and rolls. Now that Estonia is an independent country again, there are many more options. The Eesti Maja restaurant in Tallinn serves traditional Estonian foods like those described here. There are also many international restaurants in Tallinn, as Estonians love to try new things.

Estonians will be pleased and surprised that you are interested in trying the traditional dishes. Estonians are economical with their emotions, and you may not recognize from this cool manner that there is sincere appreciation for your interest. Rest assured that we will be impressed if you try the blood sausage.

RECOMMENDED LISTENING

Estonian Philharmonic Chamber Choir. *Baltic Voices 1*. 2003. HMU 907311. (Grammy Award winning classic choral music, including pieces by Estonian composers Cyrillus Kreek, Arvo Pärt, and Veljo Tormis. Estonian choral music is central to the culture. The classic composers on this CD include many elements of traditional music in their compositions. Main course music.)

Estonie: Airs anciens. Ocora C 600012. (A Radio-France collection of traditional Estonian instrumental music. Many polkas and waltzes in case you want to dance after your dinner.)

Loo, Kirile. *Saatus* [Fate]. Alula Records. ALU-1004; and *Lullabies for Husbands*. Erdenklang. 91062. (In these CDs, Kirile Loo combines ancient *regilaul*, traditional Estonian, and popular Estonian sounds. Especially good for a romantic candlelight dinner.)

Setusongs. Global Music Center. MIPUCD 104. (A collection of folk songs from the Setu region. Warning: These are not typical Estonian *regilaul*. Setu is close to the border of Russia and these are sung with a Slavic voice and close harmonies. Goes best with cabbage soup.)

Tubin, Eduard. *Violin Concerto Nr. 1*. Grammofon. AB BIS CD 286. (Classic composer Eduard Tubin's works including the *Suite on Estonian Dances for Violin and Orchestra*. Dessert music.)

FOR FURTHER INFORMATION

http://www.saku.ee (history of beer in Estonia).
http://www.laulpidu.ee/vana/eng (Estonian song festival).

SWEDEN
Theresa A. Allison

Bread and butter put color in your cheeks.

Menu: *Kåldolmar* (Cabbage Rolls), *Inlagd Gurka* (Pickled Cucumber), *Kokt Potatis* (Boiled New Potatoes), *Lingonsylt* (Lingonberry Sauce), and *Mördeg* (Butter Cookies with Seven Variations). Serve with water or soda.

Preparation Time: Approximately 4 hours total (3 hours for cabbage rolls or 1½ hours for cabbage casserole); 1–2 hours per batch of cookies.

Cooking Process: Bake the cookies days ahead of time and freeze. Make the cabbage rolls first, boil the potatoes once the cabbage rolls are baking and then make the pickled cucumber while the potatoes boil and everything will be done at the same time. Serves six people.

The Recipes

KÅLDOLMAR (CABBAGE ROLLS)

3 medium potatoes
2 large heads of cabbage
salt
2 medium yellow onions, 1 finely chopped and 1 coarsely chopped
6 T butter
1 egg
pepper
2 lb. ground beef
1 lb. ground pork
¾ c. milk
3 T flour

Boil 3 medium potatoes, peel, crush slightly, and set aside. Cut core from 2 large heads of cabbage and separate leaves. Boil the leaves briefly in salted water until soft enough for wrapping the meat (about 2 minutes); drain well. Fry the finely chopped onion in 2 T butter until browned. While the onion is frying, place the coarsely chopped onion, an egg, the potatoes, 3 t. salt, ½ t. pepper in a food processor and blend coarsely. Add 2 lb. ground beef, 1 lb. ground pork, and the fried onion to the mixture, and mix well. Then add ¼–½ c. milk until texture is smooth and forms soft meatballs. Fry a little "taster" to make sure that it tastes right. This distinctly Swedish step is essential to good cabbage rolls. Take about ½ t. meat mixture, make it into a meatball, smash it flat, fry in butter, and taste it. In particular, feed it to any little children helping in the kitchen. It should taste like a rather salty Swedish meatball. Add salt and pepper to the meat mixture and keep frying bits to taste until it has enough flavor. The salt and pepper will lose flavor during the baking. Place 2–3 T meat mixture on each cabbage leaf (may need to cut the rib out of the largest leaves in order to wrap them, or to use two of the smallest leaves for one roll). Wrap into a rectangular package. In the old days, they sewed these packages with strings, but we usually just fry them with the seam down first.

Fry in small batches with a generous amount of butter in a deep frying pan or braising pot. When brown on the surface, place in a greased Pyrex or Corningware dish. Make sure there is ½–1 cup of water in the bottom of each baking dish before baking. Bake at 350°F for about 45 minutes, and drizzle more water over the cabbage rolls every 10 or 15 minutes, as necessary, to keep them moist. Whisk out the pan occasionally by adding a little water and scraping the bottom free of drippings. Pour these over the cabbage rolls. Whisk together 3 T flour in ¼ c. of milk to form a roux, add more milk until it is easy to pour. Remove dolmas again and add milk and flour to pan to make gravy. Boil gravy well and season to taste with more milk, salt, pepper, or a little soy sauce. Either return cabbage rolls to gravy or serve separately. If you want to save 2 hours of preparation time, then make *kålpudding* instead: in a greased pan, place layers of the following: fried, chopped cabbage and onions, then meat mixture, then more cabbage and onions on top. Cook for 45 minutes, until top is nicely browned, on the dark side. It is not as pretty, but still tasty.

Inlagd Gurka (Pickled Cucumber)

¼ c. parsley
2 T white vinegar (Swedish if possible)
2 T sugar
pepper (white or black)
salt
1 English cucumber

Finely snip ¼ c. parsley with scissors and add to 2 T white vinegar (Swedish vinegar is available at specialty stores), 2 T sugar, ¼ t. white or black pepper, ¼ t. salt, and almost half a cup of water. Peel and finely slice an English cucumber; place in pickling liquid 15 minutes before serving dinner. Chill until dinner is ready.

Kokt Potatis (Boiled New Potatoes)

2 lb. tiny red, white, or fingerling potatoes
salt
1 sprig of fresh dill

Start with the smallest red potatoes that can be found at the grocery store, ideally the size of a quail's egg. Scrub thoroughly with a brush and boil in water that is both salted and flavored with a large sprig of fresh dill. When a toothpick can be stuck easily through the largest one, drain and serve. Potatoes are peeled individually at the table after they have been served.

Lingonsylt (Lingonberry Sauce)

1 jar lingonberry sauce

Once very hard to find in the United States, lingonberry sauce now appears in grocery stores and IKEA Swedish furniture stores, next to the frozen meatballs. Refrigerate the jar once it is open. You may substitute cranberry sauce in a pinch.

Mördeg (butter cookies with seven variations, Sweden). Photo by Theresa Allison.

Mördeg (Butter Cookies with Seven Variations)

For each batch of cookie dough:

2¼ c. flour
⅔ c. granulated sugar
2 sticks minus 2 T butter
2 eggs
1 t. vanilla (optional)
Miscellaneous:
¼ c. cinnamon sugar
½ c. pearl or decorator's sugar
½ c. chopped, blanched almonds
2–4 T cocoa powder
1 T heavy cream
⅛ t. raspberry jam

Place 2¼ c. flour in a heap on a clean dry surface, and make a well in the center. Pour ⅔ c. sugar into the well and slice 2 sticks (minus 2 T) butter around the edge of the sugar. Place 1 egg in the center and add 1 t. vanilla (optional). Mix all of the ingredients together (alternatively, throw everything into a food processor and blend). Adapt recipe to any of the variations below, and bake at 350°F for 7–9 minutes on greased cookie sheets until golden-brown underneath.

Variation 1: Kanelpinnar (Cinnamon Pins)

Take the basic dough. Roll the dough into long strips about a finger width in diameter. Slice into 2"–3" long pieces. Brush gently with a beaten egg and dip in cinnamon sugar. Bake as above.

Variation 2: Finska Pinnar (Finnish Pins)

Take the basic dough. Roll the dough into long strips, about a finger width in diameter. Slice into 2"–3" long pieces. Brush gently with a beaten egg and and dip in pearl or decorator's sugar and finely chopped, blanched almonds. Bake as above.

Variation 3: Choklad Brod (Chocolate Bread)

Take the basic dough and add 2–4 T cocoa powder, ¼ c. sugar, and 2 T butter. Mix well and divide the dough into quarters. Roll each quarter into a log almost as long as the cookie sheet. Place two logs on each greased cookie sheet. Spread out into a flat rectangle with your fingers (about ½" thick). Brush with a beaten egg and sprinkle with pearl or decorator's sugar. Bake as above; when still warm, slice on the diagonal into 1" wide slices.

Variation 4: Kringlor (Pretzels)

Take the basic dough. Work 1 T heavy whipping cream into the dough until easy to work with. Roll pieces of dough into a rope ½" wide x 5" long. Twist each piece into the shape of a small pretzel. Brush with beaten egg and sprinkle with pearl or decorator's sugar. Bake as above.

Variation 5: Brev (Letters)

Take the basic dough and place in refrigerator overnight. Roll out to ¼" thick on a well-floured surface. Cut into circles with a cookie cutter. In the center of each circle, place a small portion (⅛ t.) raspberry jam and fold gently in half. Seal by crimping the edges with a fork. Brush with beaten egg. Bake as above.

Variation 6: Löv (Leaves)

Take the basic dough and place it in the refrigerator overnight. Roll out to ¼" thick on a well-floured surface. Cut with a leaf-shaped cookie cutter and brush with a beaten egg. Place egg side down in bowl with ½ c. finely chopped blanched almonds and pearl or decorator's sugar to coat one side. Place sugar/almond side up on a greased cookie sheet and bake as above.

Variation 7: Schackkakor (Checkerboards)

Take the basic dough; divide dough in half and blend 2 T cocoa into one half. Divide into half again and roll out each quarter into a rope almost 1" wide. Place one vanilla rope next to one chocolate rope on a piece of plastic wrap. Place the second vanilla on top of the first chocolate rope, and place the second chocolate rope on top of the first vanilla rope (looked at from the end it should resemble a checkerboard pattern). Wrap tightly in plastic wrap and place in refrigerator overnight or until stiff. The next day, slice and place on cookie sheet, brush lightly with beaten egg, and bake as above.

Tasting across generations (Sweden). Photo by Theresa Allison.

Melodic Variations and Seven Sorts of Cookies: Family Singing and Baking in Traditional Swedish Culture

In Sweden, traditions of village folksinging and dancing have been giving way to mass-mediated popular music for decades. Still, the singing of folk songs lives on in families and in classrooms. In my family, singing traditionally belongs in the kitchen. For four generations, we have been singing as we wash the dishes. Swedish folk songs served both as a bond of communication and a way of adding entertainment to an otherwise tedious task. As Swedish immigrants trying to retain our culture while living in the United States, we have always turned to food, song, dance, and traditional holidays as a way of maintaining our heritage. Most of what I write about here, I have learned from my mother, Eva Allison, who came to America in the early 1960s and who has taught Swedish language and Swedish cooking classes for decades. Straddling the line between ethnographer and informant, I hope to share a few fundamental ideas about food and music. In addition, I would like to mention an obscure branch of ethnomusicology: gastromusicology and its theory of "just desserts," as it pertains to Swedish sweets.

According to the Theory of "Just Desserts," as defined by Bruno Nettl, "The music of a culture reflects the food of the culture." Swedish food in general, and desserts in particular, can be interpreted to be a reflection of the music. The idea of *sju sorters kakor*, or the seven kinds of cookies, epitomizes the relationship between food and culture. The premise is that a proper home has seven kinds of cookies, plus or minus sweet rolls and a cake, available to serve with coffee to even the unexpected guest in order to make them feel welcome. Making guests feel welcome, and having enough to serve, takes on greater significance considering that the climate led to recurrent famines. Swedish folk song texts tell of constant hunger as well as of the treats that can be found in the *sockerbageri* or candy store.

While the texts refer to food in many of its cultural contexts, the melodic structure of the folktunes most resemble the seven sorts of cookies. Each cookie, though tasting different from the others, consists of variations involving the same few ingredients: sugar, flour, obscene amounts of butter, and eggs. The traditional folk tunes similarly involve a single line of melody, distinctly diatonic, sweet, and using a number of well-known melodic patterns. To these charming but sometimes predictable treats, the cookies and the melodies, are added an endless variety of spices in the form of melodic variations and cardamom, minor thirds and chocolate, refrains and cinnamon. In the interest of offering your guest a "proper" welcome, the preceding recipes are for the *sju sorters kakor*, that my mother and I bake.

Traditionally, the *sju sorters kakor* are served with coffee and a pound cake in the afternoon. They stand alone as the classic accompaniment to a visit to a Swedish home. Needless to say, in today's hectic industrialized society, it is considered charming, impressive, and hopelessly old fashioned to serve seven different cookies at one coffee. Only one or two kinds might be served after a full dinner. When using the recipes, feel free to improvise further. Swedish cookbooks usually refer to having "enough" flour, assuming that the reader has already learned what is sufficient while a small child. The correct texture is almost impossible to achieve with American flour, but the cookies still taste delicious (you may add a pinch of baking powder to make them taste more Swedish).

All of the cookies freeze well. I recommend freezing them immediately to preserve the fresh taste of the butter. Substituting with margarine, or storing at room temperature, will destroy the flavor.

Swedish dishes also reflect the local produce, foods hardy enough to thrive in the short growing season while still providing nutrition and flavor. The traditional diet involved large amounts of rutabagas, pork, rye flour, yellow peas, cabbage, and a cranberry-like berry called the lingonberry. Lingonberries and apples were the primary source of vitamin C during the long winters. Into the 1950s, people living in the countryside picked lingonberries from the forest each summer, cooked them with sugar and stored them in the family root cellar in huge earthenware jars. This lingonberry sauce, *lingonsylt*, is now usually bought at the store.

To this foundation, Swedes added new foods discovered through contact with other peoples and cultures. These imported foods were welcomed and brought into the "traditional" diet. The most well-known importation, the potato, was at one point served with every meal. In an expression of the importance of the potato to Swedish life, the government erected a statue in honor of Jonas Alströmer, the man who popularized the potato in the mid-eighteenth century. As my Uncle Björn used to tell me, "If you had eaten nothing but rutabagas all winter for hundreds of years, you'd put up a statue to the man who brought the potato, too!" Today Stockholm is full of restaurants with cuisines from all over the world, and the diversification of the population with the influx of foreign workers over the last 30 years has further increased the variety in the diet.

The entrée presented here, *kåldolmar*, or cabbage rolls, has been a part of the Swedish dinner repertoire since Charles the Twelfth brought them home after spending five years in Turkey. Meat filling wrapped in cabbage leaves, *kåldolmar*, bear little resemblance to the *dolmas* found further south and east. Fully indigenized, this dish is now considered to be classically Swedish in terms of its ingredients and their complicated preparation. This dinner is rather time consuming to make and therefore isn't served very often anymore. A homestyle version, which is much quicker, involves placing alternating layers of chopped cabbage, onions, and ground meat in a greased casserole dish and then baking the casserole at 325°F for an hour or so. This relative, known as *kålpudding*, or cabbage pudding, tastes almost as good as the original, and is a traditional way of dealing with any leftover meat and cabbage. The homestyle version is better received by Americans when introduced as a cabbage casserole. Both variations are traditionally served with boiled potatoes, lightly pickled cucumber slices, and lingonberry sauce. Leftover *kåldolmar* and *kålpudding* freeze exceptionally well.

RECOMMENDED LISTENING

Babs, Alice, and Nils Lindberg. *Alice Babs sjunger Alice Tegnér.* Sweden: Grammofon AB Electra. SLT 332391975.
Barnens Julfavoriter. Oslo, Norway: Hans Edler Music, 1995. SCANACD 95066.
Best-loved Songs of Sweden. Washington, DC: Smithsonian/Folkways Recordings, 2001 (1965). MFS 440.
Christmas in Sweden: Traditional Christmas Music, Performed by the Foremost Swedish Artists. Åkersberga, Sweden: BIS, 2001. CD-1179.

FOR FURTHER INFORMATION

http://www.si.se (the website for the Swedish Institute, a link to multilingual websites providing information about the country, people, government, and customs).
http://www.skansen.se (the website for one of the most famous historical museums in Stockholm, has beautiful pictures of traditional handiworks and architecture).

NORWAY
Chris Goertzen

When I have eaten bread, I have eaten.

Menu: *Laks* (Salmon), *Poteter* (Potatoes), *Grønsaker* (Vegetables), *Brød* (Rosemary Bread), *Boller* (Rolls), and *Sjokolade-Mousse-Terte* (Chocolate Mousse Cake). Serve with any beverage of your choice.

Preparation Time: 3 hours.

Cooking Process: For this meal you will need a springform pan (for the chocolate mousse cake) and a bread machine (for the rosemary bread). Make the dessert and start the breads first, then start the potatoes. While the potatoes are cooking, wash and prepare the vegetables but do not cook until just before the salmon is finished. Serves six people.

The Recipes

LAKS (SALMON)

3 lb. fresh salmon
1 T olive oil
minced garlic
salt
pepper
pinch of paprika (optional)
1 lemon, juiced

Go to the fish market by the nearest harbor, and buy some extremely fresh salmon fillets or steaks (or any other fish that look especially good), perhaps 3 lb. for 6 adults. Salmon cooks quickly, so begin cooking it about 15 minutes before you plan to eat. First pour a film of olive oil (or a mixture of butter and oil) in two heavy frying pans, and sprinkle the oil generously with minced garlic (either fresh or dried). Heat at medium. In the meantime, set out the fish and dust with a little salt and coarsely ground pepper (and maybe some paprika) on both sides. Sauté, starting with the side down that will be up when you eat. If you're using fillets, you turn them over when a thick end has turned opaque about ⅔ the way up from the pan surface. Many diners will want to moisten their portions with lemon juice at the table. If you don't eat all you've cooked immediately, it's tasty cold the next day.

Poteter (Potatoes)

6 potatoes
1 stick butter (½ c.)

Wash six potatoes. Bake (400°F for 1 hour), or chop and boil (medium-high for 30 minutes), or chop, boil, and mash (adding butter and salt when mashing). Serve with lots of butter; don't skimp on the butter.

Grønsaker (Vegetables)

3 lb. fresh, in-season green vegetables
1 stick butter

Boil your vegetables for 3–5 minutes and serve with lots of butter. If you're stingy with the butter, you're cheating. You may substitute any cream sauce or sauce featuring dill for the butter, as long as the results aren't deliberately low fat.

Brød (Rosemary Bread)

4¼ c. bread flour
⅔ c. rye flour
2 T sugar
1½ t. salt
2 T butter
1 T dried rosemary
½ t. dried basil
Pepper
2 t. bread machine yeast

Place these ingredients in a breadmaker that will allow a two-pound loaf, and bake on the wheat setting: 1½ cups water, 4¼ c. bread flour (or substitute sunflower or other seeds for up to ¼ cup of this), ⅔ cup rye flour, 2 T sugar, 1½ t. salt, 2 T butter, 1 T dried rosemary, plus ½ t. dried basil and a little pepper, 2 t. bread machine yeast.

Boller (Rolls)

1 lb. flour
⅓ c. sugar
½ t. cardamom
4 T butter
1 package yeast
1½ c. milk

Mix 1 lb. flour, ⅓ c. sugar, and ½ t. cardamom. Crumble 4 T butter and add 1 package of yeast and 1½ c. milk. Let the dough rise to twice its original size. Divide it into 16 portions and shape each. Wait 5 minutes. Distribute on cookie sheet and bake about 15 minutes at 425°F.

Sjokolade-Mousse-Terte (Chocolate Mousse Cake)

4 eggs
½ c. sugar
⅓ c. butter
½ c. flour
2 T cocoa
8 oz. bittersweet or semisweet chocolate
3 T powdered sugar
1 orange, zested and juiced
1½ c. whipping cream
shaved chocolate (optional, for garnish)

For cake, first beat 1 egg and ½ c. sugar until light. Melt, cool, and add ⅓ c. butter. Stir in ½ c. flour and 2 T cocoa. Pour into a buttered springform pan and bake at 350°F for about 15 minutes. Let cool thoroughly in the pan. For the mousse, first melt 8 oz. bittersweet or semisweet chocolate in a double boiler (or a metal bowl placed in a saucepan that has water in the bottom). Whip 3 egg yolks (don't throw away the whites) and 3 T powdered sugar until light. Add 2 T orange juice and orange zest and then stir in the melted chocolate. Let the mixture cool completely. Whip 1½ c. cream until stiff, and add to the cooled chocolate mixture. Whip 3 egg whites until stiff; fold into the mixture. After all this is mixed well, pour over the cake base in the pan. Cool in refrigerator at least 1 hour. Decorate with shaved chocolate if you wish.

Salmon and whale meat for sale (Bergen, Norway). Photo by Sean Williams.

Eating in Norway

Norway consists of piles of rocks close to water. A tributary of the Gulf Stream makes habitation this far north reasonably practical, and also causes deep climatic contrasts between the relatively temperate coastal areas and frigid interior. Although the narrow valleys are stunningly beautiful, agriculture remains marginal, and stock raising tough too. While farms constitute a cherished part of national culture, they're as much attractive museums as viable producers of food. Most things to eat are quite expensive, but most folks eat well anyway—North Sea oil has proved to be a substantial and durable source of income, and an historical emphasis on education effectively nourishes industries that depend on brain power rather than raw materials (e.g., Norway exports computer expertise). It's an egalitarian upper-middle-class country that modernized late, and so retains palpable traces of tradition in even the most cosmopolitan lives. Through most of history, it was hard to get from here to there through much of the year, which encouraged the emergence of a mozaic of cultures over time, and promotes very, very local aspects of identity to this day. Most people are proud to speak their local dialects, however unusual, and are accustomed to translating those of individuals from elsewhere in Norway, just as Danes, Swedes, and Norwegians generally speak their own languages in conversation with one another. Similarly, musicians and dancers who focus on traditional repertoires learn "their own" styles and tunes primarily.

Nowhere is the emphasis on the "local" in culture more evident than in formal folk music venues, most of which are contests. Most contest brackets feature the fiddle. First, you play either *hardingfele* (Hardanger fiddle) or *vanleg fele* (usual fiddle), depending on which one dominates where you grew up (folks from one area in the west can legitimately play either). Then you *must* play your local tunes, many of which display their regional specificity through genre titles (*springleik* and *springdans* and *pols* and other titles describe essentially the same thing in local variants). Titles of specific pieces often include the genre name and the name of the local master fiddler whose version is being followed. Rhythms vary subtly from place to place, too, as do the dances and the folk clothing. Food served at events has some modest regional affiliation, too, though the cheapest offerings dominate: hot dogs (on bread or flat bread) and little waffles are everywhere!

What's available in grocery stores reflects the harsh climate and consequent habits of doing the most with the least, but also national affluence and the ability to import what can't be grown this far north. Foodways follow a local pattern more in the specific items consumed (fish from boats that dock locally, potatoes from "our" valley, local strawberries—a much-heralded treat—when in season) than in genres, which are fairly consistent from place to place. Both traditional habits and modern expenses mandate emphasis on processed meats and fish (that is, using the whole animal) and on root vegetables. One can buy many kinds of sausage and ground beef processed at varying levels of coarseness. Fish, while enjoyed fresh, also appears as fish balls (comparable quantities of ground white fish and flour, perhaps with egg as a binder) for soup, fish cakes to fry (fish ground up with mashed potatoes), and fish pudding to bake (fish and cream), perhaps topped with cheese. *Lutefisk* (dried cod processed with lye) is more famous (or infamous) than eaten these days, but herring variously pickled remains ubiquitous. Yes, a rainbow of fruits and vegetables decorate the small grocery stores, bins, but these expensive exotics come from southern climes (I recall wondering if the balance between veggie offerings imported from Morocco and from Israel bore a political shadow).

Bread is great in Norway. It's fresh (baguettes in paper bags), features whole grains, and you know when you've eaten some. "When I have eaten bread, I have eaten," said a friend repeatedly. (Norwegians, not a loquacious bunch, stick to a few favorite sayings; my favorite is, "There is no bad weather, only bad clothing.") While much Norwegian food remains rather plain, depending on good ingredients rather than culinary cunning for satisfactory taste, baking can be startlingly involved, and bread often forms the basis for a meal. *Smørbrød*, literally "buttered bread," is a meal consisting of lots of small pieces of bread topped with contrasting goodies, including cheeses (the brown goat and brown cow cheeses stand out), nice salamies and hams, herring, and my favorite, scrambled eggs with slivers of smoked salmon. But where otherwise staid cooks flip out is in baking desserts, especially the variety of cakes and tortes offered now and again at teatime. These are based on pan-European models; what's most surprising is how much fancier they are than the meals they punctuate. You will notice this contrast simply by cooking this meal!

RECOMMENDED LISTENING

Both these recordings can be found by visiting http://www.qualiton.com, then locating "non classical" and "world," then scrolling down. The main source for folk music recordings is Heilo Records at http://195.159.217.100/grappa/heilo2.asp. On that bilingual website, you have to know what you're seeking; it's organized by regions of Norway, since many Norwegians interested in "*folkemusikk*" want to listen primarily to their own small area's traditional repertoires.

Knut Buen [hardanger fiddle]. *Slått on Raga.*
Knut Kjøk [fiddle] and Dag Gården [accordion]. *From People to People.*

FOR FURTHER INFORMATION

Goertzen, Chris. 1997. *Fiddling for Norway: Revival and Identity.* Chicago: University of Chicago Press.

IRELAND
Sean Williams

It is easy to halve the potato where there is love.

Menu: Beef Stew with Guinness, Champ with Spring Onions, Steamed or Boiled Kale, Brown Bread, and Apple Cake. Serve with water or black tea with milk and sugar.
Preparation Time: 3 hours.
Cooking Process: Start the stew first; while it is simmering, prepare the brown bread and the apple cake. 45 minutes before eating, prepare the champ. Start the kale 10 minutes before eating. Serves six people.

The Recipes

BEEF STEW WITH GUINNESS

2 lb. beef for stewing
½ c. flour
salt
pepper
2 T vegetable oil
2 medium yellow onions
½ c. tomato sauce
1 pint Guinness (stout beer)
3 carrots, chopped

Cut 2 lb. beef into bite-sized pieces. In a plastic bag, pour ½ c. flour, 2 t. salt, 1 t. black pepper. Place the meat inside the bag and shake until thoroughly coated; brush off excess flour. Heat 2 T oil in a Dutch oven or large, solidly built pan. Quickly brown the meat, stirring and turning the pieces. Peel and chop 2 medium onions; add to the pot with ½ c. tomato sauce. Stir until the onions start to look translucent. Pour in 1 pint of Guinness (or other stout beer) and 3 carrots. Cover and simmer slowly for a couple of hours until the meat is very tender. Season to taste. If stew is too watery, add the remaining flour that you used to coat the meat.

CHAMP WITH SPRING ONIONS

4 potatoes
1 bunch spring onions or scallions
1 c. milk
4 T butter
salt
pepper

Peel and cut 4 potatoes into large chunks. Boil them with just enough water to cover until they are soft (about 20 minutes). While the potatoes are boiling, chop 1 bunch of spring onions (including the white parts) and bring to a low simmer in 1 c. milk. Remove from heat. When potatoes appear done, drain the water and mash with 4 T butter, then add the milk/onion mix. Add 1 t. salt and ½ t. pepper. Serve with more butter.

STEAMED OR BOILED KALE

1 large bunch dark green kale
2 T butter

Wash and stem 1 bunch of dark green kale. Gather all the leaves together and slice horizontally across all of them in ¼" slices. Steam or boil for 5 minutes; toss with 2 T melted butter.

BROWN BREAD

2 c. whole oats
2 c. buttermilk
salt
1 t. baking soda
2½ c. wholemeal (or whole wheat) flour

Soak 2 c. whole oats in 2 c. buttermilk overnight. The next morning, mix 1 t. salt and 1 t. baking soda with 2½ c. wholemeal flour. Shape into a round loaf in the middle of a nonsticking baking sheet (coat lightly with butter if necessary) and cut a cross in the bread right through it, keeping the shape intact. Bake at 350°F for 50 minutes. Cut into slices and slather with butter.

APPLE CAKE

2 large apples
¼ c. sugar
2½ c. flour
½ t. baking powder
¼ lb. butter
1 egg
½ c. milk
1 c. whipping cream

Peel, core, and chop up 2 large apples. Mix them with ¼ c. sugar and set aside. Whisk 2½ c. flour with ½ t. baking powder. Cut in 1 stick butter. Add ½ c. sugar. In a separate bowl, beat together 1 egg and ½ c. milk. Pour into the center of the dry ingredients and mix gently. Divide into two halves; the first half goes into the bottom of a lightly greased cake or pie pan (dough will be quite sticky, so use your fingers to shape it into the pan). Place the chopped apples on top, then stretch out the second half of the dough with your fingers and cover the apples with it, sealing the sides if possible. Cut a couple of slashes across the top and brush with beaten egg. Bake for 35–40 minutes at 350°F and serve with whipped cream if desired.

Playing the fiddle (Dublin, Ireland). Photo by Cary Black.

The Cook in the Kitchen

"The Cook in the Kitchen" (traditional Irish fiddle tune).

Tea with Singing and a Pint at the Session

Ireland, once known popularly as "The Land of Song," has a long history of its inhabitants singing or playing away the darkness of rain and winter in the comfortable confines of a cottage kitchen, near a turf fire. Songs lasting up to 15 minutes were interspersed with equally lengthy stories, serving to entertain friends and families during the cold winter months. In the summers, dances might take place at crossroads and other outdoor locations. Ireland has a much more recent history of playing host to instrumental music sessions in pubs. This newer custom had its roots in the immigrant Irish of England, the United States, and Australia needing a place to go and socialize, because the urban tenements were not hospitable to song and music sessions.

Between the time that instrumental music became associated with pubs and the recent and emphatic entry of women into the public areas of the pubs (as opposed to quietly gathering with other women in the "snug"—a private room in back), a dichotomy developed between those who sang at home—usually women, usually in the presence of children and guests—and those who played instrumental music at pubs—usually men. The beverage of choice at home was tea, and the beverage of choice at the pub was a pint of beer (often a stout beer such as Guinness). Together with the abrupt economic upswing of the 1990s, the gender-based divisions between home and pub have diminished significantly. Pub life has been increasingly dominated by the presence of televisions, and home life has been dominated by competing work schedules, leaving significantly less

Brown bread (Ireland). Photo by Sean Williams.

leisure time. The combination of laws being changed to allow married women to enter the work-force with the sudden availability of jobs has resulted in less time for music making, storytelling, and dancing.

Ireland's rapidly changing economic situation has not diminished the enjoyment of food, however. Indeed, Irish food has undergone a radical makeover since the 1990s. The economic boom spurred by Ireland's entry into the European Union brought a renewed interest in fresh local foods, including smoked wild salmon, dark greens, artisan breads and cheeses, and, of course, the potato. The Great Hunger of the 1840s, the bleak result of the Irish people's forced dependence on the potato, continues to have a powerful impact on the way people eat. A single meal at a restaurant today might include four separate potato preparations (boiled, mashed, fried, and baked) in addition to a meat dish and a green vegetable. Many people still shun foods like shellfish (once relied on in desperation) as "Famine food." Almost no one eats potato skins for the same reason: "the Famine is over." Hand in hand with the new interest in food has come an explosive growth of restaurants catering not just to wealthy tourists, but to the newly wealthy Irish themselves. While one would expect the growth of good-quality eateries to be limited primarily to the big cities of Dublin, Belfast to the north, and Galway to the west, small villages scattered throughout Ireland are increasingly home to restaurants specializing in fresh local food. One can now find organic goods in local shops.

Because tourism is one of the primary sources of Ireland's wealth, hotels and some pubs, particularly in the popular tourist havens of Dublin and Killarney, have worked hard to accommodate the unceasing need for a "roots experience" by hosting traditional music sessions. Sometimes these sessions are held on stages with full sound systems (like an Irish cabaret), and the musicians intersperse their jigs and reels with popular Irish-American hits like "When Irish Eyes are Smiling" or "Danny Boy." Other contexts for food and music outside the home include pubs that serve a limited number of dishes (bacon and cabbage, lamb stew or beef and Guinness stew, roast chicken, "chips" or fried potatoes, etc.). Locals and visitors alike might enjoy this food and pints of beer or cups of tea while three or four musicians play jigs and reels in the background. In this context, the musicians face each other, ignoring the "audience," and the audience members chat quietly among themselves. At pub sessions, singers are expected to sing only when asked, and then only to give the instrumentalists a break late in the evening. Otherwise, the place for song remains in the kitchen with the tea, brown bread with butter and marmalade, and occasional soda bread (usually served as a dessert rather than as the staple).

While beer was once the almost exclusive drink of the average Irishman (Irish whiskies and *poitín*—"moonshine"—more rarely), Australian wines are affordable and easily accessible today at all the major shops. Wine drinking has become popular in many middle-class homes, and an upwardly mobile interest in all things culinary has led to a spate of cooking classes and restaurants specializing in foreign cuisines. In addition, "hard lemonade," fortified caffeine drinks, and mixed drinks using vodka or rum are popular favorites in the urban dance scene. It is not too far of a stretch to see the ways that this experimentation with new cuisines has led some Irish people back to exploring traditional methods of cooking. People on the coasts used seaweeds, for example, as food, medicine, and fertilizer for centuries. It is no longer out of the question to see a sweetened seaweed-based dessert on the menu of a gourmet restaurant, or a soup that includes nettles.

The overwhelming sense of shame once associated with "traditional" ways of being (speaking the Irish language, singing in the old style, playing pipes and fiddles, eating wild plants and seaweed and shellfish) is no longer an automatic reaction among the Irish of the twenty-first century. Irish-language schools, for example, have grown dramatically in popularity, and more young people are enthusiastically exploring traditional music making in ways that would have shocked their elders in the 1950s. Even today, however, certain foods and musical styles invoke in some Irish a deep disdain and resentment over the dark experiences of the past. Aidan Carl Mathews wrote a poem titled, "The Death of Irish," speaking of language loss in the late twentieth century.

> The tide gone out for good
> Thirty one words for seaweed
> Whiten on the foreshore.

This concise but exceptionally revealing poem (from Mathews' 1983 collection *Minding Ruth*) may no longer apply to the Ireland of the twenty-first century. Indeed, Mathews himself recommends that one take the poem "with a grain of salt"! One can now study Irish through online tutorials, program jigs into one's cell phone ringer, and listen to live streaming broadcasts of old-style singing competitions from around the globe. And anyone halfway across the world can enjoy a hearty meal of beef and Guinness stew with champ, kale, brown bread, and apple cake. Just don't forget to sing afterward in the kitchen.

RECOMMENDED LISTENING

Classic Irish groups from the 1970s include the Bothy Band, Planxty, The Chieftains, Clannad, and others, while contemporary groups Altan, Solas, Lúnasa, and Danu represent the modern face of traditional music. All these recordings feature carefully arranged pieces interspersed with songs. In some cases, the groups have experimented with rock, jazz, punk, and world music. Many individual singers and instrumentalists have made a splash on the scene, and so many brilliant CDs have appeared in the past 10 years that it would be impossible to single out one or two without slighting all the others. Look for solo singers, fiddlers, pipers, harpers, "box" (button accordion) players, flutists, and pennywhistle players. Most importantly, support live music by attending a concert or session, or just sing in your car, your kitchen, and your child's bedroom at night.

FOR FURTHER INFORMATION

www.ceolas.org/ceolas.html
http://academic.evergreen.edu/w/williams/seannos.htm
http://academic.evergreen.edu/curricular/ireland/resources.htm

11
Encore

THE MARZIPAN WORKSHOP SONNETS

Bruno Nettl

First, blanch a pound of almonds, which you do
By boiling them—not more than half a minute;
Snap off the skins, let dry a day or two.
We're set to have the workshop. To begin it,
A pound of powdered sugar we will measure.
Get out the Cuisinart: it's time to grind
The almonds fine. Combine, and—at your pleasure—
Add water, color, flavors: any kind.

A drop of bitter almond, the quintessence
Of this prestigious candy. Mix it all,
And cook it slightly, 'til it makes a ball
To knead. It's ready now to form some crescents,
Or shapes like haystacks, spheres, like duck or swan,
And fruits traditional to marzipan.

But whence this delicacy and the word?
In youth, I thought it Czech, a kind of pan
Or "lord" of sweets. The OED—absurd? —
Derives it from the Arab *mawthaban*.
For sure, it came from Persia, Turkey, Yemen,
Or thereabouts, as Middle Eastern sweets
Are made of nuts and sugar, spiked with lemon
And saffron, rose, or cardamom—such treats!

It conquered Venice, shrine of Mark, its loaves
(In Latin *panis*) bravely ventured forth
Through Europe, reaching Lübeck in the North.
Now Germans make and purchase it in droves.
In *Buddenbrooks*, by Mann, you'll find the claim
That "Bread of Mark" gave marzipan its name.

ABOUT THE CONTRIBUTORS

Marié Abe (Tokyo, Japan; Okinawa, Japan) is a native of Tokyo, and currently a Ph.D. candidate in ethnomusicology at the University of California–Berkeley. She plans to do her dissertation research in Okinawa and Tokyo, focusing on the intersection between the street music practice called *chindon* and contemporary improvisational music scenes. Between studying, she enjoys experimenting with various culinary concoctions, hosting numerous shindigs, and playing the accordion.

Theresa A. Allison (Sweden) is an ethnomusicologist masquerading as a University of California–San Francisco family practice resident physician at San Francisco General Hospital. She is also a devoted member of the Society for Gastromusicology. While her research interests include Navajo song transmission and the use of music in residential nursing homes, she has grown up singing Swedish folk songs in the kitchen. She lives to share her cultural heritage with anyone within earshot, leading to occasional wisecracks and many smiles over shared cookies.

Julia Banzi (Andalusian Morocco; Andalusian Spain) is an ethnomusicologist, co-artistic director of the contemporary music ensemble Al-Andalus (www.andalus.com), Rotary Ambassadorial Scholar to Morocco, and one of very few professional female flamenco guitarists worldwide. Sharing in the preparation of food as well as consuming it nurtures her relationships, and she is able to learn about cultural pride, generosity, religious practices, rites of welcome, and class status in a fun (and appetizing!) environment. Good food nourishes friendships, body, spirit, and soul!

Marc Benamou (Surakarta, Java, Indonesia), associate professor of music at Earlham College in Indiana, is known as a vocalist and a passionate eater in the Javanese gamelan world. He has benefited from many fine teachers in both areas. Some of the recipes presented here were passed on by Bu Sri Kurniati and Bu Hadi (of *warung* Kelurahan Ketelan fame); his principal gurus in the Javanese gastronomy were Pak Panggah and family; and his exacting taskmaster in Javanese singing was Pak Harta, all of Surakarta. His book on rasa in Javanese musical aesthetics will be published by Oxford University Press.

Suzanne Benchimol (Judeo-Spanish Morocco) is from the Sephardic community of northern Morocco, whose roots are in medieval Spain. She has lived in Toronto for many years. Currently she is working intensively with the traditional Moroccan bridal dress.

Mark Brill (Oaxaca, Mexico) teaches music history, ethnomusicology, and film music at the University of Dayton in Ohio. One of his specialties is the music and culture of Mexico, particularly of Oaxaca and Yucatan, where he has spent much time doing research and fieldwork. One of his favorite dishes is roasted iguana in *pipian* sauce, a Yucatan specialty.

Carla Brunet (Southeastern Brazil) is a Ph.D. candidate in ethnomusicology at the University of California–Berkeley. She is currently writing her dissertation on the construction of gendered identities in Samba Schools of her native city, São Paulo, Brazil. Carla is a food enthusiast and loves cooking for her family and friends at her home in San Rafael, California.

Jennifer Caputo (Campania, Italy) is a Ph.D. candidate in ethnomusicology at Wesleyan University in Connecticut. She is currently doing fieldwork in the region of Campania, Italy, and is studying a form of local folk music called the *tammurriata*. Jennifer enjoys cooking and has been collecting recipes while living in Italy. She attributes her love of Italian music and food to all of her Italian great grandmothers who taught her one of the most important words in the Italian language: *mangia* ("eat")!

Judith Cohen (Judeo-Spanish Morocco; Ibiza and Formentera) received her doctorate in ethnomusicology from the Université de Montréal, teaches part time at York University in Toronto, and is the General Editor of the Spain series of the Alan Lomax Recordings. She works freelance as a performer, lecturer, and researcher in Spain and Portugal. Judith dislikes cooking intensely, but enjoys reading recipes and imagining that she will prepare them some day, and loves sampling the results of other people's cooking.

Jonathan Copeland (Bali, Indonesia) is an ex-lawyer and travels throughout Asia. He spends a lot of time eating at Murni's Warung in Ubud, Bali, and in between meals helps Murni with her ever-expanding website. He enjoys a tune and can be contacted at jonathan@murnis.com.

Beverly Diamond (Newfoundland and Labrador) is the Canada Research Chair in Ethnomusicology at Memorial University of Newfoundland and Director of the Research Centre for the Study of Music, Media, and Place (MMaP). Since the early 1970s, she has worked extensively in Inuit, First Nations, and Saami communities, and on diverse regional and ethnocultural traditions in Canada, including those of Newfoundland.

Mercedes DuJunco (Chaozhou, China; Luzon, Philippines) teaches ethnomusicology at Bard College in New York state. She grew up eating her favorite dishes, chicken *adobo* and fresh *lumpia*, in a Filipino-Chinese household in Manila, Philippines. She acquired her taste for Chaozhou cuisine and learned the preparation of several local dishes in the course of conducting fieldwork in the Chaozhou region in mainland China, Hong Kong, and Thailand from 1989 to the present.

Jennifer Gall (Australia) works for the National Library of Australia Oral History and Folklore/Folk Music Section, and is undertaking her Ph.D. at the School of Music, Australian National University. Her dissertation is titled "The Role of Women in the Evolution and Transmission of Australian Folk Music," and she is making a CD associated with her research to explore the hidden worlds of the women heard in old field recordings. She enjoys the way that folk music links people from the many different cultural groups who live in Australia—and she cooks a mean snake!

Mina Girgis (Egypt) is an ethnomusicologist and hotelier living in San Francisco. He is currently working on combining these two fields (ethnomusicology and hospitality) in an art and music resort. Mina's favorite latenight meal is *fool* (Egyptian beans) and *falafel* with his Cairo DJ friends at 5:00 in the morning, after they have all finished their gigs.

Chris Goertzen (Norway) teaches music history, world music, and occasionally folklore at the University of Southern Mississippi. He has cooked many Mexican meals for Norwegian fiddlers, who greet these efforts with polite wariness. He finds both the foodways and politics of Mississippi lively but frightening.

David G. Hebert (New Zealand) is an American musician who serves as Head of Music for Te Wananga O Aotearoa, New Zealand's largest tertiary institution. He previously taught music courses in Russia and Tokyo, has published in the leading research journals for music education, and serves on the editorial board of Research in New Zealand Performing Arts. He has tried many kinds of food, but is still unable to appreciate cottage cheese (U.S.), raw horse (Japan), snake meat and chicken feet (China), mystery sausages (Russia), silkworms (Korea), locusts (Thailand), and fatty beef mince pies (New Zealand).

Maria Hnaraki (Greece) dances at music events in Greece, specifically her home island of Crete, because of the abundant ambrosia and nectar served there. She prefers cooking cultural identity while she favors tasting who we are through the foods we create, coming to the conclusion that we are all amalgams of many ingredients and that the same recipes are cooked all over the world, in different ways.

Ramona Holmes (Estonia) is Chair and Professor of Music at Seattle Pacific University where she teaches ethnomusicology and music education. She plays violin and dances with the Estonian American community in Seattle, but still finds time to taste the blood sausage.

Kathleen Hood (Suwayda Province, Syria) received her Ph.D. in ethnomusicology from the University of California–Los Angeles and has conducted fieldwork in Syria, Lebanon, and Jordan, where she developed a passion for *makdus*, a side dish made of small cooked eggplants stuffed with walnuts, garlic, and hot red peppers and preserved in oil. She is completing work on a book about Druze musical traditions for the Druze Heritage Foundation. In addition to her research, she is a professional cellist, performing Arab music with MESTO (Multi-Ethnic Star Orchestra) and Western classical music with the Long Beach Symphony.

Susan Hurley-Glowa (Cape Verde Islands, Atlantic West Africa) is Assistant Professor of Music at Franklin & Marshall College in Lancaster, Pennsylvania. She began working with Cape Verdean musical communities in 1990 while living in Rhode Island and studying ethnomusicology at Brown University. She loves to cook Cape Verdean foods, and dance to *Krioulo* music whenever the opportunity presents itself.

Okon Hwang (Korea) is Professor of Music at Eastern Connecticut State University. Although her ethnomusicological interests lie primarily with music in relation to Korea, her gastronomic tendency tends to run far and wide. She is one of those rare Koreans who does not need *kimchi* (Korean pickled cabbage) as an absolute necessity for survival, and that genetic mutation has served her well over the years in her attempt to introduce more sources of pleasure into her life.

Adrienne L. Kaeppler (Tonga) is Curator of Oceanic Ethnology at the Smithsonian Institution in Washington, D.C. She has carried out field research in Tonga, Hawaii, and other parts of the Pacific. Her research focuses on the interrelationships between social structure and the arts, especially dance, music, and the visual arts.

David Locke (Northern Ghana) is Associate Professor in the Music Department at Tufts University in Boston where he teaches general courses in ethnomusicology, specialized courses in African music, and performance classes in both African music and dance. His scholarly work, rich in detailed transcriptions and analysis of sound recordings, enables a sophisticated appreciation and re-creation of African traditional music, particularly the Ewe and Dagomba heritage of West Africa. In the 1990s Locke was President of the Northeast Chapter of the Society for Ethnomusicology.

Lucy M. Long (Southern Appalachia) is Assistant Professor in the Department of Popular Culture at Bowling Green State University in Ohio, where she teaches courses in folklore and food studies. She has researched food traditions in Korea, Southeast Asia, Ireland, Spain, and throughout the United States, focusing on foods in the Midwest and the southern Appalachians as well as on ethnicity and regional identity in commercial foods. She also edited a book, *Culinary Tourism*, exploring the intersections of food and tourism.

Amelia Maciszewski (North India) believes, as an ethnomusicologist and sitarist, that food (*khana*) and music (*gana*) are virtually two sides of the same coin. Her music gurus *sarode* maestro Aashish Khan, Hindustani vocal diva Dr. Girija Devi, and the late Prof. Suresh Misra have taught her much about creating tasty dishes, which she concocts when she's not practicing, teaching, or researching Hindustani music and musicians.

Minette Mans (Namibia) is a music educator and ethnomusicologist whose main field of research is the dances and music of Namibia, where she was born. She is a "great pretender" as far as her own cooking skills are concerned, because dishes turn out to be either great or dismal—no middle road here! Minette is currently Associate Professor at the University of Namibia and has published two books, the most recent being *Discover the Musical Cultures of the Kunene* (with CD).

Peter K. Marsh (Mongolia) is an ethnomusicologist living in Ulaanbaatar, Mongolia, where he heads the American Center for Mongolian Studies. He lectures and writes on world music and is completing his second book on Mongolian music, *The Horse-head Fiddle and the Cosmopolitan Reimagination of Tradition in Mongolia* (forthcoming 2006). He plays the Mongolian horse-head fiddle and he has a personal record of consuming 21 *buuz* in a single sitting.

David McDonald (Palestine) is a Ph.D. candidate in ethnomusicology at the University of Illinois at Urbana–Champaign, studying music and nationalism among Palestinian refugees in Jordan and the West Bank. In music, as in food, McDonald has an insatiable appetite for anything Palestinian. Over the course of two years of fieldwork he has sampled from virtually every restaurant in Amman. Yet despite this, he has yet to find a better *mlukhiyyah* than at Flora Khoury's home kitchen. Her famous saying, "You can go out to eat, but why?" is sound advice.

Rosa Virgínia Melo (Brasília, Brazil) was born in Paraíba in the Northeast of Brazil and came to Brasília as a young girl. She received her BA and MA in anthropology from the University of Brasília and currently teaches at the Catholic University of Brasília. Her current research projects include the immaterial cultural heritage of Corumba, Goiás. She is also studying Ayurvedic massage and medicine.

Terry Miller (Thailand) received his first travel grant to Southeast Asia in 1970 from the U.S. Army during the Vietnam War, experiencing Thai food and music for the first time. Since then he has been increasingly spoiled, during numerous trips to Thailand, on inexpensive and delicious Thai food, while becoming increasingly alarmed at the dramatic growth of fast food, which has transmitted to the Thai the same dietary problems we have in America. At Kent State University in Ohio he founded the Thai Ensemble in 1978, which played continuously until his retirement in 2005.

Niloofar Mina (Iran) is an Iranian ethnomusicologist and teaches at New Jersey City University. Niloofar's research focus has taken her in two very different directions: the history and cultural meanings of Iranian popular music in the post-revolutionary period, and audience involvement in Western opera. Niloofar has been living in New York since 1979. *Tah chin* reminds her of home and her grandmother Khorshid Khanoom ("Ms. Sunshine"): "When served on a beautiful blue serving platter *tah chin* looks like the shining sun in a clear sky."

Ni Wayan Murni (Bali, Indonesia) is a pioneer of tourism in Bali. She is the owner of Murni's Warung, the first real restaurant in Ubud, the Kunang-Kunang shops, Murni's Villas, and Murni's Houses. Her website, www.murnis.com, is the leading Bali online resource center. She plays the gamelan in a ladies' gamelan group in Ubud and can be contacted at murni@murnis.com.

Bruno Nettl (The Marzipan Workshop Sonnets) is Professor Emeritus of Music and Anthropology at the University of Illinois in Urbana–Champaign. He has done fieldwork in Tehran, Chennai, and among the Blackfoot people in Montana, but his interest in marzipan comes from his central European background. It is believed by some that participation in a late November marzipan workshop *chez Nettl* is among the requirements for a Ph.D. in ethnomusicology at his institution.

Phong T. Nguyen (Vietnam), ethnomusicologist/musician, earned his doctorate from the Sorbonne (Paris) and has been performing worldwide. He was honored at the White House with a National Heritage Fellowship (1997) and in the *New Grove Dictionary* (2000). He served on the faculty of UCLA, University of Washington, and Kent State University. Trained as a cook during his years in Paris, he has a passionate love of French cuisine and cooks many Vietnamese and Asian dishes.

Suzel A. Reily (Minas Gerais, Brazil) is a Brazilian ethnomusicologist who for the past fifteen years has been based at Queen's University Belfast. Her research has focused on the musics of popular Catholicism in Brazil, which ultimately led her to Minas Gerais. In Northern Ireland the link to Brazil is maintained through the weekly gatherings of *"Um Pouquinho de Brasil"* ("A Little Bit of Brazil"), an ensemble made up of Brazilians living in Belfast who meet to sing Brazilian music. After rehearsals there's always a bit of food and *craic*.

Timothy Rice (Bulgaria) is Professor of Ethnomusicology at the University of California–Los Angeles and has served the Society for Ethnomusicology as editor of *Ethnomusicology* (1981–1984) and as its president (2003–2005). His research on Bulgarian music has given him the opportunity to savor and prepare real food, grown for taste not transportation, and to learn how to make wine and distill brandy from outstanding home cooks and vintners.

Thalia Rios (Bolivia), a food enthusiast with a background in dietetics/gerontology, accompanied her husband Fernando during his dissertation fieldwork, and in doing so embarked on a two-year culinary/musical tour of Bolivia, Argentina, and France. Back home, she enjoys preparing the dishes she sampled in the field. Her latest interests include baking with wild yeast starters, cooking Thai cuisine, playing classical guitar, and co-leading an Andean panpipe and duct-flute ensemble with Fernando.

Esperança Bonet Roig (Ibiza and Formentera) grew up in Dalt Vila, Ibiza's ancient fortified "Upper Town," in a family which has lived on the island for centuries. She has carried out intensive fieldwork in local traditions for many years, and is currently involved in alternative energy projects.

Philip Schuyler (Morocco) is currently Chair of the Ethnomusicology Program at the University of Washington. A specialist in the music of North Africa and the Middle East, he has lived and worked for extended periods of time in Morocco and Yemen. Having recently turned his attention to the western Pacific, he contemplated submitting a recipe for fruit bat poached in coconut milk, but, considering the difficulty of obtaining the ingredients, thought better of it.

Andrew Shahriari (Thailand) is a specialist in northern Thai music at Kent State University in Ohio. He and his wife, Christina, have mastered many Thai recipes thanks to their participation in several cooking schools while living in Chiang Mai, Thailand. They probably ate *khao nieow ma muang* (mangoes and coconut sticky rice) every day when mangoes were in season.

Christina Shahriari (Thailand) is a trombonist and former marching band director. She specializes in Thai, German, and Persian cuisine and is particularly fond of her grill for shish kebab and smoked ribs. While her husband sticks to ethnomusicological endeavors, Christina explores gastronomical pleasures during their fieldwork experiences. From ant larvae desserts to fried wasps with sticky rice, her motto is "Give me anything but sour oranges (common to Yucatecan food) and I'll give it a try."

Zoe Sherinian (Kerala, South India) is an ethnomusicologist who teaches at the University of Oklahoma. She is writing a book on the music of Dalit Christians called *The Subaltern Sing: Tamil Folk Music as Liberation Theology*. She is looking forward to going back to India to do research on Dalit drummers and to spend lots of time singing songs and proudly eating beef meals with her Indian friends.

Anna Marie Stirr (Nepal) is a Ph.D. candidate at Columbia University in New York, working on popular music in the Himalayas. She performs on *bansuri* and silver flute and can sometimes be found singing country music, occasionally in public. She credits her mother and sisters with inspiring her love of music and cooking, which must be partially attributed to nights of harmonizing in the kitchen while preparing a gourmet meal.

Jeffrey A. Summit (Romanian Jewish New York) is Associate Professor of Music at Tufts University, where he also serves as rabbi and executive director of the Hillel Foundation. He is the author of *The Lord's Song in a Strange Land: Music and Identity in Contemporary Jewish Worship*. He recorded, compiled, and annotated the CD *Abayudaya: Music from the Jewish People of Uganda* which received a Grammy nomination for best album in the category of Traditional World Music. At Tufts, he will often stop 150 students in the course of a Shabbat dinner and remind them, "Eat slowly."

Pauline "Isumatta" Tuttle (Canoe Nations of the Pacific Northwest) received her MFA at York University in Toronto and a Ph.D. at the University of Washington (both in ethnomusicology). She currently teaches ethnomusicology at the University of Victoria, and is the Director of the Kalakwáhti Studies Centre, an oral history research center in YouBou, British Columbia. Her path of field research has not only closely followed the lines of her mixed Aboriginal ancestry (Mi'kmaq, African, and Irish) but also her keen awareness of the importance of movement and relationship to place through song, dance, and story.

Jesse Samba Wheeler (Kenya; Brasília, Brazil) is a Ph.D. candidate in ethnomusicology at UCLA. He earned his MM in ethnomusicology at the University of Wisconsin–Madison and his BS in performance studies from Northwestern University. At present he lives in Brasília, Brazil, researching rock. Other projects past and present include research on various African pop musics and Louisiana zydeco. He is an amateur (in the literal sense) singer and a semiretired DJ. He voted against both Georges Bush.

Sean Williams (editor; Sunda, Indonesia; Ireland) teaches ethnomusicology, Asian studies, and Irish studies at The Evergreen State College in Olympia, Washington. She is convinced that the interdisciplinary nature of ethnomusicology lends itself perfectly to projects like this cookbook. She really liked that cuttlefish peanut brittle she tried in Eastern Indonesia, but had to draw the line at the thick, dry water buffalo lung chips and burnt rice coffee.

Abigail Wood (Dietary Modifications) teaches ethnomusicology at the University of Southampton (UK). Her research focuses on contemporary Jewish musics. She is always happy to mix ethnomusicology with cookery, and enjoys spending much of her spare time in the kitchen, continuing the quest for the perfect chicken soup.

Su Zheng (Sichuan, China) teaches ethnomusicology, East Asian music, women and music, and Asian American diaspora at Wesleyan University in Connecticut. She is curious to try out good recipes but will definitely modify them according to her likes. She believes an open taste for food, as an open taste for music, enriches one's life and creates more harmony in the world.

I CAN'T EAT THAT! DIETARY MODIFICATIONS

Abigail Wood

Sharing food, along with music, lies at the heart of the ethnomusicologist's field experience. However, many cultural and religious groups, together with a growing number of individuals, observe certain restrictions in their diets. To make sharing the food in this book as easy as possible, this list is intended to let you know which recipes are appropriate for vegetarian, vegan, and kosher diets. The key below tells you immediately what you can use and what you cannot; in some instances it may be necessary to make a small substitution (e.g., margarine for butter). If you are keeping kosher, please note that preprepared ingredients should be checked for a *hechsher* (kosher mark). Some recipes have multiple indications, such as K/VG for kosher/vegan. Any dish followed by a question mark means that it contains a prepared sauce or ingredient that may or may not contain meat or be kosher.

If you are a vegetarian or vegan (or are expecting vegetarian guests) and would like to convert an existing meat-based recipe, it is sometimes as easy as using (fermented soy) *tempeh*, tofu, beans, and cheeses (the latter does not apply to vegan cooking). Dishes that use, for example, meat-based broths can be substituted with vegetable broths, and bacon grease or lard can be substituted with olive, other vegetable oils, or margarine in the case of recipes calling for the texture of butter. If you do not eat red meat but wish to approximate the intensity of the flavor, the dark meat of chicken and turkey is an appropriate substitute; ground turkey is often easily found in supermarkets.

Key

K   Kosher (*pareve*)
Km Kosher (meat)
Kd Kosher (dairy)
NK Not kosher
V   Vegetarian
VG Vegan (no meat, dairy, or honey), automatically vegetarian

Africa

Kenya	Beef stew	Km (replace butter with margarine)
	Kidney beans	K/VG
	Greens	K/VG (if you use vegetable oil)
	Corn meal	K/VG
	Flat bread	K/VG (if you use vegetable oil)
	Coconut rice	K/VG
	Milky tea	Kd/V
	Ginger coffee	K/VG
N Ghana	Groundnut soup	NK
	Fufu	VG
Cape Verde	Hominy	Km
	Salad	K/VG
	Fruit	K/VG
Namibia	Lamb/goat	Km
	Porridge	K/VG
	Ekaka	Kd /V
	Doughnuts	Kd/V

East Asia

Chaozhou	Pork stew	NK
	Radish cake	?
	Bitter melon	NK
	Steamed fish	K
	Rice porridge	K/VG
Sichuan	Bangbang ji	?
	Eggplant	?
	Mapo tofu	?
	Shanghai cabbage	NK
	Watercress	?
	Shrimps	NK
	White rice	K/VG
Tokyo	dashi	?
	Egg custard	NK
	Sesame tofu	K (use nonmeat gelatin)
	Soybeans	K/VG
	Rice with tofu	K/VG
	Fish, steamed	K
	Kiwi jelly	K/VG
Okinawa	Stir-fry	NK
	Bean sprouts	K/VG
	Rafutê	NK
	Gourd	NK
	Fried rice	NK (unless replace broth and lard)
	Doughnut balls	K/V
Korea	Braised beef	Km
	Rice	K/VG
	Soy potato	K/VG
	Spinach	K/VG
	Mushrooms	K/VG
	Sweet Rice	K/VG
Mongolia	Dumplings	Km
	Cabbage salad	K/VG
	Salted tea	Kd/V

South Asia

Nepal	Bhaat	K/VG
	Lentils	K/VG
	Beans	K/VG
	Saag	K/VG
	Chicken	Km
	Potato salad	K/VG
	Chutney	K/VG
	Dessert	Kd/V
N India	Toor Dal	K/VG
	Chutney	K/VG
	Chicken curry	NK

	Aloo gobi	K/VG
	Raita	Kd/V
	Rice	K/VG
	Chapati	K/VG
	Kheer	Kd/V
S India	Fried beef	Km
	Rice	K/VG
	Okra	K/VG
	Yogurt	Kd/V
	Rice pudding	Kd/V

Southeast Asia

Philippines	Shrimp fritters	NK
	Spring roll	NK
	Stewed chicken/pork	NK
	Rice balls	K/VG
Java	Fried chicken	Km
	Chayotes	NK (vegan/kosher without the shrimp/shrimp paste)
	Rice	K/VG
	Shrimp crackers	NK
	Fried tofu	K/VG
	Citrus drink	K/VG
Sunda	Chicken in coconut	Km (vegan if substitute tempeh for chicken)
	Rice	K/VG
	Pickled acar	K/VG
	Shrimp crackers	NK
	Fresh fruit	K/VG
Bali	Spice paste	NK
	Pork	NK
	Green beans	NK (vegan/kosher without the shrimp paste)
	Rice	K/VG
	Shrimp crackers	NK
	Fried tofu	K/VG (with fresh oil)
	Banana fritters	Kd/V
Thailand	Curry noodle soup	?
	Chicken satay	NK
	Cucumber salad	K/VG without fish sauce
	Coconut sticky rice	K/VG
Vietnam	Noodle rolls	NK
	Spinach soup	NK
	Lemongrass chicken	NK
	Rice	K/VG

Middle East

Morocco 1	Hearty Soup	Km (replace butter with margarine)
Morocco 2	Vegetable couscous	K/VG
	Sesame cone	Kd/V
	Mint tea	K/VG

Morocco 3	Carrot salad	K/VG
	Chicken	Km
	Soup	K/VG
	Dates	K/VG
Egypt	Tea	K/VG
	Falafel	K/VG
	Eggplant	K/VG
	Koshary	Kd/V
	Sauces	K/VG
	Salad	K/VG
	Coconut sweet	Kd/V
	Tea	K/VG
Palestine	Chicken	Km
	Greens	K/VG
	Rice	K/VG
	Vegetables	K/VG
	Yogurt	Kd/V
	Ba'lawa	Kd/V
Syria	Lamb	Km
	Cucumber	Kd/V
	Lettuce	K/VG
	Olives	K/VG
	Bread	?
	Tea	K/VG
Iran	Cucumber/yogurt	Kd/V
	Eggplant	Kd/V
	Feta	Kd/V
	Chicken	NK
	Salad	K/VG
	Sour pickles	K/VG
	Yogurt drink	Kd/V
	Ice cream	Kd/V
	Tea	K/VG

South and Central America

Bolivia	Avocado	K/VG
	Quinoa soup	K/VG
	Beef tongue	Km
	Rice	K/VG (with vegetable bouillon cube)
	Squash dessert	Kd/V
Brasília	Soup	K/VG
	Salad	K/VG
	Couve	K/VG
	Rice	K/VG
	Eggplant	K/VG
	Papaya	Kd/V
	Tahine apples	K/VG

Minas Gerais	Beans	NK
	Pork	NK
	Pumpkin	K/VG
	Corn porridge	K/VG
	Rice	K/VG
	Milk fudge	Kd/V
SE Brazil	Bean stew	NK
	Rice	K/VG
	Greens	K/VG
	Vinaigrette	K/VG
	Farofa	Kd/V
	Flan	Kd/V
	Caipirinhac	K/VG
Mexico	Oaxacan mole	Km (use vegetable oil and nondairy chocolate)
	Rice w/cheese	NK/V (use vegetable broth instead of chicken)

North America

Newfoundland	Cod cheeks	K (omit pork fat)
	Jiggs Dinner	Km
	Peas pudding	Kd/V (if not cooked in meat broth)
	Figgy duff	Kd/V (if not cooked in meat broth)
	Bannock	K/VG
	Partridge soufflé	Kd/V
Jewish NY	Chicken soup	Km
	Brisket	Km
	Kasha	K/V
	Honey cake	K/V
Appalachia	Ham	NK
	Beans	NK
	Cornbread	Kd/V (use butter)
	Britches	NK
	Greens	NK
	Hominy	NK
	Sauerkraut	?
	Potatoes	NK
	Apples	NK
	Corn	Kd/VG
	Blackberry cobbler	Kd/V
Pacific NW	Raspberry juice	K/VG
	Rose hip tea	K/VG
	Fry bread	K/VG
	Venison	Km
	Salmon	K
	Rice	K/V
	Fiddleheads	K/VG
	Candied salmon	K

Oceania

Australia	Snake patties	K (use fish)
	Potatoes etc.	K/VG
	Damper	Kd/V
	Garden salad	K/VG
	Bananas	Kd/V (marshmallows use "gelatin")
	Mango ice cream	Kd/V
	Boiled fruit cake	Kd/V
	Billy tea	Kd/V
New Zealand	Mussels	NK
	Kumara	K/V
	Salad	K/VG
	Tea	Kd/V
	Port kiwis	Kd/V
	Coconut drink	K/VG
Tonga	Raw fish	K
	Corned beef	Km
	Roast pork	NK
	Sweet potatoes	K/VG
	Fruit	Kd/V

Europe

Andalusia	Gazpacho	K/VG
	Paella	K/VG (omit shellfish)
	Arroz con leche	Kd/V
	Wine	K/VG
Ibiza	Rice soup	Km
	Stew	Km
	Salsa de Nadal	Km
	Bescuit	Kd/V
Italy	Antipasti	Kd/V (omit sausage)
	Prosciutto	NK
	Pasta e ceci	Kd/V
	Bread	K/VG
	Costolette	Km (use beef)
	Verdure	K/VG
	Insalata	Kd/V
	Fruit	K/VG
	Baba	Kd/V
	Caffè	K/VG
	Liqueur	K/VG
Greece	Soup	K/V
	Eggplant	K/VG
	Lettuce/dill	K/VG
	Potatoes/chicken	Km
	Halva	K/VG

Bulgaria	Salata	Kd/V
	Yahniya	Km
	Tikvenik	K/VG
Estonia	Kurgi Salat	Kd/V
	Rosolje	NK
	Sauerkraut	NK
	Blood sausage	NK
	Semolina	Kd/V
Sweden	Cabbage rolls	NK
	Cucumber	K/VG
	Potatoes	K/VG
	Lingonberry sauce	K/VG
	Mördeg	Kd/V
Norway	Salmon	K
	Poteter	Kd/V
	Vegetables	Kd/V
	Brød	Kd/V
	Boller	Kd/V
	Mousse cake	Kd/V
Ireland	Beef stew	Km
	Champ	Kd/V
	Kale	Kd/V
	Bread	Kd/V
	Apple cake	Kd/V
Encore	Marzipan	K/VG

Index

Please note that certain ingredients are ubiquitous in these recipes, and we should all have them on hand year-round if possible: onions, scallions, and garlic appear in nearly every main dish in this cookbook, so they are not even listed here. Lemons (mostly juiced) are important nearly everywhere. Common household herbs and spices like bay leaf, basil, cayenne, cinnamon, cumin, coriander, dill, paprika, pepper, nutmeg, oregano, and turmeric find frequent mention in the recipes, but not in the index. Try to replace all of your spices at least once a year, because the quality of your cooking depends on the freshness of your ingredients. Finally, common baking items (flour, sugar, salt, pepper, cornstarch, and vegetable and other oils) are left out of the index as well.

Y

Z